Corfu

& the Ion

THE ROUGH GUIDE

There are more than one hundred Rough Guide titles
covering destinations from Amsterdam to Zimbabwe

Forthcoming titles include

Jamaica • New Zealand • South Africa
Southwest USA

Rough Guide Reference Series

Classical Music • The Internet • Jazz • Opera • Rock Music • World Music

Rough Guide Phrasebooks

Czech • French • German • Greek • Indonesian • Italian • Mandarin Chinese
Mexican Spanish • Polish • Portuguese • Spanish • Thai • Turkish
Vietnamese

Rough Guides on the Internet

http://www.roughguides.com/
http://www.hotwired.com/rough

Rough Guide Credits

Text Editor:	Paul Gray
Series Editor:	Mark Ellingham
Editorial:	Martin Dunford, Jonathan Buckley, Samantha Cook, Jo Mead, Amanda Tomlin, Ann-Marie Shaw, Vivienne Heller, Sarah Dallas, Chris Schüler, Helena Smith, Kirk Marlow, Julia Kelly, Caroline Osborne (UK), Andrew Rosenberg (US)
Online editors:	Alan Spicer (Online UK), Geronimo Madrid (Online US)
Production:	Susanne Hillen, Andy Hilliard, Judy Pang, Link Hall, Nicola Williamson, Helen Ostick
Cartography:	Melissa Flack, David Callier, Maxine Burke
Finance:	John Fisher, Celia Crowley, Catherine Gillespie
Marketing & Publicity:	Richard Trillo, Simon Carloss, Niki Smith (UK), Jean-Marie Kelly, SoRelle Braun (US)
Administration:	Tania Hummel, Mark Rogers

Acknowledgements

I owe a debt of thanks to editor Paul Gray for wrestling the text into its final shape. Innumerable other people helped, with advice, information, directions, lifts, beds and the odd beer. In particular I must thank the following:

Corfu: Ms Lia Mathioudaki of the NTOG for help beyond the call of duty; Stephan Jaskulowski for vital editorial contributions; Judith Mackrell and Mitzi Rogers for hospitality, help and that lunch in Trítsi; Sue Tsirigotis; Philip Vlasseros; and Carola Scupham. **Paxí**: Mrs Pat Stubbs, for saving my life one night; the Vassilas and Petrou families for their friendship; Don's pals; the party animals (they know who they are). **Lefkádha**: Maria and Yioryios Gazi for their kindness; the staff of the KTEL bus station – the friendliest in the Ionian; the Cafe Karfakis for those endless plates of *mezédhes*; Samba Tours in Vassilikí, for helping a stranger. **Itháki**: The Stafford brothers (beers and protection); Yioryios Moraitis. **Kefalloniá**: Mr Messaris and Mrs Vassilikis of the NTOG for their unstinting help and advice; Tassos Mazoukis for his hospitality and expertise; the Hotel Pericles; KTEL's bus drivers – the St-Exuperys of the Argostóli–Fiskárdho road. **Zákinthos**: Mrs Vicky Vitsou for advice; the Hotel Reparo for information; the Arekia taverna for a glimpse into heaven's kitchen.

I would also like to thank Iannis Tranakas, gentleman and scholar, whose gracious *filoxenía* revived my *filellinísmos* when it was evaporating in the heat; Andrew Rosenberg and Narrell Leffman for US and Oz Basics research; Nikky Twyman for proofreading; MicroMap (Romsey, Hants) for cartography; and Thorsten Fiebelkorn at Simply Ionian.

This first edition published July 1997 by Rough Guides Ltd, 1 Mercer Street, London WC2H 9QJ.
Distributed by the Penguin Group:

Penguin Books Ltd, 27 Wrights Lane, London W8 5TZ.
Penguin Books USA Inc, 375 Hudson Street, New York 10014, USA.
Penguin Books Australia Ltd, 487 Maroondah Highway, PO Box 257, Ringwood, Victoria 3134, Australia.
Penguin Books Canada Ltd, 10 Alcorn Avenue, Toronto, Ontario, Canada M4V 1E4.
Penguin Books (NZ) Ltd, 182–190 Wairau Road, Auckland 10, New Zealand.
Previous editions published in the US and Canada as The Real Guide Paris.

Printed in England by Clays Ltd, St Ives PLC.
Typography and **original design** by Jonathan Dear and The Crowd Roars.
Illustrations throughout by Edward Briant.

272pp. Includes index.

A catalogue record for this book is available from the British Library.
ISBN 1-85828-226-8

Corfu

& the Ionian Islands

THE ROUGH GUIDE

Written and researched by
John Gill

THE ROUGH GUIDES

Help Us Update

We've gone to a lot of trouble to ensure that this first edition of *The Rough Guide to Corfu & the Ionian Islands* is accurate and up-to-date. However, things inevitably change, and if you feel we've got it wrong or left something out, we'd like to know: any suggestions, comments or corrections would be much appreciated. We'll credit all contributions and send a copy of the next edition (or any other Rough Guide if you prefer) for the best correspondence.

Please mark letters "Rough Guide to Corfu & the Ionian Islands" and send to:
Rough Guides, 1 Mercer St, London, WC2H 9QJ,
or Rough Guides, 375 Hudson St, 9th floor, New York, NY 10014.

Or send email to: mail@roughguides.co.uk

Online updates about this book can be found on Rough Guides' website at http://www.roughguides.com/

Rough Guides

Travel Guides • Phrasebooks • Music and Reference Guides

We set out to do something different when the first Rough Guide was published in 1982. Mark Ellingham, just out of University, was travelling in Greece. He brought along the popular guides of the day, but found they were all lacking in some way. They were either strong on ruins and museums but went on for pages without mentioning a beach or taverna. Or they were so conscious of the need to save money that they lost sight of Greece's cultural and historical significance. Also, none of the books told him anything about Greece's contemporary life – its politics, its culture, its people, and how they lived.

So with no job in prospect, Mark decided to write his own guidebook, one which aimed to provide practical information that was second to none, detailing the best beaches and the hottest clubs and restaurants, while also giving hard hitting accounts of every sight, both famous and obscure, and providing up-to-the-minute information on contemporary culture. It was a guide that encouraged independent travellers to find the best of Greece, and was a great success, getting shortlisted for the Thomas Cook travel guide award, and encouraging Mark, along with three friends, to expand the series.

The Rough Guide list grew rapidly and the letters flooded in, indicating a much broader readership than had been anticipated, but one which uniformly appreciated the Rough Guides' mix of practical detail and humour, irreverence and enthusiasm. Things haven't changed. The same four friends who began the series are still the caretakers of the Rough Guide mission today: to provide the most reliable, up-to-date and entertaining information to independent-minded travellers of all ages, on all budgets.

We now publish 100 titles and have offices in London and New York. The travel guides are written and researched by a dedicated team of more than 100 authors, based in Britain, Europe, the USA and Australia. We have also created a unique series of phrasebooks to accompany the travel series, along with the acclaimed series of music guides, and a best-selling pocket guide to the Internet and World Wide Web. We also publish comprehensive travel information on our two web sites: http://www.hotwired.com/rough and http://www.roughguides.com/

The author

John Gill has been a regular visitor to the Ionian islands for the last 15 years, and published a book about one, *The Stars over Paxos*, in 1995. He has published several other books and works as a journalist in London.

Contents

List of Maps

MAP SYMBOLS

═	Major road	◓	Cave
=	Minor road	▲	Mountain peak
- - - - -	Path	☀	Lighthouse
━ ━	Railway	ⓘ	Tourist office
──	Wall	✉	Post office
— —	Ferry route	⊞	Hospital
········	Waterway	■	Building
━ ━ ━	National border	■+	Church
✈	Airport	† †	Cemetery
◉	Hotel	▒	Park
‡	Church (regional maps)	░	Sand/beach
♦	Point of interest		

Introduction

The **Ionian islands** comprise a core group of six – Corfu (Kérkira), Paxí (Paxos), Lefkádha (Lefkas), Itháki (Ithaca), Kefalloniá (Cephallonia) and Zákinthos (Zante) – which trace a ragged line down the west coast of Greece*. None is more than 30km from the mainland, yet this has been far enough to exclude the Ionians from many of the key events in Greek history, most notably occupation by the Ottoman Turks. However, their position at the south of the Adriatic instead put them at the mercy of northerly invaders, primarily the **Venetians** and, later, the **British**, whose cultures fused with those of the islands. The Venetians, who first arrived in the archipelago in the late fourteenth century, imported language, art, music, law and architecture; the British turned up in the eighteenth century and unpacked local government, education, civil engineering, cricket and ginger beer. To a lesser or greater degree, all these things can still be found in the islands, and the Italians and British remain the region's main summer invaders.

As the big narrative happened elsewhere, the Ionian has no major archeological sites – though Olympia, just two hours' drive from Pátra on the Peloponnese mainland, is accessible from the southern islands. However, there are some spectacular medieval fortresses, and museums on the larger islands trace the archipelago's cultures back to the Paleolithic era. Itháki is still the favourite for the disputed site of Odysseus' Homeric home, with neighbouring islands laying claim to particular settings and events from the *Odyssey*.

But the major feature that distinguishes the Ionians from the mainland and the central swarm of Greek islands in the Aegean is climatic: a reliable rainfall pattern has allowed centuries of fairly stable agriculture and nurtured olive trees, vineyards, rich fruit and vegetable crops, and even wheat and cereal farming on some islands. The Ionian islands display similar geographical characteristics, too:

---

*Isolated at the foot of the Peloponnese, Kíthira and Andíkithira are also considered part of the Ionian group. We haven't covered them in this Guide, as they bear few similarities to the core group of islands, share no transport connections with them, and would not be visited on the same trip.

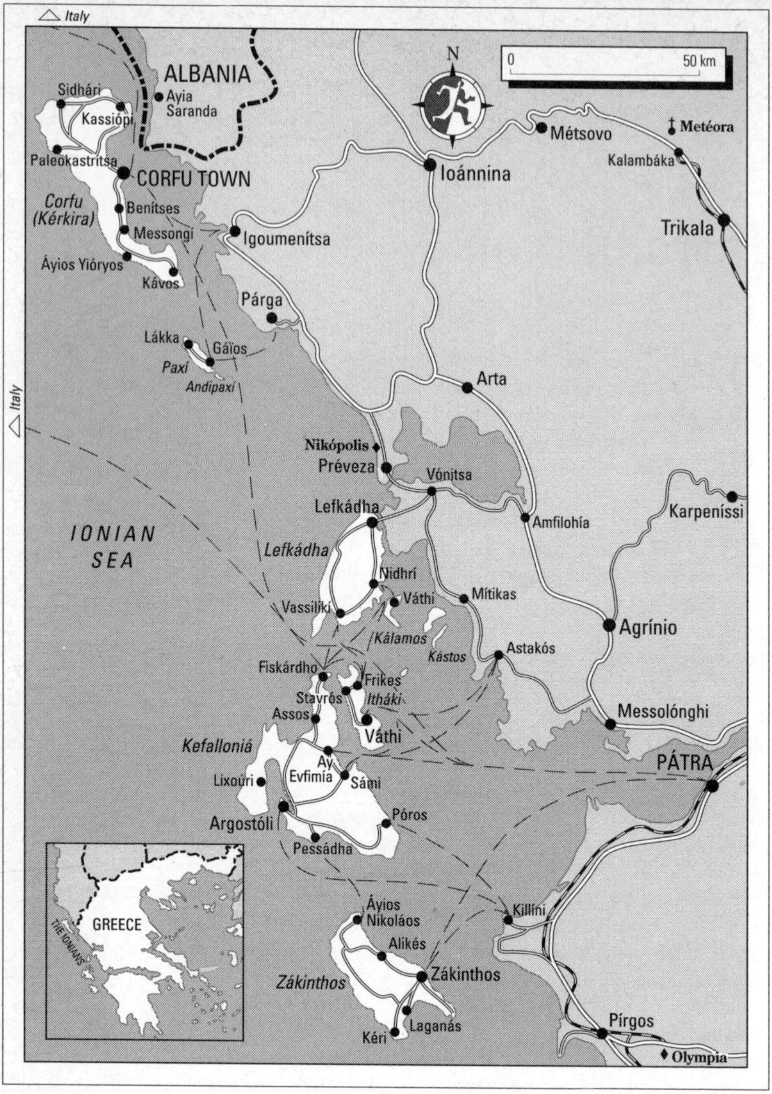

all are mountainous (even tiny Paxí has a small mountain of sorts), with their east coasts tending to be gentle dip slopes above flat, sometimes reclaimed, farm land. The west coasts are often rocky, with cliffs up to 200 metres high. This geology conspires against tourism, placing most of the best beaches on the less accessible west coasts, and the worst on the handy east coasts – where lazy developers have tended to concentrate their attentions. With the exception of Corfu's southwest and north coasts, the southwestern corner of Kefalloniá, southern Zákinthos and pockets of western Lefkádha, most beaches are pebbly, usually shelving into sand.

Corfu and **Zákinthos** are the easiest of the islands to visit: both have busy international airports, and a developed structure of package and independent tourism. In recent years, however, they have acquired a not entirely undeserved reputation as sleazepits, the blame for which can be laid at the door of unscrupulous Greek and British tourism operators. The tackier resorts on Corfu tend to be on its east coast – Ípsos and Kávos are given over to booze, bonking and bungee-jumping, although a slump in tourism has brought drastic improvements to once-notorious Benítses. On Zákinthos, Laganás is set on one of the island's finest beaches, but resembles a vast English seaside resort. However, such large-scale tourist developments take up only a small proportion of either island, and most locals and visitors remain quite undisturbed by the commerce and razzmatazz.

Kefalloniá's new airport has yet to attract the bulk of traffic of either Corfu or Zákinthos, but the island boasts some of the best unspoilt beaches and wildest mountainscapes in the Ionian. It remains a reasonably well-kept secret: chic resorts like Fiskárdho are very busy throughout the season, but others, such as Skála, never seem to fill. Its northerly neighbour **Lefkádha** has two notable pockets of development – Nidhrí and the windsurfers' paradise, Vassilikí – but the rest of the heavily indented coastline and the handsome, mountainous interior are largely untouched by tourism. It goes without saying that the farther you travel from an airport, or an island with an airport, the more you'll distance yourself from the crowds. Many landing at Corfu head at great

Transliteration

Because there's no standard system of transliterating Greek script into Roman, you're sure to find that the Greek words and proper names in this book do not always match the versions written elsewhere. Place names are the biggest source of confusion, varying from map to map, and often sign to sign. The word for "saint", for instance, one of the commonest prefixes, can be rendered Áyios, Ágios, or Ághios. To make matters worse, there are often two forms of a name in Greek – the modern, popularly used *dhimotikí* and the older, elitist *katharévoussa*. Thus, for example, you will come across the older Paxoí and the newer Paxí, as well as Anglicized Paxos. Throw in inherited Italian and English names, a boggling array of island dialects with their own variants on pronunciation, and haphazard spelling, and you have a real mare's nest.

In this book, we've used a modern, largely phonetic system in the spelling of modern Greek place names. We have, however, retained the accepted "English" spelling for familiar places like Corfu and Athens. We have also accented (with an acute) the stressed letter of each word; getting this right in pronunciation is vital in order to be understood.

speed for **Paxí**, those at Kefalloniá for **Itháki**. The former, barely 10km long and covered in olive trees, supports just three tiny (but busy) fishing village resorts; small and mountainous, the latter is the most unspoilt of the core islands.

The **satellite islands**, such as the Diapontía islets off northwest Corfu, Meganíssi off Lefkádha, and even Andípaxi south of Paxí, are becoming more accessible to adventurous travellers each year. Committed loners and misanthropes might also consider Boukári and Lefkími on Corfu; the hills around Kariá or the little-visited west coast, especially Atháni, on Lefkádha; the quieter parts of Kefalloniá, such as Skála or Ássos; or the isolated pocket of Yérakas on Zákinthos. If you want to live as the Greeks live away from the tourism racket, try the island capitals: Corfu Town has transformed itself in recent years, Lefkádha Town has the street life of a busy Manhattan neighbourhood, and Argostóli retains a spacious charm despite being razed by the 1953 earthquake. Alas, Zákinthos Town's one-way traffic system lends it all the charm of a race track after dark.

It's worth noting that nobody ever came to the Ionian islands looking for cordon bleu food or Scandinavian plumbing. In all but the smartest accommodation, bathrooms are haphazard, though rarely insanitary. And while there are excellent tavernas on many islands, most, over the decades, have been content to reach a happy medium with their foreign customers. They generally serve meals lukewarm, following the Greek nostrum that hot food is bad for the system, and on the smaller islands certain vegetables can be difficult to obtain (you could launch a career as a comedian on Paxí by asking for lettuce). Yet these shortcomings have actually entered the mythology of the thousands who return regardless to the islands year after year. One of the reasons they return – beyond some of the finest swimming and watersports in the Mediterranean, the landscape, sunshine and balmy nights out under the Milky Way – is the welcome that all but the largest resorts still manage to extend. Despite the pressure of tourism, the islanders remain a disarmingly friendly people, and reserved Britons are often embarrassed by their astonishing kindness. The traditional quality of *filoxenía*, kindness to strangers, survives, and can take the form of anything from an orange offered from someone's garden to a meal, a lift or a room for the night. And after decades of handling tourists who insist on speaking their own tongue, islanders are genuinely charmed by attempts to speak their language, even if it's just a *yá sou* or *kalí méra*.

When to go

If you can, it's best to avoid the islands in late July and most of August, when holidaying Greeks and Italians descend en masse, accommodation is scarce, and temperatures and prices soar. June and early September are just as good for those concerned about fine weather (in fact, the 1990s have seen a number of fairly unstable high summers, with rainy Augusts followed by stunning Septembers and Octobers). In June, the sea is usually warm enough for swimming; in September it can be as warm as a bath.

May, September and October are the times for bargain flights and packages, and, though you may risk short spells of inclement weather, are probably the best times to visit. In May many spring flowers are still in bloom, and villages and villagers are fresh from the winter. In late September and early October you can be blessed with fine weather, warm seas and almost no other visitors. However, bargain package deals in these low-season periods should be carefully scrutinized: some remote resorts (noted in the Guide) close early, often stranding those without the wherewithal to hire transport.

Early May and late October mark the beginning and end of charter flights to the islands. Outside these times you have to fly via Athens, but, with the exception of Paxí, every island capital has hotels open year-round, and most local accommodation companies can rustle up some suitable accommodation. When the rafts of knick-knacks are packed away until next season, even the most developed resorts resume their prelapsarian charm, and major towns – in particular, Corfu Town – are to be seen at their best. The only bars or tavernas will be those the Greeks themselves use, which is usually the best recommendation at any time of the year. The winter months, November especially, see spectacular storms in the Ionian, yet it is possible to get sunburnt on Christmas Day. Off-season travel is also the only way to catch the two biggest festivals of the year: pre-Lenten carnival, a Venetian tradition maintained with parades, parties and mischief; and Orthodox Easter, which is celebrated for up to a fortnight.

Prevailing northwesterly winds affect all the Ionian islands, commonly rising in the afternoon, occasionally developing into the *maéstro* – the Ionian equivalent of the Aegean *meltémi* – which can blow for three days or more. These winds make the Ionians ideal for yachting holidays and watersports, but can make beaches at exposed resorts hellish. The climate figures given below are averages for Corfu – if any generalizations about Ionian weather can be made in advance, they can be made only about the region as a whole. The archipelago has any number of micro-climates: Lefkádha's valleys are like little lost Shangri Las of meteorology, and Paxí gets only a fraction of the storms that gang up on nearby Corfu's Mount Pandokrátor.

Corfu climate table

	Jan	Feb	Mar	Apr	May	Jun	Jul	Aug	Sep	Oct	Nov	Dec
Average maximum daily temperatures (°C)	13	14	16	19	23	28	30	31	28	23	18	15
Average rainfall (cm)	15	14	10	6	4	1	0	0	1	15	20	18

Basics

Getting there from Britain

At roughly 2000km and three hours by air from London, Corfu is the nearest Greek island to Britain; its southerly siblings Kefalloniá and Zákinthos are barely half an hour's flight further. For most visitors, flying is the only viable option for getting to the Ionians: buses and trains can take up to four days, and are no bargain unless you're planning to work your way slowly through Europe (see p.13 for information about getting to the islands from mainland Greece and Italy).

Corfu was one of the earliest destinations for British tourism in Greece and is well connected by **summer charter flights** with British airports: as well as Gatwick and Manchester, airports at Birmingham, Belfast, Bristol, Cardiff, Edinburgh, Glasgow, Luton, Newcastle, Norwich and Stansted also have flights at least once a week to the island. More and more British airports are also developing seasonal charter connections with the region's three other airports: **Zákinthos** (the busiest and most accessible after Corfu), **Kefalloniá** and **Préveza**. Island-hoppers aiming for the hopper-friendly triangle of Lefkádha, Itháki and Kefalloniá should consider either Préveza or Kefalloniá airports: both offer good access to the islands, and Préveza, though on the mainland, is only thirty minutes by regular bus from Lefkádha Town. **Routing via Athens** is generally only a useful option if you're travelling **out of season** (when there are only a few obscure charters into the Ionians around Christmas or Easter), if you're planning to stay longer than a charter would allow and need a **scheduled ticket** (there are no direct scheduled flights from Britain to the Ionians), or as a last resort in season.

Classified ads in national papers – the *Guardian, Independent, Observer, Sunday Times* – as well as Teletext and, increasingly, a number of Internet addresses such as Campus Travel's **website** (www.campustravel.co.uk), are useful sources when shopping around for flights. Local newspapers and listings magazines also carry ads for companies selling budget flights. Among travel agents, high-street branches of the major chains tend to be geared to selling you a package holiday rather than a bargain flight, but this can be an extremely cheap way of getting to the destination of your choice if you don't mind being restricted to staying in the busy resorts.

Charter flights

Most British travellers to the Ionian will arrive by direct **charter flight**, either with a package holiday or on a flight-only deal. These flights have fixed and unchangeable outward and return dates, and are usually for one or two weeks, although most operators can offer three- or four-week flights for a nominal extra fee. Some may even agree longer periods, although these tend to be low-season deals or dependent on how busy the season is.

The cheapest charter flights to Greece are usually weekday flights leaving late at night or early in the morning. However, the days of ultra-cheap last-minute deals are – for the time being, at least – over. Sophisticated computer systems (and not a little commercial ruthlessness) have largely eliminated the situation where seats on half-empty flights were available for a song. The mid-1990s have seen a return to early booking to secure flights or holidays in a shrinking market.

Flight-only deals from Gatwick to Corfu generally **cost** between £150 and £200, although "red-eye" flights, which typically leave Britain around 11pm and arrive around 4am local time, can cost as little as £120. Flights from major provincial airports such as Manchester and Birmingham tend to be

£10–20 higher, those from Glasgow and smaller airports like Bristol £30–40 higher. Flights to Zákinthos and Kefalloniá are limited to Gatwick and the major provincial airports and are more expensive, costing between £170 and £220 depending on season. Préveza's small, semi-military airport is the worst served, with only one or two flights from the major airports per week, at prices starting from around £170. Charter flights to Athens are plentiful and cheap, from as little as £100 return.

Different regulations concerning charter tickets apply to EU nationals and those from outside the EU. **Non-EU nationals** flying charter must purchase a return ticket, valid for no fewer than three days and no more than four weeks. They should also have an accommodation voucher – a hangover from the days when flight-only deals were not meant to be sold – which should be issued by the ticketing agency but which will not actually get you accommodation. The accommodation voucher system applies to **EU nationals** too, in theory, but recent relaxation in airport practices means that few (if any) EU nationals are checked by customs and immigration.

Student/youth charters are sold as one-way flights only and are available to both EU and non-EU nationals. By combining two one-way charters you can stay for over a month. Student/youth charter tickets are available to anyone under 26, and to all card-carrying full-time students under 32.

Finally, while some carriers now regard it as a formality, **reconfirmation** of your return flight is still strongly recommended, at least 48 hours before departure. It's most common to telephone to confirm, but allow plenty of time, as the local agents who usually handle these services are often engaged. If the worst comes to the worst, contact the head office of the company you flew with. Problems are rare, but failure to reconfirm could allow the carrier to bounce you off a flight if there's a problem with overbooking.

Scheduled flights

Getting from Britain to the Ionian islands using **scheduled flights** is a roundabout process. The Greek national carrier Olympic Airways (3 daily), British Airways (2 daily) and Virgin Atlantic (1 daily) have direct flights from London Heathrow to Athens, which with advance booking can cost under £200, even in August. From Athens, there are daily internal flights on Olympic to Préveza and the Ionian island airports, costing from around £60 (return) and averaging 45 minutes flying time. Bus and ferry connections from Athens are cheaper and more frequent, but take over eight hours to reach even Corfu. Scheduled flights from British regional airports route via Heathrow in the first instance.

London–Athens flights on eastern European airlines such as Balkan have cheaper full-price fares than Olympic, BA and Virgin – £250 return for much of the year excluding high season – but are routed via their capital cities. It is not always possible to book discount flights with these airlines, who will instead pass you on to a travel agent.

The advantages of scheduled flights are that they can be booked well in advance, have long ticket validities and tend to leave at more sociable hours than charter flights. Many cheaper APEX and SuperAPEX fares, however, do have advance-purchase (usually fourteen days) and/or minimum-stay requirements, as well as restrictions on date changes and refunds, so check conditions carefully. As with charters, discount fares on scheduled flights are available from most high-street travel agents, as well as from a number of specialist flight and student/youth agencies.

If the preferred ticket is hard to find, and you have the time and money to improvise, it is also worthwhile considering flying on separate **one-way tickets** (but check p.17 regarding any visa restrictions that might affect you). Outside high season, island travel agents can often find bargain one-way tickets back to Britain (many advertise them). However, avoid coming back on national holidays and, crucially, at the end of the season, when travel companies are looking for the cheapest way to get their guest workers home.

Scheduled airlines

Balkan Airlines ☎ 0171/637 7637
British Airways ☎ 0345/222111
CSA Czech Airlines ☎ 0171/255 1898
LOT Polish Airlines ☎ 0171/580 5037
Malev Hungarian Airlines ☎ 0171/439 0577
Olympic Airways ☎ 0171/409 3400
Virgin Atlantic Airways ☎ 01293/747747

Packages and tours

The vast majority of British people visiting the Ionian islands do so on package holidays, comprising flights, transfers and accommodation. Despite the sleazy reputation of parts of Corfu and Zákinthos, the region still has no conurbations of high-rise hotels as found in parts of Spain, and consequently few half-finished-hotel horror stories. While packages to these two islands are concentrated in the most developed areas, the remaining islands are barely developed and can offer some surprisingly good-value package deals, especially if you shop around. Some package bargains are even worth taking for the flight alone, leaving you to use the accommodation as you see fit.

For a more low-key and genuinely "Greek" holiday, it's best to travel with one of the smaller **specialist agencies** listed overleaf. Most of these are more expensive than the mainstream package companies, but they tend to have found the best accommodation in the best areas, and you're also paying for a much higher standard of attention from resort staff. Best of all, however, is to contact a **local accommodation agency**, some of whom can arrange flights and even transfers. As well as plugging you straight into the local community, it also plugs your money into the local economy.

Flight agents

Alecos Tours, 3a Camden Rd, London NW1 ☎0171/267 2092. Regular Olympic Airways consolidator, plus charter flights to Corfu.

Andrews, 132 Green Lanes, London N13 5UN ☎0181/882 7153. Consolidator for CSA.

Argo Holidays, 100 Wigmore St, London W1H 9DR ☎0171/331 7000. Consolidator for Olympic, BA and Virgin Atlantic. Also charter flights and packages to the Ionian islands.

Campus Travel, 541 Bristol Rd, Selly Oak, Birmingham B29 6AU ☎0121/414 1848; 37–39 Queens Rd, Bristol BS8 3DB ☎0117/929 2494; 5 Emmanuel St, Cambridge CB1 1NE ☎01223/324283; 53 Forest Rd, Edinburgh EH1 2QP ☎0131/668 3303; 52 Grosvenor Gardens, London SW1 ☎0171/730 3402; 166 Deansgate, Manchester ☎0161/273 1721; 105–106 St Aldates, Oxford ☎01865/242067; also branches in Bradford, Brighton, Cardiff, Coventry, Glasgow, Newcastle, Nottingham, Reading and Sheffield. Student/youth travel specialists with branches also in YHA shops and on university campuses all over Britain. Campus usually has its own student/youth charter flights to Athens during the summer. Propeller-head access at www.campustravel.co.uk – a dedicated site with online booking facilities.

Council Travel, 28a Poland St, London W1V 3DD ☎0171/437 7767. Flights with student discounts to Athens, and charters to the Ionians.

Eclipse Direct ☎0990 010203. Probably the largest range of flights to the Ionians.

Springways Travel, 28 Vauxhall Bridge Rd, London SW1 ☎0181/390 5343. Scheduled and charter flights to Athens, and charters to Corfu.

STA, 25 Queens Rd, Bristol BS8 1QE ☎0117/929 4399; 38 Sidney St, Cambridge CB2 3HX ☎01223/366966; 84 Byres Rd, Glasgow G12 8SN ☎0141/338 6000; 88 Vicar Lane, Leeds LS1 7JH ☎0113/244 9212; 86 Old Brompton Rd, London SW7 3LQ, 117 Euston Rd, London NW1 2SX, 11 Goodge St, London W1 1FE, and 38 Store St, London WC1E 7BZ, all on ☎0171/361 6161; 75 Deansgate, Manchester M3 2BW ☎0161/834 0668; 36 George St, Oxford OX1 2OJ ☎01865/792800; and branches in Birmingham, Brighton, Canterbury, Cardiff, Coventry, Durham, Glasgow, Loughborough, Newcastle, Nottingham, Warwick and Sheffield. Worldwide specialists in low-cost flights and tours for students and under-26s.

Trailfinders, 22–24 The Priory, Queensway, Birmingham B4 6BS ☎0121/236 1234; 48 Corn St, Bristol BS1 1HQ ☎0117/929 9000; 254–284 Sauchiehall St, Glasgow G2 3EH ☎0141/353 2224; 42–59 Earls Court Rd, London W8 6FT ☎0171/937 5400; 194 Kensington High St, London W8 7RG ☎0171/938 3939; 58 Deansgate, Manchester M3 2FF ☎0161/839 6969. One of the best-informed travel companies around, with access to some of the best deals to Greece.

Specialist tour operators

4U Sports Tours, 11 Salterns Industrial Estate, Tenby, Dyfed SA70 7NJ ☎01834 845880. Agents for the German-run *Fanatic Board Centre* at Vassilikí on Lefkádha, who offer windsurfing packages including flight and accommodation.

Argo Holidays, 100 Wigmore St, London W1H 9DR ☎0171/331 7070. Package operator specializing in the larger hotel complexes of Corfu and Zákinthos, plus the *Paxos Beach Hotel.*

Best of Greece, 23–24 Margaret St, London W1N 8LE ☎0171/255 2320. Upmarket travel company, based in the Aegean, but offering skippered and bareboat sailing holidays in the Ionian.

Club Vassilikí, 31 Star St, Ware, Herts SG12 7AA ☎01920 484121. Windsurfing packages to Vassilikí on Lefkádha, including flights, accommodation, beginner instruction and insurance.

Corfu à la Carte, The White House, Bucklebury Alley, Cold Ash, Newbury, Berks RG18 9NN ☎01635/201140. Traditional villas on Corfu (the northeast coast) and at Longós and Gäíos on Paxí.

CV Travel, 43 Cadogan St, London SW3 2PR ☎0171/581 0851 or 584 8803. One of the big three (along with Greek Islands Club and Simply Ionian), and *the* exclusive villa company on Corfu and Paxí, with some of the islands' most luxurious (and expensive) properties on its books.

Direct Greece, Oxford House, 182 Upper Richmond Rd, London SW15 2SH ☎0181/785 4000. Villas and apartments on Lefkádha and Zákinthos (and at Párga on the mainland).

Explore Worldwide, 1 Frederick St, Aldershot, Hants GU11 1LQ ☎01252/344161. Offers a guided trekking tour of the Peloponnese, Kefalloniá and Itháki among its Greek itineraries.

Grecofile/Filoxenia, Sourdock Hill, Barkisland, Halifax, West Yorks HX4 0AG ☎01422/375999. Villa and apartment holidays on Corfu and Paxí. The company also has an unusual programme of activity holidays, including a 10-day cookery course on Corfu.

Greek Island Club, 66 High St, Walton-on-Thames, Surrey KT12 1BU ☎01932/220477. One of the longest-established villa and apartment companies in the Ionian, with prime properties on Corfu, Paxí, Itháki, Kefalloniá and Zákinthos. Also offers activity holidays: ornithology, cooking, botany, painting, photography and learning Greek, among others.

Ilios Island Holidays, 18 Market Square, Horsham, West Sussex RH12 1EU ☎01403/ 259788. Small and choosy selection of island accommodation on Zákinthos, Lefkádha and rarely visited Meganíssi.

Island Wandering, 51a London Rd, Hurst Green, East Sussex TN19 7QP ☎01580/860733. All-in holidays to Corfu, Lefkádha, Itháki (including the *Nostos* in Fríkes), Kefalloniá (the *Mouikis* in Argostóli) and Zákinthos.

Kosmar Villa Holidays, 358 Bowes Rd, London N11 1AN ☎0181/368 6833. Hotels and apartments on Corfu, Lefkádha, Kefalloniá and Zákinthos.

Manos Holidays, 168–172 Old St, London EC1V 9BP ☎0171/216 8000. One of the biggest package companies specializing in the Ionian, with a wide range of apartments and hotels on Corfu, Lefkádha, Kefalloniá and Zákinthos.

Meon Villas, Meon House, College St, Petersfield, Hants GU32 3JN ☎01730/26841. Villas and apartments on Corfu, with an emphasis on the Nissáki–Kassiópi coast and the southwest.

Planos Holidays, Whatley Farm, Whatley, Frome, Somerset BA11 3LA ☎01373 836000. Now the biggest single operator on Paxí, Planos offers bonded flight-transfer-accommodation package deals, using some of the best properties on the island, many of them in and around Lákka.

Routsis Holidays, c/o Greek Options, 4th Floor, Abford House, 15 Wilton Rd, London SW1V 1LT ☎0171/233 5233. The Lákka-based travel company now also offers bonded package deals to the island, mainly in and around Lákka, plus sailing and diving options and, uniquely to our knowledge, Easter specials.

Simply Ionian, 8 Chiswick Tce, Acton Lane, London W4 5LY ☎0181/995 1121 or 995 1541. Fastest-growing of the big three, with select properties on Corfu, Paxí, Kefalloniá and Itháki. Specializes in village and country villas, as well as sailing, painting and other activity holidays.

Something Special, 10 Bull Plain, Hertford SG14 1DT ☎01992/552231. Specializes in upmarket villas, many with pools, on the north coast of Corfu, particularly Nissáki, Áyios Stéfanos and Kalámi.

Sunvil Holidays, Sunvil House, 7–8 Upper Square, Old Isleworth, Middlesex TW7 7BJ ☎0181/568 4499. Specializes in upmarket, out-of-the-way villas and apartments on Corfu and Lefkádha (including the *Pension Ostria* in Áyios Nikítas). Also activity holidays: walking, painting, cycling and watersports.

Sunworld Sailing, 120 St George's Rd, Brighton BN2 1EA ☎01273/626284. Watersport and flotilla holidays based in Nidhrí and Vassilikí on Lefkádha.

Getting there from Ireland

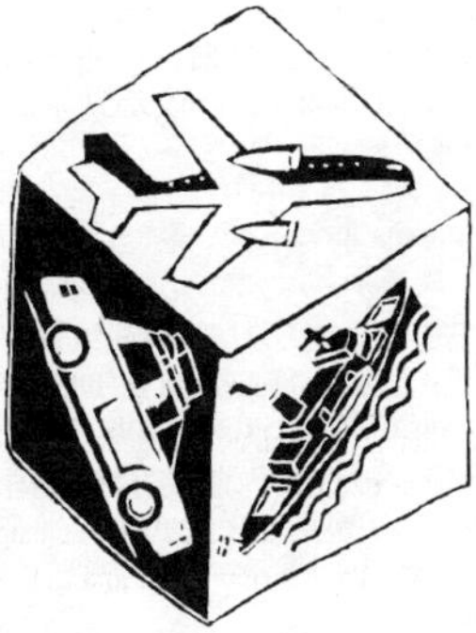

Travelling to Greece from Ireland is more expensive than from Britain, though a number of companies do offer packages to the Ionian islands and direct charter flights to Athens and Corfu. In high season, a charter flight from Dublin to Corfu currently costs around IR£280, including taxes, while a two-week package to the same island starts at IR£420, also including taxes.

A more cumbersome, though possibly cheaper, alternative is to buy a **flight to London** and a charter ticket or package from there to the Ionians (see "Getting there from Britain" above). Companies such as Ryan Air offer high-season returns from IR£69 to Gatwick, Luton or Stansted,

Airlines in Ireland

Aer Lingus, 46–48 Castle St, Belfast BT1 1HB ☎0645/737747; 2 Academy St, Cork ☎021/327155; 40–41 Upper O'Connell St, Dublin 1, and 13 St Stephen's Green, Dublin 2 ☎01/844 4777; 136 O'Connell St, Limerick ☎061/474239.

British Airways, 9 Fountain Centre, College St, Belfast BT1 6ET ☎0345/222111.

Olympic Airways, Travel Cuts, Franklin House, 142 Pembroke Rd, Dublin 4 ☎01/608 0090.

Ryan Air, 3 Dawson St, Dublin 2 ☎01/609 7800.

Travel agents in Ireland

Budget Travel, 134 Lower Baggot St, Dublin 2 ☎01/661 3122. Discount flights and package tours.

John Cassidy, 103 Talbot St, Dublin 1 ☎01/878 6888. Agents for Falcon and Budget, offering holidays and charter flights.

Link Travel, 28 Capel St, Dublin 1 ☎01/872 1444. Charter flights and package tours.

Sky Tours, 75 Talbot St, Dublin 1 ☎01/836 6677. Charter flights and package tours.

USIT, Fountain Centre, Belfast BT1 6ET ☎01232/324073; 10–11 Market Parade, Patrick St, Cork ☎021/270900; 33 Ferryquay St, Derry ☎01504/371888; 19–21 Aston Quay, O'Connell Bridge, Dublin 2 ☎01/602 1777, telesales ☎01/602 1600; Victoria Place, Eyre Square, Galway ☎091/565177; Central Buildings, O'Connell St, Limerick ☎061/415064; 36–37 Georges St, Waterford ☎051/872601. Student and youth specialists.

which all have charter connections to the Ionian islands.

Your options on **scheduled flights** from Dublin to Athens are currently limited, as there is no same-day connection through London on BA. Aer Lingus quotes a routing through London, Amsterdam or Rome, at IR£385 in low season. Far more promising is Olympic, whose high-season flights to Athens from Dublin via London start at around IR£345 return; daily internal flights to Préveza, Corfu, Kefalloniá and Zákinthos can be booked in advance through their Dublin office from IR£50 return. BA currently offers a Belfast–Heathrow–Athens flight from £232 low season. For **students and young people**, the picture is generally rosier: USIT has, for example, returns from Dublin to Athens, valid for stays of up to three months, from IR£189.

Getting there from North America

Only a few carriers fly directly to Greece from North America, and none offers direct flights to Corfu and the Ionians, so all arrangements are routed at least through Athens. If you have time, you may discover it cheaper to arrange your final Greece-bound leg of the journey in the UK, in which case your only criterion will be finding a suitable and good-value North America–Europe flight. For details of onward flights from the UK, see "Getting there from Britain".

In general there just isn't enough traffic between North America and Athens to make for very cheap fares. The Greek national airline,

Airlines in the US and Canada

Air Canada in BC, ☎1-800/663-3721; in Alberta, Saskatchewan and Manitoba, ☎1-800/ 542-8940; in eastern Canada, ☎1-800/268-7240; in US, ☎1-800/776-3000.

Air France in US, ☎1-800/237-2747; in Canada, ☎1-800/667-2747.

Alitalia in US, ☎1-800/223-5730; in Canada, ☎1-800/361-8336.

American Airlines ☎1-800/624-6262.

British Airways in US, ☎1-800/247-9297; in Canada, ☎1-800/668-1059.

Czech Airlines ☎1-800/223-2365.

Delta Airlines ☎1-800/241-4141 or 404/765-5000.

Iberia in US, ☎1-800/772-4642; in Canada, ☎1-800/221-6002.

KLM in US, ☎1-800/374-7747; in Canada, ☎1-800/361-5073.

LOT Polish Airlines in US, ☎1-800/223-0593; in Canada, ☎1-800/361-1017.

Lufthansa in US, ☎1-800/645-3880; in Canada, ☎1-800/563-5954.

Northwest Airlines ☎1-800/447-4747.

Olympic Airways in US, ☎1-800/223-1226; in Toronto, ☎416/920-2452, in Montréal, ☎514/878-3891.

TWA ☎1-800/892-4141.

Olympic Airways, only flies out of New York (JFK), Boston, Montréal and Toronto, but offers reasonably priced add-on flights from Athens to Corfu and the other islands.

Shopping for tickets

Barring special offers, the cheapest of the airlines' published fares is usually an **APEX** (Advance Purchase Excursion) ticket, although this will carry certain restrictions: you have to book – and pay – at least 21 days before departure, spend at least seven days abroad (maximum stay three months), and you tend to get penalized if you change your schedule. On transatlantic routes, there are also winter **Super APEX** tickets, sometimes known as "Eurosavers" – slightly cheaper than an ordinary APEX, but limiting your stay to between 7 and 21 days. Some airlines also issue **Special APEX** tickets to people younger than 24, often extending the maximum stay to a year. Many airlines offer youth or student fares to **under-26s**; a passport or driving licence is sufficient proof of age, though these tickets are subject to availability and can have eccentric booking conditions.

You can normally cut costs further by going through a **specialist flight agent** – either a **consolidator**, who buys up blocks of tickets from the airlines and sells them at a discount, or a **discount agent**, who, in addition to dealing with discounted flights, may also offer special student and youth fares and a range of other travel-related services such as travel insurance, rail passes, car rental, tours and the like. Some agents specialize in **charter flights**,

Discount travel agencies in the US and Canada

Air Brokers International, 323 Geary St, Suite 411, San Francisco, CA 94102 (☎1-800/883-3273 or 415/397-1383). Consolidator.

Airtech, 584 Broadway, Suite 1007, New York, NY 10012 (☎1-800/575-TECH or 212/219-7000). Standby seat broker; also deals in consolidator fares and courier flights.

Council Travel, 205 E 42nd St, New York, NY 10017 (☎1-800/226-8624), and branches in many other US cities. Student/budget travel agency. A sister company, Council Charter (☎1-800/800-8222), specializes in charter flights.

Educational Travel Center, 438 N Frances St, Madison, WI 53703 (☎1-800/747-5551 or 608/256-5551). Student/youth and consolidator fares.

International Student Exchange Flights, 5010 E Shea Blvd, Suite 104A, Scottsdale, AZ 85254 (☎602/951-1177). Student/youth fares, student IDs.

New Frontiers/Nouvelles Frontières, 12 E 33rd St, New York, NY 10016 (☎1-800/366-6387) and other branches in LA, Montréal, Québec City and San Francisco. French discount travel firm.

Skylink, 265 Madison Ave, 5th Floor, New York, NY 10016 (☎1-800/AIR-ONLY or 212/573-8980) with branches in Chicago, Los Angeles, Montreal, Toronto, and Washington DC. Consolidator.

STA Travel, 10 Downing St, New York, NY 10014 (☎1-800/777-0112 or 212/627-3111), and other branches in the Los Angeles, San Francisco and Boston areas. Worldwide discount travel firm specializing in student/youth fares.

TFI Tours International, 34 W 32nd St, New York, NY 10001 (☎1-800/745-8000 or 212/736-1140), and other offices in Las Vegas and Miami. Consolidator.

Travac Tours, 989 6th Ave, New York, NY 10018 (☎1-800/872-8800 or 212/563-3303). Consolidator and charter broker.

Travel Avenue, 10 S Riverside, Suite 1404, Chicago, IL 60606 (☎1-800/333-3335 or 312/876-6866). Full-service travel agent that offers discounts in the form of rebates.

Travel CUTS, 243 College St, Toronto, ON M5T 1P7 (☎1-800/667-2887 or 416/979-2406). Organization specializing in student fares, with branches all over Canada.

Travelers Advantage, 3033 S Parker Rd, Suite 900, Aurora, CO 80014 (☎1-800/548-1116). Full-service travel club.

UniTravel, 1177 N Warson Rd, St Louis, MO 63132 (☎1-800/325-2222 or 314/569-2501). Consolidator.

which may be cheaper than anything available on a scheduled flight, but again departure dates are fixed and withdrawal penalties are high (check the refund policy). If you travel a lot, **discount travel clubs** are another option – the annual membership fee may be worth it for benefits such as cut-price air tickets and car rental.

Don't automatically assume that tickets purchased through a travel specialist will be cheapest – once you get a quote, check with the airlines and you may turn up an even better deal. Be advised also that the pool of travel companies is swimming with sharks – exercise caution and never deal with a company that demands cash up front or refuses to accept payment by credit card.

Regardless of where you buy your ticket, fares will depend on the **season**, and are highest from May to September, when the weather is best; they drop during the "shoulder" seasons – September/October and March/April – and you'll get the best prices during the low season, November to March (excluding Christmas and New Year, when prices are hiked up and seats are at a premium). Note also that flying on weekends ordinarily adds around $75 to the round-trip fare; price ranges quoted below assume **mid-week travel**.

From the US

Nonstop Olympic Airways flights **from New York** to Athens start at around $700 return in winter (five weekly) and rise to $1040 during the summer (daily flights) for a maximum thirty-day stay; tickets must be bought at least seven days in advance. For a similar price, Olympic flies from **Boston** once a week during winter, twice a week during summer. TWA offers direct service to Athens from New York, but only once a week; flights start around $700 return in low season and jump to $1040 during the summer. Delta has just begun daily nonstop flights (year-round) from New York to Athens, though standard prices are a little more, at $815 winter, $1200 summer. American Airlines has service to Athens from the East Coast, changing carriers in London to Olympic, starting at $750 in low season and going up to $1140 in high season. Somewhat surprisingly, LOT Polish Airlines has cheap flights from New York to Athens, via Warsaw, three times a week, beginning at $700.

Since all scheduled flights to Athens from the **West Coast** go via New York or another eastern city (such as Atlanta), you basically end up paying for a transcontinental flight on top of the transatlantic fare: round-trip APEX tickets from Seattle, San Francisco or Los Angeles on TWA and Delta start at $960 in winter and go up to $1200 in the summer.

Most European airlines (Air France, Alitalia, Iberia, KLM, Lufthansa) connect selected American cities with Greece via their gateway cities in Europe, but these stopovers can mean a wait of a few hours or even a night – be sure to ask your ticket agent.

From Canada

As with the US, air fares **from Canada** to Athens vary depending on where you start your journey. The best-value scheduled round-trip fare is on Olympic, which flies nonstop out of Montréal and

Specialist tour operators in the US and Canada

Very few North American operators book group tours specifically for Corfu and the Ionians; at most, they might include one or two nights on Corfu. You can, however, get a tour operator to book you a tailor-made, independent package trip.

Cloud Tours ☎ 1-800/223-7880. Customized itineraries and honeymoon specials.

Grecian Holidays Tours ☎ 1-800/554-6281. Specializes in Greek island-hopping, and will build in Corfu and the Ionians.

Guaranteed Travel ☎ 201/540-1770. "Greece-your-way" independent travel.

Homeric Tours ☎ 1-800/223-5570. General Hellenic tour operator, with packages to Corfu via Athens.

Pharos Travel ☎ 1-800/999-5511. Mediterranean and Ionian specialists.

Triaena Travel ☎ 1-800/223-1273. Wide variety of custom-made package tours.

Zeus Tours ☎ 1-800/447-5667. Week-long Ionian island cruises.

Toronto twice a week for CDN$1190 (winter) up to CDN$1390 (summer).

KLM operates several flights a week to Athens via Amsterdam from Toronto, Montréal and Vancouver – from Toronto, expect to pay around CDN$1270 in winter, CDN$1420 in high season. Air Canada flies to Frankurt, with an onward connection on Lufthansa or Delta, at basically the same price. Numerous European carriers – Air France, Alitalia, British Airways, Iberia, Lufthansa, SwissAir and Czech Air – fly out of Montréal several times a week to Athens via major European cities, most starting at CDN$1270 in low season, some going up to as much as CDN$1800 during the summer. Keep in mind that these stopovers range from a few hours to an entire night.

Getting there from Australasia

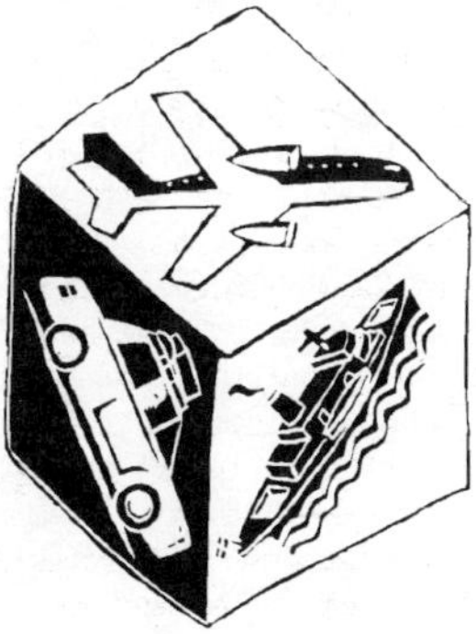

There are no direct flights from Australasia to the Ionian islands, so your best options are either to fly to Athens, where you can get a connecting flight with Olympic Airways (around A$100/NZ$120 one way) or continue your journey overland, or to fly to London where it's possible to pick up a cheap charter flight or package holiday (see "Getting there from Britain").

For both Greece and London, most airlines operate the following fare **seasons** (with some slight variations): **low** January 16 to end February; **high** May 16–31, June 1–August 31 and December 1–January 15; and **shoulder** the rest of the year. Fares from the major eastern Australian

Airlines in Australasia

Alitalia (Australia ☎02/9247 9133; NZ ☎09/379 4457). Several times a week to Athens via Bangkok and a transfer in Rome from major Australasian cities.

Britannia Airways (Australia ☎02/9251 1299; no NZ number). Charter flights to London, via Bangkok and Abu Dhabi, from major Australian cities and Auckland.

British Airways (Australia ☎02/9258 3300; NZ ☎09/356 8690). Daily flights to London via Bangkok/Singapore from major Australian cities and via LA from Auckland.

Garuda Indonesia (Australia ☎1800/800873; NZ ☎09/366 1855). Several flights a week to London, with either a transfer or stopover in Jakarta/Denpasar, from major Australasian cities.

Olympic Airways (Australia ☎02/9251 2044; in NZ, contact Air New Zealand, ☎09/366 2803). Twice weekly to Athens, with connections to Corfu, via Sydney and Bangkok from major eastern Australian cities (in conjunction with Qantas) and Auckland (in conjunction with Air New Zealand).

Philippine Airlines (Australia ☎02/9262 3333). Several flights a week to London, with either a transfer or stopover in Manila, from major Australian cities.

Qantas (Australia ☎131213; NZ ☎09/357 8900). Daily flights to London via Bangkok/Singapore from Australasian cities.

Thai Airways (Australia ☎131960; NZ ☎09/377 3886). Twice-weekly flights to Athens, with a transfer in Bangkok, from major Australasian cities.

Travel agents and consolidators in Australasia

Anywhere Travel, 345 Anzac Parade, Kingsford, Sydney (☎02/9663 0411).

Brisbane Discount Travel, 260 Queen St, Brisbane (☎07/3229 9211).

Budget Travel, 16 Fort St, Auckland, with other branches around the city (☎09/366 0061, toll-free 0800/808040).

Destinations Unlimited, 3 Milford Rd, Milford, Auckland (☎09/373 4033).

Flight Centres, Australia: Level 11, 33 Berry St, North Sydney (☎02/9241 2422); Bourke St, Melbourne (☎03/9650 2899); plus other branches nationwide.

New Zealand: National Bank Towers, 205–225 Queen St, Auckland (☎09/309 6171); Shop 1M, National Mutual Arcade, 152 Hereford St, Christchurch (☎03/379 7145); 50–52 Willis St, Wellington (☎04/472 8101); plus other branches nationwide.

Northern Gateway, 22 Cavenagh St, Darwin (☎08/8941 1394).

Passport Travel, 320b Glenferrie Rd, Malvern (☎03/9824 7183).

STA Travel, Australia: 702–730 Harris St, Ultimo, Sydney (☎02/9212 1255, toll-free 1800/637444); 256 Flinders St, Melbourne (☎03/9654 7266); other offices in state capitals and major universities.

New Zealand: Travellers' Centre, 10 High St, Auckland (☎09/309 0458); 233 Cuba St, Wellington (☎04/385 0561); 90 Cashel St, Christchurch (☎03/379 9098); other offices in Dunedin, Palmerston North, Hamilton and major universities.

Thomas Cook, Australia: 321 Kent St, Sydney (☎02/9248 6100); 257 Collins St, Melbourne (☎03/9650 2442); branches in other state capitals (local-call rate ☎131771).

New Zealand: 96–98 Anzac Ave, Auckland (☎09/379 3920).

Topdeck Travel, 65 Glenfell St, Adelaide (☎08/8232 7222).

Tymtro Travel, 428 George St, Sydney (☎02/9223 2211).

YHA Travel Centres, 422 Kent St, Sydney (☎02/9261 1111); 205 King St, Melbourne (☎03/9670 9611); 38 Stuart St, Adelaide (☎08/8231 5583); 154 Roma St, Brisbane (☎07/3236 1680); 236 William St, Northbridge, Perth (☎08/9227 5122); 69a Mitchell St, Darwin (☎08/8981 2560); 28 Criterion St, Hobart (☎03/6234 9617).

cities are common-rated, while from Perth and Darwin they're A$100–200 less if you go via Asia, A$200–400 more if you go via Canada or the US. Flying from Christchurch and Wellington costs NZ$150–300 more than from Auckland.

Tickets purchased direct from the airlines tend to be expensive, so it's best to head for a **travel agent** who, as well as offering better deals on fares, should have the latest information on limited special deals such as free stopovers en route and on fly-drive-accommodation packages. STA, who offer fare reductions for ISIC card holders and those under 26, and Flight Centres generally offer the lowest fares.

Specialist tour operators in Australasia

Since the Ionians are not a major destination for Australasians, there are no pre-packaged holidays, but the following agents can put together a holiday to suit your needs.

Eurolynx, 3rd Floor, 20 Fort St, Auckland ☎09/379 9716. Individually tailored travel itineraries.

Grecian Tours and Travel, 237a Lonsdale St, Melbourne ☎03/9663 3711. Accommodation, sailing and land tours.

Greek Island Travel and Tours, 607 Stirling Hwy, Peppermint Grove, WA ☎08/9385 4455. Greek holidays, accommodation and tours.

Kyrenia Travel Services, 92 Golburn St, Sydney ☎02/9283 2144. Accommodation, tours and cruises.

Travel Market, 11th Floor, T&G Building, 141 Queen St, Brisbane ☎07/3210 0323. Custom-made holidays, accommodation, car rental and yacht charter.

Olympic Airways, in conjunction with Qantas and Air New Zealand, have a good connecting service from Australasian cities **to Athens** and then on to Corfu, available from travel agents for around A$1950 in low season/2099 shoulder season/2199 high season (common-rated), NZ$2299/2599/2799 (from Auckland). Flights to Athens with Alitalia or Thai cost A$2000/2300/2499, NZ$2299/2530/2899. More expensive, at A$2399/2599/2899, NZ$2699/2799/3099, but a little more comfortable are Qantas and British Airways.

The lowest fares **to London** are with Britannia during their charter season from November to March (A$1289–1799; NZ$1799–2049). Failing that, try Garuda and Philippine, who operate only two seasonal bands, and at the time of writing are offering fares of A$1550 low season/1999 high season, NZ$1999/2250.

Among **round-the-world** tickets that include Athens (all valid for one year) are the BA–Qantas "Global Explorer" (A$2499 if you depart in low season/3099 if you depart in high season; NZ$2399/2999) and the Cathay–United Airlines "Globetrotter" (A$2349/2899; NZ$2999/3449), both of which allow limited backtracking and six free stopovers; additional stopovers cost A$100/NZ$110. Thai, in conjunction with Cathay, Air New Zealand and Varig, offer an RTW ticket with unlimited stopovers – except within the US and Canada – for A$3199/NZ$3299.

Getting there from mainland Greece and Italy

The Ionian islands have a wide choice of ferry connections with mainland Greek and Italian ports, as well as scheduled flights between Athens and Corfu, Préveza (for Lefkádha), Kefalloniá and Zákinthos. These links are particularly useful if you're working your way slowly around Europe and want to bypass the former Yugoslavia.

Besides the long-distance sea connections with Italy and the larger Greek ports described below, the Ionian islands are served by a variety of **local ferries** from the Greek mainland (Lefkádha, which has a land link and direct bus connections with the mainland, is the exception). Full details of each island's local ferry services are given in the "Travel details" at the end of the relevant chapter, and the more significant mainland ports are described in the Guide – **Igoumenítsa** on p.58, **Párga** on p.105, **Préveza** on p.121 and **Pátra** on p.192. Information about routes between the islands and general advice on Greek ferries can be found on p.27. If you're travelling direct to the Ionians **from Athens**, flying is the most convenient mode of transport, given the length of the bus and train journeys to the ports (8hr, for example, to Igoumenítsa), and is relatively cheap.

Flights from Athens

Olympic Airways operates daily **flights from Athens** to all the Ionian island airports: Corfu (3 daily), Kefalloniá (2 daily) and Zákinthos (2 daily), as well as Préveza (1 daily) on the mainland (for Lefkádha bus connections). Current standard one-way **prices** are Corfu 16,100dr, Kefalloniá 13,800dr, Zákinthos 13,300dr and Préveza 9700dr.

Olympic **schedules** can be picked up at their offices abroad (see "Getting there" sections) or

Ferries from Italy to the Ionians and mainland Greece

Routes

From the Italian ports, most ferries depart between 8pm and 10pm, though there are a number of afternoon departures. All voyage durations given are approximate.

From Ancona Marlines, ANEK and Minoan to Igoumenítsa (27hr) and Pátra (34hr); between them, these companies offer services Wed and Sat off season, Mon, Tues, Thurs and twice on Sat in season. Tickets to either destination start at around 16,500dr/£46 for a deck ticket 25,000dr/£70 for a vehicle. Superfast ferries also run daily to Pátra (21hr; no other stops) March–Nov (deck ticket 14,000dr/£38; vehicle 39,000dr/£108).

From Bari Ventouris almost daily year-round to Corfu and Igoumenítsa (both about 12hr; deck ticket 11,000dr/£30, vehicle 19,000dr/£53) and Pátra (20hr; deck ticket 11,000dr/£33; vehicle 19,000dr/£53). Poseidon Lines and Arkadia Lines to Igoumenítsa daily in season, Tues, Thurs, Sat, Sun in low season. Ventouris also sail from Bari to Sámi on Kefalloniá 2–3 times a week in July and August (20hr; deck ticket 10,000dr/£33; vehicle 15,000dr/£53).

From Brindisi Fragline to Corfu (10hr) and Igoumenítsa (11hr) 4–5 times a week March–Oct (deck 8000dr/£22; vehicle 15,500dr/£43). Adriatica to Corfu every other day April–Oct (7hr; deck 8500dr/£24; vehicle 13,000/£36). Strintzis daily to Corfu April–Oct (7hr; deck 7000dr/£20; vehicle 6000dr/£16). Vergina to Igoumenítsa (11hr; deck from 9300dr/£26; vehicle from 11,000dr/£30) and Pátra (21hr; deck from 10,000dr/£28; vehicle from 12,000dr/£36) Mon, Wed, Fri and Sat April–Oct. Medlink to Pátra via Sámi on Kefalloniá most days April–Sept (18hr; deck 11,000dr/£30; vehicle 14,500dr/£40).

From Otranto Rainbow Lines to Igoumenítsa (10hr) and Corfu (12hr) Thurs, Fri, Sat and Sun June–Aug (deck from 9300dr/£26; vehicle from 9300dr/£26).

UK Agents

Serena Holidays, 40 Kenway Rd, London SW5 ☎0171/244 8422. For Adriatica Lines.

Viamare Travel, Graphic House, 2 Sumatra Rd, London NW6 ☎0171/431 4560. Agents for ANEK, Arkadia, Fragline, Marlines, Rainbow Lines, Strintzis and Ventouris.

through their branch offices and representatives in Greece, which are maintained in almost every town or island of any size; Greek-only small booklets, which include prices for domestic routes, appear three times yearly (March, June & Oct) while English-language books geared more for an international readership are published twice yearly (March & Oct).

Island flights are often full in peak season; if they're an essential part of your plans, it is worth trying to make a **reservation** at least a week in advance. Domestic air tickets are non-refundable, but you can change your flight, space permitting, without penalty up to a few hours before your original departure.

Size restrictions mean that the 15-kilo **baggage weight limit** is fairly strictly enforced; if, however, you've just arrived from overseas or purchased your ticket outside Greece, you are allowed the 23-kilo standard international limit. All services operated on the domestic network are non-smoking.

Ferries from Italy

Ferries operated by a variety of companies connect four of Italy's Adriatic ports – **Ancona**, **Bari**, **Brindisi** and **Otranto** – to some or all of Greece's main Ionian Sea ports (Igoumenítsa, Corfu, Sámi on Kefalloniá, and Pátra). Some of these ferries call at more than one port en route; you can stop over at no extra charge if you get these stops specified on your ticket. All the ferries detailed in the box above also run in the opposite direction, with similar frequencies and durations.

In summer, it's essential to **book tickets** a few days ahead, especially in the peak July–August period – and certainly if you are taking a car across. During the winter you can usually just turn up at the ports, but it's still wise to book in advance if possible. **Students and under-26s** travelling with Eurail or InterRail are entitled to ten-percent discounts on certain high-season deck tickets with Medlink and Ventouris; no other companies currently offer student/youth discounts.

Travellers with disabilities

Lightweight wheelchairs are not an uncommon sight on beaches in the Ionian, proving that wheelchair users, at least, do holiday here. With planning, wheelchair users and those with sight, ambulatory or other disabilities can enjoy an inexpensive and trauma-free holiday in even the smallest of island resorts (see the box overleaf for a list of useful contacts).

It has to be admitted, though, that little in Greece, from the roads and buses to public and private buildings, is designed with the disabled in mind. There is only one public building in the Ionian designed for the disabled visitor – Corfu's excellent Archeological Museum – and the archipelago's sole public toilet with disabled access, on Corfu's Spianádha, was vandalized and out of order when last checked.

The first thing to do is spend some time gathering **information** about your choice of destination, and options for travel and accommodation. Addresses of contact organizations are published overleaf, and the Greek National Tourist Organization is a good first step, as long as you have specific questions to put to them; they publish a useful questionnaire which you can send to hotels or apartment/villa owners. Where possible, try to double-check all information, as things in Greece have a habit of changing without warning.

Planning a holiday

There are **organized tours and holidays** specifically for people with disabilities, and both Thomson and Horizon in Britain will advise on the suitability of holidays advertised in their brochures. Travelling more independently is also perfectly possible, provided you establish your parameters of ability as a traveller, plan for the worst, and don't automatically expect that assistance will always be immediately at hand. If you're not entirely confident you can manage alone, try to travel with an able-bodied friend (or two). Greek airports, in particular, can resemble rugby scrums, are not always fitted with access ramps or other aids, and airport staff may not always be able to help.

Read your travel **insurance** small print carefully to make sure that people with a pre-existing medical condition are not excluded. And use your travel agent to make your journey simpler: airlines can cope better if they are expecting you, with a wheelchair provided at airports and staff primed to help. A medical certificate of your fitness to travel, provided by your doctor, is also extremely useful; some airlines or insurance companies may insist on it.

Make a **list** of all the facilities that will make your life easier while you are away. You may want a ground-floor room, or access to a large elevator; you may have special dietary requirements, or need level ground to enable you to reach shops, beaches, bars and places of interest. You should also keep track of all your other special needs, making sure, for example, that you have extra supplies of drugs – carried with you if you fly – and a prescription including the generic name in case of emergency. Carry spares of any kind of clothing or equipment that might be hard to find in Greece.

Useful contacts for travellers with disabilities

National Tourist Organization of Greece (see p.25 for addresses). Offers general advice on terrain and climate. They have nothing specific for disabled visitors except a brief list of hotels which may be suitable.

Australia

ACROD (Australian Council for Rehabilitation of the Disabled), PO Box 60, Curtin ACT 2605 ☎06/682 4333; 55 Charles St, Ryde ☎02/9809 4488.

Canada

Jewish Rehabilitation Hospital, 3205 Place Alton Goldbloom, Montréal, PQ H7V 1R2 ☎514/688-9550. Guidebooks and travel information.

Twin Peaks Press, Box 129, Vancouver, WA 98666 ☎206/694-2462 or 1-800/637-2256. Publisher of the *Directory of Travel Agencies for the Disabled* ($19.95), listing more than 370 agencies worldwide; *Travel for the Disabled* ($19.95); the *Directory of Accessible Van Rentals* ($9.95) and *Wheelchair Vagabond* ($14.95), loaded with personal tips.

Greece

Association Hermes, Patriárchou 13, Grigoríou E, 16542 Argyroúpolis, Athens ☎01/9961 887. Can advise disabled visitors to Greece.

Evyenia Stavropoulou, Lavinia Tours, Egnatía 101, 54110 Thessaloníki ☎031/240 041. Will advise disabled visitors and has tested many parts of Greece in her wheelchair. She also organizes tours within Greece.

Ireland

Disability Action Group, 2 Annadale Ave, Belfast BT7 3JH ☎01232/491011. Information and advice group.

Irish Wheelchair Association, Blackheath Drive, Clontarf, Dublin 3 ☎01/833 8241. A national voluntary organization working with people with disabilities, with related services for holidaymakers.

New Zealand

Disabled Persons Assembly, PO Box 10, 138 The Terrace, Wellington ☎04/472 2626.

UK

Holiday Care Service, 2nd Floor, Imperial Building, Victoria Rd, Horley, Surrey RH6 7PZ ☎01293/774535. Provides free lists of accessible accommodation abroad and information on financial help for holidays.

RADAR (Royal Association for Disability and Rehabilitation), 12 City Forum, 250 City Rd, London EC1V 8AF ☎0171/250 3222; Minicom ☎0171/250 4119. A good source of advice on travel abroad; they produce a holiday guide for Europe (£5 inc. p&p) in alternate years.

Tripscope, The Courtyard, Evelyn Rd, London W4 5JL ☎0181/994 9294. This registered charity provides a national telephone information service offering free advice on international transport and travel for those with a mobility problem.

USA

Directions Unlimited, 720 N Bedford Rd, Bedford Hills, NY 10507 ☎1-800/533-5343. Tour operator specializing in custom tours for people with disabilities.

Mobility International USA, PO Box 10767, Eugene, OR 97440 (Voice and TDD: ☎503/343-1284). Information and referral services, access guides, tours and exchange programmes. Annual membership $20 (includes quarterly newsletter).

Society for the Advancement of Travel for the Handicapped (SATH), 347 5th Ave, New York, NY 10016 ☎212/447-7284. Non-profit travel-industry referral service that passes queries onto its members as appropriate; allow plenty of time for a response.

Travel Information Service, Moss Rehabilitation Hospital, 1200 West Tabor Rd, Philadelphia, PA 19141 ☎215/456-9600. Telephone information and referral service.

Visas and red tape

UK, Irish and all other EU nationals need only a valid passport for entry to Greece; you are no longer stamped in on arrival or out upon departure, and in theory enjoy the same civil rights as Greek citizens (see "Work", p.50). US, Australian, New Zealand, Canadian and most non-EU Europeans receive entry and exit stamps, effectively a "tourist visa", in their passports and can stay, as tourists, for ninety days.

Extensions

If you wish to remain in Greece for longer than three months, you should officially apply for an **extension**. This can be done in Corfu Town at the *Ipiresía Allodhapón* (Aliens' Bureau) at Alexandhrás 19 (☎0661/39 277); brace yourself for concerted bureaucracy. In other locations you visit the local police station, where staff are usually more co-operative.

Unless of Greek descent, visitors from **non-EU countries** are currently allowed only a three-month extension to the basic tourist visa, and this costs 11,000dr. In theory, **EU nationals** can stay indefinitely, but for a non-employment resident visa you will still have to present yourself every six months to the relevant authorities; only the first extension is free. In all cases, the procedure should be set in motion a couple of weeks before your time runs out. If you don't have a work permit, you will be required to present pink, personalized **bank exchange receipts** (see p.20) totalling at least 450,000dr for the preceding three months, as proof that you have sufficient funds to support yourself without working. Possession of unexpired credit cards, a Greek savings account passbook or travellers' cheques can to some extent substitute for this requirement.

Some non-EU resident individuals get around the law by leaving Greece every three months and re-entering a few days later for a new, ninety-day tourist stamp. However, with the recent flood of refugees from Albania and former Yugoslavia, plus a smaller influx of east Europeans looking for work, immigration personnel don't always look very kindly on this practice.

If you **overstay** your time and then leave under your own steam – ie are not detected within the country and deported – you'll be given a 22,000dr spot fine upon departure, effectively a double-priced retro-active visa extension; no excuses will be entertained except perhaps a doctor's certificate stating that you were immobilized in hospital. It cannot be overemphasized just how exigent Greek immigration officials often are on these issues.

Greek embassies and consulates abroad

Australia 9 Turrana St, Yarralumla, Canberra, ACT 260 ☎062/733158.

Britain 1a Holland Park, London W11 ☎0171/221 6467.

Canada 76–80 Maclaren St, Ottawa, ON K2P 0K6 ☎613/238-6271.

Ireland 1 Upper Pembroke St, Dublin 2 ☎01/676 7254.

New Zealand 57 Willeston St, 10th Floor, Wellington, PO Box 274066 ☎04/473 7775–6.

USA 2221 Massachusetts Ave NW, Washington, DC 20008 ☎202/939-5800.

Customs regulations

For EU citizens travelling between EU countries, the limits on goods already taxed have been relaxed enormously. However, **duty-free allowances** are as follows: 200 cigarettes or 50 cigars, two litres of still table wine, one litre of spirits and 60ml of perfume. Exporting **antiquities** without a permit is a serious offence; **drug smuggling**, not surprisingly, incurs severe penalties.

Costs, money and banks

The cost of living in Greece has spiralled during the years of EU membership: the days of renting an island house for a pittance are gone forever, and food prices now differ little from those of other member countries. However, outside the established resorts, travel between and around the islands remains reasonably priced, with the cost of restaurant meals, short-term accommodation and public transport still cheaper than anywhere in northern or western Europe except Portugal.

Prices depend on where and when you go. The towns and larger tourist resorts are more expensive, and costs everywhere increase sharply in July, August and at Easter. **Students** with an International Student Identity Card (ISIC) can get discounted admission fees at many museums, though these, and other occasional discounts, are sometimes limited to EU students.

Some basic costs

In most parts of the Ionian islands a **daily budget** of £20–25/US$30–38 per person will get you basic accommodation, breakfast, picnic lunch and a simple evening meal, if you're one of a couple. Camping would cut costs considerably. On £25–35/US$38–55 a day you could be living quite well, plus treating yourself and a companion to motorbike rental.

Inter-island **ferries**, one of the main expenses, are reasonably priced, subsidized by the government in an effort to preserve island communities. A deck-class ticket between any of the southerly islands and the mainland costs about £5/US$7.50, while between Corfu and the mainland or Paxí the ticket can be as little as £3/US$4.50. Long-distance journeys, such as between Corfu and Pátra, start at around £15/US$22.50.

The simplest double **room** generally costs around £12–15/US$18–23 a night, depending on the location and the plumbing arrangements. Organized **campsites** are little more than £2/US$3 per person, with similar charges per tent and perhaps 25 percent more for a camper van. With discretion you can camp for free in the more remote, rural areas.

A basic taverna **meal** with local wine can be had for around £7/US$10.50 a head. Add a better bottle of wine, seafood, or more careful cooking, and it could be up to £10/US$15 a head – but you'll rarely pay more than that, except in Corfu Town or the smarter island restaurants. Sharing seafood, Greek salads and dips is a good way to keep costs down in the better restaurants, and sharing is quite common, as is sticking to just one or two starters. Even in the most developed of resorts, with inflated "international" menus, you'll often be able to find a more earthy but decent taverna where the locals eat.

Currency

Greek currency is the **drachma** (*dhrahmí*), and the exchange rate in the islands is currently around

370dr to the pound sterling, 240dr to the US dollar. The most common **notes** in circulation are those of 500, 1000, 5000 and 10,000 drachmae (*dhrahmés*), while coins come in denominations of 5, 10, 20, 50 and 100dr; you might come across 1-drachma and 2-drachma coins and 50-drachma bills too, though they're rarely used these days. Shopkeepers rarely bother with differences of less than 10dr.

Banks and exchange

Greek **banks** are normally open Monday–Thursday 8.30am–2pm, Friday 8.30am–1.30pm. Certain branches in larger island towns or tourist centres are open extra hours in the evenings and on Saturday mornings for **exchanging money**. Outside these times, the larger hotels and travel agencies can often provide this service – though often with hefty commission. Always take your passport with you as proof of identity, and be prepared for at least one long line; sometimes you have to line up once to have the transaction approved, and again to pick up the cash.

The safest way to carry money is in **travellers' cheques**. These can be obtained from banks (even if you don't have an account) or from offices of Thomas Cook and American Express; you'll pay a commission of between one and two percent. You can cash the cheques at most banks and post offices, and (often at poorer rates) at quite a number of hotels, travel agencies and tourist shops. Each transaction in Greece will incur a **commission** charge of 400–800dr, so you won't want to change too many small amounts.

Small-denomination **foreign banknotes** are also extremely useful, and relatively unlikely to be stolen in Greece (see "Police and trouble", p.49). Since the lifting of all remaining currency controls for Greek residents in early 1994, a number of authorized brokers for exchanging foreign cash have emerged in Athens and major tourist centres. Choose those that charge a flat percentage commission (usually one percent) rather than a high minimum when you're changing small amounts.

Most British banks can issue current-account holders with a **Eurocheque** card and chequebook; these are accepted in some shops in the larger towns and resorts and, if you know your PIN number, they can also be used for withdrawing drachmae from cash machines or Greek banks. An annual card fee is payable for this service, plus a two percent processing charge on the debit facility subject to a minimum of about £1.75, but there's no on-the-spot commission levied on straightforward transactions. The current limit is 45,000dr per cheque, and the bank or merchant does not need to know the prevailing exchange rate – useful if bank computers have gone down.

Exchanging money at the **post office** has considerable advantages in Greece. There are post offices in all the island capitals and some larger resorts, and mobile ones in resorts such as Nidhrí, giving you access to exchange almost anywhere you go. In addition, commissions levied for exchanging cheques or cash tend, at a flat rate of about 300dr per transaction, to be much lower than at banks or travel agencies. If you have a UK-based Girobank account, you can also use your chequebook to get money at remote post offices.

Finally, there is no need to purchase large amounts of drachmae **before arrival**. Airport arrival lounges will usually – though not always – have an exchange booth open for passengers on incoming international flights. If travelling independently, it's wise to bring a small stash of drachmae with you, for taxis, drinks or meals. If you're stuck, remember that hotel-owners rarely expect payment up front and will usually accept your passport as surety.

Credit cards and ATMs

Major **credit cards** are rarely accepted by tavernas or hotels: notable hotel exceptions are the *Bella Venezia* and *Atlantis* in Corfu Town, *Mentor* on Itháki, *Mouikis* and *Mirabel* in Argostóli, and *Reparo* in Zákinthos. However, credit cards are useful – indeed almost essential – for renting cars, for example. Diners and Amex are the most common, Visa less so and Mastercard rare. If you run short of money, you can get a **cash advance** on a credit card, but be warned that the minimum amount is 15,000dr. The *Emborikí Trápeza* (Commercial Bank) handles Visa, and the *Ethnikí Trápeza* (National Bank) services Mastercard customers. However, there is usually a two-percent credit-card charge, often unfavourable rates and always interminable delays while transaction approval is sought by telex.

It is far simpler to use the growing network of Greek **cashpoint machines** (**ATMs**) that are now found in most large ports and island capitals, though not yet on any of the smaller islands. The most useful and well distributed are those of the National Bank which take Cirrus and Mastercard, and those of the Commercial Bank which handles Plus System and Visa cards; Visa is also compatible with ATMs at the *Trápeza Pistéos* (Credit Bank) and the *Ioníki Trápeza.* (Ionian Bank). Most capitals and mainland ports will also have 24-hour automated exchange machines – with a poor exchange rate, but useful in emergencies.

Emergency cash

All told, learning and using the **PIN** numbers for any debit or credit cards you have will be the quickest and least expensive way of securing moderate amounts of emergency funds from abroad. In an emergency, however, you can arrange to have **money sent** from home to a bank in Greece. Receiving funds via telex takes a minimum of three days and often up to six days, so be prepared for delays. From the UK, a bank charge of three percent, or minimum £17, maximum £35, is levied. Bank drafts can also be sent, with higher commission rates. You can retrieve the amount in foreign currency, or even as travellers' cheques, but heavy commissions apply.

Funds can also be sent via **Western Union Money Transfer** (☎0800/833833 in the UK, ☎1-800/325-6000 in the US or Canada), which is represented by the Ergo Bank, Alexandhrás 31, in Corfu Town (Mon–Fri 8am–2pm; ☎0661/25449). Fees depend on the amount being transferred, but as examples, wiring £400–500 should cost around £37, wiring $1000 should cost around $75; the funds should be available for collection within minutes of being sent. American Express's MoneyGram facility is now only available to Amex card holders; the American Express Bureau de Change is at Kapodístriou 20a, Corfu Town (Mon–Fri 8am–2pm; ☎0661/30883).

Currency regulations

Since 1994, Greek **currency restrictions** no longer apply to Greek nationals and other EU member citizens, and the drachma is freely convertible. Arcane rules may still apply to arrivals from North America, Australia or non-EU nations, but you would have to be extremely unlucky to run foul of them.

If you have any reason to believe that you'll be acquiring large quantities of drachmae – from work or sale of goods (the latter illegal, incidentally) – declare everything on arrival, then request (and save) pink, personalized receipts for all **exchange transactions**. Otherwise you may find that you can only re-exchange a limited sum of drachmae on departure; even at the best of times many banks stock a limited range of foreign notes, though you can usually strike lucky at airport exchange booths. These pink receipts are also essential for obtaining a non-employment resident visa (see p.17).

Health matters

There are no required inoculations for Greece, though it's wise to ensure that you are up to date on tetanus and polio. Don't forget to take out travel insurance (see p.23), so that you're covered in case of serious illness or accidents.

Water quality is variable in the Ionian islands and, although the larger hotels have a good drinking water supply, that cannot be said of smaller and more out-of-the-way places. Villa and apartment companies often warn you to boil tap water before drinking it. On smaller islands such as Paxí, many properties use undrinkable *glýpha*, desalinated seawater, in bathrooms. Bottled water is widely available if you're uncertain.

Specific hazards

The main health problems experienced by visitors have to do with **overexposure to the sun**, and the odd nasty from the sea. To combat the former, don't spend too long in the sun, cover up and wear a hat, use high-factor sunblock (preferably not the waterproof variety: this simply bastes you) and drink plenty of fluids in the hot months to avoid any danger of sunstroke. Remember that even a hazy sun can burn. For sea wear, goggles or a diving mask are useful, as well as footwear for walking over slippery rocks.

Hazards of the deep

In the sea, you may have the bad luck to meet an armada of **jellyfish** (*tsoúkhtres*), especially in late summer; they come in various colours and sizes, from tiny purple ones to some the size of a large pizza. Various over-the-counter remedies are sold in resort pharmacies; baking soda or diluted ammonia also help to lessen the sting. The welts and burning usually subside of their own accord within a few hours; there are no deadly man-of-war species in Greek waters.

Less venomous but more common are black, spiky **sea urchins** (*ehíni*), which infest rocky shorelines year-round; if you step on or graze one, a sewing needle (you can crudely sterilize it by heat from a cigarette lighter) and olive oil are effective for removing spines from your anatomy; if you don't extract them, they'll fester.

The worst maritime danger – fortunately very rare – is the **weever fish** (*dhrakéna*), which buries itself in tidal zone sand with just its poisonous dorsal and gill spines protruding. If you tread on one, the sudden pain is excruciating, and the exceptionally potent venom can cause permanent paralysis of the affected area. The imperative first aid is to immerse your foot in water as hot as you can stand, which degrades the toxin and relieves the swelling of joints and attendant pain, but you should still seek medical attention as soon as possible.

Somewhat more common are **stingrays** (Greek names include *platí, seláhi, vátos* or *trígona*), who mainly frequent bays with sandy bottoms, against which they can camouflage themselves. Though shy, they can give you a nasty lash with their tail if trodden on, so shuffle your feet a bit on entering the water.

Sandflies, mosquitoes, snakes, scorpions

If you are sleeping on or near a beach, a wise precaution is to use insect repellent, either lotion or wrist/ankle bands, and/or a tent with a screen to guard against **sandflies**. Their bites are potentially dangerous, as the flies spread visceral leishmaniasis, a rare parasitic infection characterized by chronic fever, listlessness and weight loss.

Mosquitoes (*kounóupia*) in Greece carry nothing worse than a vicious bite, but they can be infuriating. The best solution is to burn pyrethrum incense coils (*spíres* or *fidhákia*), which are widely and cheaply available. Better, if you can get them, are the small electrical devices (trade name *Vape-Net*) that vaporize an odourless insecticide tablet; many "rooms" proprietors supply them routinely. Insect repellents, such as Autan, are available from most general stores and kiosks on the islands.

Adders (*ohiés*) and **scorpions** (*skorpií*) are found throughout the Ionian; both species are shy, and the latter usually quite small and harmless, but take care when climbing over dry-stone walls where snakes like to sun themselves, and don't put hands or feet in places (eg shoes) where you haven't looked first.

Pharmacies and drugs

For **minor complaints** it's easiest to go to the local **farmakío**. Greek pharmacists are highly trained and dispense a number of medicines that elsewhere could only be prescribed by a doctor. In the larger towns and resorts there'll usually be one who speaks good English. Pharmacies are usually closed evenings and Saturday mornings, but are supposed to have a sign on their door referring you to the nearest one that's open. **Homeopathic and herbal remedies** are quite widely available, too, and the larger island towns have dedicated homeopathic pharmacies, delineated by the green cross sign.

If you regularly use any form of **prescription drug**, you should take a copy of the prescription together with the generic name of the drug – this will help should you need to replace it and also avoid possible problems with customs officials. In this regard, it's worth pointing out that codeine is banned in Greece. If you import any you might find yourself in serious trouble, so check labels carefully; it's the core ingredient of Panadeine, Veganin, Solpadeine, Codis and Empirin-Codeine, to name just a few compounds.

Contraceptive pills are more readily available every year, but don't count on getting them outside of a few large island towns (over the counter from *farmakía*). **Condoms**, however, are inexpensive and ubiquitous – just ask for *profilaktiká* (the slangy *lastiká* or slightly vulgar *kapótes* are even better understood) at any pharmacy or corner *períptero* (kiosk). It's also quite common to find them prominently displayed in supermarkets, sometimes with the blunt legend "Anti-AIDS".

Lastly, **hay fever** sufferers should be prepared for the early Greek pollen season, at its height from April to June. If you are taken by surprise, pharmacists stock tablets and creams, but it's cheaper to travel prepared: commercial antihistamines such as Triludan are difficult if not impossible to find in the islands, and local brands can cost around £12/US$18 for a pack of ten.

Doctors and hospitals

For **serious medical attention**, phone ☎166 for an ambulance. You'll find English-speaking doctors in any of the bigger towns or resorts; travel agencies or hotel staff should be able to come up with some names if you have any difficulty.

In **emergencies** – for cuts, broken bones, etc – treatment is given free in **state hospitals**, though you will only get the most basic level of nursing care. Greek hospitals expect patients' families to feed and care for them in hospital, so as a tourist you'll be at a severe disadvantage. Somewhat better are the ordinary state-run **outpatient clinics** (*yatría*) attached to most public hospitals and also found in rural locales; these operate on a first-come, first-served basis, so go early – hours are usually 8am to noon.

Don't forget to obtain **receipts** for the cost of all drugs and medical treatment; without them you won't be able to claim back the money on your travel insurance.

Insurance

UK and other EU nationals are, officially at least, entitled to free medical care in Greece (see "Health matters", p.21), upon presentation of an E111 form, available from most post offices. "Free", however, means just admittance to the lowest grade of state hospital (known as a *yenikó nosokomío*), and does not include nursing care or the cost of medication. In practice, hospital staff tend to greet E111s with uncomprehending looks, and you may have to pay and request reimbursement by the NHS upon return home. In any case, if you need prolonged medical care, you're better off using private treatment, which is expensive – 8000dr minimum for a brief clinic consultation. Costs of prescription drugs and anything beyond basic medical equipment – bandages, splints, etc – escalate from there.

Some form of **travel insurance** is therefore advisable – indeed essential for **North Americans** and **Australasians**, whose countries have no formal healthcare agreements with Greece (other than allowing for free emergency treatment). For **medical claims**, keep receipts, including those from pharmacies. You will have to pay for all private medical care on the spot (insurance claims can be processed if you have hospital treatment), but it can all be claimed back eventually. Travel insurance usually provides cover for the **loss of baggage, money and tickets**, too. If you're thinking of **renting a moped** or motorbike on the islands (many people do), make sure the policy covers motorbike accidents. Some policies exclude hired bike or car accidents, others will cover such events but only if you were acting within local traffic laws when the accident hap-

TRAVEL INSURANCE COMPANIES AND AGENCIES

BRITAIN AND IRELAND

Campus Travel ☎ 0171/730 3402.

Columbus Travel Insurance ☎ 0171/375 0011.

Endsleigh Insurance ☎ 0171/436 4451.

Frizzell Insurance ☎ 01202/292333.

Link Travel (Dublin) ☎ 01/872 1444.

Sky Tours (Dublin) ☎ 01/836 6677.

STA Travel ☎ 0171/361 6161.

USIT (Belfast) ☎ 01232/324073.

NORTH AMERICA

Access America ☎ 1-800/284-8300.

Carefree Travel Insurance ☎ 1-800/323-3149.

Desjardins Travel Insurance – Canada only ☎ 1-800/463-7830.

International Student Insurance Service (ISIS) – sold by STA Travel ☎ 1-800/777-0112.

Travel Assistance International ☎ 1-800/821-2828.

Travel Guard ☎ 1-800/826-1300.

Travel Insurance Services ☎ 1-800/937-1387.

AUSTRALASIA

AFTA (Sydney) ☎ 02/9956 4800.

Cover More (Sydney) ☎ 02/9202 8000; toll-free 1800/251881.

Ready Plan (Victoria) toll-free ☎ 1800/337 462; (Auckland) ☎ 09/379 3399.

UTAG (Sydney) ☎ 02/9819 6855; toll-free 1800/809462.

pened. Check whether any policy excludes **"risk" pastimes**, which may include scuba diving and even trekking.

Britain and Ireland

In **Britain and Ireland**, travel insurance schemes (from around £26 a month) are sold by almost every travel agent or bank, as well as by specialist insurance companies. Policies issued through the companies listed in the box on p.23 are all good value. Columbus also does an annual multi-trip policy which offers twelve months' cover for £47.

Most **banks** and **credit card** issuers also offer some sort of vacation insurance, often automatic if you pay for the holiday with a card. Travel agents and tour operators are also likely to recommend insurance when you book; indeed some will insist you take it. These policies are usually reasonable value, though as ever you should check the small print. If you have a good "all-risks" home insurance policy it may well cover your possessions against loss or theft even when overseas, and many private medical schemes also cover you when abroad – make sure you know the procedure and the helpline number.

US and Canada

Before buying an insurance policy, check that you're not already covered. **Canadians** are usually covered for medical mishaps overseas by their provincial health plans. Holders of official **student/teacher/youth cards** are entitled to accident coverage and hospital inpatient benefits. Students will often find that their student health coverage extends during the vacations and for one term beyond the date of last enrolment. **Bank and credit cards** (particularly American Express) often have certain levels of medical or other insurance included, and you may automatically get travel insurance if you use a major credit or charge card to pay for your trip. **Home-owners' or renters' insurance** often covers theft or loss of documents, money and valuables while overseas, though conditions and maximum amounts vary from company to company.

After exhausting the possibilities above, you might want to contact a specialist **travel insurance company** (see box on p.23); your travel agent can also usually recommend one, though most can arrange the insurance themselves at no extra charge. Policies are comprehensive (accidents, illnesses, delayed or lost luggage, cancelled flights, etc), but maximum payouts tend to be meagre. Premiums vary, so shop around. The best deals are usually to be had through student travel agencies – ISIS policies, for example, cost $80–105 for a month. If you're passing through Britain in transit, you may prefer to buy a British policy (see above), which is usually cheaper and wider in scope, though some British insurers may require a permanent UK address.

Most North American travel policies apply only to items lost, stolen or damaged while in the custody of an identifiable, responsible third party such as a hotel porter, an airline or a luggage consignment. In all cases of theft or loss of goods, you must contact the local police – often within a certain time limit – to have a complete report made out so that your insurer can process the claim. This can occasionally prove tricky in Greece, since many officials simply won't accept that anything could be stolen on their turf, or at least don't want to take responsibility for it. Be persistent, and if necessary enlist the support of the local tourist police or tourist office. Note that very few insurers will arrange on-the-spot payments in the event of a major expense or loss; you will usually be reimbursed once you're home.

Australia and New Zealand

Travel insurance is put together by the airlines and travel agent groups (see box on p.23) in conjunction with insurance companies. They are all comparable in premium and coverage – a typical insurance policy will cost A$190/NZ$220 for one month, A$270/NZ$320 for two months and A$330/NZ$400 for three months. Most adventure sports are covered, but check your policy first.

Information and maps

The National Tourist Organization of Greece (*Ellinikós Organismós Tourismós*, or EOT; GNTO abroad) has offices in most European capitals, and major cities in Australia and North America (see box below for details). It publishes an impressive array of free, glossy, regional pamphlets that are good for getting an idea of where you want to go, even if the text is usually in brochure-speak. The EOT also has a reasonable map of Greece, and brochures on special interests and festivals.

Tourist offices

Tourist offices in the Ionian are actually on the decline: with the closure of the one in Lefkádha, only Corfu and Argostóli now have offices, though both are friendly and keen to help. They keep lists of rooms and other accommodation, can advise on trips to island sights, and may know certain tricks about buses and ferries that don't appear on the timetables. Elsewhere, local travel companies, hotels and other businesses are usually happy to help with information.

Maps

The Ionian is probably the worst-served region in Greece in terms of cartography. Local **maps** are often inaccurate and out of date, and even the widely available Toubi's series can be relied on for little more than confirming that a road or path connects A with B. Few maps can be used for orienteering, either on foot or by vehicle, as zigzag hill roads are sometimes drawn as a straight line, and relationships between such trifling geographical details as hills, sea and towns can be wildly out.

Maps on a par with Britain's Ordnance Survey do exist in Greece, but are regarded as a military secret. Earlier maps, from British surveys during World War II, are held in the Map Room of the Royal Geographical Society, Kensington Gore, London SW7 2AR (☎0171/591 3000), which is open to the public, but copies of the maps are only available if you obtain written permission from the Ministry of Defence, and then pay for copies to be made. Given the age of the detail,

Greek national tourist offices abroad

Australia 51 Pitt St, Sydney, NSW 2000 ☎02/9241 1663.

Britain 4 Conduit St, London W1R 0DJ ☎0171/734 5997.

Canada 1300 Bay St, Upper Level, Toronto, ON M5R 3K8 ☎416/968-2220; 1233 rue de la Montagne, H3G 1Z2 Montréal, Quebec ☎514/871-1535.

Denmark Vester Farimagsgade 1, DK 1606-Kobenhavn V ☎325-332.

Netherlands Leidsestraat 13, NS 1017 Amsterdam ☎20/254-212.

Norway Ovre Slottsgate 15B, 0157 Oslo 1 ☎2/426-501.

Sweden Birger Jarlsgatan 30, PO Box 5298, S10246 Stockholm ☎8/679 6480.

USA 645 Fifth Ave, New York, NY 10022 ☎212/421-5777.

NB If your home country isn't listed here, apply to the embassy. Note that there are no Greek tourist offices in Ireland or New Zealand.

MAP OUTLETS

AUSTRALIA

Bowyangs, 372 Little Bourke St, Melbourne ☎03/9670 4383.

The Map Shop, 16a Peel St, Adelaide ☎08/8231 2033.

Perth Map Centre, 891 Hay St, Perth ☎09/9322 5733.

Travel Bookshop, 20 Bridge St, Sydney ☎02/9241 3554.

CANADA

Open Air Books and Maps, 25 Toronto St, Toronto, ON M5R 2C1 ☎416/363-0719.

Ulysses Travel Bookshop, 4176 St-Denis, Montréal ☎514/289-0993.

World Wide Books and Maps, 1247 Granville St, Vancouver, BC V6Z 1E4 ☎604/687-3320.

IRELAND

Easons Bookshop, 80 Middle Abbey St, Dublin 1 ☎01/873 3811.

Fred Hanna's Bookshop, 27–29 Nassau St, Dublin 2 ☎01/677 1255.

Hodges Figgis Bookshop, 56–58 Dawson St, Dublin 2 ☎01/677 4754.

Waterstone's, Queens Building, 8 Royal Ave, Belfast BT1 1DA ☎01232/247355.

NEW ZEALAND

Specialty Maps, 58 Albert St, Auckland ☎09/307 2217.

UK

Daunt Books, 83 Marylebone High St, London W1 ☎0171/224 2295.

National Map Centre, 22–24 Caxton St, London SW1 ☎0171/222 4945.

John Smith and Sons, 57–61 St Vincent St, Glasgow G2 5TB ☎0141/221 7472.

Stanfords, 12–14 Long Acre, London WC2 ☎0171/836 1321; 52 Grosvenor Gardens, London SW1W 0AG; 156 Regent St, London W1R 5TA. Maps available by mail or phone order.

The Travel Bookshop, 13–15 Blenheim Crescent, London W11 2EE ☎0171/229 5260.

US

The Complete Traveler Bookstore, 199 Madison Ave, New York, NY 10016 ☎212/685 -9007; 3207 Fillmore St, San Francisco, CA 92123 ☎415/923-1511.

Forsyth Travel Library, 9154 W 57th St, Shawnee Mission, KS 66201 ☎1-800/367-7984.

Map Link Inc, 25 E Mason St, Santa Barbara, CA 93101 ☎805/965-4402.

Phileas Fogg's Books & Maps, #87 Stanford Shopping Center, Palo Alto, CA 94304 ☎1-800/233-FOGG in California; ☎1-800/533-FOGG elsewhere in the US.

Rand McNally, 444 N Michigan Ave, Chicago, IL 60611 ☎312/321-1751; 150 E 52nd St, New York, NY 10022 ☎212/758-7488; 595 Market St, San Francisco, CA 94105 ☎415/777-3131; 1201 Connecticut Ave NW, Washington, DC 20003 ☎202/223-6751. For maps by mail order, call ☎1-800/333-0136, ext 2111.

Sierra Club Bookstore, 730 Polk St, San Francisco, CA 94109 ☎415/923-5500.

Travel Books & Language Center, 4931 Cordell Ave, Bethesda, MD 20814 ☎1-800/220-2665.

Traveler's Bookstore, 22 W 52nd St, New York, NY 10019 ☎212/664-0995.

these would be of little use to anyone except the off-road hiker (or as a work of art). Most pertinently, though, mere possession of such detailed maps is itself an **offence** in Greece: two Dutch visitors were arrested as "spies" in 1996 for possession of such a map in the vicinity of an airfield.

The most reliable **general map** of the Ionian region is the *Bartholomew Corfu & Ionian islands Holiday Map* (1:100,000), which is as geographically accurate as possible at this scale, even on the smaller islands. Also serviceable are the AA-MacMillan and Globetrotter maps at a similar scale.

On **Corfu**, an independent mapmaker, Stephan Jaskulowski, has produced a beautiful set of hand-drawn maps to sections of the island, which should soon be available in book form.

The maps detail all roads, tracks and main paths, with lines of elevation and navigational features. At the moment, each island section map costs 800dr in the form of a colour photocopy. A map of the whole island, the *Precise Road Map of Kérkira*, costing around 1000dr, is expected to be published under the aegis of the *Corfiot* monthly English-language magazine.

A similar island map is available on **Paxí**. Produced in recent years by cartographers Elizabeth and Ian Bleasdale and sold by most tourism businesses on the island, it is chiefly a detailed walking map, but is the best, and certainly the most accurate, of any of the maps of Paxí.

Walkers should also check out Noel Rochford's two books, *Landscapes of Paxos* and *Landscapes of Corfu* (Sunflower), which detail walks around both islands. Available on Corfu, at least in the better bookshops, Hilary Whitton Paipeti's *Second Book of Corfu Walks* (Hermes Press) details over thirty island walks researched by the author, a long-term resident on the island. As yet, there are no such maps or guides covering the other Ionian islands.

Getting around

Island-hopping isn't as easy in the Ionian as it is in parts of the Aegean, although there are ferry connections throughout the archipelago. Particularly well served are Lefkádha, Itháki and Kefalloniá, within an hour's voyage of each other and with regular ferries to a choice of destinations on each island daily. Zákinthos is also connected to Kefalloniá, and to Killíni on the mainland. Ferries between Corfu and Paxí are currently in a state of flux: at one point in the summer of 1996, there was only one public ferry a week to the island.

There are now no inter-island flights in the Ionian region, although Corfu, Kefalloniá, Zákinthos, and Préveza on the mainland near Lefkádha have daily connections to Athens. However, sheer expense and poor connections make this an unlikely way to travel between islands. For getting around the islands themselves, there are basic bus services, which many tourists choose to supplement at some stage with moped, motorbike or car rental.

Ferries

Shuttle **ferries** from the islands **to the nearest mainland ports** – which, except in the case of Lefkádha, are the islands' primary links with the outside world – are usually relatively stable (see "Travel details" at the end of each island chapter in the Guide). However, apart from the Four Islands line services between Lefkádha, Itháki, Kefalloniá and Zákinthos, **inter-island ferries** cannot be trusted from one year to the next. The high-speed catamaran between Brindisi, Corfu, Paxí and Lefkádha has been discontinued; Corfu–Itháki links were cut two years ago; and the Corfu–Kefalloniá Minoan sailing may not be continued. As a result, most people wanting to travel between Corfu or Paxí and the southern Ionian islands go via the mainland and bus.

The situation between Corfu and **Paxí** is little short of a public scandal: tour operators often have to improvise lifts on small private boats for clients staying on Paxí, and in 1996 one British firm went as far as switching airports from Corfu to Préveza. While cynical businessmen continue to play games with the ferry service, it's only possible to confirm a Monday morning sailing from

Inter-island ferry routes

All the ferries detailed below also run in the opposite direction, with similar frequencies and durations. See p.14 for details of Corfu–Pátra and Kefalloniá–Pátra ferries which begin their voyages in Italy.

From Corfu: To **Paxí** weekly (3hr; deck ticket 1000dr; vehicle 4000dr). Strintzis/Minoan to Sámi on **Kefalloniá** weekly (9hr; deck ticket 4800dr; vehicle 17,000dr). Strintzis/Minoan to **Pátra** daily April–October (9hr; deck ticket 4800dr; vehicle 17,000dr).

From Lefkádha: To **Meganíssi** 7 daily (20min; deck ticket 600dr; vehicle 1000dr). To Fríkes on **Itháki** 2 daily April–October (1hr 10min; deck ticket 1000dr; vehicle 2000dr). To Sámi on **Kefalloniá** 4 daily April–October (50min; deck ticket 1000dr; vehicle 2000dr).

From Kefalloniá (Sámi): To Váthi on **Itháki** 8 daily (30min; deck ticket 1000dr; vehicle 2000dr); daily ferries from Sámi to Astakós on the mainland (2hr; deck ticket 1200dr; vehicle 3000dr) also stop at Váthi.

From Zákinthos: To Pessádha on **Kefalloniá** daily (1hr; deck ticket 1000dr; vehicle 2000dr).

Paxí to Corfu (6am), returning at 2.30pm the same day. In season, one or two ferries – the *Pegasus, Paxos Star* or *Dolphin* – will probably continue the daily (except Sun) afternoon run between Corfu and Paxí, but independent travellers are advised to contact travel agencies on Paxí, such as Gaios Holidays, Planos and Routsis, for the latest information.

Ferry services are drastically reduced in the **off season**, but with the exception of Paxí each island has at least a daily connection to a neighbouring island or mainland port. Only the worst weather conditions – a force six upwards, which few would want to sail in anyway – prevent large ships leaving. The **types of ferries** you'll encounter vary enormously, from the landing-craft lookalikes that shuttle between Corfu and Igoumenítsa, or Argostóli and Lixoúri, which have little more than a cabin, snack bar, toilet and open upper decks, to the comparatively luxurious vessels that ply international routes, and between the southerly islands and mainland, which have restaurants, shops and cinemas.

If planning to travel on any of the long-distance ferries, it is advisable to check availability with more than one ferry company – some agents will tell you theirs is the only ferry available, despite the fairly sizeable evidence to the contrary moored perhaps only a few metres from their office. Tickets are **deck class** unless you request otherwise, and on the larger ferries also allow use of bars, restaurants and public seating areas. Pullman or aeroplane-type seating, allowing you to sleep, costs slightly more. **Cabins**, worth considering in high season, bad weather, or particularly if travelling in a group of two to four people, cost between double and quadruple the price of a basic ticket. **Motorbikes and cars** are issued extra tickets; slightly less than the cost of a deck ticket for the former, up to three or four times that for the latter. Pets and bicycles commonly travel free. Technically, written permission is required to take rental vehicles on ferries, although this is rarely if ever policed.

It's common to pay on board most inter-island ferries, although the larger ferries and lines have recently introduced computerized **ticketing**, which often requires pre-purchase at a quayside ticket agency. Most ferries run their own ticketing systems, and your ticket will probably commit you to a specific sailing on a named vessel, although on journeys such as Igoumenítsa–Corfu, it's easy to transfer tickets at the dockside ticket offices. If you're uncertain whether you'll make a specified departure, check if the ticket is transferable.

As independent fishing is gradually elbowed out by factory fishing, so the romantic notion of hiring a **kaíki** also sails off into the sunset. As with sea taxis, which command around £70-90 for an hour's journey one-way between islands, *kaíkia*, when available, tend to be very expensive. It is still possible, however, especially in smaller ports and at quieter times of the season, so ask around.

Buses

The mythical boneshakers you had to share with livestock have for the most part been replaced by the modern cream and green **buses** of the national company, KTEL (*Kratíko Tamío Elliníkon Leoforíon*). On small islands like Itháki, one island bus trundles back and forth from end to end several times a day; larger islands like Corfu and Kefalloniá are served by fleets of buses based in the capital. Note that almost all routes radiate out from the capital, and there are few if any connections between outlying towns and villages except along the radial routes. In some places, however, there are weekday early morning and early afternoon services connecting outlying communities to collect or drop off students attending schools and colleges in larger towns. These are not always advertised on timetables, so it's worth asking, particularly if you've spotted a bus where the timetable said there wasn't a service.

As elsewhere in Greece, **timetables** tend to be unreliable, although you can normally bank on the last inbound service running, if only to get vehicle and driver back to base. Most buses turn round immediately or after a short break, and can be flagged down anywhere along the road. Bear in mind that KTEL also has buses in its fleet with livery other than the cream and green, normally for private hire, but sometimes used on normal routes. If in doubt, stick your hand out at anything that has your destination on the front.

You **pay** on board nearly all buses in the Ionians. Exceptions include those originating in Lefkádha Town which, like the mainland bus stations, has a computerized ticketing system, with numbered seats. Corfu's suburban blue bus system is a confusing mix of pay-on-board and prepay (from the ticket kiosk by the bus ranks in Platía San Rócco). Pre-pay buses are those with "*horis eíspraktor*" (without conductor) signs in the driver's window. **Prices** on island buses are extremely cheap – an hour's journey the length of an island may cost less than £1/US$1.50 – although mainland bus journeys are slightly more expensive.

There are no **airport bus** services in the Ionian.

Car rental

Car rental in the Ionian costs a minimum of £160/US$240 a week in high season for the smallest, Group A vehicle, including unlimited mileage and insurance; prices on the smaller islands are usually higher. Tour operators' brochures threaten alarming rates of £220/US$330 for the same period but, except in mid-August, no rental company in the islands expects to fetch that price for a car. Outside peak season, at the smaller local outfits in less touristed resorts, you can often get terms of about £25/US$37 per day, all inclusive, with better rates for a rental of three days or more. Shopping around agencies in the larger resorts – particularly on Corfu – can yield a variation in quotes of up to 15 or 20 percent for the same conditions over a four-to-seven-day period; a common hidden catch, however, is to charge extra for kilometres in excess of 100 per day. Open **jeeps**, an increasingly popular extravagance, begin at about £30/$US45 per day, rising to as much as £45/US$68 at busy times and places.

Many basic-rate rental prices in Greece don't include tax, collision damage waiver (CDW) and personal insurance, so check the fine print on your contract. Be careful of the hammering that cars get on minor roads; tyres, windscreen and the underside of the vehicle are almost always excluded from even supplementary insurance policies. All agencies will want either a credit card or a large cash deposit up front; minimum age requirements vary from 21 to 25. In theory an

INTERNATIONAL CAR RENTAL AGENCIES

NORTH AMERICA

Avis ☎ 1-800/331-1084.

Budget ☎ 1-800/527-0700.

National ☎ 1-800/CAR-RENT.

Hertz US ☎ 1-800/654-3001; Canada ☎ 1-800/263-0600.

UK

Avis ☎ 0181/848 8733.

Budget ☎ 0800/181181.

Europcar-InterRent ☎ 0345/222525.

Hertz ☎ 0990/996699.

Holiday Autos ☎ 0990/300400; stations on Corfu, Kefalloniá, Zákinthos.

AUSTRALASIA

Avis Australia ☎ 1800/225533; NZ ☎ 09/579 5231.

Budget Australia ☎ 13 2848.

Hertz Australia ☎ 13 3039; NZ ☎ 09/309 0989.

International Driving Licence is also needed, but in practice European, Australasian and North American ones are honoured.

In peak season only you may get a better price (and, more importantly, better vehicle condition) by booking through one of the **international companies**, rather than arranging the rental once you're in Greece; this may also be the only way to get hold of a car at such times. In the Ionian, Avis (Corfu, Kefalloniá, Zákinthos), Budget (Corfu, Lefkádha, Kefalloniá, Zákinthos), Europcar-InterRent/National (Corfu, Lefkádha, Kefalloniá) and Hertz (Corfu, Lefkádha, Kefalloniá, Zákinthos) all have outlets, mainly in island capitals or major resorts.

In terms of **models**, the more competitive companies tend to offer the Subaru M80 or Subaru Vivio and the Suzuki Alto 800 as A Group cars, and Opel Corsa 1200 or Nissan Cherry in the B Group. The Suzuki Alto 600, Fiat Panda 750 and Seat Marbella should be avoided at all costs. More acceptable are the Fiat Cinquecento as an A Group choice or the Fiat Uno in the B Group. The standard four-wheel-drive options are Suzuki jeeps – great for bashing down rutted tracks to remote beaches.

Driving in Greece

Greece has the highest **accident rate** in Europe after Portugal, and many of the roads can be quite perilous: asphalt can turn into a one-lane surface or a dirt track without warning on secondary routes, and you're heavily dependent on magnifying mirrors at blind intersections in congested villages. Uphill drivers insist on their right of way, as do those first to approach a one-lane bridge – **flashed headlights** mean the opposite to what they do in the UK or North America, here signifying that the driver is coming through or overtaking.

Wearing a **seatbelt** is compulsory, and children under the age of 10 are not allowed to sit in the front seats. It's illegal to drive away from any kind of accident, and you can be held at a police station for up to 24 hours. If this happens, you have the right to ring your consulate immediately to summon a lawyer; don't make a statement to anyone who doesn't speak, and write, very good English.

Tourists with proof of membership of their home-motoring organization are given free **road assistance** from ELPA, the Greek equivalent, which runs breakdown services on the larger islands (not Paxí or Itháki); in an emergency ring their road assistance service on ☎104. Many car rental companies have an agreement with ELPA's equally widespread competitors Hellas Service and Express Service, but they're prohibitively expensive to summon on your own – over 25,000dr to enrol as an "instant member".

Buying fuel

Fuel currently costs around 210dr a litre for unleaded (*amólivdhi*), 215dr for super; so-called "regular" is on its way out, and even pricier when available. Beware that most stations in island towns and rural areas close at 7pm sharp. Nearly as many are shut all weekend, and though there will always be at least one pump per district open, it's not always apparent which that is. Filling stations run by international companies (BP, Mobil and Shell) usually take **credit cards**; Greek chains like EKO, Mamidhakis and Elinoil don't.

Incidentally, the smallest grade of motor **scooters** (Vespa, Piaggio, Suzuki) consume "mix", a red- or green-tinted fuel dispensed from a transparent cylindrical device. This contains a minimum of three-percent two-stroke oil by volume; if this mix is unavailable, you brew it up yourself by adding to "super" grade fuel the necessary amount of separately bottled two-stroke oil (*ládhi dhío trohón*). It's wise to err on the side of excess (say five percent by volume); otherwise you risk the engine seizing up.

Motorbikes, mopeds – and safety

The cult of the **motorcycle** is highly developed in the Greek islands, presided over by a jealous deity apparently requiring regular human sacrifice. **Accidents** among both foreign and local motorbikers are common, and some package companies have taken to warning clients in print against renting motorbikes or mopeds. However, with a bit of caution and common sense – plus an eye to increasingly enforced traffic regulations – riding a bike on holiday should be a lot less hazardous than, say, riding in central London or New York.

Many tourists come to grief on rutted dirt tracks or astride mechanically dodgy machines. In many cases accidents are due to attempts to cut corners, in all senses, by riding two to an underpowered scooter. Don't be tempted by this apparent economy – and bear in mind, too, that you're likely to be charged an exorbitant sum for any repairs if you do have a wipeout.

One precaution is to wear a **crash helmet** (*kránio*); many rental outfits will offer you one, and may make you sign a waiver of liability if you refuse it. Helmet-wearing is in fact required by law, and though very few people comply at present, it's likely to be more strictly enforced in the future. Above all, make sure your travel **insurance policy** covers motorcycle accidents. Reputable establishments require a full **motorcycle driving licence** for any machine over 75cc, and you will usually be required to leave a passport as security.

Mopeds and small motor scooters, known in Greek as *papákia* (little ducks) after their characteristic noise, are good transport for all but the hilliest islands. They're available for rent in most main towns or ports, and at the larger resorts, for 3000dr (mopeds) or 3500–4000dr (scooters) a day. Rates can be bargained down out of season, or if you negotiate for a longer period of rental. Before riding off, make sure you check the bike's mechanical state, since many are only cosmetically maintained. Bad brakes and worn spark plugs are the most common defects; dealers often keep the front brake far too loose, with the commendable intention of preventing you going over the handlebars. If you break down it's your responsibility to return the machine, so it's worth taking down the phone number of the rental agency in case the bike gives out and you can't get it back, or if you lose the ignition key.

As far as **models** go, the three-speed Honda 50, Suzuki Townmate and Yamaha Birdie are workhorse favourites; gears are shifted with a left-foot pedal action, and (very important) they can be push-started if the battery fails. These carry two people easily enough, though if you have a choice the Cub series gives more power at nominal extra cost. A larger Vespa scooter is more comfortable, but less stable; the Suzuki Address is thirsty on fuel and cannot be push-started. Smaller but surprisingly powerful Piaggio Si or Monte Carlo models can take one person only along almost any road and are automatic. Bungy cords (*khtapódi* in slang) for tying down bundles are supplied on request.

Cycling

Cycling on the Ionian islands is not such hard going as you might imagine, unless you're planning to traverse island hill or mountain ranges, in which case a mountain bike and a mountain biker's stamina are essential. Away from the busier resorts and arterial roads, which are hellish for cyclists and pedestrians alike, cycling is an ideal form of transport. Virtually every resort will have bikes for hire, at around 1000–1500dr a day.

If you have your own mountain or touring bike, you might consider bringing it with you: bikes fly free on most airlines, if within your twenty-kilo luggage limit, and are free on most ferries. Any spare parts you might need, however, are best brought along, since there are no specialist bike shops in the islands beyond rental agencies, and parts are difficult to obtain.

Hitching

Hitching on the Ionian islands is a hit-and-miss affair, and carries the usual risks and dangers, particularly for solo women travellers. However, Greece is in general one of the safest places to hitch. These days, though, the key question is whether you'll find anyone prepared to stop. On the larger islands and in larger resorts, especially, it's almost taken for granted (not unreasonably) that foreigners should hire or pay for their own transport. In Greece's increasingly car-mad culture, the idea of not driving anywhere baffles most islanders under donkey-owning age. That noted, hitching is a great way to meet islanders and see the landscape, particularly in outlying areas, where it's not uncommon for villagers to stop and offer lifts unasked. Just don't expect to get very far very fast.

Taxis

Greek **taxis** and tariffs are a law unto themselves. Most vehicles in the Ionians are fitted with meters, and there are various regulations on metering, but for most visitors the back of a cab is hardly the place to start arguing the toss about Greek transport law. Always request and negotiate a price beforehand, ideally in Greek, however basic your Greek is. Expect to be overcharged on journeys from airports to capitals (around 2000dr at Corfu, 4000dr at Kefalloniá). Away from airport rides, taxis are still roughly half the price paid to cover a similar distance in Britain. In rural areas, taxis respond to hailing, and will even return to collect you if full. Taxi-sharing is common, and cheap.

Accommodation

With the recent drop in the number of visitors to Greece, there are a great number of beds available for tourists in the Ionian islands. At most times of the year you can rely on turning up anywhere and finding a room – if not in a hotel, then in a private house or block of rooms (the standard island accommodation). All the larger islands have at least one basic but inexpensive campsite, too.

However, from late July to early September, when large numbers of Greeks and Italian visitors arrive in the islands, you may well experience problems if you haven't booked accommodation in advance. Some resorts can literally fill up, and in busy periods room owners, and even hoteliers, are less inclined to rent for one or just a few nights; some won't even contemplate stays of less than a week. At these times, it's worth looking away from the obvious tourist areas, turning up at each new place early in the day, and taking whatever is available in the hope of exchanging it for something better later on.

Out of season, there's a different problem: rooms close from November to March (campsites even earlier), leaving hotels your only option, probably in the island's main town or port; there'll be very little life outside these places, anyway, with all the seasonal bars and restaurants closed. Just one hotel, the *Mentor*, stays open on Itháki; there are none on Paxí. If you're set on travelling out of season, local travel companies can sometimes help to find suitable accommodation, often at bargain prices.

Private rooms

The most common form of island acommodation is **privately let rooms** – *dhomátia*. These are regulated and officially classified by the local tourist police, who divide them into three classes (A down to C), according to their facilities. These days the bulk of them are in new, purpose-built low-rise buildings, but a few are still in people's homes, where you'll occasionally be treated to disarming hospitality.

Rooms are almost always scrupulously clean, whatever their other qualities. At their simplest, you'll get a bare, concrete or wood room, with basic furnishing and shared toilet facilities (cold water only). At the fancier end of the scale, you'll find modern, purpose-built and fully furnished rooms with a smart modern bathroom attached. Sometimes there's a choice of rooms at various prices – owners will usually show you the most expensive first. Room prices and standards are not necessarily directly linked, so always ask to see the room before agreeing to take it and settling on the price.

Areas to look for rooms, along with recommendations of the best places, are included in the Guide. But as often as not, the rooms find you: owners descend on ferry or bus arrivals to fill any space they have, sometimes waving photos of the premises. In smaller places you'll often see rooms advertised – sometimes in German (*Zimmer*). The Greek signs to look out for are "*Enoikiázontai dhomátia*" or "*Enoikiazómena dhomátia*" – "Rooms to let". If you can't find rooms or, as is sometimes the case, there are no signs for them, ask in a shop, *kafenío* or taverna: if they don't have rooms themselves, they'll often know someone who does. Even in small villages, there is often someone prepared to earn some money by putting you up.

It's quite usual for room owners to ask to keep your passport – ostensibly "for the tourist police", but in reality to prevent you departing without paying. Some owners will be satisfied with taking your passport details, or simply ask you to pay in advance. They'll usually return the documents once they've got to know you, or if you need them for another purpose (to change money, for example).

Accommodation price codes

Rooms and hotels listed in this book have been price-coded according to the scale outlined below. The rates quoted represent the cheapest available double room in high season. Out of season, rates can drop by as much as fifty percent or more, especially if you negotiate for a stay of three or more nights. Single rooms, where available, cost around seventy percent of the price of a double.

① up to 4000dr
② 4000–8000dr
③ 8000–12,000dr
④ 12,000–16,000dr
⑤ 16,000–20,000dr
⑥ 20,000–30,000dr
⑦ 30,000 upwards

Very little accommodation beyond campsite bungalows and drastically simple, cold-water rooms fall into the ① category. Most private rooms tend to fall into the ② or ③ categories, some (falling mostly in the latter category) with en-suite toilet and shower facilities. These overlap in price terms with C-category hotels, the smarter or more recently built of which edge into the ④ bracket. Most ④ hotels are B-class, with en-suite facilities, air conditioning, phone and TV. ⑤–⑦ are A or Luxury, top-of-the-range hotels which can charge as much as £150/US$230 a night or more.
Prices in any establishment should by law be displayed on the back of the door of your room. If you feel you're being overcharged at a place that is officially registered, threaten to report it to the tourist police, who will generally adopt your side in such cases. Small increases over the listed prices may be legitimately explained by local tax or outdated lists. Out of high season, you may well find yourself paying much less than the listed amount.

Hotels

There are **hotels**, from basic to luxury, in most island towns, ports and resorts in the Ionian. In the larger resorts, however, many are block-booked by package holiday companies.

Like private rooms, hotels are **categorized** by the tourist police. They range from Luxury down to E-class, and all except the top category have to keep within set price limits. Letter ratings are supposed to correspond to facilities available, though in practice categorization often depends on location and other, less obvious criteria (some decent hotels in quieter areas, because they are away from the main resorts, receive a relatively low categorization, and are therefore surprisingly good value). D-class usually have attached baths, while in C-class this is mandatory, along with a bar or breakfast area. The additional presence of a pool and/or tennis court will attract a B-class rating, while A-category hotels must have a restaurant, bar and extensive common areas. Luxury hotels are in effect self-contained holiday villages; both they and A-class outfits usually back a private beach. **Prices** have to be displayed in the room, although outside the high season you will normally find yourself paying less than the advertised price. As a rough guide, D- and E-class hotels usually cost around £20–25/US$30–38 for a double room, only slightly less for single occupancy.

In terms of **food**, C-class hotels are required only to provide the most rudimentary of continental breakfasts – in practice, most now let you choose whether to take a room with or without breakfast – while B-class and above will usually offer some sort of buffet breakfast including cheese, cold cuts, sausages, eggs, etc. With some outstanding exceptions, noted in the Guide, lunch or supper at hotel-affiliated restaurants is bland and poor value.

Villas and long-term rentals

The easiest – and usually most reliable – way to arrange a **villa rental** is through one of the package holiday companies detailed in the "Getting there" sections above. They can offer some superb places, from simple to luxury, and costs can be very reasonable, especially if shared between four or more people. Several of the companies we list will arrange "multi-centre" stays on two or more islands.

On the islands, a few local travel agents arrange villa rentals, mostly places not booked or listed by the overseas companies, and sometimes representing excellent value. **Out of season**, you can sometimes get a good deal on villa or apartment rental for a month or more by asking around locally, though in these days of EU convergence and the increasing desirability of the islands as year-round residences, "good deal" means anything under 45,000dr per month for a large studio (*garsoniéra*) or small one-bedroom flat.

Camping

Officially recognized **campsites** in the Ionian are restricted to Corfu (six), Paxí (one), Lefkádha (four), Kefalloniá (one) and Zákinthos (two); see the Guide for full descriptions. Most places cost from 700dr a night per person, the same fee per tent, and 1200dr per camper van, but at the fanciest sites, rates for two people plus a tent can add up to the price of a basic room. Generally, you don't have to worry about leaving tents or baggage unattended at campsites; the Greeks are one of the most honest nationalities in Europe. The main risk comes from other campers.

Freelance camping – outside authorized campsites – is such an established element of Greek travel that few people realize that it's officially illegal. Since 1977 it has actually been forbidden by a law originally enacted to harass gypsies, and regulations are increasingly enforced. If you do camp rough, it's vital to exercise sensitivity and discretion. Police will crack down on people camping (and especially littering) around popular tourist beaches, particularly when a large community of campers develops. Off the beaten track, however, nobody is very bothered, though it is always best to ask permission locally in the village taverna or café. During high season, when everything may be full, attitudes towards freelance camping are more relaxed. At such times the best strategy is to find a sympathetic taverna, which in exchange for regular patronage will probably be willing to guard small valuables and let you use their facilities.

Eating and drinking

Greeks tend to socialize mostly outside their homes, and sharing a meal is one of the chief ways of doing it. The atmosphere is always relaxed and informal, with an accent on celebration, usually with children, grandparents, other relatives and friends in tow. Greeks are not big drinkers – what drinking they do is mainly to accompany food, as an appetizer or *digestif* – though in the resorts a whole range of bars, pubs and cocktail joints have sprung up principally to cater for tourists.

Breakfast, picnic fare and snacks

Greeks don't generally eat **breakfast**, so the only egg-and-bacon kind of places are in resorts where the British congregate; this can be fairly good value (1100–1600dr for the works), especially where there's competition. More indigenous alternatives are sweet or savoury pies and pretzel rings from a street stall (see "Snacks", opposite), or the fare on offer at *galaktopolía* or *zaharoplastía* (see "Sweets and desserts", p.39).

Picnic fare is good, cheap and easily available at bakeries and *manávika* (fruit-and-veg stalls). **Bread** is often of minimal nutritional value and inedible within a day of purchase. It's worth paying extra at the bakery (*foúrnos*) for *olikís* (wholemeal), *sikalísio* (rye bread), *oktásporo* (eight-grain), or even *enneásporo* (nine-grain), which are particular specialities of wheat-growing Lefkádha. Although the

Ionian archipelago is an olive-producing region, local **olives** are hard to find; they take forty days of daily rinsing with salted water before they leach natural poisons and become edible, so don't try tasting one off a tree. Local **olive oil** is, however, available – and delicious – usually from oil-pressing factories or the older shops. However, it rarely makes it into tavernas or restaurants. **Fétta cheese** is ubiquitous – often, these days, imported from Holland or Denmark, though local brands are usually better and not much more expensive. The goat's milk variety can be very dry and salty, so ask for a taste before buying; if you have a fridge, leaving the cheese in water overnight will solve both problems. This sampling advice goes for other indigenous cheeses as well, the most palatable of which are the expensive Gruyère-type *graviéra*. Despite the presence of farmland and the rainy winters, **fruit and vegetables** are fairly basic in the islands: roots like potatoes, carrots and onions and legumes such as courgettes and aubergine form the staple in shops on small islands such as Paxí, with little variation on the larger islands. Salad vegetables are more widely available, although lettuces are as rare as hen's teeth on some islands, hence the ubiquity of *horiátiki* (peasant) salad: cucumber, onion, tomato, olives and fétta cheese. Apples, pears, peaches, bananas, grapes and mountains of various melons are also plentiful and usually cheap. Useful **phrases** for shopping are *éna tétarto* (250g) and *misó kiló* (500g). If you're self-catering and know your herbs by sight or smell, they're often available for free in the open countryside, in particular thyme, rosemary and oregano. Cheap local red wines are unbeatable with oil in salad dressings.

Snacks

Traditional **snacks** can be one of the distinctive pleasures of Greek eating, though they are being increasingly edged out by an obsession with *tóst* (toasted sandwiches) and pizzas. However, small kebabs (*souvlákia*) are widely available, and in most larger resorts and towns you'll find *yíros* – doner kebab with garnish in thick, doughy *píta* bread that's closer to Indian nan bread, often with *patátes* (the Greek equivalent of chips) and a spicy sauce.

Other common snacks include *tirópites* (cheese pies) and *spanakópittes* (spinach pies), which can usually be found at the baker's, as can *kouloúria* (crispy pretzel rings sprinkled with sesame seeds) and *voutímata* (heavy biscuits rich in honey or cinnamon). Snack bars in towns and resorts usually also sell savoury pies with sausages (*loukánika*), and sweet ones with cream (*kréma*), fruit (*froúta*) or chocolate (*sokoláta*), and are an excellent source of cheap fuel food at any mealtime.

Restaurants

Greek cuisine and **restaurants** are simple and straightforward. There's no snobbery about eating out; everyone does it some of the time, and it's still reasonable – around 3000–4000dr per person for a substantial meal with a measure of house wine.

In choosing a restaurant, the best strategy is to go where the Greeks go. They eat late: 2pm to 3pm for **lunch**, 9pm to 11pm for **dinner**. You can eat earlier, but you're likely to get indifferent service and cuisine if you frequent establishments catering to tourist timetables. Chic appearance is not a good guide to quality; often the more ramshackle, traditional outfits represent the best value – one good omen is the waiter bringing a carafe of refrigerated water, unbidden, rather than pushing you to order bottled stuff.

In resort areas, it's wise to keep a wary eye on the **waiters**, who are inclined to urge you to order more than you want, then bring things you haven't ordered. They often don't actually write anything down and may work out the **bill** by examining your empty plates. Although cash-register receipts are now required in all establishments, these are often only for the grand total, and even if they are itemized will probably be illegible. Where prices are printed on menus, you'll be paying the right-hand (higher) set, inclusive of all taxes and usually **service charge**, although a small tip (150–200dr) is standard practice for the lad who lays the table, brings the bread and water, and so on.

Bread costs extra (around 200dr), but consumption is not obligatory; you'll be considered deviant for refusing it (just say you're on a diet or diabetic), but be warned that outside the very smartest places and those with a predominantly Greek clientele, much restaurant bread might be better taken home to build a sauna. **Children** are normally very welcome at restaurants and tavernas, day or night, and owners have a high tolerance of children playing around tables – although this may not be the case with neighbouring tables. Feeding the inevitable crowd of mendicant cats is frowned on – and unhygienic, anyway.

Estiatória

There are two basic types of restaurant: the **estiatório** and the taverna. Distinctions between the two are minimal, though the former is more commonly found in town centres and tends to have slightly more complicated dishes. An *estiatório* will generally feature a variety of oven-baked casserole dishes: *moussakás, pastítsio*, stews like *stifádho, yemistá* (stuffed tomatoes or peppers), the oily vegetable casseroles called *ladherá*, and oven-baked meat or fish. Choosing these dishes is commonly done by going back to the kitchen and pointing at the desired trays.

Batches are cooked in the morning and then left to stand, which is why the food is often lukewarm or even cold. Greeks don't mind this (most believe that hot food is bad for you). If you do mind, ask for it *zestí* or *zestós* (hot). Some meals actually benefit from being allowed to marinate in their own juices before warming again.

Similarly, you have to specify if you want your food with little or no oil (*horís ládhi*), but once again you will be considered a little strange, since Greeks regard good olive oil as essential to digestion.

Desserts (*epidhórpia* in formal Greek) of the pudding-and-pie variety don't exist at *estiatória*, and yoghurts only occasionally. Fruit is always available in season – watermelons, melons and grapes are the summer standards.

Tavernas

Tavernas range from the smart and fashionable to rough-and-ready huts set up behind a beach,

Food and drink glossary

Basics

Aláti	Salt
Avgá	Eggs
(Horís) ládhi	(Without) oil
Hortofágos	Vegetarian
Katálogo/lísta	Menu
Kréas	Meat
Lahaniká	Vegetables
Méli	Honey
Neró	Water
O logariazmós	The bill
Psári(a)	Fish
Psomí (olikis)	Bread (wholemeal)
Thallassiná	Seafood (non-fish)
Tirí	Cheese
Yiaoúrti	Yoghurt
Záhari	Sugar

Cooking terms

Akhnistó	Steamed
Psitó	Roasted
Saganáki	Rich red sauce
Skáras	Grilled
Stí soúvla	Spit-roasted
Stó foúrno	Baked
Tiganitó	Pan-fried
Tís óras	Grilled/fried to order
Yahní	Stewed in oil and tomato sauce
Yemistá	Stuffed (squid, vegetables, etc)

Soups and starters

Avgolémono	Egg and lemon soup (rare in the Ionian)
Dolmádhes	Stuffed vine leaves
Fasoládha	Bean soup
Melitzanosaláta	Aubergine/eggplant dip
Skordhaliá	Garlic dip for certain fish
Soúpa	Soup
Taramosaláta	Cod roe paté
Tzatzíki	Yoghurt, garlic and cucumber dip

Vegetables

Angoúri	Cucumber
Bámies	Okra, ladies' fingers
Bouréki	Courgette/zucchini, potato and cheese pie
Briám	Ratatouille
Domátes	Tomatoes
Fakés	Lentils
Fasolákia	French (green) beans
Frésko kremídhi	Spring onions
Horiátiki (saláta)	"Greek salad" (usually cucumber, onion, tomato, olives and fétta cheese)
Hórta	Greens (usually wild)
Kolokithákia	Courgettes/zucchini
Maroúli	Lettuce
Melitzána	Aubergine/eggplant
Papoutsákia	Stuffed aubergine/eggplant
Patátes	Potatoes
Rízi/piláfi	Rice (usually with *sáltsa* – sauce)
Saláta	Salad
Spanáki	Spinach
Yígandes	White haricot beans (usually in tomato sauce)

under a reed awning. Basic taverns have a very limited menu, but the more established will offer some of the main *estiatório* dishes mentioned opposite, as well as the standard taverna fare. This essentially means *mezédhes* (hors d'oeuvres) and *tís óras* (meat and fish, fried or grilled to order).

Since the idea of courses is foreign to Greek cuisine, starters, main dishes and salads often arrive together unless you request otherwise. The best thing is to order a selection of *mezédhes* and salads to share, in true Greek fashion. Waiters encourage you to take the *horiátiki* **salad** – the so-called "Greek salad" with *fétta* cheese – because it is the most expensive. If you only want tomato, or tomato and cucumber, ask for *domatosaláta* or *angourodomáta*. *Láhano* (cabbage) and *maroúli* (lettuce) are the typical winter and spring salads.

The most interesting **mezédhes** are *tzatzíki* (yoghurt, garlic and cucumber dip), *melitzanosaláta* (aubergine/eggplant dip), *kolokithákia tiganitá* (courgette/zucchini slices fried in batter) or *melitzánes tiganités* (aubergine/eggplant slices fried in batter), *yígandes* (white haricot beans in vinaigrette or hot tomato sauce), *tiropitákia* or *spanakópittes* (small cheese and/or spinach pies) and *okhtapódhi* (octopus).

Among **meats**, *souvláki* (shish kebab) and *brizóles* (chops) are reliable choices. In both cases, pork (*hirinó*) is usually better and cheaper than veal (*moskharísio*). The best *souvláki*, though not often available, is lamb (*arnísio*). The small lamb cutlets called *païdhákia* are very tasty, as is

Meat and meat-based dishes

Arní	Lamb
Biftéki	Hamburger
Brizóla	Pork or beef chop
Hirinó	Pork
Keftédhes	Meatballs
Kokorétsi	Liver/offal kebab
Kotópoulo	Chicken
Loukánika	Spicy home-made sausages
Moskhári	Veal
Moussakás	Aubergine/eggplant, potato and meat pie with béchamel sauce topping
Païdhákia	Lamb chops
Pastítsio	Macaroni baked with meat
Sikóti	Liver
Soutzoukákia	Mincemeat rissoles/beef patties
Stifádho	Meat stew with tomato sauce
Youvétsi	Baked clay casserole of meat and pasta

Sweets and desserts

Baklavás	Honey and nut pastry
Bougátsa	Creamy cheese pie served warm with sugar and cinnamon
Galaktobóureko	Custard pie
Halvás	Sesame or semolina sweetmeat
Karidhópita	Walnut cake
Kréma	Custard pudding
Pagotó	Ice cream
Pastélli	Sesame and honey bar
Rizógalo	Rice pudding

Fruit and nuts

Fistíkia	Pistachio nuts
Fráoules	Strawberries
Karpoúzi	Watermelon
Kerásia	Cherries
Lemóni	Lemon
Míla	Apples
Pepóni	Melon
Portokália	Oranges
Rodhákino	Peach
Síka	(Dried) figs
Stafília	Grapes
Kristália	Green miniature pears

Cheese

Fétta	Salty, white cheese
Graviéra	Gruyère-type hard cheese
Kasséri	Medium cheese
Katsikísio	Goat's cheese
Mizíthra	Sweet cream cheese
Próvio	Sheep's cheese

Drinks

Bíra	Beer
Boukáli	Bottle
Gála	Milk
Gazóza	Generic fizzy drink
Kafés	Coffee
Krasí	Wine
Áspro/levkó	White
Mávro/kókkino	Red
Rosé/kokkinéli	Rosé
Limonádha	Lemonade
Metalikó neró	Mineral water
Portokaládha	Orangeade
Potíri	Glass
Stinyássas!	Cheers!
Tsáï	Tea

roast lamb (*arní psitó*) and roast kid (*katsíki stó fournó*) when obtainable. *Keftédhes* (meatballs), *biftékia* (a sort of hamburger) and the homemade sausages called *loukánika* are cheap and good. *Kotópoulo* (chicken) is also usually a safe bet.

Seafood dishes such as *kalamarákia* (fried baby squid) and *okhtapódhi* (octopus) are a summer staple of most seaside tavernas, and in some places *mídhia* (mussels) and *garídhes* (small prawns) will be on offer at reasonable prices. Keep an eye out, however, for freshness and season – mussels in particular are a common cause of stomach upsets in mid-summer. Seaside tavernas also offer **fish**, though the choicer varieties, such as *barboúni* (red mullet), *tsipoúra* (gilt-head bream), or *fangrí* (common bream), are expensive. The price is usually quoted by the kilo, which should be not much more than double the street market rate – eg if squid is 2000dr a kilo at the fishmongers, that sum should fetch you two 250-gramme portions. It is procedure to go over to the cooler and pick your own, but if this isn't an option you should always specify how little or much you want.

As in *estiatória*, traditional tavernas offer fruit rather than **desserts**, though nowadays these are often available, along with coffee, in tavernas frequented by foreigners.

Specialist tavernas – and vegetarians

Some tavernas specialize. **Psarotavérnes**, for example, feature fish, while **psistariés** serve spit-roasted lamb, pork or goat (generically termed *kondosoúvli*), grilled chicken (*kotópoulo skáras*) or *kokorétsi* (grilled offal).

If you are **vegetarian**, you may be in for a hard time, and will often have to assemble a meal from various *mezédhes*. Even the excellent standbys of yoghurt and honey, *tzatzíki* and Greek salad begin to pall after a while, and many of the supposed "vegetable" dishes on the menu are cooked in stock or have pieces of meat added to liven them up. Restaurants wholly or largely vegetarian are slowly on the increase in touristed areas; this guide highlights them where appropriate, as well those with a decent range of vegetable alternatives.

Wines

Both *estiatória* and tavernas will usually offer you a choice of bottled **wines**, and many have their own house variety: kept in barrels, sold in bulk by the quarter-, half- or full litre, and served either in glass flagons or brightly coloured tin "monkey-cups". Not as many tavernas stock their own wine as once did, but always ask whether they have wine *varelísio* or *híma* – respectively meaning "**from the barrel**" and "**bulk**". Non-resinated bulk wine is almost always more than decent. **Retsina** – pine-resinated wine, a slightly acquired taste – is also usually better, and startlingly cheap, straight from the barrel. Some of the older village shops stock it as well as tavernas. Kourtaki retsina in the small tin-top bottles is the most basic, and best served extra-chilled. The cork-bottle, 75cl version, is slightly more palatable.

Among the more common bottled wines, Calliga, Boutari and Lac de Roches are good, inexpensive whites, while Boutari Nemea is perhaps the best mid-range red. If you want something better but still moderately priced, Tsantali Agioritiko is an excellent white or red, and Boutari has a fine "Special Reserve" red.

The kafenío

The **kafenío** is the traditional Greek coffee shop or café, found in every town, village and hamlet in the country. Although its main business is Greek coffee – prepared *skéto* or *pikró* (unsweetened), *métrio* (medium) or *glikó* (sweet) – it also serves spirits such as *oúzo* (see opposite), brandy (Metaxa or Botrys brand, in three grades), beer and soft drinks. Another refreshing drink sold in cafés is *kafés frappé*, a sort of iced instant coffee with or without milk and sugar – uniquely Greek despite its French-sounding name. Like Greek coffee, it is always accompanied by a welcome glass of cold water. Standard fizzy soft drinks are also sold in all *kafenía*.

Usually the only **snacks** available are variants on those in the street snack bars, or biscuits, cakes and sweets – increasingly pre-packaged, as a new generation of Greeks discover their sweet teeth and a taste for junk food.

Like tavernas, *kafenía* range from the plastic and sophisticated to the old-fashioned, spit-on-the-floor variety, with marble or brightly painted metal tables and straw-bottomed chairs. An important institution anywhere in Greece, they are the focus of life in more remote villages. You get the impression that many men spend most of their waking hours there. Greek women are rarely to be seen in the more traditional places –

and foreign women may sometimes feel uneasy or unwelcome in these establishments. Even in holiday resorts, you will find there is at least one coffee house that the local men have kept intact for themselves.

Some *kafenía* close at siesta time, but many remain open from early in the morning until late at night. The chief socializing time is 6–8pm, immediately after the siesta. This is the time to take your pre-dinner *oúzo*, as the sun begins to sink and the air cools down.

Oúzo and mezédhes

Oúzo is a simple spirit of up to 48 percent alcohol, distilled from the grape-mash residue left over from wine-making, and then flavoured with herbs such as anise or fennel. It's comparable to a very rough schnapps, aqua vit or genever. When you order, you will be served two glasses: one with the *oúzo*, and one full of water that's tipped into the latter until it turns a milky white. You can drink it straight, but the strong, burning taste is hardly refreshing if you do. It is increasingly common to add ice cubes.

Until not long ago, every *oúzo* you ordered was automatically accompanied by a small plate of **mezédhes**, on the house: bits of cheese, cucumber, tomato, a few olives, sometimes octopus or even a couple of small fish. Unfortunately these days you usually have to ask, and pay, for them, although bars on some of the islands – notably Lefkádha and Kefalloniá – have preserved the tradition. As these tend to be some of the best such establishments, we list them where we find them.

Sweets and desserts

Similar to the *kafenío* is the **zaharoplastío**, a cross between café and patisserie, which serves coffee, alcohol, yoghurt with honey, and sticky cakes.

The better establishments offer an amazing variety of pastries, cream and chocolate confections, honey-soaked Greco-Turkish sweets like *baklavás*, *kataífi* (honey-drenched "shredded wheat"), *galaktoboúreko* (custard pie), and so on. The latter is something of a rarety nowadays, and when encountered should be tried.

If you want a stronger slant towards the dairy products and away from the pure sugar, seek out a **galaktopolío**, where you'll often find *rizógalo* (rice pudding – rather better than the English school-dinner variety), *kréma* (custard) and home-made or at least locally made *yiaoúrti* (yoghurt), best if it's *próvio* (from sheep's milk).

Ice cream, sold principally at the gelaterias which have carpeted Greece of late, can be very good and almost indistinguishable from their Italian prototypes. A scoop (*baláki*) costs 250–300dr; you'll be asked if you want it in a cup (*kípello*) or a cone (*honáki*), or with *santí* (whipped cream) on top. By contrast, mass-produced stuff like Delta or Evga brand is pretty trashy, with the honourable exception of Mars and Opal Fruit ices and Dove Bars.

Both *zaharoplastía* and *galaktopolía* are more family-oriented places than the *kafenío*, and many also serve a basic continental-type **breakfast** of *méli me voútiro* (honey poured over a pat of butter) or jam (all kinds are called *marmeládha* in Greek; ask for *portokáli* – orange – if you want proper marmalade) with fresh bread or *friganiés* (melba-toast-type slivers). You are also more likely to find proper (*evropaïkó*) tea and non-Greek coffee. *Nescafé* has become the generic term for all instant coffee, regardless of brand; it's generally pretty vile, and in resort areas smart proprietors have taken to offering genuine filter coffee, dubbed "*gallikós*" (French).

Bars – and beer

Bars (*barákia*), once confined to towns, cities and holiday resorts, are now found all over Greece. They range from clones of Parisian cafés to seaside cocktail bars, by way of imitation English pubs, with satellite and MTV-type videos running all day. Once twenty-hour-a-day operations, most bars now close between 2am and 3am, depending on the municipality; during 1994 they were required by the Ministry of Public Order to make an admission/cover charge which included the first drink. This decree, met with a storm of street protests and other mass civil disobedience, is presently in abeyance but could be revived at any time.

For that and other reasons, drinks are invariably more expensive than in a café. Bars are, however, most likely to stock a range of **beers**, all foreign labels made locally under licence, since the indigenous Fix brewery closed in 1984. Kronenbourg and Kaiser are the two most common of these, with the former available in both light and dark; since 1993 a tidal wave of even pricier, imported German beers, such as Bitburger and Warstein, has washed over the fancier resorts. Amstel and Henninger are the two ubiquitous cheapies, rather bland but inoffensive; the Dutch themselves claim that the former is better than the Amstel available in Holland. A possible compromise in both taste and expense is the sharper-tasting Heineken, universally referred to as a "*prássini*" by bar and taverna staff after its green bottle. Incidentally, try not to get stuck with the 330ml cans, vastly more expensive (and more of a rubbish problem) than the returnable 500ml bottles.

Communications: mail, phones and the media

Postal services

Most **post offices** are open Monday to Friday from about 7.30am to 2pm, though certain large towns – for example Corfu, Lefkádha and Argostóli – also have evening and weekend hours. They exchange money in addition to handling mail.

Airmail **letters** from the islands take three to seven days to reach the rest of Europe, five to twelve days to North America, and a little longer to Australia and New Zealand. Generally, the larger the island (and the planes serving its airport, if it has one), the quicker the service. Aerograms are slightly faster, and for a modest fee (about 500dr), you can further cut delivery time to any destination by using the express (*katepígonda*) service. Registered (*sistiméno*) delivery is also available, but it is quite slow unless coupled with express service. If you are sending large purchases home, note that **parcels** should, and often can only, be handled in the main island capitals.

For a simple letter or card, **stamps** (*grammatósima*) can also be purchased at a *períptero* (kiosk). However, the proprietors charge ten percent commission on the cost of the stamp, and never seem to know the current international rates. Ordinary **postboxes** are bright yellow, with the hunting horn logo, and express boxes dark red; if you are confronted by two slots, "*esoterikó*" is for domestic mail, "*exoterikó*" for overseas.

Receiving mail

The **poste restante** system is reasonably efficient, especially at the post offices of larger towns. Mail should be clearly addressed and marked "poste restante", with your surname underlined, to the main post office of whichever town you choose. It will be held for a month and you'll need your passport to collect it.

Telephones

Telephone calls are relatively straightforward. Street-corner call boxes work only with **phone cards**; these come in three denominations – 100, 500 and 1000 units – and are available from kiosks, OTE offices (*Organismós Tilepikinoníon tis Elládhos*) and newsagents. Not surprisingly, the more expensive cards are the best value.

If you won't be around long enough to use up a phone card, it's probably easier to make **local calls** from a *períptero*, or **street kiosk**. Here the phone is connected to a meter, and you pay after you have made the call. While local calls are reasonable (20dr for the first six minutes), long-distance ones have some of the most expensive rates in the EU – and definitely the worst connections, owing to the lack of digitized exchanges in the islands. Other options for local calls are from a *kafenío* or **bar** (same 20dr charge as at kiosks), but you won't be allowed to use these for trunk or overseas calls unless the phone is metered: look for a sign saying *"tiléfono meh metrití"*.

For inter-island and **international** (*exoterikó*) **calls**, it's better and cheaper to use either card phones or visit the nearest **OTE** office, where there's often a digitally wired booth reserved for overseas calls only; make your call and pay afterwards. **Reverse charge** (collect) or person-to-person calls can also be made here, though connections are not always immediate – be prepared to wait up to half an hour. In the larger island capitals, the OTE is open from 7am to 10pm or 11pm; in smaller towns their offices can close as early as 3pm, though in a few resorts OTE operates Portakabin booths that keep weird but useful schedules such as 2–10pm. **Faxes** can also be sent from OTE offices, post offices and some travel agencies – at a price. Receiving a fax may also incur a small charge. **Avoid** making long-distance calls from a hotel, as they slap a fifty-percent surcharge onto the already outrageous rates.

Calls through OTE booths start at around 950dr for three minutes to all EU countries and much of the rest of Europe, and around 2000dr for the same time to North America or Australasia. **Cheap rates**, a reduction of 20–30 percent at the most, apply from 3–5pm and 9pm–8am daily, plus all weekend, for calls within Greece.

British Telecom, as well as North American long-distance companies like AT&T, MCI and Sprint, provide **credit card call** services from Greece, but only back to the home country. There are now local-dial numbers with some cards, such as BT, which enable you to connect to the international system for the price of a one-unit local call, then charge the international call to your home phone – cheaper than the alternatives.

Phoning Greece from abroad

Dial the international access code (given below) + 30 (country code) + area code (minus initial 0) + number

Australia ☎ 0011

Canada ☎ 011

Ireland ☎ 010

New Zealand ☎ 00

UK ☎ 00

US ☎ 011

Phoning abroad from Greece

Dial the country code (given below) + area code (minus any initial 0) + number

Australia ☎ 0061

Canada ☎ 001

Ireland ☎ 00353

New Zealand ☎ 0064

UK ☎ 0044

US ☎ 001

Useful Greek telephone numbers

ELPA Road Service ☎ 104

Fire brigade ☎ 199

Medical emergencies ☎ 166

Operator ☎ 132 (domestic)

Operator ☎ 161 (international)

Police/Emergency ☎ 100

Speaking clock ☎ 141

Tourist police ☎ 171

Phone credit card operator access numbers from Greece

AT&T USA Direct ☎ 00 800 1311

MCI ☎ 00 800 1211

Sprint ☎ 00 800 1411

Canada ☎ 00 800 1611

British Telecom ☎ 00 800 4411

The media

British **newspapers** are fairly widely available in Greece at a cost of 450–600dr, or 800–900dr for Sunday editions. You'll find day-old copies of the *Independent* and the *Guardian*'s European edition, plus a few of the tabloids, in all the resorts as well as in major towns. American and international alternatives include the turgid *USA Today* and the more readable *International Herald Tribune*; *Time* and *Newsweek* are also widely available. There are a number of English-language publications on Corfu, but these are little more than parish magazines pitched at the expat market.

Greek publications

Although you will probably be excluded from the **Greek print media** by the double incomprehensibilities of alphabet and language, you can learn a fair bit about your Greek fellow-travellers by their choice of broadsheet, so a quick survey of Greek magazines and newspapers won't go amiss.

Many papers are funded by **political groups**, which tends to decrease the already low quality of Greek dailies. Among these, only the centrist *Kathemerini* – whose former proprietor Helen Vlakhos attained heroic status for her defiance of the junta – approaches the standards of a major European newspaper. *Eleftherotypia*, once a PASOK mouthpiece, now aspires to more independence, and has editorial links with Britain's *Guardian*; *Avriani* has now taken its place as the PASOK cheerleading section; *Ta Nea* is mostly noted for its extensive small ads. On the **left**, *Avyi* is the Eurocommunist forum with literary leanings, while *Rizospastis* acts as the organ of the KKE (unreconstructed Communists). *Ethnos* was also shown some years back to have received covert funding from the KGB to act as a disinformation bulletin. At the other end of the political spectrum, *Apoyevmatini* generally supports the **centre-right** Néa Dhimokratía party, while *Estia*'s no-photo format and reactionary politics are both stuck somewhere at the turn of the century. The **nationalist**, lunatic fringe is staked out by paranoid *Stokhos* ("Our Goal: Greater Greece; Our Capital: Constantinople"). Given the generally low level of journalism, there is little need for a soft-porn or gutter press, unlike in Germany or the UK.

Among **magazines** not merely translations of overseas titles, *Takhydhromos* is the respectable news-and-features weekly; *Ena* is more sensationalist, *Klik* a crass rip-off of *The Face*, and *Toh Pondiki* (The Mouse) a satirical weekly revue in the same vein as Britain's *Private Eye* or *Spy*; its famous covers are spot-on and accessible to anyone with minimal Greek. More specialized niches are occupied by low-circulation titles such as *Adhesmatos Typos* (a muck-raking journal) and *Andi*, an intelligent biweekly somewhat in the mould of Britain's *New Statesman and Society*.

Radio

If you have a **radio**, playing dial roulette can be rewarding. As the government's former monopoly of wavelengths has ended, regional stations have mushroomed and the airwaves are now positively cluttered. On Corfu, frequencies around 100 FM play host to a variety of fairly forgettable local radio stations. The **BBC World Service** broadcasts on short-wave throughout Greece; 15.07 and 12.09 MHz are the most common frequencies.

TV

Greece's two centralized, government-controlled **TV stations**, ET1 and ET2, nowadays lag behind private, decidedly right-wing channels – Mega-Channel, New Channel, Antenna, Star and Seven-X – in the ratings. On ET1, news summaries in English are broadcast daily at 6pm. Programming on all stations tends to be a mix of soaps (especially Italian, Spanish and Latin American), game shows, Westerns, B-movies and sports. All foreign films and serials are broadcast in their original language, with Greek subtitles. Except for Seven-X, which begins at 7pm, and Mega and Antenna (24hr channels), the main channels broadcast from breakfast time, or just after, until the small hours. Numerous **cable and satellite** channels are received, including Sky, CNN, MTV, Super Channel, French Canal Cinque and Italian Rai Due. The range available depends on the area (and hotel) you're in.

Opening hours and public holidays

The one constant about Greek opening hours is change. Hours may alter for reasons that elude those who happily alter them. The traditional timetable starts at a relatively civilized hour, with shops opening between 8.30 and 9.30am, then runs through until lunchtime, when there is a long break for the hottest part of the day. Things may then reopen in the mid- to late afternoon (but not banks).

Tourist areas tend to adopt a slightly more northern timetable, with shops and offices, as well as the most important archeological sites and museums, usually open throughout the day.

Business and shopping hours

Most **government agencies** are open to the public on weekdays from 8am to 2pm. In general, however, you'd be optimistic to show up after 1pm expecting to be served the same day. Private businesses, or anyone providing a service, frequently operate a 9am–6pm schedule. If someone is actually selling something, then they are more likely to follow a split shift as detailed below.

Shopping hours during the hottest months are theoretically from approximately 9am to 2.30pm, and from 6 to 9pm. During the cooler months the morning schedule shifts slightly forward, the evening trade a half-hour or even a full hour back. There are so many exceptions to these rules, though, that you can't count on getting anything done except from Monday to Friday, between 9.30am and 1pm. It's worth noting that delis and **butchers** are not allowed to sell fresh meat during summer afternoons (though some flout this rule); similarly **fishmongers** are only open in the morning, as are **pharmacies**, which additionally are shut on Saturday.

All of the above opening hours will be regularly thrown out of sync by the numerous **public holidays and festivals**. The most important, when almost everything will be closed, are listed in the box below.

Ancient sites and monasteries

Opening hours of **ancient sites** vary considerably. As far as possible, individual times are quoted in the text, but bear in mind that these change with

Public holidays

January 1	May 1
January 6	Whit Monday (usually in June)
March 25	August 15
First Monday of Lent (Feb/March; see below)	October 28
Easter weekend (according to the Orthodox festival calendar; see below)	December 25 & 26

There are also a large number of local holidays, which result in the closure of shops and businesses, though not government agencies.

Variable religious feasts

	Lent Monday	Easter Sunday	Whit Monday
1998	March 2	April 19	June 8
1999	Feb 22	April 11	May 31
2000	Mar 13	April 23	June 12

exasperating frequency and at smaller sites may be subject to the whim of a local keeper. The times quoted are generally summer hours, which operate from around late April to the end of September. Reckon on similar days but later opening and earlier closing in winter. Reductions on entry fees of approximately 25 percent often apply to senior citizens, 50 percent to students with proper identification.

Smaller sites tend to close for a long lunch and siesta (even where they're not supposed to), as do **monasteries**. The latter are generally open from about 9am to 1pm and 5 to 8pm (3.30–6.30pm in winter) for limited visits. Most operate a fairly strict **dress code** for visitors; shorts on either sex are unacceptable, and women are often expected to cover their arms and wear skirts – wraps are sometimes provided on the spot.

Festivals

Many of the big Greek festivals (see the box overleaf) have a religious basis, and are observed in accordance with the Orthodox calendar. Give or take a few saints, this is similar to the regular Catholic liturgical year, except for Easter, which can fall as much as three weeks on either side of the Western festival.

Easter

Easter is by far the most important festival of the Greek year – infinitely more so than Christmas – and taken much more seriously than elsewhere in western Europe. The festival is an excellent time to be in Greece, both for its beautiful religious ceremonies and for the days of feasting and celebration that follow. Corfu, in particular, is a good place to be, but each village celebrates the event, and in the smaller villages you're more likely to find yourself invited to join in. Similarly, each island and village has its own variations on the main ceremonies. Corfu continues its tradition of pottery-smashing from windows around the old town on Easter Saturday morning (Lefkádha and Zákinthos have a similar tradition), and the spectacular firework display at midnight over the Spianádha. Each town and village parades its saints' icons in great panoply and, on Paxí, islanders strew the country lanes with flowers from their gardens. Zákinthos has a tradition dating from the Middle Ages of practical jokes played on shop-owners through the Easter period.

The first great public ceremony takes place on **Good Friday** evening as the Descent from the Cross is lamented in church. At dusk the *Epitáfios*, Christ's funeral bier, lavishly decorated with flowers by the women of the parish, leaves the sanctuary and is paraded solemnly through the streets.

Late Saturday evening sees the climax in a majestic *Anástasis* Mass to celebrate Christ's triumphant return. At the stroke of midnight all lights in each crowded church are extinguished, plunging the congregation into the darkness that envelops Christ as he passes through the underworld. Then there's a faint glimmer of light behind the altar screen before the priest appears, holding aloft a lighted taper and chanting "*Avtó to Fos*" (This is the Light of the World). Stepping down to the level of the parishioners, he touches his flame to the unlit candle of the nearest worshipper, intoning *"Dhévteh, láveteh Fos"* (Come, take the Light). Those at the front of the congregation and on the aisles do the same for their neighbours until the entire church is ablaze with burning candles and the miracle reaffirmed.

Even the most committed agnostic is likely to find this moving. The traditional greeting, as an arsenal's worth of fireworks explode around you in the street, is *"Hristós Anésti"* (Christ is risen), to which the response is *"Alithós Anésti"* (Truly He is Risen). In the week up to Easter Sunday you should wish people a Happy Easter: *"Kaló Páskha"*; after the day, you say *"Hrónia Pollá"* (Many Happy Returns).

Worshippers then take the burning **candles** home, and it brings good fortune on the house if they arrive still lit. On reaching the front door it is common practice to make the sign of the cross on the lintel with the flame, leaving a black smudge visible for the rest of the year. The **Lenten fast** is traditionally broken early on **Sunday** morning (usually just after midnight) with a meal of *mayarítsa*, a soup made from lamb tripe, rice and lemon. The rest of the lamb will be roasted on spits for Sunday lunch, and festivities often take place through the rest of the day.

The Greek equivalent of **Easter eggs** are hard-boiled eggs (painted red on Holy Thursday), which are baked into twisted, sweet bread-loaves (*tsourékia*) or distributed on Easter Sunday. People rap their eggs against their friends', and the owner of the last uncracked one is considered lucky.

The festival calendar

Most of the other Greek festivals are in honour of one or another of a multitude of **saints**. The most important are detailed in the box overleaf: a village or church bearing one of the saint's names mentioned here is a sure sign of celebrations – sometimes right across the town or island, sometimes quiet, local and consisting of little more than a special liturgy and banners adorning the chapel in question. Saint's days are also celebrated as **name days**; if it's a friend's name day, you wish them *"Hrónia Pollá"* (Many Happy Returns). Also detailed are a few more **secular holidays**, most enjoyable of which are the pre-Lenten carnivals.

In addition to the specific dates mentioned, there are literally scores of **local festivals** (**paniyíria**) celebrating the patron saint of the village church. With hundreds of possible name-saints' days (liturgical calendars list two or three, however arcane, for each day) you're unlikely to travel around Greece for long without stumbling on something.

It is important to remember the concept of the **paramoní**, or eve of the festival. Most of the events listed overleaf are celebrated on the night before, so if you show up on the morning of the date given you will very probably have missed any music, dancing or drinking.

Festivals

January 1

New Year's Day (*Protohroniá*) in Greece is the feast day of Áyios Vassílios (Saint Basil), and is celebrated with church services and the making of a special loaf, *vassilópitta*, in which a coin is baked which brings its finder good luck throughout the year. The traditional New Year greeting is "*Kalí Hroniá*".

January 6

Epiphany (*Áyia Theofánia*, or *Fóta* for short), when the *kalikántzari* (hobgoblins) who run riot on earth during the twelve days of Christmas are banished back to the nether world by various rites of the Church. The most important of these is the blessing of baptismal fonts and all outdoor bodies of water.

Pre-Lenten carnivals

These span three weeks, climaxing during the seventh weekend before Easter. All the islands in this guide have the most elaborate festivities, parties and parades, usually based around the capital towns – in the Ionian, the tradition harks back to the Venetian era, and is dubbed Carnival.

March 25

Independence Day and the Feast of the Annunciation (*Evangelismós*) is both a religious and a national holiday, with, on the one hand, military parades and dancing to celebrate the beginning of the revolt against Turkish rule in 1821 and, on the other, church services to honour the news being given to Mary that she was to become the Mother of Christ. There are major festivities at any locality with a monastery or church named *Evangelístria* or *Evangelismós*.

April 23

The feast of **Saint George** (*Áyios Yióryios*), the patron of shepherds, is a big rural celebration, with much dancing and feasting at associated shrines and towns. If April 23 falls before Easter, ie during Lent, the festivities are postponed until the Monday after Easter.

May 1

May Day is the great urban holiday when townspeople traditionally make for the countryside for picnics and return with bunches of wild flowers. Wreaths are hung on their doorways or balconies until they are burnt on Midsummer's eve. There are also large demonstrations by the Left, claiming the *Ergatikí Protomayiá* (Working Class First of May) as their own.

May 21

Ionian Day is the anniversary of the islands' union with Greece in 1864, celebrated on Corfu with marches, wreath-laying, flybys and much military pageant.

June 29

The **Holy Apostles** (*Ayíi Apostolí*), Petros and Pavlos (Peter and Paul). Two of the more widely celebrated name days.

July 26

Ayiá Paraskeví; celebrated in the many parishes and villages bearing that name.

August 1 onwards

Lefkádha Festival of Language and Arts. Launched in a postwar atmosphere of internationalism, this aims to bring together disparate cultures to enhance understanding. Spread out over a three-week period, the festival mixes music and dance from South America, Europe and the Mediterranean countries.

August 11

Áyios Spirídhon. The one fixed date of the Corfiot patron saint's four festival days, each remembering the saint's intervention in disaster threatening the island. The gold casket containing the saint's mummified remains is paraded around the centre of the town. (The other days, floating in the calendar, are Palm Sunday, Easter Saturday and the first Sunday in November.) The saint's day is also a major celebration in Kariá on Lefkádha.

August 15

Apokimísis tis Panayías (Assumption or Dormition of the Blessed Virgin Mary). This is the day when people traditionally return to their home village, and in many places there will be no accommodation available on any terms. Even some Greeks will resort to sleeping in the streets. There are major festivities throughout the islands – strangest of all is the ritual **snake-handling** at the village of Markópoulo on Kefalloniá.

August 24

Áyios Dioníssios. One of two days (the other is the visitor-unfriendly December 24) for the saint, with major celebrations held around Áyios Dioníssios churches, notably in Zákinthos Town.

September 8

Yénisis tis Panayías (Birth of the Virgin Mary) sees special services in churches dedicated to the event.

September 14

A last major summer festival, the **Ípsosis tou Stavroú** (Exaltation of the Cross).

October 26

The Feast of **Áyios Dhimítrios**, another popular name day. New wine is traditionally tapped on this day, a good excuse for general inebriation.

October 28

Ókhi Day, the year's major patriotic shindig – a national holiday with parades, folk-dancing and speechifying to commemorate Metaxas's apocryphal one-word reply to Mussolini's 1940 ultimatum: "*Okhi*!" (No!).

November 8

Another popular name day, the feast of the **Archangels Michael and Gabriel** (Mihaíl and Gavriíl, or Taxiárhon), marked by rites at the numerous churches named after them, particularly at the rural monastery of Taxiárhis on Itháki.

December 6

The feast of **Áyios Nikólaos**, the patron of seafarers, with many chapels dedicated to him.

December 25

A much less festive occasion than Greek Easter, **Christmas** (*Hristoúyenna*) is still an important religious feast. In recent years it has acquired all of the commercial trappings of the Western Christmas, with decorations, trees and gifts. December 26 is not Boxing Day as in England, but the **Sínaxis tis Panayías** (Meeting of the Virgin's Entourage), a legal holiday.

December 31

New Year's Eve (*Paramoní Protohroniá*), when, as on the other twelve days of Christmas, children go door to door singing the traditional *kálanda* (carols), receiving money in return. Adults tend to play cards, often for money. The *vassilópitta* is cut at midnight (see January 1).

Watersports

The Ionian islands can claim some of the finest water-sports facilities in the Mediterranean. Water-sport equipment – from the humble pedalo to top-of-the-range competitive windsurf boards and sails – can be rented out in most resorts, and larger resorts have waterskiing and parasailing facilities.

The last few years have seen a massive growth in the popularity of **windsurfing** in Greece. The country's bays and coves are ideal for beginners, and boards can be rented in literally hundreds of resorts. Because of the shared geography and prevailing winds of the Ionian islands, it is typically the sandy or pebbly parts of the west coasts, often inaccessible except by boat, that provide the best conditions. Only Paxí and Zákinthos are exceptions to this rule, with west coasts dominated by high, hostile cliffs. Morning winds are gentle, ideal for novices, and the afternoon winds will test even the most experienced. Rentals start from around £6/US$9 an hour. Fully inclusive windsurf holidays on islands such as Lefkádha start at around £350/US$425 a week.

Waterskiing is available at a number of the larger resorts, and even on the smaller islands. By the rental standards of the ritzier parts of the Mediterranean, it is a bargain, with twenty minutes' instruction often available for around £8–10/US$12–15. At many resorts, **parasailing** (*parapént*) is also possible; rates start at £10/US$15 a go.

A combination of steady winds, appealing seascapes and numerous natural harbours has long made the Greek islands a tremendous place for **sailing**. Holiday companies offer all sorts of packaged and tailor-made cruises (see the "Getting there" sections above). Locally, small boats and dinghies are rented out by the day at many resorts. Larger craft can be chartered by the week or longer, either bareboat or with skipper, from marinas on Corfu and bases in most of the islands. Where the Aegean has its notorious *meltémi*, the Ionian has its equivalent **maéstro**, which can blow for up to three days and make for pretty nauseating sailing, most often at either end of the season, but sometimes at points during it. More and more companies are offering sailing as options, and there are numerous agencies who will organize skippered or bareboat charters. For more details, contact the Hellenic Yachting Federation, Aktí Navárhou Koundourióti 7, 185 34 Pireás (☎01/41 37 351, fax 41 31 119).

Scuba diving is still a minority sport in the Ionian, but growing fast because of its popularity among north European visitors. Many schools are in fact run by visitors from Germany and the Nordic countries. We list diving schools in the Guide, most notably on Corfu, and more extensive information can be obtained in Britain from the British Sub-Aqua Club (Seymour Leisure Centre, Seymour Place, London SW1 ☎0171/723 8336) or from GNTO offices in other countries.

Public beaches, sunbeds and umbrellas

Not many people realize that all **beaches** in Greece are public land; that's understandable, given the extent to which luxury hotels encroach on them, and the sunbeds and umbrellas that carpet entire strands. Greek **law**, however, is very clear that the shore from the winter high-tide mark down to the water must be freely accessible, with a right of way provided around hotels or resorts, and that no permanent structures be built in that zone. Accordingly, you should resist pressure to pay rental for unwanted **sunbeds** or **umbrellas**, particularly the latter, which are often anchored with permanent, illegal concrete lugs buried in the sand.

Police and trouble

Greece is one of Europe's safest countries, with a low crime rate and an almost unrivalled reputation for honesty. If you leave a bag or wallet at a café, you'll most likely find it scrupulously looked after, pending your return. Similarly, Greeks are relaxed about leaving possessions unlocked or unattended on the beach, in rooms or on campsites. However, in recent years there has been a large increase in theft and crimes, perpetrated mainly by fellow tourists, particularly in the cities and resorts, so it's wise to lock things up and treat Greece like any other European destination. Below are a few pointers on offences that might get you into trouble locally, and some advice on sexual harassment – all too much a fact of life given the classically Mediterranean machismo of Greek culture.

Offences

The most common causes of a brush with authority are nude bathing or sunbathing, and camping outside an authorized site.

Nude bathing is legal on only a very few beaches, and is deeply offensive to the more traditional Greeks. You should exercise considerable sensitivity to local feeling: it is, for example, very bad etiquette to swim or sunbathe nude within sight of a church. Generally, though, if a beach has become fairly established as naturist, or is well secluded, it's highly unlikely that the police are going to come charging in. Where they do get bothered is if they feel a place is turning into a "hippie beach" or nudity is getting too overt on mainstream tourist stretches. Most of the time, the only action will be a warning, but you can officially be arrested straight off – facing up to three days in jail and a stiff fine.

Topless (sun)bathing for women is technically legal nationwide, but specific locales often opt out of this by posting signs, which should be heeded.

Very similar guidelines apply to **freelance camping** – though for this you're still unlikely to incur anything more than a warning to move on. The only real risk of arrest is if you are told to move on and fail to do so. In either of the above cases, even if the police do take any action against you, it's more likely to be a brief spell in their cells than any official prosecution.

Incidentally, any sort of **disrespect** towards the Greek State or Orthodox Church in general, or Greek civil servants in particular, may be construed as offences in the most literal sense, so it's best to keep your comments on how things are working (or not) to yourself. This is a society where words count, with a consistent backlog of court cases dealing with the alleged public utterance of *malákas* (wanker). While you'll hear it bandied about, don't be tempted to use it yourself: you may well land yourself in hot water.

Drug offences are treated as major crimes, particularly since there's a growing local use and addiction problem, even on the smaller islands. The maximum penalty for "causing the use of drugs by someone under 18", for example, is life imprisonment and at least a ten-million-drachma fine. Theory is by no means practice, but foreigners caught in possession of even small amounts of grass do get long jail sentences if there's evidence that they've been supplying the drug to others.

If you get arrested for any offence, you have a right to contact your **consulate**, who will arrange a lawyer for your defence. Beyond this, there is little they can or (in most cases) will do.

In an **emergency**, dial ☎ 100 for the police; ☎ 171 for the tourist police; ☎ 166 for an ambulance.

Sexual harassment

Thousands of women travel independently about the Ionian without being **harassed** or feeling intimidated. Greek machismo, however, is strong, if less upfront than in Southern Italy, for example. Most of the hassle you are likely to get is from a small minority of Greek males, known as *kamákia* (fish harpoons), who migrate in summer to the beach bars and discos of the main resorts and towns, specifically in pursuit of "liberated, fun-loving" tourists. Indigenous Greeks, who are increasingly protective of you as you become more of a fixture in any one place, treat these outsiders with contempt. Words worth remembering as unambiguous responses include *pápsteh* (stop it), *afístemeh* (leave me alone) and *fíyeteh* (go away), the latter intensified if followed by *dhrómo*! (road, as in "hit the road"). **Hitching** is not advisable for lone women travellers, but **camping** is generally not a problem, though away from recognized sites it is often wise to attach yourself to a local family by making arrangements to use nearby private land. On the more remote islands you may feel more uncomfortable travelling alone. The intensely traditional Greeks may have trouble understanding why you are unaccompanied, and might not welcome your presence in their sometimes exclusively male *kafenía* – often the only place where you can get a drink. Travelling with a man, you're more likely to be treated as a *kséni*, a word meaning both (female) stranger and guest.

Work

Since Greece's full accession to the European Union in early 1993, a citizen of any EU state has (in theory) the right to work in Greece. In practice, however, there are a number of bureaucratic hurdles to overcome. Formerly, the most common job for foreigners was teaching English in the numerous private cramming academies (*frondistíria*), but lately severe restrictions have been put on the availability of such positions for non-Greeks, and you will more likely be involved in a commercial or leisure-orientated trade.

If you plan to work for someone else, you first visit the nearest Department of Employment and collect two forms: one an **employment application** which you fill in, the other for the formal offer of work by your prospective employer. Once these are vetted, and revenue stamps (*hartósima*, purchased at kiosks) applied, you take them to the Aliens' Bureau (*Ipiresía Allodhapón*) or, in its absence, the central police station, to support your application for a **residence permit** (*ádhia paramonís*). For this, you will also need to bring your passport, two photographs, more *hartósima* and a stable address (not a hotel). Permits are given for terms of three or six months (white cards), one year (green triptych booklets), or even five years (blue booklets) if they've become well acquainted with you. For one- or five-year permits, a **health examination** at the nearest public hospital is required, to screen for TB, syphilis and HIV.

EU nationals who do not wish to work in Greece but still need a residence permit will still get a "white" pass gratis, but must present evidence of financial solvency; personalized pink exchange receipts, travellers' cheques or credit cards are all considered valid proof.

At the present time, **non-EU nationals** who wish to work in Greece do so surreptitiously, with the ever-present risk of denunciation to the police and instant deportation. Having been forced to accept large numbers of EU citizens looking for jobs in a climate of rising unemployment, Greek immigration authorities are cracking down hard on any suitable targets, be they Albanian, African, Swiss or North American. That old foreigners' stand-by, teaching English, is now available only to TEFL certificate-holders, preferably Greek, non-EU nationals of Greek descent, or EU nationals in that order. If you are a non-EU foreign national of Greek descent, you are termed *"omólogos"* (returned Greek diaspora member) and in fact have tremendous employment and residence rights – you can, for example, open your very own *frondistírio* without any qualifications (something painfully evident in the often appalling quality of English instruction in Greece).

Directory

BARGAINING This isn't a regular feature of life, though you'll find it possible with private rooms and some hotels out of season. Similarly, you may be able to negotiate discounted rates for vehicle rental, especially for longer periods. Services such as shoe, watch and camera repair don't have iron-clad rates, so use common sense when assessing charges (advance estimates are not a routine practice).

CHILDREN Kids are worshipped and indulged in Greece, and present few problems when travelling. Baby foods and nappies (diapers) are ubiquitous and reasonably priced, plus concessions are offered on most forms of transport. Private rooms and luxury hotels are more likely to offer some kind of babysitting service than the mid-range hotels.

CINEMA Greek cinemas show a large number of American and British movies, always in the original language, with Greek subtitles. They are highly affordable, currently 1100–1600dr depending on location and plushness of facilities. In the Ionians, however, there are only cinemas on Corfu and Lefkádha, with occasional showings in town halls on Zákinthos and elsewhere. An outdoor movie in summer is worth catching at least once for the experience alone, though it's best to opt for the earlier screening (approximately 9pm) since the soundtrack on the later show tends to be turned down or even off to avoid complaints from adjacent residences.

DEPARTURE TAX This is levied on all international ferries – currently 1500dr per person *and* the same again for any car or motorbike within the EU. There's also an airport departure tax, currently 2800dr for destinations under 1200km away, 5600dr for remoter ones, but it's always included in the price of the ticket – there's no collection at the airport itself.

ELECTRICITY 220 volt AC throughout the country. Wall outlets take double round-pin plugs as in the rest of continental Europe. Three-to-two-pin adaptors should be purchased beforehand in the UK, as they can be difficult to find in Greece; the standard five-amp design will allow use of a hairdryer. North American appliances will require both a step-down transformer and a plug adapter.

FILM Fuji and Agfa print films are reasonably priced and easy to have processed – you practically trip over "One Hour Foto" shops in some resorts. Fuji and Ektachrome slide film can be purchased, at a slight mark-up, on the larger islands, but it cannot be processed there – whatever you may be told, it will be sent to Athens, so it's best to wait until you return home.

FOOTBALL (Soccer) By far the most popular sport in Greece. The most important (and most heavily sponsored) teams are Panathanaïkós and AEK of Athens, Olympiakós of Pireás, and PAOK of Thessaloníki.

GAY LIFE Male homosexuality is legal over the age of 17 in Greece, but still very covert. Male bisexuality is common but rarely admitted, as in any society where in terms of sexuality men are granted carte blanche and women are rigorously policed. Out gay Greeks are rare, and out lesbians rarer still: they suffer harassment and even violence from peers, although thanks to the culture of *filoxénia* (hospitality) gay visitors will encounter few, if any, problems. Most Greeks regard same-sex couples with bemusement, although younger males have adopted the homophobia of some British visitors. Gay and lesbian tourists are visible on virtually all the Ionian islands (although Zákinthos is mainly Family Hols Hell). There are gay-owned/run bars and businesses in the islands, but they rarely advertise the fact. Greek men are terrible flirts – cruising them is a semiotic minefield and definitely at your own risk (references in gay guides to male cruising grounds should be regarded with great caution). Native lesbians are virtually invisible in Greece, and are unusually absent from Lefkádha, despite its claim to a major role in queer history – proto-dyke Sappho is said to have committed suicide by throwing herself from the cliffs of Cape Lefkáta.

HIKING Greeks are just becoming used to the notion that anyone should want to walk for pleasure, yet if you have the time and stamina it is probably the best way to see many of the islands. This guide includes tips on good bases and routes; for advice on maps see p.25.

LAUNDRETTES (*plindíria*) are rare in the Ionian, except in main towns, but they are beginning to crop up in some of the main resort towns; sometimes an attended service wash is available for little or no extra charge over the basic cost of 1300–1500dr per wash and dry. Dry cleaning can run to 300dr an item. Otherwise, ask room-owners for a *skáfi* (laundry trough), a bucket (*kouvás*), or the special laundry area; they freak out if you use bathroom washbasins, Greek plumbing and wall mounting being what they are.

PERÍPTERA These are street-corner kiosks, or sometimes a hole-in-the-wall shop front. They sell everything from pens to disposable razors, stationery to soap, sweets to condoms, cigarettes to plastic crucifixes – and are often open when nothing else is.

TIME Greek summertime begins at 4am on the last Sunday in March, when the clocks go forward one hour, and ends at 4am the last Sunday in September, when they go back. Be alert to this, as the change is not well publicized, leading scores of visitors to miss planes and ferries every year. Greek time is two hours ahead of Britain, but one hour for a few weeks in October when the countries' respective changes back to wintertime fail to coincide. For North America, the difference is seven hours for Eastern Standard Time, ten hours for Pacific Standard Time, with again an extra hour plus or minus for those weeks in April and October when one place is on daylight savings and the other isn't. A recorded time message (in Greek) is available by dialling ☎141.

TOILETS Public ones in towns are usually in parks or squares (such as Corfu Town and Argostóli), often subterranean; otherwise try a bus station. Public toilets tend to be pretty filthy – it's best to use those in restaurants and bars. Note that throughout Greece you drop toilet paper in the adjacent waste bins, not in the bowl.

USEFUL THINGS A small alarm clock for early buses and ferries, a flashlight if you're camping out, sunscreen of high SPF (15 and above; generally unavailable in Greece), and earplugs for noisy ferries or hotels.

Part 2

The Guide

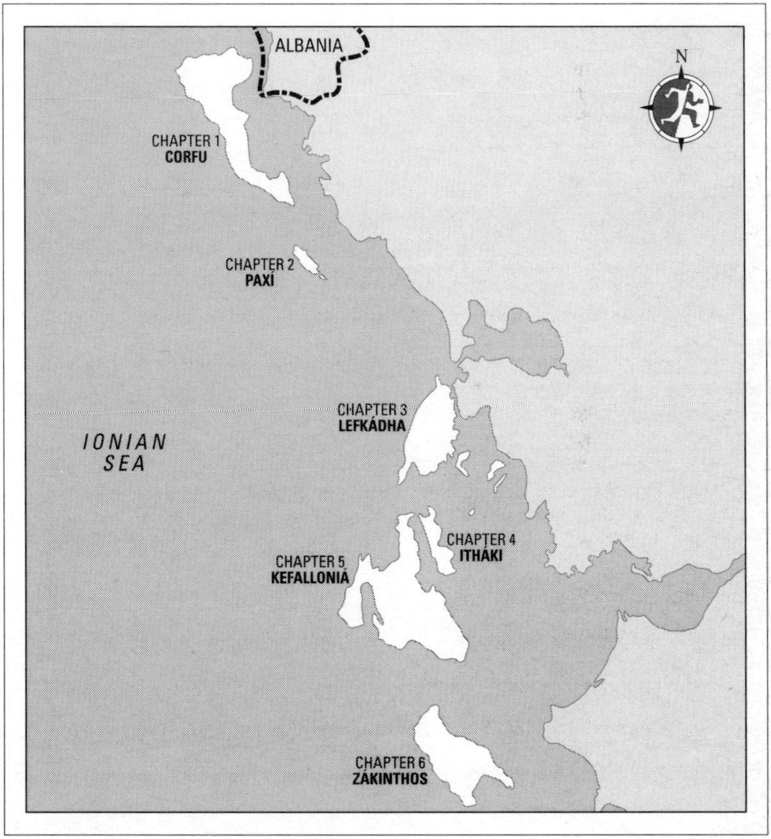

Chapter 1

Corfu (Kérkira)

Dangling between the southern tip of Italy and the west coast of mainland Greece, at the point where the Adriatic meets the Ionian Sea, the lush green sickle of **Corfu (Kérkira)** was one of the first Greek islands to attract mass tourism in the 1960s. It now has probably the sleaziest reputation among the islands, although much of this is exaggerated and due more to snobbery than actual fact. It's true that indiscriminate exploitation by package tour operators and their willing Corfiot partners turned parts of Corfu into eyesores, but many of the island's resorts have hardly been touched by tourism, and even in those that have, unspoilt parts of the coast and interior are often only a few minutes away on foot. The island has some of the best beaches in the whole archipelago, and idyllic bays that still resemble the "delectable landscape" Lawrence Durrell described in *Prospero's Cell*. The main settlement, **Corfu (Kérkira) Town**, for many years a mess of collapsing tenements and traffic congestion, was renovated for the 1994 EC summit in the town and is now one of the most elegant island capitals in the whole of Greece.

Tourism has tended to stick to the coasts, in clusters that are handy either to base yourself in or to avoid. There are no high-rise hotels here in the Spanish mould: **accommodation** tends to be in apartments,

Accommodation price codes

Rooms and hotels listed in this book have been price-coded according to the scale outlined below. The rates quoted represent the cheapest available double room in high season. Out of season, rates can drop by as much as fifty percent or more, especially if you negotiate for a stay of three or more nights. Single rooms, where available, cost around seventy percent of the price of a double. For further information, see p.32.

① up to 4000dr
② 4000–8000dr
③ 8000–12,000dr
④ 12,000–16,000dr
⑤ 16,000–20,000dr
⑥ 20,000–30,000dr
⑦ 30,000dr upwards

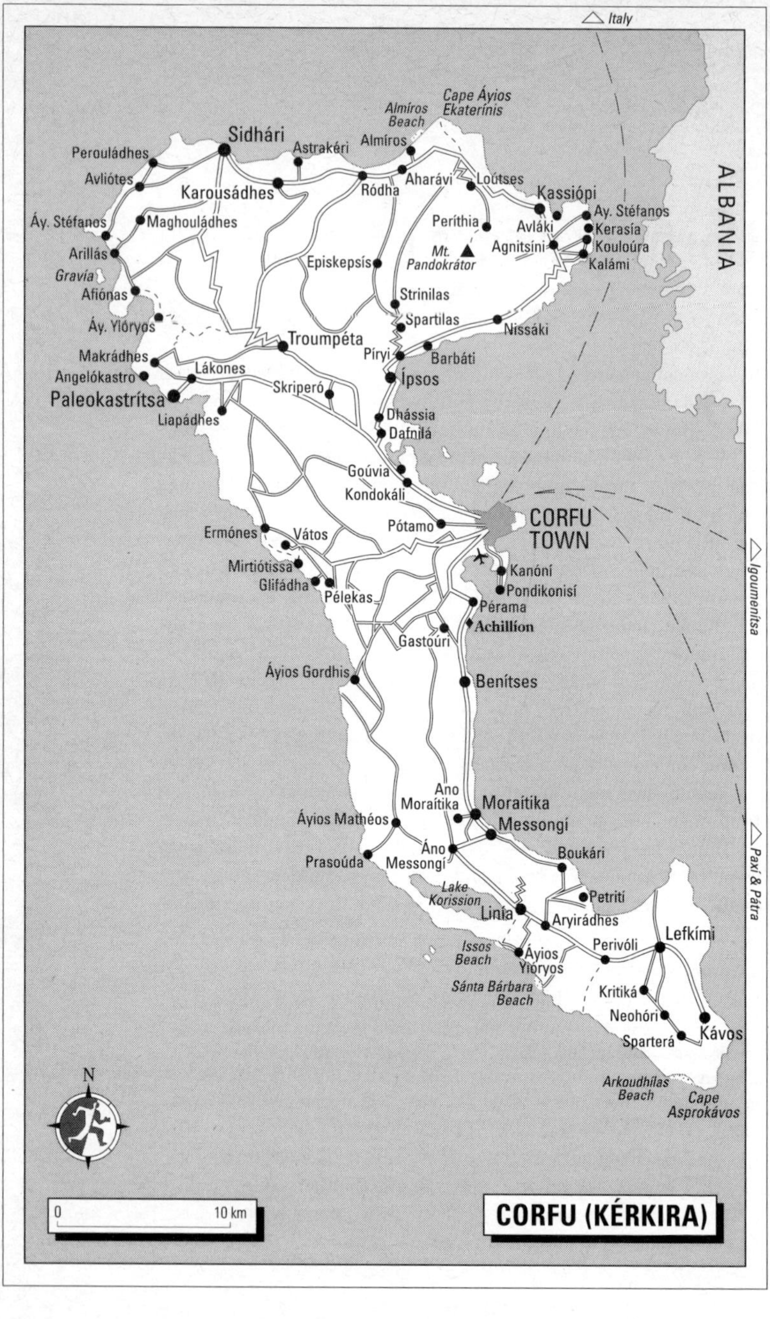
CORFU (KÉRKIRA)
Italy
ALBANIA
Igoumenitsa
Paxí & Pátra
Sidhári
Astrakéri
Almíros
Almíros Beach
Cape Áyios Ekaterínis
Peroulådhes
Avliótes
Karousádhes
Ródha
Aharávi
Loútses
Kassiópi
Áy. Stéfanos
Maghouládhes
Períthia
Avláki
Kerasía
Arillás
Mt. Pandokrátor
Agnitsíni
Kouloúra
Kalámi
Gravía
Episkepsís
Afiónas
Strinílas
Spartílas
Áy. Ylóryos
Nissáki
Troumpéta
Makrádhes
Píryi
Barbáti
Lákones
Angelókastro
Ípsos
Skriperó
Paleokastrítsa
Liapádhes
Dhássia
Dafnilá
Goúvia
Kondokáli
CORFU TOWN
Pótamo
Ermónes
Vátos
Kanóní
Mirtiótissa
Glifádha
Pondikonisí
Pélekas
Pérama
Achillíon
Gastoúri
Áyios Gordhis
Benítses
Áno Moraítika
Moraítika
Messongí
Áyios Mathéos
Áno Messongí
Prasoúda
Boukári
Lake Korission
Petrití
Linía
Aryirádhes
Lefkími
Issos Beach
Áyios Yióryos
Perivóli
Sánta Bárbara Beach
Kritiká
Neohóri
Kávos
Sparterá
Arkoudhílas Beach
Cape Asprokávos
N
0
10 km

rooms, villas and small hotels, while the larger resort hotels are horizontal rather than vertical, rarely more than five storeys high. Transport on the island's **bus** system is cheap, reliable and will get you to almost every village or resort. Buses stop at around 6pm, and restricted services run on Sundays. The system radiates out from Corfu Town, and a few hundred drachmas will get you to the furthermost points at the north or south of the island in an hour and a half.

The island's finest scenery is along the northeast coast, served by a single mountain road with turnings leading down to small pebbly bays and clear blue water, and in the northwest, with its towering cliffs and wide sandy bays. The north is dominated by the bulk of **Mount Pandokrátor** and neighbouring peaks, whose foothills and summits offer great walks and even better views – though the mountain attracts more than its fair share of bad weather, particularly in low and shoulder seasons. The centre and south is less hilly and more verdant: the lush farmland of the **Ropa Plain** which extends south from just below the resort of Paleokastrítsa is the island's fruit (and veg) basket. The south, the most developed part of the island, has two distinct sides: narrow stony beaches and a few hidden beauty spots face the mainland, while the southwest-facing coast is backed by verdant countryside and features some of the best sandy beaches on the island.

If you're intending to try to see the whole island, it's probably best to get the south out of the way first, which, apart from a handful of beauty spots detailed below, is the most developed and spoilt region – things can only get better elsewhere. Hardened **beach** nuts go west, to Mirtiótissa and other strands to the south. If you want scenery and unspoilt bays, head for the northeast coast between Nissáki and Kassiópi. Resorts for **nightlife** include Kassiópi, Sidhári, Ípsos and, notoriously, **Kávos**, still a favourite with teenage ravers. If you're on a tight schedule, spend a day in Corfu Town, move north to Kalámi, Kouloúra and Áyios Stéfanos, and then head for the west coast.

Despite the complaints of overdevelopment, many northern Europeans have been returning to the island for twenty or thirty years. The Corfiots' friendliness and kindness to strangers, the quality of *filoxenía* that has been eroded in some larger resorts, can still astonish with its generosity and grace. In particular, the Corfiots retain a great affection for the British – something the island's former rulers didn't actually earn or deserve – and the absence of British visitors during the tourism slump in recent years has left many Corfiots perplexed. In the mid-1990s, many islanders have accused British travel operators of virtually blockading the island, by cutting flights and reducing the length of the season. Paradoxically, this slump actually benefits the independent traveller, both in terms of lack of crowds and the bargains available in accommodation (happily, it also benefits the small operators in the local tourism economy). The island authorities have taken steps – a little late in the day, some would say – to reverse its fortunes. Throughout the 1990s,

Igoumenítsa

IGOUMENÍTSA is Corfu's major link with mainland Greece, and a key stop on **ferry routes** between Italy, Corfu Town and Pátra; boats also run to Paxí at least twice a week (Wed and Thurs; 4hr). The town is an important crossroads for mainland **bus services**, with connections to Athens and Thessaloníki, inland to Ioánnina, and south to Párga and Préveza (the **bus station** is a few blocks along Kyproú, the main shopping street, from the southeast corner of the town's main square, Platía Dimarkíou, which stands two blocks back and a few blocks east of the port). There's little in this busy industrial port to detain travellers, and most people travelling in either direction will find connections onwards: ferries to Corfu Town's New Port run from 4.30am to 10pm daily, although buses to Athens stop at 6pm, to Ioánnina at 8pm. At the time of writing, the one Thessaloníki bus leaves at 11.45am (Mon–Sat).

It's possible, however, that bad connections, or a tiring journey, may force you to **stay** in Igoumenítsa. **On the quayside**, the large international-standard *Hotel Aktaion*, Áyion Apostólon 17 (☎0665/22 330 or 22 707; ④) offers comfortable and modern en-suite rooms. Further along the seafront, on Ethníki Antistásis, is the *Hotel El Greco*, slightly cheaper but also very modern, with an outdoor lift and striking design (☎0665/22 245 or 25 070, fax 25 073; ④). The bargain for rooms in Igoumenítsa is *Rouzaki* (☎0665/23 612 or 24 000; ②), visible a short block across from the Corfu dock, while the *Xenia* motel at the far end of the seafront (☎0665/22 282, fax 23 282; ④) is useful if you're arriving with a vehicle. Accommodation **away from the quay** is quieter and, on the whole, cheaper. There are decent rooms on the south side of Platía Dimarkíou (Dimitroula Tsimouri: ☎0665/22 248; ②), and a couple of hotels on Elefthéria leaving the northwest corner of the square: the basic *Ignatia* (☎0665/23 648; ②), and the smarter *Stavrodromi* (☎0665/22 343; ②).

A walk away from the Corfu dock west along the seafront will bring you to a marina used by visiting yachts, where the concrete quay has recently been transformed into an elegant, illuminated promenade. Here on Antistásis, you'll find some stylish **bars**, catering to high-spending Greeks who hang out at *Art*, *Memphis*, *Metropole* and *Opera*, and some of the better **restaurants**, such as the *Petros* and *Emilios psistariés*. Next to the large, open-air *Traffic Bar*, there's a **cinema**, *Pame*, which sometimes screens English-language films.

There are **banks** and 24-hour autotellers opposite the ferry docks on Apostólon, as well as **international ferry offices**. **Corfu ferries** dock at the open quay beyond the secured international terminal; different boats operate their own ticketing systems, with the name of the ferry posted on one of two ticket kiosks opposite the loading ramps. If you miss or skip a sailing, a ticket for one sailing may not be valid for a later one, though usually you can change it. Crossing times depend on the boat: the regular open-topped ferries take just under two hours; the larger *Áyios Spirídion* is slightly more expensive (1000dr) but cuts the journey time in half.

Corfu Town has been gradually renovated, a renewal programme that is now spreading to other parts of the island. The authorities have made determined, if vain, attempts to attract a more moneyed, middle-class breed of tourist, but it is too early to see if this will succeed. Many of the British family holidaymakers who helped build

Corfu's tourism economy have been lured away to cheaper deals in Turkey and Florida. But it may be that the island really is undergoing a sea change because of the current downturn. **Benítses**, once reviled as the home-from-home of lager-loutism, has, under a new mayor, begun to revert to a whitewashed island village splashed with purple bougainvillea.

Some history

Although the Middle Ages saw important defensive structures built at outposts such as Kassiópi and Paleokastrítsa, the island's history is essentially that of its main town. Indeed, the name Corfu is an Italian corruption of the ancient Greek word *koryphai*, the "hills" on which the town's two forts were built.

Archeological finds carbon-dated to the middle Palaeolithic age – when the island was still part of the mainland, and much of the Adriatic was dry land covered by vast forests – indicate that there's been a settlement of sorts on the site of the town for over fifty thousand years. Much of prehistoric Corfu has been discovered around the sites of two ancient natural harbours: one at the opposite end of Gáritsa Bay to the town centre, near Mon Repos; and the other in the Hyllaic Harbour, now the Chalikiópoulos Lagoon, bisected by the airport runway. The latter is also thought to have been the site of settlements of **Eretrians**, mainland Greeks who overran tribes of Liburnians, in what is now Albania, in 750 BC. They were soon followed, and displaced, by invaders from **Corinth**, who made Corfu Town (which they called Corcyra, from which modern Greek Kérkira is derived) one of the most powerful forces in ancient Greece, turning it into a mighty walled city and a major sea power in the region. During the Persian Wars of the fifth century BC, Corfu provided the second largest naval force after Athens and, along with other Ionian islands, it fought alongside Athens against the Spartans in the Pelopponesian War, which was in part caused by political tensions beween Corfu and Corinth to the south.

Much to the relief of the inhabitants, who had been overrun by Illyrian pirates, the city was taken over by the **Romans** in 229 BC. It remained under Rome's rule, supplying men and ships in its wars, until 395 AD, when both city and island passed into the **Byzantine Empire**. Corfu was nominally Byzantine for over eight centuries, but as one of the most distant outposts of the empire, it was prone to raids by Vandals, Goths, Saracens, Normans and others. It was seized, briefly, by the Venetians in 1205, who were followed by the Despots of Epirus and the Angevins. After further suffering at the hands of pirates, the islanders asked for help from **Venice** in 1386, under whose rule they remained until 1797. The Venetians imposed their own laws, language, art and architecture, and began the construction of the town as it is seen now, including structures on both the Paleó and Néo Froúrio hills.

Following Bonaparte's defeat of the Republic of Venice in 1797, Corfu and the other Ionian islands were acquired by **France**. The French began what was proposed as an extensive plan of development, which resulted in the construction of the famous Listón, modelled on the rue de Rivoli in Paris. Bonaparte's true legacy to the islanders, however, was a taste for independence and republicanism, which was vigorously and even violently discouraged when the city and island were taken by the **British** in 1814. The British began the last notable stage of civic construction, building the Palace of Saints George and Michael, as well as various public amenities, under lords Guildford and Maitland. Despite these efforts, the British rulers were not liked by the general populace; Maitland, in particular, was despised for his arrogant attitude towards the islanders, who nicknamed him "The Abortion". The Ionian islands were finally offered to Greece by Queen Victoria – whose great-great-great-nephew Prince Philip was born in the Mon Repos estate in Gáritsa Bay – in her speech at the opening of Parliament in 1864.

During **World War II**, Corfu was occupied by the Italians and Germans between 1941 and 1944, and was heavily bombarded by Nazi planes. Over a quarter of Corfu Town was destroyed, including the library, parliament and numerous churches. Most, if not all, of the town's Jewish population, who had found refuge here over the centuries after pogroms elsewhere in Europe, were arrested and shipped off to the Nazi death camps. The elegant Listón makes a haunting appearance in Claud Lanzman's epic holocaust documentary, *Shoah*, as the place where Corfu's Jews were rounded up.

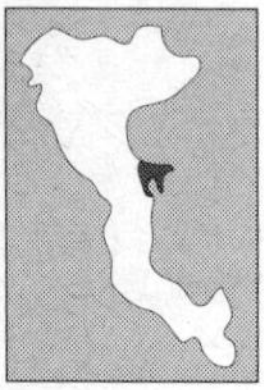

Corfu Town

CORFU TOWN (Kérkira in Greek) is the place where the island's heritage and commerce collide with an almighty bang. In high summer it can seem hellish, with a seemingly endless stream of tour coaches, dumping even more tourists on a town that's already overflowing with its own hotel guests and a native population heading for 35,000. It's not a place to come for peace and quiet, and certainly not a place to arrive without checking on accommodation beforehand; even in deep winter some hotels are fully booked. Yet if you intend to see much of the island by bus, it's the only place to base yourself, and the recent renovations to its older buildings, and the appearance of new restaurants, galleries and other attractions, have made Corfu Town more attractive than it has been for decades.

Beneath all the bustle there remains a beautiful city in miniature, fortified since Byzantine times, developed by the Venetians, added to by the French – and, some would say, desecrated by the British. It's one of the most attractive towns in the Greek islands, and certainly the most stunning in the Ionian. When the crowds subside, at siesta time and in low season, it's well worth ambling around its elegant arcades,

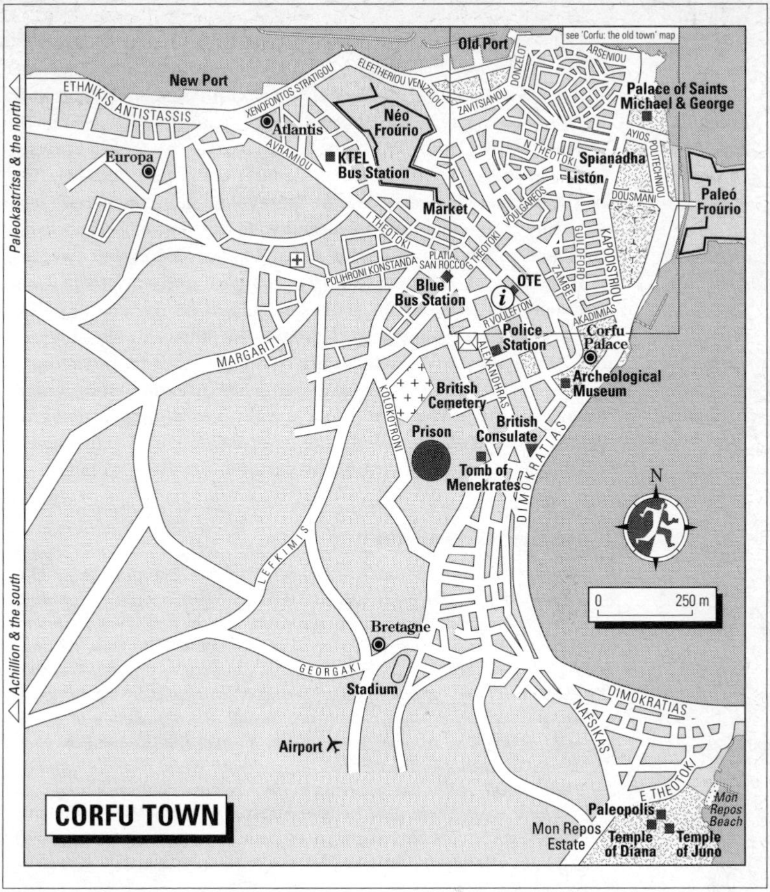

boulevards and squares. If you're just visiting on a day-trip, you shouldn't miss, first of all, the two forts, both now open daily, the warren of alleys in the Campiello and the old streets behind the Listón. Coach trips almost invariably take in tiny but overrun Mouse Island, but independent travellers would be better advised to track down the newly excavated Doric temples in the recently opened Mon Repos estate, seek out the British cemetery or hop on a boat to Vído Islet.

Arrival and information

Most visitors arrive at Corfu's notorious **airport** (see the box on p.62), 2km south of the centre of the town. There are no airport buses, and taxis have a tradition of overcharging (expect to pay around 2000dr); car rental agencies at the airport are listed on p.72.

Corfu Town

For details of the frequencies and journey times of buses, ferries and domestic flights from Corfu Town, see p.101. For information on buying tickets, see "Listings" on p.72.

Corfu has two distinct ports, though they're near to each other on the same straight seafront. The **new port (Néa Limáni)**, just beyond Platía Athínagora in the old town, serves the major ferry links with Brindisi, Bari and Ancona in Italy, and with Igoumenítsa and Pátra on the Greek mainland. Shuttle ferries from Igoumenítsa on the mainland (Corfu's key link with the rest of Greece), as well as ferries from Paxí in the south, arrive at the **old port (Paléo Limáni)**, right by the *platía*. Either port is little more than ten minutes' walk from the heart of the town, and the island-wide bus station is a short walk from either. Taxis meet ferries day and night, as do room owners.

Buses from Athens and the island's outlying towns and communities arrive at the main bus station on Avramíou, behind the agricultural co-operative building; the suburban bus station is in Platía G. Theotóki (aka San Rócco Square). For those visiting in a rented vehicle, a new one-way system has further complicated the town's traffic system, with an anticlockwise flow around the arterial road that runs along the seafront. Much of the centre is inaccessible by car, and poor for **parking** – it's best to park away

Surviving Corfu airport

Described by one respectable British newspaper as "European air travel's answer to the Black Hole of Calcutta", **Corfu airport** has come to present a special challenge to seasoned aeronauts. The airport doubled in size when an extension was built for the 1994 EC summit, but that was only opened to the general public late in 1996, with little to offer the traveller beyond more floor space. Passage through what is basically one big glass box is invariably traumatic, with occasional air-traffic delays of up to twelve hours or more exacerbating the problem. A few tips can ease your passage through the "Black Hole".

On **arrival**, unless you're racing to catch a ferry, don't rush to get off the plane. Even if you were lucky enough to get one of the few seats in Arrivals, you'd only be doing what you can do in the cool of the plane. Baggage takes ages at Corfu and Arrivals is an airless glasshouse, even in winter.

When **departing**, do not go through passport control unless you know your plane home has landed. Once through, you won't get back out, and if delayed you'll be stuck with a choice of naff snacks and expensive drinks from a tiny bar with long queues, and no shop or exchange facilities – no fun if that twelve-hour delay has your name on it. Things worsen as people departing on other flights come in behind you (the so-called Black Hole effect), until the departure lounge and tiny balconies begin to resemble the rock festival of your nightmares. It's far better to wait in the areas outside passport control or in the cafeteria upstairs. Keep an eye on the passport gate, though: it opens and closes at whim, so leave time to get through (at least thirty minutes before takeoff). If you are facing a long delay, you can escape the building and go back into town, or to the shops and bars of Gáritsa ten minutes' walk back from the airport; however, you should only leave the airport if you can confirm a departure time or length of delay with an airline representative.

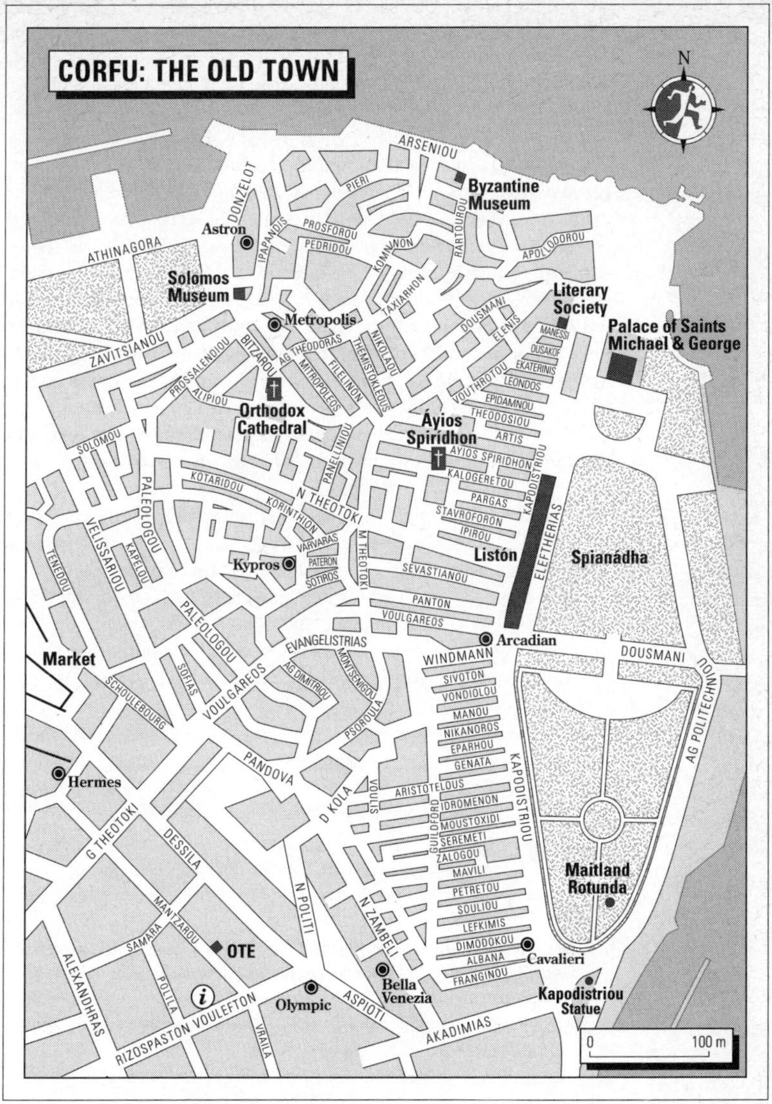

from the centre, or choose the quieter side streets in the Gáritsa district. The **tourist office** (Mon–Fri 8am–2pm; ☎0661/37 520 or 37 638), long based in the Néo Froúrio, has moved to a first-floor office on the corner of Vouléfton, the main street between Zambéli and Alexandhrás. The office is very friendly, and keeps accommodation details.

Accommodation

Accommodation in Corfu Town is notoriously hard to come by and, when found, notoriously expensive and cramped – it's cold comfort to know that, because of the town's topography, even middle-class apartments in the old town tend to be tiny. The surrounding bluffs hinder further construction, and the airport and adjacent farmland prevent much more expansion, so new accommodation developments have been squeezed north to Kondokáli and beyond, and south to Pérama and further. And even in midwinter the hotels can fill up with mysterious crowds of businesspeople and visitors who don't seem visible on the streets. At any time of year, it's best to call ahead.

Both the tourist office (see p.63) and the tourist police (see p.73) keep lists of private rooms.

Private rooms tend to be in the old town and Mandoúki area by the two ports; a small crowd of room-owners meets each ferry arrival in the New Port. If you want to phone ahead, try George Scordilis (☎0661/24 252 or 43 421; ②) or K. Nikis (☎0661/35 827 or 26 956; ②). A number of agencies near the Néo Froúrio offer rooms in the Mandoúki area, including the seafront *Katsaros Travel*, Andrea Kalvoú 6 (☎0661/27 002, fax 42 413).

Budget travellers might be advised to head straight for the **campsite** (☎0662/91 202) 2km north at Kondokáli – or, even further out, the superior campsite with cheap bungalows at Dhássia (see p.75). The nearer campsite is in a leafy garden set back from the road, signed on the left at the edge of Kondokáli, and, though basic, has a shop, café and small pool. The one drawback is that the neighbouring area looks like a half-finished motorway and sounds like a finished one.

Inexpensive hotels

Arcadian, Kapodhistríou 44 (☎0662/37 670). Mid-range hotel in a central setting, with en-suite rooms with balconies and views over the Listón and Spianádha. Street noise can be a problem, especially at weekends. ③.

Astron, Dónzelot 15 (☎0662/39 505, 39 983 or 33 708). A travellers' favourite over the decades, and it's unlikely that much of the decor has changed since the 1960s. Basic but reliable – apart from the hot water supply. Open year round. ③.

Atlantis, Xenofóntos Stratígou 48 (☎0662/35 560–2). Large and spacious air-conditioned hotel, with a bar and taverna attached. Open year round. Most credit cards accepted. ③.

Europa, Yitsiáli 10 (☎0662/39 304). Small family hotel one block back from Néo Froúrio quay; ideal if arriving by ferry. ②.

Hermes, Markóra 14 (☎0662/39 268). A longtime favourite with budget travellers, open year round, with basic rooms, and friendly staff who do not always speak English. Its main drawback is that it overlooks the lively market behind San Rócco. Open year round. ②.

Kypros, Áyion Patéron 13 (☎0662/40 675). Basic but one of the best bets in the town, dead centre; be prepared for noise. ②.

Metropolis, Leofóros Konstantínou (☎0662/31 156). Tucked away on the side of the steps up to the Orthodox cathedral, a small basic hotel. ②.

Olympic, Ioníou Voúlis 4 (☎0662/30 532 or 30 534). Big international-style hotel with large and comfortable en-suite rooms, set in a relatively quiet cross-street between the top of Kapodhistríou and Alexandhrás. ③.

Upmarket hotels

Bella Venezia, Zambéli 4 (☎0662/46 500 or 44 290). Smart and very good value if you're packing plastic: just behind the *Cavalieri*, with all the *Cavalieri*'s comforts but far cheaper. Most credit cards accepted. ③.

Bretagne, Georgáki 27 (☎0662/30 724, 31 129 or 35 690). Not the place for a quiet night, barely 100m from the airport runway, but useful if arriving late or leaving early. A comfortable modern hotel with en-suite rooms with balconies, a restaurant and bar; also recommended to those escaping the airport or sitting out a flight delay. ③.

Cavalieri, Kapodhistríou 4 (☎0662/39 041 or 39 336). Smart and friendly, with great views and a roof bar open to the public. Credit cards not accepted. ④.

Corfou Palace Hotel, Dimokratías (☎0662/39 485–7). After roughing it round the islands, this could be a great end-of-holiday treat, with its gardens, pools and luxury rooms, but beware: the bed linen is sadistically rubberized and the restaurant operates a dress code. ⑥.

Corfu Holiday Palace, Náfsica, Kanóni (☎0662/36 540–4, fax 36 551). Formerly the Hilton, a vast, international luxury hotel, used by Argo and other operators, although it's parked right at the end of the airport runway. ⑥.

The Town

Corfu Town is best explored on foot, but if you're flagging, you might consider catching the bizarre, theme park-style miniature train that runs from the far end of the Listón, circling the old town and the Néo Froúrio (800dr, or 1200dr including admission to the Néo Froúrio).

Though compact, in parts claustrophobically so, Corfu Town is actually a collection of quite different areas, each with a distinct character. The **Campiéllo**, the oldest district, sits on the hill above the old port (roughly between the Palace of Saints Michael and George, the Listón and the cathedral), while the streets running between the Campiéllo and Velisáriou, to the west, are what remains of the town's **Jewish Quarter**. These districts form the core of the old town, and their tall, narrow alleys conceal some of Corfu's most beautiful Venetian architecture. **Mandoúki**, beyond the old port, is a commercial and dormitory area for the port, and well worth exploring, not least for its small bars and restaurants.

The town's main **commercial area** lies inland from the **Spianádha** (Esplanade), roughly between G. (Georgíou) Theotóki, Alexandhrás and Kapodhistríou streets, with most shops and boutiques around the meeting of Voulgaréous and G. Theotóki and the streets radiating off Platía Theotóki. The alleys between Theotóki and Platía Athínagora, in particular, cater to Corfu's most feared latter-day invaders, shoppers with attitude: windows sparkle with gold, silver and jewellery, and craft stores recycle the island's surplus olive wood into as many shapes as tourists can be persuaded to buy. Tucked behind the corner of Platía San Rócco and Odhós Theotóki is the old **morning market**, specializing in farm produce, fish and other comestibles. The smarter areas of **San Rócco** and **Gáritsa**, to the west and south, give a good idea of the town's thriving nineteenth-century lifestyle, especially in the mansions of Odhós Alexandhrás and the Gáritsa seafront.

The Paleó Froúrio and the Néo Froúrio

The Paleó Froúrio (800dr) and the Néo Froúrio (400dr) are open daily 9am–9pm.

Jutting up above its rooftops like two miniature volcanoes, Corfu Town's most obvious sights are the forts, the **Paleó Froúrio** and the **Néo Froúrio**. Their designations (*paleó* – "old", *néo* – "new") are a little misleading, since what you see of the older structure was begun by the Byzantines in the mid-twelfth century, a mere hundred years before the Venetians began work on the newer citadel. They have both been modified and damaged by various occupiers and besiegers since, including the Neoclassical shrine of **St George**, built by the British in the middle of the Paleó Froúrio in the 1840s; the latest contribution was an extensive but rather sterile renovation of the older fort at the time of the 1994 EC Summit in the town.

Looming above the old port, the Néo Froúrio, which has only been opened to the public this decade, is by far the more interesting of the two forts. The entrance, tucked away at the back of the fort up steps beyond the *Tenedos Taverna* on Odhós Solomoú, gives onto a complex of cellars, dungeons, tunnels and battlements, with excellent views over the old town and bay, and a small gallery and café at the summit.

The Listón and the Spianádha

The **Listón**, an arcaded street designed during the French occupation, and the green **Spianádha** (Esplanade) it overlooks, are the focus of town life, even if the *kafenía* here charge exorbitant prices. People still play cricket on the Spianádha some afternoons, a tradition (like the local *tsintsí bírra*, "ginger beer") left over from the British administration, and it's possible to linger for hours over one drink. This is the venue for Corfu Town's evening *vólta*, a relaxed parade of strolling friends, couples and overdressed teenage posers. At the south end of the Spianádha, the **Maitland Rotunda**, now covered in graffiti, was built to honour the first British High Commissioner of Corfu and the Ionian islands. The neighbouring **statue of Ioannis Kapodistrias** celebrates the local hero and consummate statesman (1776–1831) who led the diplomatic efforts for Greek independence and was made its first president in 1827.

The Palace of Saints Michael and George

Renovated for the 1994 summit – hence the incongruously space-aged glass structure to the rear – the **Palace of Saints Michael and George** is currently barred to the public, except for the Sino-Japanese Museum and the new Modern Art Museum, at the rear of the building (accessed via the gardens). The palace was built between 1819 and 1824, to honour British civil servants in the

Ionian and on Malta; the imposing statue on a moated pedestal in the gardens is of the British High Commissioner of the time, Sir Frederic Adam.

Said to be the only one of its kind in Greece, the **Sino-Japanese Museum** is a must for aficonados of Oriental culture, and has more than enough to detain the casual visitor. Amassed by Corfiot diplomat Gregorios Manos (1850–1929), the collection of over 10,000 pieces was given to the Greek government in 1926, and is displayed in elegant staterooms on the first floor of the palace. It includes Noh theatre masks, exquisite woodcuts, erotic wood and brass statuettes, samurai weapons, and decorated screens and fans, as well as art works from Thailand, Korea and Tibet.

The Sino-Japanese Museum is open Tues–Sat 8.30am–3pm, Sun 9.30am–2.30pm; 500dr.

Opened in 1996, the **Modern Art Museum** holds a small but growing collection of contemporary art, much of it local. It's well worth a visit to see what Greek artists are currently producing, and to take in the gardens and pleasant cafe-bar, a quiet haven away from the busy tourist routes through the old town.

The Modern Art Museum is open Tues–Sat 8.30am–3pm, Sun 9.30am–2.30pm; 500dr.

The Solomos and Byzantine museums

In a nearby backstreet off Arseníou, five minutes' walk from the palace, a former private house, restored in 1979, houses a museum dedicated to modern Greece's most famous poet, **Dionisios Solomos**. Born on Zákinthos, Solomos was author of the poem *Hímnos yiá Éleftheria* (*Hymn to Liberty*), which was to become the Greek national anthem. He studied at Corfu's Ionian Academy, and lived in a house on this site for much of his life (it was destroyed in the war and rebuilt). The museum contains a small collection of Solomos manuscripts and effects but, frustratingly, is labelled solely in Greek.

The Solomos Museum is open Mon–Fri 5–8pm; 200dr. The Byzantine Museum is open Tues–Sun 9am–3pm; 200dr.

Up a short flight of steps on Arseníou, the **Byzantine Museum** is housed in the restored church of the Panayía Andivouniótissa (by which name it is also known). Despite its name, it houses Christian and pre-Christian artefacts, religious and secular, including sculptures and sections of mosaic floors from Paleópolis, sections of Byzantine church frescoes, a collection of ninety icons dating from the fifteenth to nineteenth centuries, and other religious paraphernalia from around the island.

Áyios Spirídhon Church

A block behind the Listón, down Odhós Spirídhonas, is the most famous structure on the whole island: the **church of Áyios Spirídhon**, whose maroon-domed campanile dominates the town and serves as a handy navigation mark. The church is dedicated to **Spiridhon**, a second-century BC bishop of Cyprus, whose relics were kept in Constantinople until the fall of the Byzantine Empire, when refugees managed to salvage them. Having finally arrived on Corfu in 1489, the relics were credited with saving the islanders from a

Áyios Spirídhon is open daily, but should be avoided during services.

famine in 1553: a sea captain carrying grain claimed that the saint appeared to him in a dream and told him to take it to Corfu. Since then Spiridhon has been credited with saving the island from numerous plagues, invasions and other disasters.

The saint's mummified body is kept in a silver sarcophagus near the altar, and on Palm Sunday, Easter Saturday, August 11 and the first Sunday in November, he is paraded through the city. Corfiots visiting the shrine on his name day (December 12) kiss his robe to petition for good luck. Spiridhon is believed by some to be a peripatetic saint, given to the odd *vólta* around town by himself, and each year he's given a new pair of slippers; apocryphal lore holds that the old slippers have been found scuffed from use.

This "new" church was built in 1590, after the original, founded in the fifteenth century in the suburb of San Rócco, had to be destroyed because of structural faults. The ceiling features ornate gilt-framed scenes from the saint's life, nineteenth-century copies of earlier works by the painter Panayiotis Doxaras, leader and instigator of the Ionian School, which were destroyed by damp.

The Archeological Museum

The Archeological Museum is open Tues–Sun 9am–3pm; 800dr, free on Sun. Full wheelchair access.

Corfu Town's **Archeological Museum**, a few blocks south from the Maitland Rotunda, is the biggest and best in the archipelago, and the ideal place to catch a glimpse of ancient Corfu, at least in the form of architectural details and artefacts from the era. It contains fragments of Neolithic weapons and cookware, coins and pots from the Corinthian era, and Roman architectural features. However, its most impressive exhibit is a massive Gorgon pediment excavated from the Archaic temple of Artemis at Paleópolis, just south of Corfu Town: at around 17m long, this dominates an entire room, its central Gorgon figure flanked by panthers and battle scenes between the gods.

The British Cemetery

South of Platía San Rócco and signposted on the corner of Methodíou and Kolokotróni, just beyond the psychiatric hospital, the **British Cemetery** – which is still used for civilian burials – features some elaborate civic and military memorials. Most notable is a memorial to the seamen killed in a naval incident in 1946, when an Albanian vessel sank two British warships, killing 44 men, leading to the severing of diplomatic ties between the countries. Despite its grim history, the cemetery is a quiet green space away from the madness of San Rócco at any time of the year, and in spring and early summer it's alive with dozens of species of orchids and other exotic blooms.

Around Corfu Town

Each of the following sights on the outskirts of the city is easily seen in a morning or afternoon, and best visited from the town rather than outlying resorts.

Mon Repos

Mon Repos is open daily 8am–8pm; free.

Around the bay from the Rotunda and Archeological Museum, and tucked behind Mon Repos beach, the estate around **Mon Repos** villa contains the most accessible archeological remains on the island. The villa itself, a Neoclassical structure built by British High Commissioner Frederic Adam in 1824, became the property of the Greek royal family when Britain ceded the island to Greece in 1864. The Corfu authorities stirred up a minor international spat in 1996 – at least in right-wing British tabloids – when they unilaterally took over the property where Prince Philip was born and began to redevelop it for public visits. The grounds are already open to the public, accessible via the gate just beyond Mon Repos beach, and the building itself is due to open in the summer of 1997.

The estate makes a pleasant shady walk, its thick woodlands concealing the remains of two **Doric temples**, dedicated to Hera and Artemis. The first has some recognizable features such as an altar and fragments of columns. The second, near the low cliffs overlooking the coast, is better preserved, with walls, foundations, columns and other details partly excavated in a pit.

Vlahérna and Pondikoníssi

The most famous excursion from Corfu Town is to the islets of **Vlahérna and Pondikoníssi**, 2km south of town – either walk there, along the road past Mon Repos beach or over the causeway that crosses the lagoon from Pérama, or take a suburban bus from Platía San Rócco to the suburb of Kanóni (20min). Joined to the mainland by a short causeway, the tiny white convent of Vlahérna is surrounded by tall cypresses and has to be one of the most photographed images in Greece. The crowds, however, as well as the roar from planes at the nearby airport, significantly detract from what can look like an idyllic setting through a camera lens. Nearby, the small wooded island of Pondikoníssi (aka Mouse Island) can be reached by a short boat trip from the dock (500dr). It's reckoned to be the petrified remains of one of Odysseus' ships, an act of revenge by Poseidon after the blinding of Polyphemus in the cave – although it's only one of a number of rocks in the region that are said to be this vessel. Barely a hundred metres across, Pondikoníssi also suffers from brief but intense overpopulation by day-trippers.

Vído

A far quieter destination than Vlahérna and Pondikoníssi is **Vído**, the larger wooded island visible from the port in Corfu Town. Vído has been a strategic point in defending, and attacking, Corfu over the centuries, and over the years has been the site of a prison, a cemetery and an execution ground. Regardless of its history, it's a pleasant place for a picnic, and part is now a privately run bird sanctuary. A shuttle *kaíki* runs back and forth between the Paleó Froúrio (far end of the quay) and Vído hourly. Hard by the Vído *kaíki* moors the *Calypso Star*, a large, glass-bottomed semi-submersible boat, which, for 3000dr a head (children half-price), takes parties out to explore the waters around Vído and to see divers at work.

Achillíon Palace

The Achillíon Palace is open daily 9am–3pm; 700dr.

Built in 1890–91 for Empress Elizabeth of Austria, this Neoclassical folly of a summer residence attracts a huge number of coach tours, despite an alarming mishmash of styles that led Henry Miller to describe it (in *The Colossus of Maroussi*) as a "madhouse" and "the worst piece of gimcrackery I have ever laid eyes on". It's certainly a curiosity in its setting, but no more interesting than an average minor country house in England – those on a tight schedule could avoid it with few qualms. If you're tempted, at 4km through the badlands of suburban Corfu, it's best reached on the dedicated bus from Platía San Rócco.

The **house** itself is small, and only four ground-floor rooms are open. On display you'll find furniture, portraits, statuary, jewellery and bas reliefs, as well as personal effects of the Empress and of Kaiser Wilhelm II, who bought the Achillíon after her assassination by an Italian anarchist in 1898. It's difficult to really appreciate the displays as, like much of the building, they're roped off and festooned with "Don't touch" signs.

Apart from the surrounding flowerbeds and a beautiful double pergola leading to Herter's monumental statue of **The Dying Achilles**, from whom the building takes its name ("I want a palace . . . worthy of Achilles," the empress is reported to have said), the **gardens** are off-limits and unremarkable, planted mainly with indigenous flora. Herter's statue and the marble balcony seat in the upper courtyard do, however, afford fine views over town and coast. The closed gardens lead down to the remains of **Kaiser's Bridge**, which used to span the coast road and led to an elegant Neoclassical stone jetty, which still survives.

Eating and drinking

A town where most visitors return to outlying resorts after dark, and where the population eat in or at small neighbourhood tavernas, doesn't offer much to the hapless hungry visitor. Most **restaurants** are in or around the old town, with some hard-to-find places favoured by locals concealed in the maze of the Campiéllo. Restaurants on the main thoroughfares – the Listón, Arseníou, around Theotóki/San Rócco – tend to be fast, snacky and indifferent. The Gáritsa seafront has a number of excellent fish restaurants with outdoor seating and views of the bay, although in summer the area is troubled by powerful odours from the drains.

Averof, in the alley leaving the cathedral steps behind Zavitsiánou. Long-running Corfu institution, offering above-par if fairly unimaginative taverna cuisine.

Faliraki, below the Palace of Saints Michael and George, down a sunken slope that passes through an arch onto the Faliráki jetty. Crumbling medieval buildings renovated as a restaurant, reasonably priced for its setting and with an imaginative menu: marinated salmon, cod croquettes, steamed mussels, designer pasta, prosciutto and other dishes not normally spotted in Corfu. The restaurant's large patio overlooks the bay, and when not busy is a good place for just a drink and a rest.

Orestes, Xenophóntos Stratígou, in Mandoúki. Probably the best fish and seafood restaurant in town, and better priced than the central restaurants.

Pizzeria, Guildford Street (Town Hall end). A wide range of pizzas with a pleasing choice for vegetarians.

Quattro Stagione, in an alley on the north side of N. Theotóki. A mix of Italian and Greek but, as the name implies, it concentrates on a range of pastas.

Rex, Zavitsiánou behind the Listón. Pricey, but some of the best food in the centre, mixing Greek with north European.

Venetian Well Bistro, Platía Kremásti. One of the best-kept secrets in Corfu, mainly because is it's so difficult to find, tucked away in a tiny square a few alleys to the south of the cathedral. This is the nearest you're likely to get to Greek *nouvelle cuisine*, but with large portions, and exotica such as Albanian calves' livers done in ouzo. One warning: beyond the house, the wine-list prices climb alarmingly. Sometimes closes Mon.

Nightlife

Corfu's self-proclaimed **Disco Strip** lies a few kilometres north of town, en route to Kondokáli, a trip best made by bus or taxi – on foot along the road, it's a game of chicken with the local daredevils. Here, at the (unofficial) *Hard Rock Café*, the *Hippodrome* disco complex (the town's biggest, with its own pool), the bizarrely decorated *Apokalypsis* and *Coco Flash*, party animals dress up for wild and fairly expensive nights out with gaggles of friends.

The Pallas cinema, on G. Theotóki, and the Orfeus, on the corner of Akadimiás and Aspióti, regularly show English-language films.

If that's not your bag, Corfu Town has plenty to offer in the way of **bars**, outdoor restaurants and streetlife at night. The Listón stays open until late, and has its own special atmosphere at night, with prices to match: if you're drinking here, avoid the eyebrow-raising mark-ups at the *Magnet*, and follow the locals to *Koklia*, *Aegli* or *Olympia*. Platía San Rócco's bars are bedevilled by traffic noise and fumes, but you will find some quieter open-air spots around Zavitsiánou. Another alternative is to drink in one of the smarter hotels, which all open their bars to outsiders: the *Cavalieri* rooftop in particular can be a dream at night.

If you're looking for a little local atmosphere, try the cheap and cheerful *Dirty Dick's*, on the corner of Arseníou and Zavitsiánou (below the old *Hotel New York*, which is closed at the time of writing). Less funky is the *Mermaid*, on Ágíon Pantón off the Listón, and for over fifteen years a friendly hangout for expats, which will give you a different spin on island culture.

Listings

American Express Kapodístriou 20a (Mon–Fri 8am–2pm; ☎0661/30 883).

Banks and exchange The town's banks are almost all based on G. Theotóki, and around Platía San Rócco; most have cash machines that accept international credit and debit cards. There are two 24hr automatic currency exchange machines on Alexandhrás, on the left leaving San Rócco.

Beaches and lidos There are no beaches in town, but two lidos offer deep-water swimming off jetties and platforms. The main lido is at Faliráki, below the palace, reached by the sunken road leading down from the corner of Arséniou and Kapodhistríou. It has loungers, changing facilities and a café, and charges 100dr entry. The second is the public swimming area below the Old Fort near the *Corfu Palace Hotel*. Mon Repos Beach, a small private beach of imported sand at Gáritsa, 15min walk south of the Spianádha (daily 9am–6pm; 150dr), is very popular with townspeople, despite what looks like a sewage outfall just metres outside its northern boundary. There's a bar and taverna, changing rooms, showers, toilets, sunbeds and a diving jetty.

Bus departures Corfu Town's suburbs, and outlying resorts as far south as Benítses and north to Ípsos, are served by the blue bus system, which is based in Platía San Rócco (Platía G. Theotóki). Some services, notably to Benítses, leave from a stop 100m down Methodíou, the road leaving the square by the bus stand. For those buses signed *horís eispráktor*, "without conductor", you'll have to buy tickets either at the San Rócco bus stand or the *kafenío* by the Methodíou bus stop. Island-wide and mainland services leave the KTEL green bus station on Avramíou near the new port. Here, tickets are bought on board, apart from Athens and Thessaloníki departures.

Car rental Avis, Ethníkis Antistásseos 42 (☎0661/24 404), plus an office at the airport; Budget, Venízelou 22 (☎0661/49 100), and at the airport (☎0661/44 017); Hertz, at the airport (☎0661/33 547). Among local companies, try Sunrise, Ethníkis Antistásseos 14, in the new port (☎0661/44 325).

Consulates Belgium, Alexandhrás 44 (☎0661/33 788); Denmark, Ethníkis Antistásseos 4 (☎0661/35 698); France, Iákanou Pólyla 22 (☎0661/26 312); Germany, 57 Guildford Street (☎0661/31 453); Italy, Alexandhrás 10 (☎0661/37 351); Netherlands, Idroméneu 2 (☎0661/39 900); Norway, Donzelot 9 (☎0661/39 667); UK, Menékratou 1 (☎0661/30 055).

Ferry offices There are ticket agencies inside the new port buildings, and franchises of the major ferry companies on Ethníkis Antistásseos opposite: Minoan/Strintzis (☎0661/25 000 or 253 32); Anek (☎0661/32 664); Adriatica (☎0661/38 089). High-season ferries to Italy fill quickly, especially car spaces, so phoning ahead is advised. Tickets for old port ferries are available in the row of offices near the Paxí ferry jetty, and also on Odhós Dónzelot above it.

Hospital On the corner of I. Andreádi and Polichroníou Konstánta, off Platía San Rócco (☎0661/45 811 or 25 400).

Laundry There are at least three ancient *plindíria* hidden in the alleys of Corfu Town. Most central is the Kyknós on Néa Palaíologou, behind the Pistea Bank on Voulgaréou. Also handy is the Periotéri, in the first block of I. Theotóki off Platía San Rócco. And tucked in an alleyway to the left of the Orthodox Cathedral's front entrance stands the Chrísto *plindírio*. None of their staff speak English.

Motorbike rental Most bike rental firms are based in or around the new port: Sunrise, Ethníkis Antistásseos 14 (☎0661/44 325), is a good place to start, but if you have time shop around.

Olympic Airways Kapodhistríou 20 (☎0661/38 694).

OTE Mantzárou 3 (daily 6am–midnight; ☎0661/45 699 or 34 131).

Police Alexandhrás 19 (☎0661/38 661).

Post office Corner of Alexandhrás and Zafirópoulos (Mon–Fri 7.30am–8pm).

Taxis There are taxi ranks at the airport, by the new and old ports, at the Spianádha end of the Listón, and on Theotóki.

Tourist police Arseníou 31 (☎0661/30 265).

The northeast and the north coast

The northeast is the most stereotypically Greek part of Corfu: mountainous, with a rocky coastline chopped into pebbly bays and coves, above a sea that's often as clear as a swimming pool. A green **bus** route between Corfu Town and Kassiópi serves the resorts along the single coastal road, along with some blue suburban bus services as far as Dhássia and Ípsos. A bus from the island capital connects Kassiópi to the family-oriented resort of Aharávi, but otherwise the north coast resorts – as far west as brash Sidhári and the nearby hill town of Avliótes – are served by direct buses from Corfu Town that travel via often spectacular inland routes.

Kondokáli and Goúvia

The landscape immediately to the north of Corfu Town as far as Kondokáli is little more than motorway and industrial sites, and has about as much rural charm as Brooklyn or Lewisham. Things don't improve much at **KONDOKÁLI** itself, a small village overrun by holiday developments, which serves the nearby marina at Goúvia. The old town consists of a short street with a number of bars and traditional *psistariés* – notably, *Gerekos* and *Takis* – and one international restaurant, *Flags*, with an imaginative menu (fish and steaks in exotic sauces) aimed at the yachting fraternity, who comprise much of Kondokáli's passing trade. There's very little accommodation here: holiday lets have tended to revert to domestic tenancies due to the tourism slump.

Kondokáli's neighbouring resort, **GOÚVIA**, is the site of Corfu's largest yachting marina, and the launching point of most flotilla and bareboat holidays. As the first half-decent resort north of Corfu, it also tends to fill up with tourists off the ferries, particularly in high summer. Besides the marina facilities, the village boasts a couple of small **hotels**, notably the *Hotel Aspa* (☎0661/91 303 or 91 155; ④), and some **rooms** – try Maria Lignou (☎0661/91 348; ②) or Yorgos Mavronas (☎0661/91 297 or 90 297; ②). Catering largely to the flotilla culture are a number of decent **restaurants**, including *The*

Captain's Table and *Aries Taverna*, and a couple of pizzerias, *Bonito* and *Palladium*, as well as the curious Spanish-themed *Borracho* bar and the *Adonis* disco. The very narrow shingle **beach**, barely 5m wide in parts, shelves into sand, but given the amount of yacht traffic in the area, water quality must be at best uncertain. Behind the fenced-in marina are the skeletal remains of a **Venetian armoury**, an almost surreal collection of stone buttresses standing in a meadow.

Curiously, Goúvia's marina has become the target of armed Albanian criminals, who steal yachts either to sell on or to strip for equipment. Although the problem has been blown out of proportion in the British media, early in 1996 the Foreign Office issued a warning that the marina was unsafe from dusk to dawn, and indeed a British yachtsman was shot dead by one such gang aboard a yacht off Cape Komméno to the north of Goúvia in September 1996. The Albanian criminals are becoming more audacious (as are the small number of Corfiots rumoured to be using the cover to commit copy-cat crimes), but land-based visitors should have no need to worry about the threat.

Danília Village is open 10am–3pm & 6pm–midnight (☎0661/91 621–2 or 36 833).

Goúvia is the turn-off point for the **Danília Village** "Corfu Experience", the Ionian's first theme park, about 2km inland. Built two decades ago by a Greek family – some time before the craze for historical theming took off – it's an earnest attempt to capture Greek village architecture and culture, akin to British working-history museums. It's set around a reproduction village and examples of vernacular architecture, and includes an authentic olive press and craft workshops, as well as the inevitable gift shops. At night, it hosts "Greek evenings", which are hugely popular with coach parties.

Dhássia and Dafnilá

Two kilometres beyond Goúvia are **DHÁSSIA** and **DAFNILÁ**, set in two small wooded bays where developments have largely merged into one. The beaches here are pebble, with two outfits, Corfu Ski Club and Club 2001, offering paragliding and other **water sports** at either end of the Dhássia beach (expect to pay from 7000dr for a single session with either company). Two large A-class **hotels**, the *Dasia Chandris* (☎0661/33 871–4; ⑦) and *Corfu Chandris* (☎0661/97 100–3; ⑦), dominate Dhássia. The hotels are next to each other but in their own extensive grounds, with pools and sports facilities, shops, restaurants, bars and beach frontages. Both take block bookings from north European package companies, but have rooms available for most of the season.

More reasonably, the *Hotel Amalia* (☎0661/93 523; ③) has pleasant en-suite rooms and its own pool and garden, set back from the main road opposite the *Chandris* hotels. Private **rooms** are scarce in the resort, although Spiros Rengis, who runs the local mini-market, has a few (☎0661/90 282; ②), and *Hermes Apartments*

(☎0661/93 314, fax 93 373; ④) can offer studios and apartments. Dhássia does, however, have the best **campsite** on the island, *Dionysus Camping Village* (☎0661/91 417 or 93 785, fax 91 760). While it doesn't have direct access to the sea, it's only a few hundred democratic metres from the beach the two *Chandris* joints use. As well as camping space under terraced olive trees, *Dionysus* has simple bungalow huts (①), a pool, shop, bar and restaurant. The camp attracts an international crowd, some of whom appear still to be on their way home from the Isle of Wight pop festival, and the friendly, multilingual owners will offer a ten percent discount if you wave this book at them (nicely).

Ípsos

ÍPSOS, 2km and one bay north of Dhássia, can't really be recommended to anyone but hardened bar-hoppers. There isn't room to swing a cat on the long, thin pebble beach, which lies right beside the busy coast road, and the atmosphere suggests the resort has been twinned with Southend or Coney Island. The seafront comprises a kilometre-long row of snack joints, vehicle rental firms, one laundromat (the subversively named *My Beautiful Laundrette*), and cocktail bars with names like *Alcoholics Anonymous*, *The Shamrock* and *The Victoria Pub*, which draw a young, boozy crowd with adverts for "Sex on the Beach" cocktails – and, on the irregular visits by the US Navy on R&R shore trips, bar notices asking "Fancy a date with four thousand sailors?"

Most **accommodation** has been taken over by British package companies, although *Ipsos Travel* (☎0661/93 661 or 93 920–1) can offer rooms, as well as car rental and other facilities. *Ipsos Ideal* **campsite** has closed, leaving just *Corfu Camping Ipsos* (☎0661/93 579 or 93 246) in the centre of the strip, which has a motel-style reception with bar and restaurant, and offers standing tents to those without their own equipment. Ípsos is also the base for probably the island's major **diving centre**, *Waterhoppers* (☎0661/93 876), which is registered with the British Sub-Aqua Club and run on BSAC guidelines. Claiming to be the only dive outfit in Greece with a 54-inch decompression chamber, the club caters for beginners and advanced divers, as well as offering a number of BSAC and CMAS courses. The daily trips on its own *kaíki* also welcome snorkellers and those who prefer to remain dry.

Eating on Ípsos main drag is a hit-and-miss affair, although it does have a large and stylish Chinese, the *Peking House*, looming over it. A more traditional meal and a quieter setting can be found in the *Akrogiali Psistaria* and *Asteria Taverna*, by the small marina at the southern end of the strip. **Drinking** in Ípsos is mandatory, but if you want to avoid droves of bevvied-up lads searching for TV football, head for one of the quieter bars at the southern end of the seafront.

Mount Pandokrátor

Ípsos has now all but engulfed the neighbouring hamlet of Píryi, at the end of the strip, which is the main point of access for the hill villages and routes leading up to the island's largest mountain, **Mount Pandokrátor**. The access road, initially signposted "Spartílas", is 200km beyond the main junction in Píryi. A popular base for walkers is the village of **STRINÍLAS**, 16km up the road from Píryi. Accommodation is basic but easy to come by: most of it is in private houses, but the *Elm Tree Taverna* in Strinílas, a longtime favourite with walkers, can point you in the direction of rooms.

The presence of an unattractive communications station on the top of Mount Pandokrátor, complete with two large radio masts, has meant that the path leading up to the neighbouring Pandokrátoras monastery has now become a (fairly rough) road. Cars and tour coaches can almost reach the summit, stopping at the hamlets of Petália, if coming from the south, or Períthia from the north. In summer the main routes become quite busy, but there are quieter walks to be had by taking in the handsome Venetian village of Episkepsís, 5km northwest of Strinílas; quietest of all is the trail from Agnitsíni (on the main northeast coast road by the turn-off for Áyios Stéfanos), which leads to the tiny hamlet of Tritsí and on to the near-deserted Venetian village of Áno Períthia, from where a path leads up to the summit. Anyone interested in walking the Pandokrátor paths is advised to get the **map** of the mountain by island-based cartographer Stephan Jaskulowski, which should be available in Corfu's bookshops from the summer of 1997.

In spring and early summer, the route up to the summit blossoms with dwarf cyclamen, irises and orchids, and birds of prey – including the rarely seen golden eagle – patrol thermals above the slopes. Rules about hill walking – taking liquids, cover, sensible clothing, leaving note of your destination – should be followed. Pandokrátor is a magnet for bad weather, so take local advice if it looks at all changeable. Storms and low cloud are not uncommon in all but the driest of high seasons.

Barbáti and Nissáki

The coast road beyond Ípsos mounts the lower slopes of Pandokrátor towards **BARBÁTI**, some 4km on. Here you'll find the best beach on this stretch of coast: long and wide, away from traffic, with a gently shelving shore of pebbles and sand, and ample facilities. It's a favourite with families, and much of the **accommodation** here is booked throughout the summer by north European travel companies. However, there are some rooms – *Paradise* (☎0663/91 320; ②) and *Geranou Roula* (☎0663/92 397; ②) – and a friendly travel agency on the main road, named *Helga* after its owner, that has a range of accommodation (☎0663/91 547; ②–③). Apart from these places and a number of **tavernas** – including the *Lord Byron*, and the more traditional *Alexiou* and *Chryso Varelli* – there's not much else. Barbáti gets the morning sun, but the steep mountain bluffs behind it lose light early, and when bad weather is snagged by Mount Pandokrátor, the coast here tends to get dumped on.

The mountainside becomes steeper and the road higher above the sea beyond Barbáti, as the population of the coastline thins drastically. **NISSÁKI** is more a vague area than a place: three excellent pebble beaches, one dominated by the gigantic and rather soulless *Nissaki Beach Hotel* (☎0663/91 232–3, ⑦), a couple of shops and a bakery, and a few travel and **accommodation agencies**. The British-owned *Falcon Holidays* (☎0663/91 318) rents out apartments above the first beach, a tiny, white-pebble affair with deep-blue water that's home to a trio of fine tavernas. Also worth contacting for apartments and villas are the *Nissaki Holidays Center* (☎0663/92 106) and *Vally's Tours* (☎0663/91 294, fax 91 071), or for rooms, *Studios Aliki* (☎0663/91 041) by the bus stop. One **restaurant** on the main road deserves a mention: *Taverna Giorgos*, opposite Club Med's quasi-military security gates, which specializes in Italian and German dishes.

At Nissáki and beyond, watch out for blue signs saying "to paralía" *(the beach), which point out short-cut paths to the beaches below.*

Kalámi and Kouloúra

The two places no one visiting the northeast coast should miss are neighbouring Kalámi and Kouloúra: the first for its Durrell connection, the latter for its exquisite bay and sole taverna (though it has to be said that neither has a beach worth mentioning). Sadly, **KALÁMI** is on the way to being spoiled – already, the hillside above the bay is scarred by ugly purple apartment blocks that must have been designed with the help of hallucinogenic drugs – but the village itself is still small and, if you squint, you can imagine how it would have been in the year Lawrence Durrell spent there on the eve of World War II, when, according to Henry Miller, "days in Kalámi passed like a song". The beach is stony, and pebbly in the water, but many who holiday here hire boats to explore nearby coves. The **White House**, where Durrell wrote *Prospero's Cell*, is now split in two: the ground floor is an excellent taverna; the upper floor is let by the week through CV Travel (see p.6), although it tends to be prebooked months in advance.

Most of the **accommodation** in Kalámi – like much of the strip between Nissáki and Kassiópi – has been sewn up by blue-chip villa companies such as CV Villas, Simply Ionian and Corfu à la Carte; anything left over for independent travellers probably needs to be booked in advance. The owner of the White House, Tassos Athineos (☎0663/91 251), has rooms, and Yannis Vlachos (☎0663/91 077–8 or 91 094, fax 91 077) has rooms, apartments and studios in the bay, as do *Sunshine Travel* (☎0663/91 170 or 91 572–3) and *Kalami Tourism Services* (☎0663/91 062, fax 91 369). These agencies also

The Durrells and Corfu

Between them, brothers **Gerald and Lawrence Durrell** unwittingly persuaded untold hundreds of thousands of Britons to visit Corfu – a fact the former would live to rue. Gerald (1925–95) described the family's arrival on the island in the early 1930s in his *My Family and Other Animals;* the "strawberry-pink" villa the family moved into was in Pérama, although later they would move to another house in the hills above Kalámi. Lawrence (1912–90) was in his twenties and had already published a first novel (*Panic Spring*) pseudonymously when he arrived in 1937 to spend a year and a half living in "an old fisherman's house in the extreme north of the island – Kalamai". The book he produced describing this idyll, *Prospero's Cell* – the title taken from the theory that Corfu was the setting for Prospero and Miranda's exile in Shakespeare's *The Tempest* – remains in print half a century on and portrays an island that can still be glimpsed in the more remote corners of the northeast coast. Lawrence left the island at the outbreak of World War II – Henry Miller's *Colossus of Maroussi* describes a holiday with Durrell on the eve of war – but returned later, and shorter pieces on the island can be found in his collected prose works, *Spirit of Place*. *Prospero's Cell* would form part of an island trilogy – joined later by *Reflections on a Marine Venus*, based on his postwar visit to Rhodes, and *Bitter Lemons*, on a later visit to Cyprus. While Lawrence travelled widely, eventually settling in France, Gerald retained his contact with Corfu up until his death. The environmentalist and author was particularly outspoken about the dangers of chemical pesticide sprays on the olive trees, particularly when an alfresco lunch party of his was "accidentally" sprayed with noxious chemicals. The aerial spraying continues, as does research to substantiate environmentalists' claims that the sprays may be carcinogenic.

offer car, bike and boat rental, and exchange facilities. *Matella's* restaurant at the back of the village can also find you a room.

The **restaurant** at the White House is recommended, as is *Matella's* for its range of vegetarian and north European dishes, even though it's away from the view. The *Kalami Beach Taverna* also has a lengthy list of vegetarian alternatives to Greek staples. *Pepe's* on the beach offers a mix of pizzas and local dishes, and holds traditional Greek music nights.

The tiny harbour of **KOULOÚRA** has managed to retain its charm, set at the edge of a (so far) totally undeveloped bay with nothing in it but pine trees and *kaíkia*. The fine **taverna** here has to be the most idyllic setting for a meal in the whole of Corfu, which accounts for its great popularity, particularly with drivers: if you're coming for lunch, arrive early, as it fills up quickly even in low season.

Kerasiá, Áyios Stéfanos and Avláki

Two pleasant kilometres by lane beyond Kouloúra, the large, shady cove of **Kerasiá** shelters the friendly, family-run *Kerasia Beach Taverna* and a strip of villas along the shore, handled by CV Travel and others. The beach has a jetty, and with reason: it tends to attract day-trip boats most summer afternoons, when those staying here leave as fast as their outboards will take them.

Without doubt the most attractive resort on this stretch of coast, some 3km down a winding lane from the village of Agnitsíni on the main coast road, is **ÁYIOS STÉFANOS**, not to be confused with the resort of the same name on the west coast above Paleokastrítsa. Buses marked "Áyios Stéfanos" from Corfu Town go to the latter; this Áyios Stéfanos is only ever served by the Kassiópi bus, which will drop you at Agnitsíni. From there, it's a beautiful walk down to the resort, through olive groves and then open country with views across to nearby Albania – though quite a slog on the way back up.

Áyios Stéfanos is probably the most remote resort on Corfu, and the bare countryside around it and across in Albania increases this pleasant – and, for Corfu, rare – sense of isolation. Most **accommodation** here is upmarket villas and apartments run by British travel companies, and the village has yet to succumb to any serious development, which means that available space is thin on the ground; so far, only the *Kochili* pizzeria and snack bar has rooms and apartments for independent travellers (☎0663/81 522; ③). The handful of **tavernas** reflect this upmarket exclusivity in their pricing and the fact that they almost all take credit cards. Recommended are the *Garini* and *Kaporelli* tavernas on the seafront, which mix high-class Italian and Greek, and the *Eucalyptus* over by the village's small and rather gravelly beach.

Half an hour's walk from the coastguard station above Áyios Stéfanos, along a path that at present resembles jungle lorry track, is the beach of **Avláki**. In season, it's favoured by those fleeing the crowds on the more accessible beaches to the south and at Kassiópi. The pebble bay faces north-northwest, and its cliffs scoop up the prevailing winds, providing lively conditions for the **windsurfers** who visit the beach's small windsurf club (board hire starts at around 2000dr). There are two **tavernas**, the *Barbaro* and *Avlaki*, and some **rooms** a few hundred metres back from the beach (*Mortzoukos*, ☎0663/81 196, and *Tsirimiagos*, ☎0663/81 522), but nothing else.

Áyios Stéfanos is connected to Kerasiá by a two-kilometre lane passing through olive groves and an estate owned by the Rothschild clan.

Kassiópi and around

About 2km around the coast from Avláki is **KASSIÓPI**, a small fishing village with a long history that's been transformed into a major party resort. Emperor Tiberius had a villa here, and the village's sixteenth-century church, locked and a little careworn these days, is believed to be on the site of a temple of Zeus, once visited by Nero. Very little evidence of Kassiópi's longevity survives, however, apart from a sadly abandoned Angevin *kástro* on its headland. Most visitors come for the nightlife – clubs, video bars, restaurants – and some small pebbly beaches around the headland. Package tourism dominates, and the Greek language is on its way out, but the original architecture of some of the streets around the harbour is still attractive.

Kassiópi's **beaches** are hidden below its ruined castle, and reached by paths leaving the harbour and the village church. They are small but well protected and, because of their geographical distribution, at least two of them should be sheltered regardless of which way the wind is blowing. Only a few minutes' walk from the town centre, Kalamíonas is the largest, Pipítos the smallest, and Kanóni and Batariá the quietest, although even these two fill up very easily.

Inland from Kassiópi, the tiny village of **Loútses** has no shops, tavernas or other facilities (though buses run there from Corfu Town), but the open countryside around is excellent walking terrain, mainly grazing land or wild maquis, free of trees and with fine views over Albania. The walk from Kassiópi, a simple stroll along the coast road to the signed turning for Loútses, can be done in under an hour. For more serious walkers, the Loútses route continues to Seríthia, where a path leads onto the summit of Mount Pandokrátor.

Practicalities

Most **accommodation** in Kassiópi is through village agencies who, because they're in the marketplace with cut-price package operators, tend to be cheaper than in the tonier resorts to the south. The largest, *Travel Corner* (☎0663/81 220 or 81 213, fax 81 108; ②), is a good place to start if you're planning to stay a while in Kassiópi and want a choice of accommodation. *Beri's Travel* (☎0663/81 682 or 81 681), *Salco Holidays* (☎0663/81 040) and *Cosmic Tourist Centre* (☎0663/81 624 or 81 686) also have a range of rooms, apartments and villas. An independent alternative, the rather smart *Kastro* café-pension, is set away from the hubbub of town, overlooking the beach behind the castle (☎0663/81 045; ④). And if they aren't overrun by package bookings, *Theofilos* (☎0663/81 261; ①) offers good rooms on Kalamíonas beach at a bargain price.

Anglicized cuisine and fast food dominates **eating** in Kassiópi. For something more traditional, head for the *Three Brothers* taverna on the harbourfront, which has a vast menu, and the neighbouring *Porto* fish restaurant. At night, Kassiópi rocks to the cacophony of its music and video **bars**. Flashest has to be the gleaming hi-tech *Eclipse*, closely followed by the *Baron*, *Angelos* and *Jasmine*, all within falling-over distance of the small town square. The *Axis Club* (daily 11pm–late; entrance free) specializes in house, techno and other dance strains mixed by imported British DJs; frolics sometimes extend onto the beach until dawn.

Almirós and Aharávi

The coastline on from Kassiópi becomes slighty overgrown and marshy, until reaching the little-used **Almirós beach**. Almirós is in fact an extension of the same beach as at Aharávi and Ródha, and as such is one of the longest on the island. So far, it is also the most undeveloped, with only a few apartment buildings under construction at the hamlet of **ALMIRÓS**, which currently comprises a pair of snack bars and some package-tour rooms. The beach is wild and near deserted, although it gets busier as it approaches Aharávi. The far eastern end, towards Cape Áyios Ekaterínis, is backed by the **Antinióti lagoon**, smaller than Korissíon in the south of the island, but still a haven for waterfowl, waders, marsh species and any number of other birds lured by the fish farms in the lagoon.

With its wide main road, **AHARÁVI** at first sight resembles a rather unappealing American Midwest truck stop, but the village proper is in fact tucked away behind this new highway, in a small, quiet crescent of old tavernas, bars and shops. The sand-and-pebble beach is very popular with family holidaymakers, who arrive in their coachloads with the British travel majors, but also attracts German and north European tourists to a number of seriously expensive resort hotels.

On the whole, Aharávi makes a decent, quieter alternative to the beaches in the southwest, and should also be considered by those looking for alternative routes up onto **Mount Pandokrátor** (see p.76). Signposted roads leaving the Aharávi main road for small mountain hamlets such as Áyios Martínos and Lafkí connect with well-signed routes up onto the mountain, and even a walk up from the backstreet of Aharávi will find you on the mountain's upper slopes in under an hour. The dip slopes around Aharávi also have some excellent walks through them, although, given the maze of paths through the olive groves and lack of identifying topography, these are almost impossible to identify. As elsewhere in the region, though, the olive grove paths are there for a specific purpose, and will invariably bring you out to another road or village, although not always the one you might expect. The views from the open roads around Lafkí, down over Aharávi and Cape Áyios Ekaterínis, are stunning, sometimes vertiginous.

Aharávi practicalities

Independent **accommodation** isn't too easy to find in Aharávi, but a good place to start is *Castaway Travel* (☎0663/63 541 or 63 843, fax 63 376). Run by a long-term English resident of the village, Sue Tsirigoti, and her husband Theo, the company handles a wide range of rooms and apartments, and offers other services such as currency exchange and excursions. The village's other travel company, *Oracle* (☎0663/63 265 or 63 262, fax 63 441), has a smaller range of mainly upmarket accommodation, much of it committed to German holidaymakers, and offers car rental.

Day-trips to Eríkoussa (see p.100), run weekly by Castaway Travel, cost around 3000dr per person.

There are a number of good **restaurants** on Aharávi's main drag, among them the *Pump House* steak and pasta joint, which also offers a wide range of Italian, German and Greek dishes. There's a similarly catholic choice at *Gloo Gloo* (only ask them the meaning of the name if you've got time on your hands), and the traditional tavernas *Chris's* and *George's* are also recommended. A few hundred metres out of town towards Ródha, the smaller *Young Tree* specializes in Corfiot dishes such as *sofríto* and *pastitsáda*. The bar-restaurants tend to get quite rowdy at night, although the light and airy *Captain's Bar*, where the counter is actually the owner's old *kaíki*, is a pleasant place to drink. For a quieter drink still, head for the leafy awning of the friendly *Vevaiotis Kafenio* in the old village.

Ródha

Where Aharávi pulls up short of overdevelopment, **RÓDHA** has tipped over into it, and can't really be recommended to the independent traveller. Its central crossroads has all the charm of a motorway service station, and the beach, though an extension of Aharávi's, is rocky in parts and swampy to the west. "Old Ródha", as the signposts call it, is a small triangular warren of alleys between the main road and the seafront, where you'll find the best **restaurants and bars**: the *Taverna Agra*, oldest in Ródha, overlooking the beach, is the best for fish, and both the *Rodha Star Taverna* and *New Harbour* are also recommended. For bars, try *Nikos* near the *Agra* and the upmarket bar-club *Skouna*.

For **accommodation**, try the Anglo-Greek *NSK UK Travel* (☎0663/63 471, fax 63 274; UK office ☎01792 790662), which offers a wide range of rooms, villas and apartments, and also rents cars. *Yuko Travel* on the main drag (☎0663/63810; ②) rents rooms and handles car rental, as does *Spitias Travel* (☎0663/63 014, fax 63 974). The large *Hotel Afroditi* (☎0663/63 147, fax 63 125; ②) has decently priced en-suite rooms with sea views, but the only campsite, *Rodha Camping*, was moribund when last visited. *Yuko* and *Myron's* by the crossroads rent bicycles, useful for exploring this relatively flat region.

Sidhári and Avliótes

The next notable resort, **SIDHÁRI**, is expanding rapidly under the influence of travel companies such as Thomson and First Choice. It has a small but pretty town square, with a bandstand set in a small garden, but this is lost in a welter of bars, snack joints and some very well-stocked shops. It's extremely popular with British package visitors, whose presence makes it a busy and fairly noisy party resort most nights.

The main beach is sandy but not terribly clean, and many people tend to head west to the various coves near Sidhári's star attraction, the direly named **Canal d'Amour**. This area is noted for its coves walled by wind-carved sandstone cliffs, which give the coastline a curious, almost science fiction landscape. One of these coves was once almost enclosed as a cave, and local legend claimed that if a woman swam its length she would win the man of her dreams. Erosion has completely reshaped the channel, but it has become known as the Canal d'Amour, and many local tour operators offer "romantic" evening cruises there. The nickname may have something to do with its reputation – at least in local rumour – as the setting for some fairly scandalous late night parties in recent years. A more functional, and probably more enjoyable watery experience is provided by Sidhári's much-advertised water slide (2000dr), away from the beach off the main road.

There is little about Sidhári that will captivate the first-time visitor, although it gets its fair share of returnees. The main reason the independent traveller would probably want to visit or stay is en route to the **Diapontia islands** to the northwest. Day-trips to Mathráki, Othoní and Eríkoussa (see p.99) tend to leave weekday mornings at around 9am, so unless you're able to catch the 5.30am Sidhári bus from Corfu Town, your only option is to stay in the area. The boats are run by Nearchos Seacruises (☎0663/95 248) and cost around 3000dr return per person.

Practicalities

Kostas Fakiolas at the *Scorpion* café-bar at the west end of the main road (☎0663/95 046; ②) and Nikolaos Korakianitis's minimarket on the main road (☎0663/95 058; ②) are the best sources of **rooms**. *Princess Travel* (☎0663/95 667; ②) and *Alkinoos Travel* (☎0663/95 012 or 95 550; ②) also have good-value rooms in town, and Dimitrios Vlasseros can offer larger self-catering apartments, with a snack bar and pool (☎0663/95 313, fax 95 737; ④). The biggest accommodation agency in Sidhári is run by can-do young tycoon Philip Vlasseros, whose *Vlasseros Travel* (☎0663/95 695 or 95 062) also handles car rental and a boggling range of excursions, including horse riding. Sidhári's **campsite**, *Dolphin Camping* (☎0663/31 846), is some way inland from the T-junction at the western end of the main drag. The site is small and pleasant, with cleaning facilities and a shop, and is positioned to avoid the worst of Sidhári's night-time noise.

Eating in Sidhári is often an event for which people dress up: most restaurants are pitched at those looking for a great night out rather than a quiet meal in a taverna. The *Olympic* is the oldest taverna in Sidhári, but has gone upmarket and provides ersatz folk entertainment most evenings. Quieter are the traditional *Diamond* and *Sea Breeze* tavernas, while the *Romana* pizzeria is recommended for simple refuelling. There are no quiet bars in Sidhári, and two **nightclubs** vie for your custom, the *Remezzo* and its younger rival, the dodgily named *Ecstasy*.

Avliótes

The Sidhári bus usually continues to **AVLIÓTES**, a handsome hill town with bars and tavernas but few other concessions to tourism. Avliótes is noteworthy for two reasons, however: its accessibility to the quieter beaches below Perouládhes just over a kilometre away, which make a welcome alternative to the rather cramped sandstone coves of Sidhári; and the fact that Áyios Stéfanos on the west coast is under half an hour's walk from here, downhill through lovely olive groves. Indeed, given the scarcity of buses to Áyios Stéfanos from Corfu Town (only 2 a day), going via Avliótes might be a useful way of approaching this remote resort.

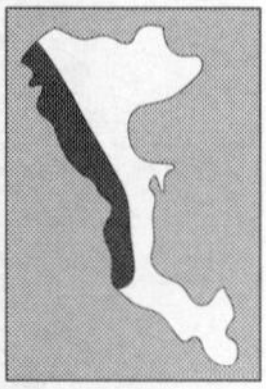

Paleokastrítsa and the west coast

The northwest of Corfu conceals some of the island's most dramatic coastal scenery and, in the interior, violent mountainscapes jutting out of the verdant countryside. Its resorts are fairly developed, though not on the same scale as the southeastern coast, probably because the craggy northwestern landscape just doesn't have much accessible terrain. Further down the west coast, the terrain opens out more to reveal long sandy beaches, such as delightful Mirtiótissa and the backpackers' haven of Áyios Górdhis. Given the structure of the bus system, travel along the west coast is at best haphazard: virtually all buses ply dedicated routes from Corfu Town, only rarely linking resorts.

Paleokastrítsa

PALEOKASTRÍTSA is the honeypot attraction on the west coast, with hotels spreading so far up into the surrounding area that some are a taxi ride from town. The village itself is small, surrounded by dramatic hills and cliffs – an idyllic setting which led British High Commissioner Sir Frederic Adam to popularize Paleokastrítsa in the nineteenth century. It has been suggested as a possible site of the Homeric city of Scheria, where Odysseus was washed ashore, discovered by Nausicaa and her handmaidens, and welcomed by her father King Alcinous, although it's a claim shared by a number of other sites in the islands. The thirteenth-century **Paleokastrítsa monastery** overlooks the town, and a circuitous 6km or so north is the **Angelokástro** castle, one of the most impressive ruins on the island.

Unfortunately, these days – at least in high season – Paleokastrítsa has a mean and even grasping air about it. This is probably due to the intensity of commerce in such a confined space, but there's an attitude about parts of Paleokastrítsa that is almost hostile. Some businesspeople are plainly contemptuous of visitors, although this is counter-balanced by displays of *filóxenia* elsewhere.

Accommodation

Accommodation is at a premium in Paleokastrítsa, both in terms of price and sheer availability. However, there are good-value independent **rooms** for rent above Alipa beach on the road down into Paleokastrítsa: try Andreas Loulis at the *Dolphin Snackbar*

(☎0663/41 035; ②), Spiros and Theodora Michalas (☎0663/41 485 or 41 643; ②), or George Bakiras at the *Green House* (☎0663/41 311; ②). Above the centre, past *Nikos' Bikes*, the friendly Korina family also have rooms (☎0663/44 0641; ②). Alternatively, some room-owners have formed the misleadingly named *Paleokastritsa Tourism Information Office* (☎0663/41 673), which rents out a wide range of accommodation in and around town, from an office on the road outside Paleokastrítsa. The town's **campsite**, imaginatively named *Paleokastritsa Camping* (☎0663/41 204, fax 41 104), is just off the main road into town, a ten-minute walk from the centre, but has a restaurant, shop and bike rental.

If you opt to stay in Paleokastrítsa, you may find room-owners reluctant to let for less than a week, especially in high season.

Hotels in Paleokastrítsa tend to be in the upper grades, and to cater for package tourism. A reasonable independent exception, easily accessible from the town, is the small, family-run *Odysseus* (☎0663/41 209 or 22 280, fax 41 342; ③), a mid-range hotel with pool, restaurant and sea views. The first-class *Akrotiri Beach Hotel* (☎0663/41 237 or 41 275, fax 41 277; ⑥) has rooms aside from its block bookings, is friendly and unpretentious for such a large, modern hotel, and accessible on foot.

The beaches and boat trips

The focal point of modern Paleokastrítsa is a large car park on the seafront, which backs onto the longest and least attractive of three town **beaches**, home to sea taxis and *kaíkia*, and plagued by flurries of windborne sand. The second, to the right of the main beach and signed by flags for *Mike's Ski Club*, is preferable, a stony beach with clear water. The best of the three, however, is a small, relatively secluded strand reached along the path from the *Astakos Taverna*. Protected by surrounding cliffs, it's undeveloped apart from the German-run *Korfu-Diving Centre* (☎0663/41 604) at the end of the cove. The centre runs daily trips (bar Saturdays) for beginners and advanced divers to over twenty sites, taking in reefs, arches, canyons and caves. It can also offer night dives, cave diving and advanced training.

From the beach in front of the main car park, **boat trips**, starting at around 2000dr per person, leave for the blue grottoes, a trip worth taking for the spectacular coastal views alone. These trips also serve as a taxi service to three neighbouring beaches, Áyia Triánda, Platakía and Alípa, each a pebbly strand over blue water, and served by beach bars and snack bars on the slopes above.

Paleokastrítsa Monastery is open daily 7am–1pm & 3–8pm; free, donations welcome. Go early or near either closing time to avoid the crowds.

Paleokastrítsa Monastery

On the rocky bluff above the beaches, the beautiful, whitewashed **Paleokastrítsa Monastery** (also known as the Theotókos monastery) is believed to have been established in the thirteenth century, though the current buildings date from the eighteenth. It's a favourite with coach parties and, despite being within walking distance of the town's main car park below, has had to have traffic lights installed to ease the flow of vehicles up and down the bluff.

The small church has a number of impressive icons, including a depiction of Saint George and the Dragon, while the ceiling features a woodcarving of the Tree of Life. There's also a museum, resplendent with further icons, jewel-encrusted silver-bound Bibles and other impedimenta of Greek Orthodox ritual, as well as a curious "sea monster", with very large vertebrae and tusks, said to have been killed by fishermen in the last century. The real highlight of a visit, however, is the beautiful paved gardens, which afford spectacular views over the coastline.

The Angelokástro

Paleokastrítsa's castle, the **Angelokástro**, is in fact around 6km from the town up the coast. There are short-cut paths through open country from Paleokastrítsa, but the main approach, and certainly the only one by car, involves doubling back to the Lakonés turning and heading for the village of Makrádhes, a route with some of the finest views in the region, and cafés like the *Bella Vista* to enjoy them from. Makrádhes itself is a pleasant little village built in the Venetian style, with a curious tradition of roadside stalls whose energetic owners could probably sell refrigerators to Eskimos. The route to the *kástro* leaves the smaller, dead-end hamlet of Kriní. Angelokástro is only approachable by path (the walk from the car park takes about 30min), but the ruined castle has stunning, almost circular views of the surrounding sea and land – presumably why its Byzantine builders and later Venetian developers chose the site to defend. On a clear day, it's possible to see Corfu Town some 25km away; however, little remains of the fort except for parts of the main walls.

Eating and nightlife

There isn't a huge choice of **restaurants** in the centre of Paleokastrítsa, considering the number of visitors the town entertains. The *Astakos Taverna* and *Corner Grill* are two traditional places, the former with the rather unusual habit of closing early in the siesta. *Il Pirata* has a raised balcony with sea views and offers a wide range of Italian and Greek dishes, including local fish and seafood. Beachside restaurants tend to suffer from the same problem of windborne sand as the beach itself, but the largest, the curiously named *Smurfs*, has awnings to beat the winds and an excellent, if expensive, seafood menu, featuring live trout and salmon, which you can choose from tanks. Also recommended are the very smart *St Georges on the Rock*, and the restaurant of the *Odysseus Hotel*.

Nightlife hangouts include the restaurant-bars in the centre, and those straggling up the hill towards Lákones. By the Lákones turning is Paleokastrítsa's one nightclub, *The Paleo Club*, a small disco-bar with a garden, which opens and closes late.

Áyios Yióryios

ÁYIOS YIÓRYIOS is reached by road via the hill town of Troumpéta, one of the largest in the interior, but with few facilities beyond the shops, tavernas and bars used by townspeople; it is worth a stop, however, to see how island life proceeds away from the tourism racket. Like many of the west coast resorts, Áyios Yióryios isn't actually based around a village (it's not to be confused with the Áyios Yióryios near the island's southern tip). The resort has developed in response to the popularity of its three-kilometre sandy bay, which cuts deep into the land between Cape Arilás to the north and Cape Falákron to the south. It's a major **windsurfing** centre, with schools and rental companies on the beach, and tends to be quite busy even in low season. There are several good **hotels** – the *Alkyon Beach Hotel* (0663/96 222; ④), the *Chrisi Akti* (0663/96 207; ④) and the *Tehos* (0663/96 482; ④) – and some rooms, but unless you're after a watersports holiday, with little to do at night, Áyios Yióryios is best visited as a day-trip. The village of Afiónas at the north end of the bay has been suggested as the likely site of **King Alcinous' castle** – there are vestigial Neolithic remains outside the village – and the walk up to the lighthouse on Cape Arilás has excellent views both over Áyios Yióryios and Arilás bay to the north.

Arilás, a small settlement in the neighbouring bay, has a long but rather scruffy pebble beach, inferior to the great sweep of sand at Áyios Stéfanos in the next bay. The barren rocky islets of **Graviá** out to sea are yet another on the list of places claiming to be the petrified remains of Odysseus' ship.

Áyios Stéfanos

The most northerly of the west coast's resorts, and the most distant from Corfu Town, **ÁYIOS STÉFANOS** is a family-oriented resort that's still very low-key despite a tourism presence for some decades. It takes its name from the beautiful eighteenth-century **chapel** dedicated to the saint at the southerly end of the village. Gentle hills give onto a large sandy beach, although there's a small marshy area at the centre of the beach with a stream running into the sea which, given Corfiot farming techniques, might spell chemicals. The terrain militates against too much development; the bay is tucked into an amphitheatrical hillside that precludes any further building. At present, it's still a fairly quiet place, even in high season. There is little to do here, which is probably one of the place's strengths, and it would make a quiet base from which to explore the northwest and the Diapóntia islands, visible on the sea horizon. Day-trips to Mathráki, Othoní and Eríkoussa (see p.99), run every Thursday in season, and cost around 3000dr per person.

Its distance from any major settlements and, hence, major traffic flow, makes Áyios Stéfanos a particularly good base for walking. As well as Avliótes and Perouládhes to the north, Magouládhes – which boasts one of the area's finest village tavernas, 3km to the east – and other small villages in the gently rolling hinterland are well within hiking distance of Áyios Stéfanos.

Practicalities

Áyios Stéfanos' long-standing **hotel**, the *Nafsika* (☎0663/51 051, fax 51 112; ②), is a pleasant, purpose-built structure with en-suite rooms and balconies overlooking the sea. It has a large restaurant on the ground floor, a favourite with villagers, and gardens with a pool and bar. In recent years, it has been joined by the twinned *Thomas Bay* (☎0663/51 787, fax 51 553; ④) and *Romanza* hotels (☎0661/22 873, fax 41 878; ④), upmarket places with pools, cocktail bars, tennis courts and, in the *Romanza*, self-catering apartments. Both take block bookings from package operators, but keep some rooms free throughout the season.

For those on a tighter budget, Peli's and Maria's gift shop, on the northern edge of the village, offers bargain purpose-built **rooms** (☎0663/51 424; ②), and the *Restaurant Evnios* (☎0663/51 766; ②) and *Hotel Olga* (☎0663/71 252; ②) have apartments on a rise above the village with excellent views over bay and open sea. A number of travel agencies handle accommodation, among them *San Stefano* (☎0663/51 157) and *Mouzakitis Travel* in the centre (be warned, however, that virtually everyone in Áyios Stéfanos is called Mouzakitis). The English-owned While Away Holidays (☎0663/51 910), which has a representative based in the village's *Margerita* supermarket, has a range of villas around Áyios Stéfanos, and produces a brochure that's available in the UK (While Away, New Inn Farm, West End Lane, Henfield, West Sussex, BN5 9RF; ☎01273/493841).

Besides the *Nafsika*, good options for **eating** include the large, varied menu at the *Golden Beach Taverna*, and the *Waves Taverna*, which is ideal for lunches on the beach. The *Taverna O Manthos*, with a garden above the beach, serves Corfiot specialities like *sofríto* and *pastitsáda*, and has a barbecue. For **nightlife**, there's a pair of lively music bars, the *Condor* and the *Athens*, in the centre of the village, plus the small but smart *Enigma* nightclub, towards the chapel.

Ermónes

ERMÓNES, the first major settlement south of Paleokastrítsa, is one of the busiest resorts on the island. Its lush green bay is backed by the mountains above the Ropa River, which empties into the sea here. The beach is a mix of gravel and sand, often hectic with water-sports activities, and the sea bed shelves quite steeply, making it ideal for good swimmers but not so for children or uncertain swimmers.

The resort is dominated by the extensive grounds of the upmarket *Ermones Beach* **hotel** (☎0661/94 241; ⑥), which is unique in the entire archipelago in providing its guests with a small funicular railway down the cliff to the beach (which rather scars the view). More reasonable accommodation can be found near the beach at the *Pension Katerina* and *Georgio's Villas*. Further back from the shore is the Corfu Golf and Country Club (☎0661/94 220), the only golf club in the archipelago, and said to be the finest in the Mediterranean. Head for *George's* **taverna** above the beach for some of the best Greek food here: the *mezédhes* are often enough for a meal in themselves.

Mirtiótissa and Vátos

Far preferable to Ermónes are the sandy beaches just south, at Mirtiótissa and Glifádha. Half a century ago in *Prospero's Cell*, Lawrence Durrell described **Mirtiótissa** as "perhaps the loveliest beach in the world" – though he qualified that by adding that the sand has the consistency of tapioca. Difficult to reach down a path from Vátos (see below), it's been a long-guarded secret among aficionados, a shallow, safe strand with rollers, spotted with vast boulders and overlooked by tall tree-covered cliffs. Nowadays, however, the secret has been passed on to more than enough people to fill the beach on a summer's day. Nudists and freelance campers now have to share the sand with the increasing numbers who risk the steep clamber down, or invade from the sea on day-trip boats from nearby resorts such as Glifádha. There are also a couple of refreshment stalls and sunshade concessions. The charm of the place hasn't been entirely swamped, but it's best visited at either end of the day or out of high season entirely. Above the beach is the tiny whitewashed **Mirtiótissa Monastery**, dedicated to Our Lady of the Myrtles, which is open in the daytime and has a curious little gift shop attached.

The small village of **VÁTOS** has a couple of tavernas, a disco and rooms, and is on the Glifádha bus route from Corfu Town. Spiros Kousounis, owner of the *Olympic Restaurant and Grill* (☎0661/94 318; ②) has rooms and apartments, as does Himarios Prokopios (☎0661/94 503; ②), next to the Doukakis café-minimarket in the traditional centre of the village. The steep, half-hour path to Mirtiótissa beach is signposted just beyond the extremely handy, if basic, *Vatos Camping* (☎0661/94 393).

Glifádha and Pélekas

GLIFÁDHA is thoroughly dominated by the *Louis Grand* (☎0661/94 140–5, fax 94 146; ⑦), a large A-class **hotel** in its own spacious grounds, with a residents-only pool, and a bar and restaurant open to non-residents. The hotel, which takes up a good quarter of the available beachfront, is used by the major package tour operators, but has rooms for independent travellers throughout the season. There's another hotel at the far north end of the bay, the *Hotel*

Glifada Beach (☎0661/94 258; ③), a small, family-run affair with en-suite rooms and balconies overlooking the beach, and set away from the action to avoid most of the noise. Its owners, the Megas family, also have a fine traditional taverna attached to the hotel. Most of the other accommodation at Glifádha is block-booked by tour operators – this is a very popular family beach – but the *Gorgona* pool bar and *Restaurant Michaelis* might have rooms. There's another, unnamed, family taverna midway along the beach, while nightlife centres on two music bars, the *Kikiriko* and *Aloha*, both of which open onto the beach. At night, however, Glifádha begins to look slightly tacky, and with a five-kilometre hike uphill just to reach tiny Vátos, you really are stuck here.

The attractive hilltop village of **PÉLEKAS**, inland and 2km south of Glifádha, has long been popular for its views – particularly at sunset – and for its welcome summer breezes. The **Kaiser's Throne** viewing tower, a thirty-minute walk along the road to Glifádha, was Wilhelm II's favourite spot on the entire island. However, Pélekas is fast going the way of Kávos, with new developments beginning to swamp the town. There are still some good **hotels**, including the elegant, upmarket *Pelekas* (☎0661/94 230; ⑤) and the friendlier, budget-oriented *Nicos* (☎0661/94 486; ③), as well as rooms at the *Alexandros* taverna (☎0661/94 215; ②). Out towards the Kaiser's Throne, the *Sunset Hotel* (☎0661/94 230; ⑥) is a top-class establishment, with views out over the sea and coastline which are unlikely to be bettered anywhere else on the island. Its restaurant, whose balcony shares the view, is open to non-guests. Among **tavernas**, the *Alexandros* and *Roula's Grill House* are highly recommended.

Pélekas' long, sandy **beach** can be reached down a small path; quieter neighbouring Kontogíalos beach is down another path, signposted off the Vátos road. At the former, *Maria's Place* is an excellent family-run **taverna** with a reputation for the fish caught daily by the owner's husband, Costas. There are **rooms** above the taverna (☎0661/94 601; ②), and at *Tolis Rooms* (☎0661/94 059; ②), 50m back from the beach.

Áyios Górdhis and Áyii Dhíka

Around 7km south of Pélekas, **ÁYIOS GÓRDHIS** is one of the key play beaches on the island, largely because of the activities organized by the startling **Pink Palace** complex (☎0661/53 101 or 53 104) which fairly dominates the resort. The beach itself is one of the finest on the island, a long, sandy strand backed by pine-clad hills. The *Pink Palace*, covering much of the hillside, has swimming pools, games courts, restaurants, a shop and disco, and some seventy staff to run beach sports and other activities. It's hugely popular with backpackers, who cram into communal rooms for up to ten (although smaller rooms, and singles, are also available) for a bargain 5000dr a night including breakfast and evening meal. People booking for four or more days also get free scooter hire. Other accommodation is available on the beach, notably at the quieter *Michael's Place* taverna (☎0661/53 041; ②) at the end of the beach road. The neighbouring *Alex-in-the-Garden* **restaurant** is also a favourite.

Inland from the resort is the south's largest prominence, the hump back of **Áyii Dhíka**, at 576 metres officially a mountain. Reached by path from the hamlet of Áno Garoúna (signposted on the road between Sinarádhes and Áyios Górdhis), the mountain is the island's second largest after Pandokrátor. The lower slopes are wooded, and it's possible to glimpse buzzards wheeling on thermals over the high slopes. Its peak affords panoramic views across the south and to the mainland. Those with the stamina – and a good map and a compass – might consider following the path that leads from the summit down into the village of Stávros and on to Benítses, whose regular bus connections to Corfu Town make this a viable, if taxing, day's hike from Áyios Górdhis.

Pentáti, Paramonás and Áyios Mathéos

Around 2km south of Áyios Górdhis as the crow flies, but reached by a country lane skirting around the hills for 5km, the fishing hamlet of **PENTÁTI** sits on a narrow coastal plateau 200m above sea level. Small, winding tracks north and south of the hamlet lead down to tiny inlets from where the local fishermen ply their trade. There is no accommodation in the village, but *Angela's* café and mini-market and the *Strofi* grill cater to villagers and the few tourists who stray here.

Walkers and careful drivers are recommended the four-kilometre coastal road between here and **PARAMONÁS**, mostly unsurfaced and potholed where it is surfaced, but affording excellent views over the coastline. Paramonás itself is slightly larger than Pentáti, but still has only a few businesses geared to tourism. Situated on sandy Makroúla Bay, the hamlet is, however, beginning to develop an infrastructure: the *Paramonas Bridge* restaurant (☎0663/75 761; ②), by the small ford through the stream that bisects the beach, has **rooms and apartments** to rent, as does the *Areti Studios* (☎0661/75 838; ③) on the road in from Pentáti.

The town of **ÁYIOS MATHÉOS**, 3km inland and shadowed by its eponymous mountain, has little truck with the tourism trade. Chiefly an agricultural centre, its busy, narrow main road is often thronged with local traffic – so much so that visiting motorists have had their vehicles manhandled aside to allow the Corfu Town bus to pass. There is still no noticeable accommodation in the town, although a number of **kafenía and tavernas**, still unused to tourism, offer a warm if bemused welcome to passers-by: head for the *Mouria* snack bar-grill, or the modern *Steki*, which maintains the tradition of spiriting tasty *mezédhes* onto your table unasked.

On the other side of Mount Áyios Mathéos, 2km by road, is the **Gardíki Pírgos**, the ruins of a thirteenth-century castle built in this unlikely lowland setting by the Despots of Epirus. Little remains of the castle apart from its outer walls, and the enclosure is nowadays employed to house cattle. Just off the road south of the castle, a large cave, now empty, was the site of some of the oldest archeological finds on the island, dated back to the Palaeolithic age. The road continues on to the northernmost tip of the beach on the sea edge of Lake Korissíon.

Benítses and the south

Corfu's southeast coast was the first to develop tourism on the island, back in the 1960s, and became synonymous with some of the worst excesses of package tourism, in terms of both tacky development and the behaviour of some visitors. There are still echoes of this at **Kávos**, which is almost entirely given over to beach, bar and (if you're lucky) bonking, but the slump in tourism has wrought many changes. Ten years ago, the idea of casting even a sympathetic eye at **Benítses** would have been unthinkable. Yet the crowds of drunks and people screwing in the streets have vanished, and, though it's now at the bottom of an economic slump, the village is slowly being transformed.

Beaches along this stretch of coast, at least as far as Messóngi, tend to be narrow pebble or stone and, near the centres of habitation, water quality can be doubtful. Unfortunately, the best beach in the area involves running the gauntlet of Kávos for its two-kilometre stretch of sand. Beyond Messóngi, the road south turns inland, and is more or less equidistant from the coasts, putting spectacular beaches such as Íssos on the southwest-facing shore within easy reach.

Benítses

Heading south from Corfu Town, there's little point in recommending anything much before **BENÍTSES**: accommodation in the suburb of Pérama and on the edge of the swamps around the Chalikópoulos lagoon is just too close to the airport and its approach paths. Once you reach Benítses, you'll still see signs of its grim heyday – the southern end still boasts music-bars such as *B52s* and *Alcoholics Anonymous* – but the old town at the north end is reverting to a quiet, whitewashed, bougainvillea-splashed Greek village. A few minutes' walk through the alleys of the old town and you're in thick woodland with streams. Benítses' beach, however, is at best serviceable; most people congregate on the small spit of land below the *Hotel Corfu Maris* at the southern end of town.

There's little to see in Benítses, beyond some small, and rather disappointing, Roman remains, a small corner of a bathhouse buried in weeds behind fences at the back of the village, and the curious **Shell**

Museum, on the main road north of the village (daily 9am–5pm; free). This contains over two thousand items of shell, coral and skeleton, and is a little tacky, but worth a quick peek.

Practicalities

Rooms are plentiful in Benítses, but often rented through agencies. *Bargain Travel* (☎0661/72 137, fax 72 031; ②) and *All Tourist* (☎0661/72 223; ②), both in the heart of the village, have decently priced options in and around the village. With the decline in visitor numbers, however, some **hotels** are almost as cheap. The *Corfu Maris* (☎0661/72 035; ②), on the beach at the southern end of town, has modern en-suite rooms with balconies and views, while the *Hotel Benitsa* and neighbouring *Agis* in the centre (both ☎0661/39 269 or 92 248, ②) can offer quiet rooms, also en suite, set back from the main road; the *Benitsa* was the first hotel in the resort, and is still owned by the friendly, Anglophone Spinoulas family. Seemingly conceived as an ironic tilt at the nearby Achillíon, the larger *Hotel Potamaki* (☎0661/71 140 or 72 201, fax 72 451; ④) revels in eye-popping Neoclassical detail in its large courtyard bar-restaurant and interior halls, although the en-suite rooms, most with views, are more demure.

On the coast road 2km north of Benítses is one of the smartest hotels on the island, the *San Stefano* (☎0661/71 117, fax 72 272; ④), a vast, international ziggurat-style hotel with pools, restaurants and its own beachfront, but reasonably priced for what you get. Also worthy of note, on the road to the Achillíon just north of the *San Stefano* – though a steep 2km from the sea – is the quiet *Hotel Montagnola* (☎0661/56 205 or 56 789; ③), with pool, tennis court, restaurant and en-suite rooms with sea views.

Benítses always catered to a free-spending crowd and it has its fair share of decent if not particularly cheap **tavernas**, notably *La Mer de Corfu* and the Corfiot specialist, *Spiros*, as well as the plush *Marabou*, which specializes in steaks, seafood, pasta and north European dishes. There's also a curiously popular hybrid of Chinese, Indian and Greek in the extravagantly decorated *Flower Garden*, and decent pizzas and pasta at *Bravo*. The **bars** at the southern end of town are still fairly lively at night, despite new rules controlling the all-night excesses, and the *Stadium* **nightclub** still opens occasionally. If you're looking for a quiet drink, head for the north end of the village, away from the traffic.

Moraítika and Messóngi

The coast road south of Benítses is speckled with rooms and small hotels above scraps of beach, although negotiating any length of this road on foot can be a nightmare due to the traffic. The next two resorts of any note, Moraítika and Messóngi, have now more or less merged into one. **MORAÍTIKA'S** main street is an ugly strip of bars, restaurants and shops you could find anywhere in the islands, but the beach behind it is the best between Corfu Town and Kávos, a mixture of shingle and sand, and very busy in high season. The usual range of wind sports is on offer, as well as a small water slide, with chutes made of soft plastic, which charges an exorbitant 3000dr per hour.

Much accommodation is block-booked for families on package tours, but there are **rooms** for independent travellers between the main road and beach, and up above the main road, all within a minute or two of the centre: try Alekos Bostis (☎0661/75 637; ②) or Kostas Vlachos (☎0661/55 350; ②), both near the beach. For a wider range, it's worthwhile trying the *G & S Moraítika Tourist Centre* (☎0661/75 723 or 30 977, fax 76 682) and *Budget Ways Travel* (☎0661/75 664 or 76 768, fax 75 664), which both offer rooms from 6000dr a night. Reasonable beachside **hotels** likely to have space for the independent traveller include the *Margarita Beach* (☎0661/76 267; ④) and the *Three Stars* (☎0661/92 457; ④), both of which have comfortable en-suite rooms with balconies, some with sea views. Much of the main drag is dominated by souvenir shops and mini-markets, as well as a range of **bars**: flash joints like *Scorpion*, *Crocodile*, *Rainbow* and *Cotton Club*, and the village's oldest surviving bar, *Charlie's*, which opened in 1939. *Islands* **restaurant** on the main drag is recommended for its mix of good vegetarian, Greek and international food, as is the beach restaurant named, with charming innocence, *Crabs*, where the seafood and adventurous salads are excellent.

Áno Moraítika

The garish main drag is by no means all there is to Moraítika: the village proper, **ÁNO MORAÍTIKA**, is signposted a few minutes' hike up the steep lanes inland, and is virtually unspoilt. Its tiny houses and alleys are practically drowning in bougainvillea, among which you'll find two **tavernas**: the *Village Taverna*, with a catholic range of island specialities, and the *Bella Vista*, which offers a contrastingly limited blackboard menu, but which justifies its name with a lovely garden and view out over the coast – on hot days, it's a great place to park yourself in front of a breeze. There's little **accommodation** in the village, apart from *Corifo Apartments* (☎0661/32 891) on its southern edge.

Messóngi

Barely a hundred metres on from the Moraítika seafront, **MESSÓNGI** is disappointing even in comparison to its larger northerly neighbour: large parts of the resort are sadly moribund, and the beach is minor, a narrow tract of gravelly sand, bisected at the north end by a small river. The sand is dominated by the vast *Messonghi Beach* **hotel** complex (☎0661/76 684–6, fax 75 334; ⑥), one of the plushest on the island, with pools, bars and extensive grounds. Both the cheaper *Hotel Gemini* (☎0661/75 221 or 75 212, fax 75 213; ③) and *Pantheon Hall* (☎0661/75 802 or 75 268, fax 75 801; ②) also have pools and gardens, and en-suite rooms with balconies. *Christina's* (☎0661/75 294, fax 76 515; ④) is very popular with British tourists, who get a special deal, if booked independently, on weekly and fortnightly rates, and a Sunday roast on the hotel restaurant's menu. There are good, cheap **rooms** right on the beach (Dinos Ramos: ☎0661/75 695; ②) and at *Olga's Apartments* at the southern end of the village (②; the owner speaks no English, so declines to give her telephone number), and the village travel agency, *Pandora Travel* (☎0661/75 329), has a range of apartments and villas. Half a kilometre inland from Messóngi, flagged by vast road signs, the *Sea Horse* **campsite** (☎0661/75 364 or 76 212) is a trek from the beach, but, along with the *Odysseus* at Dhassía, is one of the best on the island. Secluded from any noticeable development, it has a pool, restaurant and shops, and offers a choice of pitches shaded by olive trees or basic but modern cabins (①).

Despite several closures, Messóngi still has a number of good **restaurants**, notably the *Memories Taverna*, which specializes in Corfiot dishes and serves its own barrel wine, and the upmarket *Castello*, which mixes local dishes like *sofríto*, with seafood (including mussels) and – a rarity on Corfu – asparagus. *Christina's Hotel* and the neighbouring *Rossi's* taverna have bars that open onto the beach, but a better option at night, offering seafood under the stars, is to head for the two popular beachside tavernas, *The Almond Tree* and *Sparos*, a short walk south on the road to Boukári.

Boukári and around

The road from Messóngi to **BOUKÁRI** is barely used by traffic even in high season, and follows the seashore for about 3km, often only a few metres above it. The few available plots of land here have been snapped up by wealthy Greeks, whose discreet villas testify to the appeal of the area. The hamlet of Boukári itself comprises little more than a handful of tavernas, a shop and a few small, family-run hotels. The *Boukari Beach* is the best of the **tavernas**, though it tends to attract *kaíkia* tour parties, who moor at its tiny jetty. The very friendly Vlachopoulos family who run the taverna also manage two small, smart hotels nearby, the *Boukari Beach* and *Penelopi* (☎0662/51 269 or 51 792; ④), as well as good rooms attached to the taverna (②). Just back from the *Karidis Taverna* is the *Helios Hotel* (☎0662/51 824; ②), which also has a taverna. Boukári is out of the way, but an idyllic little strip of unspoilt coast for anyone fleeing the crowds elsewhere on the island. Inland from here is the unspoilt wooded farming region around Aryirádhes, rarely visited by tourists and a perfect place for undisturbed walks.

Aryirádhes and Perivóli are both good watering holes when heading south, but have few amenities.

Petríti

Back on the coastline, the friendly, seemingly prosperous village of **PETRÍTI** fronts onto a small but busy dirt-track harbour, but in general is mercifully free of noise and commerce. Maps claim Petríti has a beach, but this is a cartographical fancy: the littoral is variously bulldozed rock, thick mud and a small stretch of sand above more mud – though local children do swim in the sea. In its setting among low olive-covered hills, with tree-covered rocks in the bay, Petríti would be perfect if you wanted to disappear somewhere quiet for a while.

The *Pension Egrypos* here (☎0662/51 949; ④) has **rooms** and a **taverna**, set back a hundred metres or so from the harbour, among trees near a beautiful white church framed by a large free-standing campanile. At the harbour, which is the departure point for yacht flotilla holidays, three tavernas serve the trickle of sea traffic: the smart waterfront *Limnopoula*, guarded by two handsome caged parrots, with a wide range of locally caught fish and seafood, and the more basic but friendly *Dimitris* and *Stamatis*. Some way back from the village, moored in the middle of woodlands near the hamlet of Vassilátika, is the elegant *Regina* **hotel**, with gardens and pool (☎0662/52 132, fax 52 135; ②), which specializes in full-board holidays for German tourists, but also has room-only availability.

Áyios Yióryios and around

With its beach spreading as far south as Mága Khóro Point, and north to encircle the edge of the Koríssion lagoon, **ÁYIOS YIÓRYIOS** (not to be confused with the Áyios Yióryios just north of Paleokastrítsa) can lay claim to around 12km of uninterrupted and fairly unspoilt sand. The village itself, however, is an unprepossessing sprawl that's in danger of becoming a real mess. British package tour operators have arrived in force, with bars and tavernas competing to present bingo, quizzes and video nights.

The *Golden Sands* (☎0662/51 225; ③) can offer a pool, open-air restaurant and gardens, but the best **hotel** bargain, for its setting and size, has to be the smaller *Blue Sea* (☎0662/51 624, fax 51 172; ②). Much of the resort's accommodation is block-booked, even in those places that advertise rooms on street signs (no doubt, hedging against the possibility of the package tourism business going pear-shaped). The most likely place to head for in search of good **rooms** is at the southern end of the strip: the *Barbayiannis* taverna-bar (☎0662/52 110 or 52 377; ②). The *Status* travel agency in the centre of the main strip (☎0662/51 661) also has rooms, apartments and villas, as well as car rental. This far from Corfu's banks, a number of local agencies, notably the *St George*, offer bank-rate exchange.

Besides the *Barbayiannis*, Áyios Yióryios has a number of good **restaurants**: *La Perla's*, mixing Greek and north European in a walled garden; the *Napoleon psistariá*; and the *Florida Cove*, a grill and barbecue taverna with a beachcomber sea theme. **Nightlife** centres around music and pool bars like the *Gold Hart* and *Traxx*, although the best bar in Áyios Yióryios is the sea-edge *Panorama*, which has views as far south as Paxí.

Íssos beach

A few minutes' walk north of Áyios Yióryios, **Íssos** is by far the best beach in the area, a largely deserted stretch of sand and dunes; it's so quiet that the dunes that continue north of Íssos remain an unofficial nude bathing area. Further on, the beaches towards the channel that cuts into the Korissíon lagoon (which makes it impossible to circumnavigate on foot) also see very few visitors. Parts of Íssos and the Korissíon beach are turtle nesting grounds, so should be treated with due care. Avoid nests, stay off the beach at night, don't dig or use spiked beach furniture in the day, and never approach a turtle, young or old, if you see one.

For further information on the Issos Beach Windsurfing School, contact, in winter in the UK, ☎015396/25385.

Facilities around Íssos are drastically limited: one **taverna**, the *Rousellis Grill* (which sometimes rents out rooms), a few hundred metres from the beach on the lane leading to Linía on the main road, and the *Friends* snack bar in Linía itself. An English-run **windsurfing school**, operating from a caravan on the beach, has a wide range of boards of different sizes for rent (starting at 2500dr an hour), as well as a beach simulator and rescue craft, and offers tuition for beginners and upwards – prevailing cross-beach winds make it a safe place to learn.

The Korissíon lagoon

The nature reserve of **Korissíon lagoon** is most easily reached by walking from the village of Linía (on the Kávos bus route) via Íssos beach; other, longer routes trail around the north end of the lagoon from Ano Messóngi and Hlomatianá. The lagoon is in fact man-made, excavated, with a channel opened to the sea, by the Venetians. Over 5km long and 1km wide at its centre, Korissíon is home to turtles, tortoises, lizards and numerous indigenous and migrating birds, including ducks, waders, herons and other species that feed on wetlands. Migratory birds are more often observed towards the end of the season (even though rifle-hunting of birds is allowed in the autumn), but they can also be seen in early season as well.

Lefkími

Most guides either ignore or dismiss **LEFKÍMI**, but anyone interested in how a Greek town works away from the bustle of tourism should not miss it. The charm of the place, where donkeys are still a common form of travel and some women retain traditional costume, lies in its almost perverse resistance to tourism.

Maps distinguish between Áno Lefkími and Lefkími proper, but in fact the two flow into each other. The second largest town after

Corfu, Lefkími is the administrative centre of the south of the island, and has some fine architecture, including two striking (but usually locked) churches: **Áyios Theodóros**, whose beautiful campanile sits on a mound above a small village square, and **Áyios Arsénios**, with a vast orange dome that can be seen for miles around. Lefkími is also the major commercial port in the south, fitted up with a startling new stretch of sodium-lit four-lane highway – once you get to the harbour, however, you'll find no facilities apart from a coffee stall that opens to serve lorry drivers awaiting boats.

There are some **rooms** at the *Cheeky Face* taverna (☎0662/22 627; ②) and the *Maria Madalena* apartments (☎0662/22 386), both by the bridge over the canal that carries the Chimáros River through the centre of town, but little other accommodation. A few **bars and restaurants** sit on the edge of the canal – try the *River Psistaria* – and, while it's hardly Amsterdam, the canal and the facades of the main street and surrounding alleys are very attractive. Away from the centre, the *Hermes* bar has a leafy garden, and there are a number of other good local bars where tourists are rare enough to guarantee you a friendly welcome, including the *Mersedes* and *Pacific*, and tavernas, notably *Kavouras* and *Fontana*.

Kávos and around

The very name **KÁVOS** can make most regular island visitors – and not a few islanders – cross themselves in dread. There are no ambiguities here: either you like 24-hour drinking, clubbing, bungee-jumping, go-karts, video bars named after British sitcoms and chips with almost everything, or you should avoid the place altogether. The resort is sizeable, stretching over 2km of decent, if not particularly clean, sandy beach, with water sports, pedalos, ringoes and serried sunbeds. The bulk of tourism here is package, with a heavy preponderance of young and unattached English males giving the place the air of a not very friendly football crowd; if you want independent **accommodation**, *Britannia Travel* (☎0662/61 400) and *Island Holidays* (☎0662/23 439) have decent, cheap rooms and apartments. The nearest to genuine Greek **food** you'll find is at the *Two Brothers Psistaria*, well away from the crowds at the south end of town. *Future* is still the biggest **club**, with imported north European DJs mixing techno and house, and these days jungle and trip-hop, followed by *Whispers*. *JCs*, *Jungle*, *The Face* and *Net* are the favourite **bars**, usually self-policed but still prone to the off-their-face antics of Britons unused to Greek licensing hours. Away from the core, the hip *Jazz Bar* at the southern end of town adds a welcome note of cool. It's no coincidence that in season there's an English-speaking doctor on duty around the clock at the medical centre opposite the *Fountain Bar* in the middle of town (☎0662/61 161 or 61 555).

Beyond the limits of Kávos, where few visitors stray, a path leaving the road south to the hamlet of Sparterá heads on south through unspoilt countryside; after around thirty minutes it reaches the cliffs of **Cape Asprokávos** and the crumbling monastery of Arkoudhílas, which retains its bell tower and supporting walls. The cape looks out over the straits to Paxí, 19km away, and down over deserted **Arkoudhílas beach**. The beach, however, is inaccessible from here, though it can be reached from Sparterá, 5km by road but only 3km by the signed path from Kávos. Even wilder is **San Górdios beach**, 3km further on from Spartéra, one of the least visted beaches on the island.

Corfu's satellite islands

Corfu's three (barely) inhabited satellite islands, **Eríkoussa**, **Othoní** and **Mathráki**, in the quintet of **Diapontía islands**, are situated a good 20km off the far northwest coast. Each is distinct in character from the others: Eríkoussa is flat and sandy, Othoní rocky with a hilly interior, Mathráki, the most attractive for island collectors, a green hill surrounded by almost volcanic sandy beaches. Some travel agencies, for example in Aharávi, offer **day-trips** to Eríkoussa only, often with a barbecue thrown in – fine if you want to spend the day on the beach. A trip taking in all three from Sidhári or Áyios Stéfanos is excellent value, if a little hurried: the islands are between thirty and sixty minutes apart by boat, and most trips allow you an hour on each (though usually longer on sandy Eríkoussa).

It's now possible to **stay** on all three islands, although travel between them is difficult. Islanders themselves use day-trip boats, so it's possible to hitch (or offer to pay for) a lift if the craft is going your way: out of Sidhári, from where day-trips are most frequent, *kaíkia* usually travel Mathráki–Othoní–Eríkoussa. There is also a twice-weekly **ferry** from Corfu Town, the *Alexandros II*, which brings cars and goods to the islands, but given that it has to sail halfway round Corfu first, it's the least attractive option for reaching them.

Mathráki

Hilly, densely forested and with a long, deserted beach, beautiful **MATHRÁKI** is the least inhabited of the three islands. Its tiny harbour is on the east coast, facing Corfu, and at present sports little more than a taverna. The beach begins at the edge of the harbour, and extends south for 3km of fine, dark-red sand. A single road rises from the harbour into the interior and the scattered village of Káto Mathráki (walkable with time for refreshments on most day-trip stops), where just one friendly taverna-*kafenío*-shop overlooks the beach and Corfu. The views are magnificent, as are the sense of isolation – few day visitors make it even this far – and the pungent smell of virgin forest. The road continues to the small settlement of Áno Mathráki, but this is beyond walking distance on a day visit.

Sadly, the population on Mathráki has dwindled: about 700 people used to live here, but many have moved away to America, Australia and elsewhere, leaving mainly the elderly behind. Most homes are only used in the summer, when the diaspora or their children return. Construction work above the beach suggests this may be about to turn, however, and islander Tassos Kassimis (☎0663/71 700; ②) is already renting **rooms**. Apart from the village *kafenío* with its basic provisions, there are no shops on Mathráki, so if you plan to stay be prepared for limited taverna menus.

Othoní

Six kilometres north of Mathráki, **OTHONÍ** doesn't come with the same recommendation as its southerly neighbour. The island has a handful of good tavernas and some rooms for rent in the main village, Ámmos, on the southern coast, but the reception from islanders who aren't in the tourism trade is rather unfriendly, an observation shared by regular visitors from Corfu's north coast.

The island's interior is dramatic, and a path up out of the village leads through rocky, tree-covered hills to the dwindling central hamlet, Hório, after about half an hour. Paths also run to the telecommunications station at the north end of the island, and the lighthouse at the south, journeys of around an hour, although the distances mean these would only be accessible to those staying on the island. The main village has two beaches, both pebbly, one of them part of the harbour, which is used by fishermen and visiting yachts. The village *kafenío* serves as a very basic shop, and there's one smart **restaurant**, *La Locanda dei Sogni*, which also has **rooms** (☎0663/71 640; ④) – though these tend to be prebooked by Italian visitors. Three tavernas, *New York*, *Mikros* and tiny *Rainbow*, offer decent but fairly limited menus; Alex Katechis, owner of the *New York*, offers rooms for rent (☎0663/71 581; ②).

Eríkoussa

East of Othoní, **ERÍKOUSSA** is the most populous of the Diapontía islands, and the most frequent destination of day-trips from the northwestern resorts. It's invariably hyped as a "desert island" trip, although this is a desert island with a medium-sized hotel, rooms, tavernas, a year-round village community, a paved road and an ugly aggregates plant overlooking its small harbour. In high season, it's far from deserted: Eríkoussa has a large diaspora living in America and elsewhere, who return to family homes in their droves in summer, so you may find your *yia sou* or *kaliméra* returned in a Brooklyn accent.

Eríkoussa has an excellent golden sandy beach right by the harbour, with great swimming off it, and another, quieter, beach reached by a path across the wooded island interior. Even when the day-trip craft arrive in high season, the main beach is rarely busy and, when they depart in mid-afternoon, Eríkoussa reverts to something approaching the "desert island" promised by the tour companies. The island's small cult following keep its one **hotel**, the *Erikoussa* (☎0663/71 555 or 71 110; ②), fairly busy through the season; it has a good restaurant and bar, and rooms are en suite with balconies and views. Simpler rooms are available from the main **taverna** on the beach, *Anemomilos* (☎0663/71 647; ②). If you're hoping to stay, phoning ahead is essential, as is taking anything you might not be able to buy on an island where there are no conventional shops, only a snack bar selling basic groceries.

Travel details

Buses

Corfu Town to: Aharávi (4 daily; 1hr 45min); Arílas (2 daily; 1hr 15min); Athens (3 daily; 12hr); Áyios Górdhis (8 daily; 1hr); Áyios Mathéos (4 daily; 1hr); Áyios Stéfanos (on the west coast; 2 daily; 1hr 45min); Áyios Yióryios (in the south; 4 daily; 1hr 15min); Glifádha (8 daily; 1hr 15min); Ípsos (5 daily; 30min); Kassiópi (6 daily; 1hr 30min); Kávos (11 daily; 1hr 45min); Lefkími (11 daily; 1hr 30min); Messóngi (5 daily; 45min); Paleokastrítsa (4 daily; 1hr 30min); Petrití (2 daily; 1hr 30min); Píryi (5 daily; 30min); Ródha (4 daily; 1hr 45min); Sidhári (9 daily; 1hr 45min); Thessaloníki (2 daily; 18hr); Vátos (8 daily; 1hr 15min).

Ferries

Every 2hr or so (4.30am–10pm) between Corfu Town (new port) and Igoumenítsa (1–2hr). Also in season roughly daily departures to Bari (12hr), Brindisi (10hr), Otranto (12hr) and Pátra (9hr); weekly to Sámi on Kefalloniá (9hr); most services reduced off season (for further information, see p.14 and p.27). Ferry services to Paxí are in a state of flux: both the *Zefiros* and *Pegasus* services have been discontinued, as has the high-speed Brindisi–Corfu–Paxí–Lefkádha catamaran. At present, only one ferry a week is confirmed, on Monday mornings (3hr). However, it is likely that other ferries, such as the *Anna Maria* or *Paxos Star*, will resume daily (not Sun) services between Corfu's old port and Paxí.

Flights

Corfu Town on Olympic to: Athens (3 daily; 45min); Thessaloníki (1 daily; 1hr).

Chapter 2

Paxí

Small, unusually green and surprisingly underdeveloped, **Paxí (Paxos)** is the most badly kept secret in the Ionian, perhaps in all Greece. It has the least to offer of all the major Ionian islands – no sandy beaches, no historical sites, only two hotels, and a serious water shortage – yet it is one of the most sought-after destinations in the archipelago. Despite these privations, Paxí draws a vast crowd of return visitors, who can make its three harbour villages rather cliquey. It's also very popular with yachting flotillas, whose shopping, eating and drinking habits have brought a certain sophistication to shops and tavernas with a long tradition of telling their customers to be thankful for what they get given. It's the most expensive place to visit in the Ionian – just about everything consumed on Paxí has to be imported by ferry from Corfu or the mainland – yet so popular in high season that casual visitors are warned to book ahead before boarding a ferry to the island. There is only one, remote, official campsite (although there are pockets of freelance camping), and most accommodation is block-booked by upmarket north European travel companies – though there are local tour operators whose holidays might cost half the price.

Although it gets only a fraction of the bad weather that is regularly visited on neighbouring Corfu, Paxí is remarkably verdant. Its abundant

Accommodation price codes

Rooms and hotels listed in this book have been price-coded according to the scale outlined below. The rates quoted represent the cheapest available double room in high season. Out of season, rates can drop by as much as fifty percent or more, especially if you negotiate for a stay of three or more nights. Single rooms, where available, cost around seventy percent of the price of a double. For further information, see p.32.

- ① up to 4000dr
- ② 4000–8000dr
- ③ 8000–12,000dr
- ④ 12,000–16,000dr
- ⑤ 16,000–20,000dr
- ⑥ 20,000–30,000dr
- ⑦ 30,000dr upwards

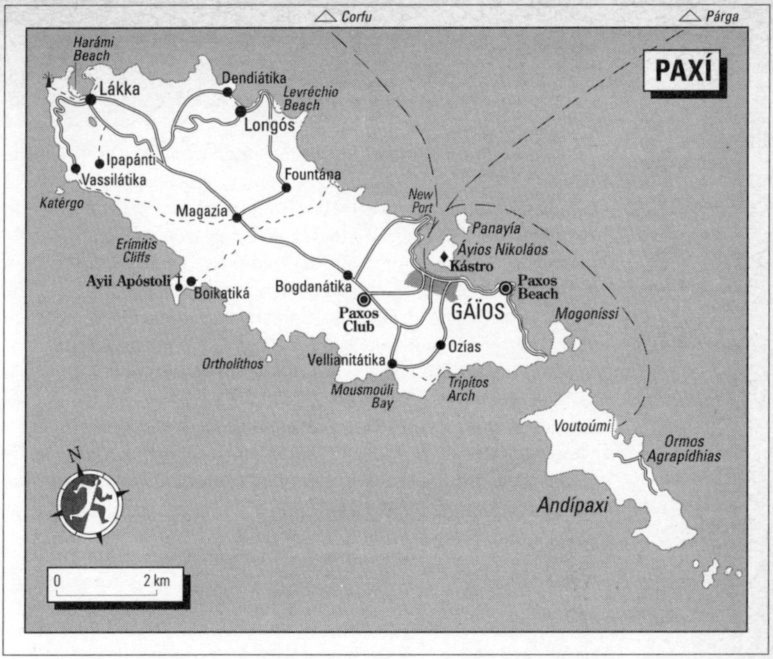

flora and **bird life** make it a favourite haunt of ornithologists, botanists, walkers and watercolourists, particularly in spring. Drenching winter rains produce carpets of dwarf cyclamen in spring; daffodils and antirrhinums flower in February, and by Easter the island's woods and olive groves are full of wild lilies, irises and orchids. Despite the unwanted attentions of gun-mad hunters, the island is home to numerous native and migratory species of bird. Barn owls and the tiny Scops owl are heard at night, and peregrine falcons nest on remote hilltops.

Walking routes on Paxí are detailed on the comprehensive map produced by cartographers Elizabeth and Ian Bleasdale and sold by most tourism businesses on the island (3000dr).

Barely 8km long by 3km wide, Paxí has only three villages of any size, all of them ports: its capital, **Gáïos**, towards the southern end, **Lákka**, at the northern tip, and tiny **Longós**, 2km south of Lákka. Gáïos is where most visitors will arrive, although many immediately head off to quieter Lákka and Longós. The island's best bathing is around Longós and Lákka, or further afield in the desert island coves and beaches of **Andípaxi**, Paxí's sibling 2km south. Many of Paxí's beaches are not accessible by road or foot, which is where a boat with outboard motor comes in handy. Most village travel agencies and some of the larger international companies offer boat rental by week or day.

Some history

There are two overlapping myths about Paxí's origins. In one, Poseidon needed a place to hide his lover, Amphitrite, and struck the sea with his trident – now Paxí's emblem – to create an island. In the other, the sea god simply wanted somewhere to rest while travelling between islands (odd, given that Homer credits the gods with the power to traverse the Med in a flash) and so created this hideaway between Corfu and Itháki.

Paxí is believed to have first been settled by shepherds from the mainland in the sixth century AD; a ruined chapel near the hamlet of Ozías in the south of the island has been dated back this far. Ancient history seems to have passed the island by, apart from a walk-on role in a few key moments. In the third century BC, Paxí was the site of a sea battle between Corcyreans, as Corfiots were then known, and the Illyrian fleet, which resulted in Corcyra becoming the first Greek state to surrender to Roman rule. Antony and Cleopatra are believed to have dined on Paxí on the eve of the ill-fated Battle of Actium in 31 BC, when they were decisively defeated by the emperor Octavian's fleet. Paxí is also associated with a piece of Christian mythology, retold by Plutarch in his *Moralia* and interpreted by Spenser and Milton, which cites the island as the place where the

Párga

Spread over three wooded, hilly coves, **PÁRGA** is the most attractive coastal resort in the mainland region of Epirus. Its jumble of low, red-tiled buildings faces out towards Paxí, over vegetation-tufted rocks and islets a short swim off some of the best beaches in the region. Unfortunately, Párga is also Epirus' most popular resort: even in low season it can be hectically busy, and in high summer it heaves. All the same, it can be a welcome change of scene on one of the **day-trips** that leave Gáïos most days of the week (from around 3000dr per person).

As a stopover on the way to or from the islands, however, it leaves a lot to be desired: accommodation is hard to come by in season, and its **ferry connections** – to Paxí (twice weekly, taking two hours, although you could negotiate to return with one of the daily excursion boats from Paxí) and Corfu (Thursdays, taking three hours) – are far inferior to services from Igoumenítsa 70km to the north. **Buses** to Igoumenítsa (4 daily; 1hr 30min) and Préveza (4 daily; 1hr 30min) leave from the crossroads in the centre of town, on Odhós Skoúfa. This crossroads is the commercial heart of the town, with post office, banks, shops and travel agencies.

Of Párga's **beaches**, the pebble strand immediately below the quay is probably the poorest; the smaller **Krióneri** and **Píso Krióneri** beaches just to the north are cleaner and quieter; best, however, is the long, sandy **Váltos beach** to the south, beyond the massive *kástro* that towers above the town. Sea taxis connect Váltos and Párga every fifteen minutes from 9am onwards for those reluctant to slog twenty minutes over the headland. The **kástro**, open all day, is the ruined skeleton of a major Venetian fort, built when Párga was Venice's sole mainland settlement during its rule of the Ionians from the fourteenth to eighteenth centuries. It has excellent views, as well as some rather dangerous unguarded precipices, and makes an excellent stroll or picnic destination.

Accommodation in Párga is notoriously difficult to find, except at a price. Phoning ahead is near obligatory, but anyone who finds themselves

death of paganism and the birth of Christ were announced. An Egyptian captain taking his craft north through the Ionian found himself becalmed off Paxí, when a mysterious voice called him by name from the island and told him to shout out to the inhabitants of a mainland port as he passed that "the great god Pan is dead". The captain reluctantly obeyed, and reported an unearthly wailing from the mainland at this news.

Shortly after its first likely settlement in the sixth century, Paxí was subsumed into the Byzantine Empire along with Epirus and the rest of the northern Ionian. The **Venetians**, after their invasion of the region from 1386 onwards, proved to be more forward-thinking rulers. They planted **olive trees** throughout the archipelago, including an estimated quarter million on Paxí alone, which, as well as producing a bumper crop, would bind topsoil to allow the cultivation of fruit, vegetables and vines. Islanders were paid the equivalent of a drachma for each tree planted, and under Venetian auspices produced the extraordinary terracing and intricate dry-stone walling that covers much of Paxí. The invaders also initiated the construc-

here without accommodation should first try the friendly *Souli* taverna on the seafront (☎0684/31 658; ②), which has **rooms** in town, or some of the rooming houses on the whitewashed lane leading past the *kástro*, such as Christos Katsavanis (☎0684/31 408; ②). At the back of the town, there's *Aleca's House* (☎0684/31 920; ②), a traditional town house with rooms, or the modern, purpose-built *Lina* rooms (☎0684/31 660; ③). The **hotels** *Rezi* (☎0684/31 417; ③) and *Kalypso* (☎0684/31 316; ③), set back from Krióneri beach, are also reasonable alternatives, with en-suite rooms and balconies. If you're planning to spend a few days in Párga and want to be close to the beach, head for Váltos and either the *Parga Beach Hotel* (☎0684/31 287; ⑤) or the *Valtos Beach Hotel* (☎0684/31 610 or 31 005; ⑥). For a splurge, the *Achilleas Hotel* (☎0684/31 600 or 31 878, fax 31 879; ⑥), on Krióneri beach, is the most elegant in town. Two **travel agencies** on the seafront with access to a variety of accommodation are *Kryoneri Travel* (☎0684/32 488, fax 32 400) and *IYS Travel* (☎0684/31 833 or 31 683, fax 31 834). **Campers** should head for either *Parga Camping* or *Elea Camping* fifteen minutes walk from the centre on the main road into Párga.

Párga's two best **restaurants** are secreted in the lane ascending towards the *kástro*: the smart, and fairly expensive, *Kastro*, near the fort itself, and in a courtyard nearer the town, the cheaper, but if anything superior *Kastello*, whose reputation has spread to Paxí and even Itháki. In town, as well as the traditional *Souli* taverna, the *Tzima* restaurant at the far end of the quay is recommended for its vast range of vegetarian-friendly, Greek and north European food, as are the *Three Stars* and *To Kyma* tavernas. The seafront **bars** tend to fill quickly at night, but some of the best drinking spots are to be found at the upper end of the lane leading up to the *kástro*, including the aforementioned *Kastro*, with stunning views down over the town.

tion of basic civic amenities: a harbour at Gáïos, various official buildings, and several small water reservoirs still seen, and some still in use, around the island. The distinctive Venetian architectural style can be observed on the seafront at Gáïos, and as ruins in a few isolated parts of the island's interior.

Venetian rule finally came to an end after more than four hundred years with the arrival of the French, but not before Paxí had suffered a particularly brutal maritime raid, when in 1537 Turkish admiral **Barbarossa** enslaved most of the islanders in a revenge attack, after failing in a siege on Corfu. When the **British** took over in 1809, they improved on the Venetians' building schemes, as well as instituting the basis of a government infrastructure and education system. Britain ceded the Ionian islands to the Greek government in 1864, at which point Paxí slipped into the mainstream of Greek history. During **World War II**, garrisons of German troops were stationed in Gáïos and Lákka, and, it's claimed, the Luftwaffe used Paxí for practice bombing runs from Corfu. Along with the rest of Greece, the island was liberated in 1944 – a popular local story has German troops in Lákka attempting to arrest arriving British troops, only to be told it was they who were being arrested.

Arrival and getting around

Most **ferries** arrive at Gáïos, with larger vessels from Corfu Town and Igoumenítsa on the mainland docking at the new port, 1km north of Gáïos. There's no bus connection at the new port, so people either walk into Gáïos (15min) or take a taxi (500dr). Smaller ferries, when they are running, moor a hundred metres or so along the quayside from Gáïos's tiny town square.

There is no tourist office on Paxí, but local travel agencies in the three ports are usually happy to help with information, even if you're not travelling or staying with their company.

Buses shuttle between Gáïos and Lákka six times a day (45min), with alternate departures travelling via Longós. Timetables are posted in each village and in most travel agencies. Gáïos's bus stop is at the back of the village, 100m from the square, in a small dirt car park where the village alleys meet the island's one main road. In Lákka buses stop by the *Petrou kafenío* at the back of the village; in Longós on the quay. There are **taxi** stands in Gáïos (by the church in the main square) and Lákka (by the *Petrou kafenío*); an average one-way fare between Lákka and Gáïos is 1500–2000dr. Both buses and taxis, which are often shared, can be flagged down anywhere you see them on the island's roads.

There are **motorcycle** rentals in all three villages: by the dock in Gáïos, 50m back from the ferry ramp behind the *Dionysus* taverna in Lákka, and on the northern end of the quay at Longós. Rental starts at around 3000dr a day. However, riders should beware Paxí's treacherous gravelly roads, which are often slicked with oil from the olive trees – accidents are a daily occurrence in season.

A limited number of **cars** can be rented in Gáïos and Lákka, with established companies such as *Planos* and *Gáïos Travel* getting first choice of what's available. It's also fiendishly expensive: between 90,000 and 110,000dr a week for a saloon, depending on season, and between 130,000 and 160,000dr for a four-wheel drive. British-based travel companies such as CV Villas and Greek Islands can hire cars ahead for clients; an alternative for independent travellers is to rent a car on Corfu and bring it to Paxí by ferry.

Gáïos and around

Named after Saint Gaius, who is said to have brought Christianity to the island, **GÁÏOS** is the one of the most attractive villages in the Ionian. It's extremely compact, consisting of little more than a crescent-shaped quay, the small Venetian town square – hub of life in the village – and a handful of narrow alleys leaving the square. It's the island's administrative centre (two banks; one magistrate's court; Paxí's sole police station), its major port of arrival, and shopping centre, including several mini-markets, two delis and a pharmacy.

The town is protected from the open sea by two islands, **Áyios Nikoláos** and **Panayía**. The former is little more than 20m across from the harbourfront and crowned by a magnificent stand of pines. Beyond the pines stands a ruined Venetian fortress built in 1423 and renovated by the French in the eighteenth century. Panayía is named after a white-walled church dedicated to the Virgin Mary (*Panayia*), the site of a major festival every August 15. Both islands are well worth exploring: a sea taxi (there's a desk on the seafront) will take you to either for around 1000dr. Smoking is discouraged on Áyios Nikoláos to prevent fires on its tinder-dry pine forest floor.

Accommodation

Much accommodation in Gáïos – and elsewhere on Paxí – is block-booked by British and other northern European travel companies, and the range of freelance accommodation dwindles near high season, when a call ahead is essential. However, a few villagers offering **rooms** meet ferries arriving at the quay in season, and a few metres from the ferry is one of the biggest Paxiot-run tourism and accommodation companies, *Gaïos Travel* (☎0662/32 033), run by the friendly, English-speaking Ioannis Arvanatakis. The company shares an office with *CV Villas* and can also help with money exchange, trips and other business. Also worth contacting for accommodation is *Paxos Tourist Enterprises* (☎0662/31 675), also situated on the seafront.

Freelance camping on Paxí is frowned on, largely because of the fire risk, but there is a campsite at Mogonissi – see p.110.

Paxí's two seasonal **hotels** are both near Gáïos. They are heavily used by package companies in high season, but will often have rooms available to independent travellers. The secluded *Paxos Beach Hotel* (☎0662/31 211; ⑤) is sited on a hillside above a small pebbly beach 2km south of Gáïos. Accommodation is in bungalows, spread out through the trees, though the place has an unfriendly and rather regimented air. The hotel has its own irregular minibus service into Gáïos; otherwise access is by taxi or on foot.

The newer *Paxos Beach Club* (☎0662/32 450, fax 32 097; ⑤), 2km outside of Gáïos on the main road towards Bogdanátika, is fairly luxurious. On an island with a severe water shortage, it boasts a large fancy-shaped pool which, along with its bar and restaurant, welcomes non-residents. Rooms are en suite with balconies, and some large, suite-style apartments are also available. However, the hotel currently has a fairly short season, and has been known to close in early September.

Eating and drinking

Eating out is not one of Paxí's strong points. Over the years, many tavernas have operated on the basis that on a small island customers are a captive audience, and most islanders would be embarrassed to serve in their own kitchens the sort of food that gets served in the village squares. If you're used to the fare on other islands, or the predominantly Cypriot food in British Greek restaurants, you'll be surprised by the lack of choice and poor quality of cooking. When the large number of return visitors to the island started switching to self-catering in the early 1990s, the taverna owners' response to the fall in business was simply to raise their prices.

In Gáïos itself, however, there are a number of decent **tavernas**, best of them *Carcoleggio's*, 1.5km out of town on the main road to Bogdanátika. Menu and wine list are limited, and opening hours unpredictable, but it fills up with islanders who flock for its *souvláki*. Tucked away to the left at the back of the village square, the longstanding *Blue Grotto* is a good second choice for its grills and pan-cooked meat and fish dishes. *Spiro's*, to the right at the top of the square, opposite the alley leading to the *Blue Grotto*, offers friendly service and excellent meat, fish and veggie dishes in a pleasant, arcaded Venetian square. *Dodo's*, up the alley leading out of the square, is a welcoming taverna with outdoor seating, serving pizza, pasta and indigenous food, while the *Gaïos Grill* behind provides a conventional range of lamb, chicken and fish dishes. The one traditional taverna in the line of eating houses running down to the quayside, the *Volcano* has been family-run for decades, with vegetarian-friendly alternatives such as stuffed vegetables as well as conventional taverna dishes.

For self-caterers, the picture is rosier. Thanks to the demands of picky yacht crews, Gáïos now offers as sophisticated a range of foodstuffs as you're likely to encounter in the Ionian islands. The **deli** at the top left of the town square offers the widest range of cured meats, dairy products, wines and other delicacies, while the supermarket directly opposite the ferry dock (nicknamed Harrod's by some expats) also stocks a wide range of alcohol and deli/dairy foodstuffs. The spread of high-class *zaharoplastía* has now reached

Gáïos, with a mouthwatering **cake shop** a stone's throw from the ferry dock, and a larger, even fancier store opposite *Spiro's* taverna in the arcade to the right at the top of the town square. The **bakery** a few doors uphill on the main road out of the square is the only one on the island to stock a daily supply of brown as well as white bread.

Nightlife

As on most small Greek islands, visitors soon discover that evening entertainment on Paxí consists largely of lotus-eating outside tavernas and bars. The *Carnayo* on Gáïos's seafront, a source of much amusement and scandal over the years, has now closed, but the range of booze, desserts and snacks available in Gáïos's square – *Red Chairs* is a local favourite – should provide ample diversion.

From May through to September, the taverna at Mogoníssi (see p.110) stages special "Greek nights", with music, dancing and free sea-taxi transport from Gáïos quayside. Joiners-in will enjoy themselves; others might find this enough reason to give Mogoníssi a wide berth.

There are two **discotheques** outside Gáïos: the *Castello*, a moribund barn that opens only fitfully, on the first turning out of town on the main road; and the *Phenix*, out of harm's way just past the new port, a lively and popular late night venue with a terrace for sub-lunar fun, dodgy music policy and pricey bar list.

Listings

Banks and exchange The branches of the National Bank of Greece and the Agricultural Bank in Gáïos, the only banks on the island, are for domestic accounts rather than foreign exchange. Most travel companies, however, will change travellers' cheques at rates checked daily with banks, although with commission.

Doctors and medical emergencies The island's surgery (☎0662/31 466), in the village of Bogdanátika, 3km west of Gáïos, opens weekday mornings – attendance avoids the doctor's call-out fee of around 10,000dr. The two doctors both speak English. Serious injuries are taken to Corfu by sea taxi or helicopter. There are no dental services on Paxí.

Ferry agent A tiny caravan at the new port is the only dedicated ferry office on Paxí, although any travel agency (see p.106 or p.113 for examples) will be able to make reservations.

Police station One block back from the quayside at the southern end of the waterfront, behind the schoolhouse (☎0662/31 222).

Post office The only proper post office and OTE on the island is by the bus stand at the back of the village (Mon–Fri 9am–1pm & 6–9pm).

Beaches around Gáïos

Gáïos is poorest served of the island's villages in terms of beaches. Apart from a tiny pebble strand dynamited a few years back just south of the town, the only true beach is at the micro-resort of

Mogoníssi, 3km south of Gáïos. Mogoníssi is in fact an island, attached to Paxí by a short causeway, set in the dullest landscape on the entire island – flat, part scrubby and part rocky. It has a small **campsite** set in trees above a beach of imported sand, a **taverna** and water sports. There is no bus service beyond Gáïos, however, so it's either foot or taxi.

There are, however, numerous rocky coves between Gáïos and Mogoníssi, popular with those staying in the capital, with large slabs of rock sloping into the sea, ideal for swimming and sunbathing. One bay south of Gáïos, the taverna *Klis* overlooks a bay with safe swimming and, sometimes in season, a floating bathing platform with its own bar. Further bays are accessible from the road north beyond the new port, but they're a good few kilometres' walk through a landscape akin to a building site. They're also uncomfortably close to the island's eco-unfriendly municipal dump, a hill of smouldering garbage that glows orange at night while slipping slowly into the sea.

Southwest Paxí

The comparative flatness of the landscape around Gáïos makes the surrounding countryside easy walking terrain. A circular two-to-three hour route leaving the southern end of Gáïos takes in some of the oldest hamlets on the island: through Ozías, Vellianitátika, neighbouring Zenebissátika and on to **Bogdanátika** on the main road. The chief interest in these hamlets is the architecture, much of it from Venetian times and before, but there are hardly any facilities along the way – only Bogdanátika has a *kafenío* and bar.

The walk can be augmented by taking a path leading from near the church in Vellianitátika. This cuts across fairly rough country to the cliffs above Mousmoúli bay and on to the dramatic **Tripítos arch**, a hundred-metre limestone sea stack attached to the island by a walkway. It's a strenuous and even dangerous trip, with vertiginous drops, and should only be attempted by the sure-footed (and never in bad weather).

Longós and around

The smallest of the island's three ports, **LONGÓS** is also the most picturesque and, for its size, blessed with the best ratio of amenities. Its pocket-sized, east-facing harbour is perfectly sited to catch the morning sun (making alfresco breakfasts idyllic), the handful of tavernas are among the best on the island, and the nightlife is lively. The one drawback to staying here, which should be taken seriously in high and shoulder seasons, is the lack of space, with bars, restaurants and other tourists right on your doorstep, and at night the noise. Indeed, the extent of Longós's facilities can be taken in simply by looking around its harbour: with the exception of one mini-market and a restaurant tucked into an alleyway, the village's few amenities, including another well-stocked mini-market and a bakery, are all here on the quay. Note that there is no bank or post office – exchange transactions are dealt with by the travel agencies.

Longós's seclusion has made it a favourite with upmarket villa companies like CV and Simply Ionian, whose properties are in the hills above the port. The village has a small and scruffy beach, but most people swim from pebbly **Levréchio beach**, around ten minutes' walk away in the next bay south. Above the village to the north, reached by steps rising above the disused factory on the beach, is the small Venetian hamlet of **Dendiátika**. While there are no tavernas or *kafenía* here, it has excellent views over the port and makes a diverting short walk, probably best taken from the Dendiátika road signposted off the Lakká–Longós road and then down into Longós.

Accommodation

Of Paxí's three ports, Longós has the least accommodation for independent travellers, and in the high season months of July and August, the supply all but dries up. You should be prepared to move on to Lákka if Longós is full or, as has happened in at least one drought year, has been forced to "close" because of water shortages.

The bulk of villas and apartments here are controlled by companies such as *Greek Islands* and *CV Villas*, though *Planos Holidays*, now the island's largest local accommodation agency, with its main office in Lákka, has an increasingly large stake. *Planos*'s office in Longós (☎0662/31 530) is probably the best place to start looking for accommodation hereabouts, from village **rooms** to country **villas**, especially if phoning ahead. It's also possible to rent rooms from Gamal's shop (☎0662/31 929) and from the Dendias mini-market (☎0662/31 597). A certain amount of unofficial **camping** takes place on Levréchio beach, but it's nowhere near as hidden as at Lákka – it's best to ask for advice at the beach taverna.

Eating and drinking

The **restaurants** in Longós are good but there aren't many of them, so people often head for Lákka by bus, taxi or, if there's light, on foot (taxis run until well after midnight). Some more diplomatic visitors spread their favour among Longós's tavernas to avoid offending the owners. The *Nassos* is probably the best restaurant in Longós, with a wide variety of fish and seafood dishes, including things like prawns with a side order of mayonnaise (unusually for Paxí, they'll bring hot water and lemon finger bowls, if you ask). The seafront *Vassilis* is immortalized in thousands of holiday tales as the restaurant where you have to squeeze in for the island bus when it rumbles by; it has a basic taverna menu, but done with imagination and more veg than you'll ever find in Lákka. Tucked behind the *Vassilis*,

Kakarantzas offers a range of fish, meat and vegetarian dishes far more adventurous than the majority of tavernas on the island.

Nightlife is largely limited to the few bars facing the seafront, and the promised new *Piano Bar*: the old, and infamous, *Piano Bar* on the quay, which used to offer live small-combo jazz, rock and funk until well after you should have been in bed, closed in 1996, but already a newer version, with the same name and party policy, is under construction on the edge of the village. Those who like to greet the dawn with a drink in their hand should still be able to follow the hard core to *Dino's* all-night bar on the edge of the village.

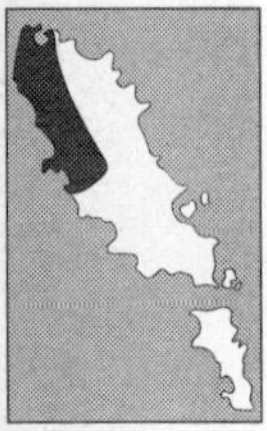

Lákka and around

LÁKKA is the funkiest and friendliest of the island's ports, attracting a large crowd of loyal return visitors, as well as a fair share of roustabouts, who give the place a faintly racy edge – especially at night. The sea approach into the horseshoe bay has to be one of the most magnificent views in Greece, though arriving from elsewhere on Paxí is disappointing: you're greeted by a jumble of half-built apartment blocks at the back of the village. Beyond these, however, a compact grid of narrow alleys around the village's one small square, lined with two-storey houses in the Venetian style, comprises the village's charming centre. It's full of surprise details and strange corners and turns – not least Platía Edward Kennedy, commemorating, probably with tongue in cheek, a visit by members of the Kennedy clan (including, rumour insists, Jackie O) in the 1960s. The *platía* is in fact only a tiny, triangular alley, signalled by a blink-and-you'll-miss-it wall sign hard by the *Ubu Bar*, a favoured late-night hangout at the village's western edge.

Lákka is so compact that you'll trip over most of what there is here in the first five minutes. Shops are based around the back of the village, bars along the seafront, and restaurants around the village square. Taxis and buses stop metres from each other near the *Petrou Kafenio* at the back of the village. There's no bank or post office, but the two main travel agents, *Planos* and *Routsis*, both on the quayside, change money, sell stamps and operate quiet payphones, as well as renting water sports equipment; Planos also offers car rental.

Lákka and its bay offer the best swimming and water sports on Paxí, with its two public **beaches** on the western side of the bay – **Kanóni** and **Harámi**, which has a snack bar-taverna – and a small beach by the schoolhouse opposite. As elsewhere on the island, the beaches are pebble, with occasional tar deposits, but shelve into sand at the edge of the clear, shallow water. In recent years, however, questions have been raised about the quality of the water at high season. Eye and ear infections, stomach upsets and infected cuts and abrasions have led some to suspect that untreated sewage is finding its way into the bay. Take local advice on whether to swim or not.

Paxí olive oil

Paxí's prize-winning **olive oil** is regarded by some as being on a par with, or even superior to, Italian brands. The olive trees originally planted by the Venetians still dominate the island's economy and landscape; olive oil remains the largest business after tourism, and the trees cover around eighty percent of the island.

Unlike crops elsewhere, Paxí's olives are allowed to fall before being harvested, and until nets were introduced a few decades ago, this was done by hand. The biennial crop would be hand-picked, winnowed, bagged and carried to olive presses in each village. The traditional stone mills were driven by donkeys and sometimes by women and children: a generation of islanders still remembers this back-breaking work. Mechanization of the mills and the introduction of nets has transformed the industry, and most of the stone presses have fallen into disuse, their overgrown masonry and machinery visible at points throughout the island.

Mechanized presses operate in Gáïos, Fountána and, most visibly, Lákka. The olive oil sells at around 2000dr a litre, but it is rarely seen in shops, less still in restaurants. However, it's a staple in the kitchens of the islanders, most of whom have a stake, if only a few trees, in the crop. The oil is sold chiefly in the presses themselves, which only open when deliveries from the olive groves require processing. If you're planning to take some home, buy early to avoid finding the press closed on your day of departure.

Accommodation

Accommodation is easier to come by in Lákka than either Gáïos or Longós, although even here rooms are scarce at the height of the season. The village has a large number of return visitors, many of whom book the same accommodation year after year. Rooms in the village itself are generally noisy, especially as some bars stay open until dawn.

The growth of the two main village travel companies has resulted in a healthy choice of accommodation that directly benefits islanders rather than anonymous multinational corporations. *Planos* (☎0662/31 744 or 31 821, fax 31 010) is the larger of the two, and can offer anything from a village room the size of a cupboard to a villa with pool up in the hills. It also offers complete holiday packages from its British office (see p.6), inclusive of flights and transfer. *Routsis* ((☎0662/31 807 or 31 162, fax 31 161) is fast catching up with *Planos*, and also has a wide range of rooms, apartments and villas in the village and outlying areas. It now also offers bonded flight and holiday deals through its British agents (see p.6). Of the two, *Routsis* is more likely to have basic village accommodation and, because *Planos* presells much of its accommodation, probably more choice for the independent traveller.

Between them, these two companies and several overseas operators have sewn up much of the accommodation in and around Lákka; even the "hotels" *Ilios* and *Lefcothea* (in fact basic rooming houses) are run by *Routsis*. At a pinch, independent travellers are advised to enquire about rooms at Marigo's food store at the landward end of the main square, or to ask for directions to Maria's rooms, set in a paradisiacal garden but difficult to find in a lane rising out of the west end of the village.

Camping

A large sign on the path leading beyond Platía Kennedy to the main beach, Harámi, explains that **camping** is strictly forbidden, although this has never deterred the backpackers who happily pitch tent in the glade above Kanóni, the smaller beach reached a few minutes before Harámi. In fact, it's tolerated locally provided that campers take care with litter and fires: there's no fire brigade on Paxí, and islanders are understandably paranoid about the threat to the olive groves.

Eating and drinking

In recent years, **tavernas** have proliferated in Lákka to a capacity beyond the numbers of tourists arriving: bad news for the restaurant-owners, good news for customers. Restaurants are sited in the central square or visible two or three minute's walk away. Late night **bars** are also proliferating in Lákka, often run by the new generation of would-be tourism moguls.

Restaurants

The Butterfly. The best of the conventional tavernas, with friendly family service and plenty of veggie alternatives to taverna staples.

Dionysus. This specializes in grills – chicken, chops, *souvláki*, even whole baby lamb – for the flotilla crowd; telltale signs of when the fleet's in (tables lined up for twenty or more) should warn you to eat elsewhere.

Nautilus. Under a blue-striped awning on the far side of the bay, this has the most breathtaking view of any taverna on Paxí. It specializes in seafood (expensive), salads, and conventional fare prepared with effort and imagination, not least a classic bean soup.

Rosa di Paxos. The most stylish restaurant on the island, with prices to match (which is why they're left off the menu outside). Good choice of designer Greek and international cuisine, well worth a special night out.

Souris. A Lákka institution, and the oldest surviving traditional family taverna in the village. The Souris brothers field a wide range of grilled fish and meats, as well as pan-cooked staples. A favourite with villagers and hardened returnees.

Ubu. This drop-dead cool bar-restaurant actually had people queueing for tables in past seasons, when some dishes passed into local legend. Each year, owner Luciano decides whether or not to do food this season: when he does, *Ubu* offers imaginative Italianate specialities.

Bars

Spiro Petrou's *kafenío*, by the bus stop at the back of the village, has been the hub of Lákka society since anyone can remember, and remains the place to eavesdrop on village life. It's the friendliest *kafenío* in the whole archipelago, with none of the usual macho atmosphere. Among the new generation of venues, *Akis's* seafront bar is a smart cocktail bar overlooking the harbour. It's noisy but popular with younger islanders and visitors. The *Harbour Lights* is the liveliest bar in town, a hangout for night creatures with a soundtrack that tends towards heavy metal. The village's premier cocktail joint, the *Romantica*, has moved back to the seafront, and offers the biggest nightcap list in town, as well as a cool jazz soundtrack. *Serano's*, in the square, serves homemade sweets and cakes to induce sugar shock, and is a favourite among guest workers, who park their tape collections behind the bar. *Basta's*, on the seafront, has the best views, especially when storms crack open over Corfu.

Around Lákka

Lákka is perfectly sited for the finest walking on the island. For a simple, short hike, take the track leaving the far end of Harámi beach. This mounts the headland and leads on to the **lighthouse**, where a goat track descends through tough scrub to a sandy open-sea beach with rollers best left to confident swimmers.

Another good walking route heads west into the hills above the village to **Vassilátika**, high on the west coast cliffs, which has stunning views out to sea. From here, the path to the left of the blue-painted stone archway leads on to the most dramatic cliff-edge views (vertigo sufferers beware) and continues to **Magazía** in the centre of the island, where you can flag down a bus or taxi.

The best walk on Paxí, however, especially good under a clear early evening sky, is to the church at **Áyii Apóstoli**, almost halfway down the west coast, next to the hamlet of Boikátika. The rough track is signposted a few hundred metres south of Magazía, and takes less than half a hour on foot. The church and surrounding vineyards overlook the sheer 150-metre **Erimítis cliffs**, which at sunset are transformed into a seaside version of Ayers Rock, turning from dirty white to pink and gold and brown. If you visit Áyii Apóstoli at sunset, take a torch and prepare to return from the trailhead by bus or – more likely – taxi, either of which can be waved down on the main road. Tourism agencies in Lákka and the other ports organize coach trips to the cliffs involving "Greek night" meals in a village taverna afterwards.

Andípaxi

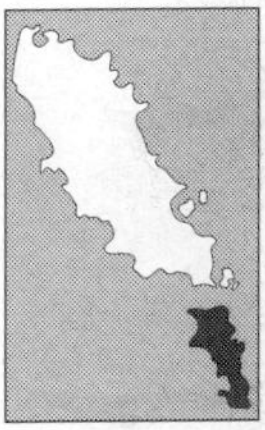

The neighbouring island of **Andípaxi** is a flawed paradise, with the clearest blue coves in the entire archipelago – and some of the best snorkelling in Greece – but some rather indifferent beaches. Unfortunately, even the quieter low-season afternoons will see you sharing the more popular coves such as **Voutoúmi** with large numbers of day-trippers from various resorts on Corfu. Even so, this doesn't entirely dent the charms of Andípaxi, and the island still has space to accommodate its invaders. The trick is to head south away from the pleasure-boat moorings – and the tavernas that have sprung up in the last decade at Voutoúmi – to find the quieter spots. Sunny Octobers can leave you with a bay to yourself and a clear sea as warm as a bath.

High-speed sea taxis and more leisurely *kaíkia*, which take in the sea-stacks and blue-water caves of the west coast as well as the east coast bays, leave all three of Paxí's ports for Andípaxi each morning in season (around 3000dr a head). The **sea caves** are the finest in the Ionian: large enough to be entered by pleasure craft, one even big enough, according to local legend, to have concealed an Allied submarine during World War II. The sea taxis tend to buzz in and out, while *kaíkia* enter and cut their engines to scare faint hearts.

While a limited number of **villas** are now being made available on Andípaxi, mainly by tourism agencies in Gáïos such as *Gáïos Travel*, this is still for hard-core loners who are expected to transport provisions with them: there are no shops or bars, only two beach **tavernas** open in season. They close once the day-trip craft depart, and there's little else on Andípaxi apart from a smattering of summer houses owned by Paxiots. Paths marked on some maps penetrate the interior, but require serious footwear and long trousers. The west coast has no beaches of note and few points of access.

Travel details

For advice on Paxí's skeletal **bus** service, see p.106.

Ferries

Ferry routes between **Corfu** (the main port of entry by air) and Paxí have been in a state of flux: both the *Zefiros* and *Pegasus* ferry services have been discontinued, as has the high-speed Brindisi–Corfu–Paxí–Lefkádha catamaran. At present, only one ferry a week is confirmed, between Corfu Town old port and Gáïos new port on Mondays (3hr). However, it is likely that other ferries, such as the *Anna Maria* or *Paxos Star*, will resume daily (except Sun) services on this route. **Sea taxis** are available to the rich or desperate (phone a travel company in your preferred destination; they'll rustle one up), but, at anything between 30,000dr and 35,000dr one way from Corfu Town, are best shared with as many as you can get into the boat. They'll also pick up from Lefkími or Kávos in the south of Corfu, reducing travel time and cost.

There are at present only two ferries a week to **Igoumenítsa** (Wed & Thurs; 4hr; vehicle-carrying), and two a week to **Párga** (2hr).

Chapter 3

Lefkádha

Although it's home to two very busy resorts, Nidhrí and Vassilikí, **Lefkádha (Lefkas)** is the least developed of the larger Ionian islands. Its terrain – almost ninety percent is defined as mountainous or semi-mountainous and just ten percent as lowland – provides little land on which tourism might develop, and its typically Ionian geography – cliffs on the west coast and flat land to the east – leaves a poor endowment of beaches: the best are difficult, often nearly impossible, to get to, while the more accessible are stony or pebbly, and sometimes rather scruffy. Much of the island's tourism straggles along the east coast road heading south from Lefkádha Town. **Nidhrí**, overlooking Lefkádha's satellite islands, is a popular package destination, and has been commercialized to meet this demand. **Vassilikí**, set on the vast bay of the same name at the south of the island, has some of the finest windsurfing in Europe. The mountainous **west coast** is less developed but shelters some of the most attractive smaller resorts, notably the pretty village of **Aï Nikítas**, and the sandy beaches of **Káthisma** and **Pefkoúlia**.

Away from the coast, the island conceals breathtaking valleys and hill ranges, offering some of the best **walking** terrain in the entire archipelago. Serious hikers should base themselves in **Kariá**, dead

Accommodation price codes

Rooms and hotels listed in this book have been price-coded according to the scale outlined below. The rates quoted represent the cheapest available double room in high season. Out of season, rates can drop by as much as fifty percent or more, especially if you negotiate for a stay of three or more nights. Single rooms, where available, cost around seventy percent of the price of a double. For further information, see p.32.

① up to 4000dr
② 4000–8000dr
③ 8000–12,000dr
④ 12,000–16,000dr
⑤ 16,000–20,000dr
⑥ 20,000–30,000dr
⑦ 30,000dr upwards

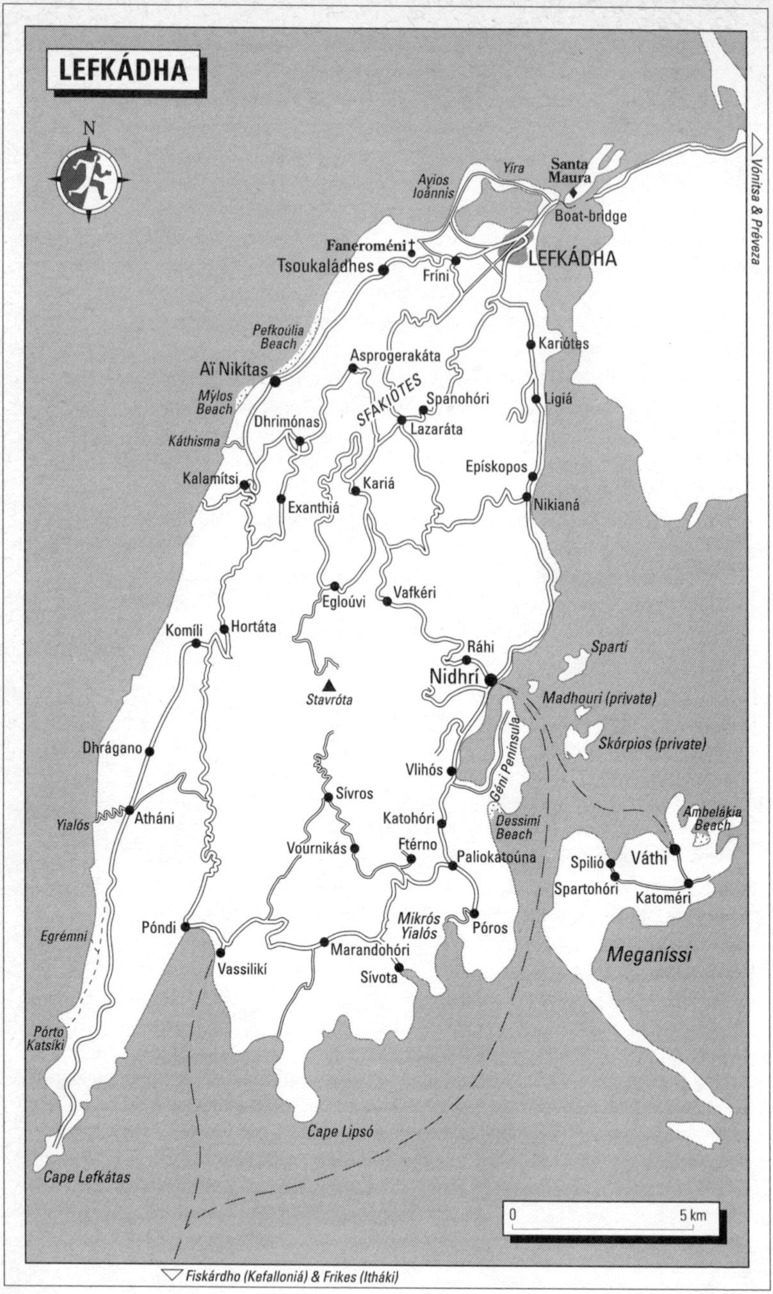
LEFKÁDHA
N
Yíra
Santa Maura
Ayios Ioánnis
Boat-bridge
Vónitsa & Préveza
Faneroméni
Tsoukaládhes
Fríni
LEFKÁDHA
Pefkoúlia Beach
Aï Nikítas
Asprogerakáta
Kariótes
SFAKIOTES
Spanohóri
Ligiá
Mýlos Beach
Dhrimónas
Lazaráta
Káthisma
Epískopos
Kalamítsi
Kariá
Exanthiá
Nikianá
Vafkéri
Egloúvi
Komíli
Hortáta
Ráhi
Spartí
Nidhrí
Stavróta
Madhouri (private)
Skórpios (private)
Dhrágano
Géni Peninsula
Vlihós
Sívros
Athání
Yialós
Katohóri
Dessimí Beach
Ambelákia Beach
Vournikás
Ftérno
Paliokatoúna
Spilió
Váthi
Spartohóri
Katoméri
Egrémni
Póndi
Mikrós Yialós
Póros
Vassilikí
Marandohóri
Meganíssi
Sívota
Pórto Katsíki
Cape Lipsó
Cape Lefkátas
0
5 km
Fiskárdho (Kefalloniá) & Frikes (Itháki)

centre of a whole network of easily walkable villages set in an almost alpine landscape. Similarly, the road to Vournikás and Sívros in the south has fine mountain views, and the west coast route beyond Káthisma is also recommended, although probably in sections; the walk from Atháni to Cape Lefkátas is particularly fine, with primeval mountainscapes and empty arable land.

Lefkádha is also notable for its **satellite islands**. The proximity of the main quartet gives Nidhrí the finest sea views on the island, but only two of these – **Spartí**, and the larger and more interesting **Meganíssi** – are accessible to visitors. Some 20km away are the further satellites of **Kálamos**, **Kástos** and **Átokos**, nowadays inaccessible from Lefkádha and reached only by occasional ferries from the Greek mainland.

Lefkádha's **history** largely follows that of the archipelago as a whole. Excavations have produced evidence of settlement on the island dating back to the Palaeolithic Age, around 8000 BC. According to local mythology, Lefkádha was given to Arcadius, father of Penelope, as a gift from Laertes, on her marriage to his son Odysseus. It is this, along with a close geographical reading of Homer's *Odyssey* and the discovery of Mycenean remains in the hills above Vassilikí, that led archeologist **Wilhelm Dörpfeld** (Heinrich Schliemann's assistant at the excavations of Troy and Mycenae) to spend many years in the late nineteenth century vainly attempting to identify Lefkádha as the home of Odysseus. Some of Dörpfeld's excavations are still visible on the roads just south and north of Nidhrí, but amount to little more than rather forlorn collections of architectural details fenced into small gardens which are locked to the public.

The island's **name** derives from the ancient Greek for "white", referring to the colour of its cliffs and barren mountain ranges. Under the Corinthians, Lefkádha became a major seat of power, and played an important part in the Peloponnesian War in the fourth century BC; however, much of the archeological detail from this period has disappeared beneath farmland and more recent settlements. During the Byzantine period, the island fell into the same Byzantine "theme", or regional administration, as Kefalloniá and Zákinthos. Venetian rule on Lefkádha was shorter than elsewhere in the Ionian, lasting just over a hundred years from 1684 to 1797, and was interrupted, briefly, when the Turks captured the island – not for the first time – in 1715.

Like other Ionian islands, Lefkádha developed an extensive olive industry under the Venetians, but it also built its wealth on currants and wine grapes. The island's other **specialities** include honey (often produced by bees fed on thyme), mandolato nougat, almonds, and strong island wines and retsina. Lefkádha also has its own tradition of **kantáthes** and other folk-song forms, which can only be heard in village festivals and in certain tavernas in Lefkádha Town.

There has been much pedantic debate over whether Lefkádha is a real island at all. It appears originally to have been joined to the mainland by a narrow isthmus, through which the Corinthians excavated a channel in the sixth century BC – although those who argue in favour of its island status suggest that the Corinthians may simply have been clearing a pre-existing channel that had silted up. The northernmost tip of the island at Lefkádha Town, barely a hundred metres from the mainland, is connected to the region of Akarnanía by a causeway with a boat bridge built into it, which is opened every hour on the hour to allow yachts and small boats to pass through. This makes Lefkádha very accessible to Greeks from the mainland, who invade the island in high summer, and it's also very popular with Italian drivers arriving in the region by ferry. Buses connect Lefkádha Town to Préveza, half an hour's drive north, and there are ferry connections to Itháki (from Nidhrí) and Kefalloniá (from Vassilikí). These connections have given an unusual configuration to tourism on Lefkádha. In high season, especially the first two weeks of August, when the island hosts an **international folkloric festival**, the place is packed, and rooms can

Préveza

Though the majority of tourists visiting Lefkádha use its airport, few ever see the town of **PRÉVEZA**, 2km to the east. The airport actually stands on, and takes its name from, the sandy peninsula of Áktio, off which the Battle of Actium was fought in 31 BC, when the emperor Octavian's fleet decisively defeated that of Antony and Cleopatra. Anyone staying in Préveza itself is advised to walk (about 15min) or take a taxi from the airport only as far as the ferry across the entrance to the Amvrakíkos Gulf; after the ten-minute crossing (80dr), everything in Préveza is within short walking distance of the ferry quay.

Préveza can boast a pleasant seafront and a newly renovated centre, and is very popular with Greek holidaymakers, even though there are no beaches beyond a thin strip of imported sand. It's also a useful base for visiting either **Nikópolis**, the ancient city whose walls and foundations can be seen 2km north of town, or the **Amvrakíkos wetlands** skirting the Gulf of Amvrakíkos which extends 20km inland from the town. The wetlands are one of the biggest wildlife sanctuaries in Greece, but are only really accessible with your own vehicle.

The town is built on a grid system, with most facilities – tavernas, bars, shops, hotels – a few minutes' walking distance from the quay. It's book-ended by two large medieval forts, the **castles of St George and St Andrew**, but both are in use by the armed forces (who have quite a presence in Préveza) and off limits to the public.

Buses arrive at the KTEL station on Ioánninon, the first true road reached through the grid of alleys behind the seafront. Services are basic: 4 daily from Athens (6hr); 1–2 daily from Igoumenítsa (not Sun; 3hr); 8–10 daily from Ioánnina (not Sun; 3hr); 3–4 daily from Lefkádha Town (30min); 3–4 daily from Párga (not Sun; 2hr); and 1 daily from Thessaloníki (not Sat or Sun; 7hr). The **tourist office** (Mon–Fri 8am–1pm) is in the government building at the west end of the seafront. There are

be almost impossible to find in the main resorts. Outside these resorts, however, Lefkádha is the least Anglophone of the Ionian islands, and even in the four-star hotels in Lefkádha Town staff will often expect you to speak Greek. A few years ago, the island took the unusual step of closing its only tourism information office, and the tourism police are unable to offer any more assistance than the phone numbers of rooms in the town. That said, after Corfu, **Lefkádha Town** is the most sophisticated of the island capitals, with a cinema, clubs, bookshops, and a main shopping street where you can buy anything from a cowbell to a computer.

Arrival and getting around

Most visitors arrive via **Préveza (Áktio) airport**, 40km to the north on the mainland and only 2km west of Préveza town across the narrow entrance to the Amvrakíkos Gulf (see box). There are no dedicated buses from the airport to the town of Préveza or to Lefkádha, although the bus from Préveza to Lefkádha Town passes the airport four times daily (3 on Sun). The bus can be flagged down

various **banks** on Odhós Ethnikí Antistásis, the pedestrian precinct two alleys back from the seafront, plus a 24-hour money exchange machine on Ioánninon.

Because Préveza is very popular with Greek tourists, there are no cheap hotels and no rooms in the centre. The nearest **rooms** are in the suburb of Pantokrátoras, 3km northeast of town: try Evgenia Peroni (☎0682/27 745 or 26 640), Elias Katsimbokis (☎0682/24 227), or Gerasioula Rouga (☎0682/29 454 or 28 965). The best-value **hotels** are the newly renovated apartment-hotel *Urania*, at Irínis 33, the diagonal thoroughfare through the centre of town (☎0682/27 123 or 24 307; ③), and the simple but pleasant *Minos*, in an alley off Odhós XXI Octóvrios in the centre of town (☎0682/28 424 or 27 424; ②). The large, modern *Preveza City* (☎0682/27 370 or 27 365, fax 23 872; ④) is away from the hubbub of the seafront, although on busy Ioánninon, and is the only hotel in Préveza that accepts a wide range of credit cards. More upmarket again are the *Dioni* on Platía Papageórgiou (☎0682/27 381–2, fax 27 384; ⑤), a small, comfortable hotel tucked away from the crowds in the centre of town, and the smart *Hotel Avra* (☎0682/21 230, fax 26 454; ④), across the road from the ferry quay and consequently in the middle of the action. Two **travel agencies** offer a wide variety of accommodation and other services: *Kiss Travel* (☎0682/23 753 or 23 157, fax 28 846) and *Elias Stamatis* (☎0682/23 003 or 21 025), both on the seafront.

Préveza has a trio of fine **taverna-psistariés**: *Ambrosia* and *Stavaraka* behind the Club Mercedes and *Néa Demokratía* building on the seafront, and the *Psistaria Delfinaki* on Zapountzáki off the front. The seafront is lined with a number of garish music and cocktail **bars**, but the best places for a night out are the *Cafe Amico* gelateria-pizzeria near the ferry dock and neighbouring *Orange Mecanique*, and the *Olympia Kafenio* on the front by the fountain, which does splendid *mezédhes* with drinks at night.

outside the airport entrance, barely 200m from Arrivals. Taxis to Lefkádha Town from the airport are negotiable, but expect to pay 4000–5000dr.

It's worth pointing out that Préveza airport is still largely a military base, home to SEAC early-warning planes with their distinctive disc-like radar, and the high-tech jets that streak through the islands on training runs. The authorities are particularly sensitive about security, and the armed guards are extremely strict with queues for outbound flights and even people chatting to friends through the fences that bound the tiny airport building. Photography is banned, as at other Greek airports. Beyond a small bar and exchange kiosk, there are no other services at the airport.

Lefkádha Town's **bus station**, on Odhós Dimítri Golémi opposite the small yacht marina, has connections from Athens and Thessaloníki, and is the hub of island transport. The station's new computerized system issues tickets with numbered seats, which you should use to avoid potential confusion, although outside the town it's normal to pay on board and sit anywhere. The bus station is the most efficient and friendly in the islands, although the more remote services sometimes vary wildly from the faded timetable in the waiting room. It's worth remembering that services to remote destinations such as Atháni stop early, and last buses frequently turn round immediately, with no later return service. There's also a smaller ticket office and bus stop where Golémi turns into Odhós Merárchias, but this is favoured by locals using longer-distance island buses to get to the suburbs, and often resembles a small-scale riot.

Taxis are easy to find outside the siesta, and even the smaller villages in the interior have at least one resident taxi driver; a cab from Lefkádha to Vassilikí, a distance of some 38km, will cost in the region of 8000dr. In emergencies, bars, shops and travel agencies will usually telephone a cab for you. Cars and motorbikes can be rented in Lefkádha Town and the main resorts.

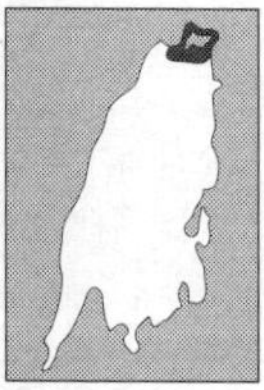

Lefkádha Town and around

LEFKÁDHA TOWN is compact, squeezed between a seawater lagoon – the *Ichthiotrofrío*, quite literally "fish pond" – and the foothills on the north side of Mount Stavróta. Like neighbouring Kefalloniá and Itháki, it was devastated by the 1953 earthquakes, and little remains of the original town beyond a number of small, private chapels. Sitting on a stunted peninsula, the town comprises one central thoroughfare, **Odhós Dörpfeld**, a trio of seafront roads (Golémi, Panagoú and Sikeliánou), and a warren of minor streets and mainly pedestrian alleys that vein the heart of the town. As a precaution against further earthquake damage, few buildings are above three storeys. The dormitory area of the town, west of Dörpfeld, took even greater precautions: most houses are built of

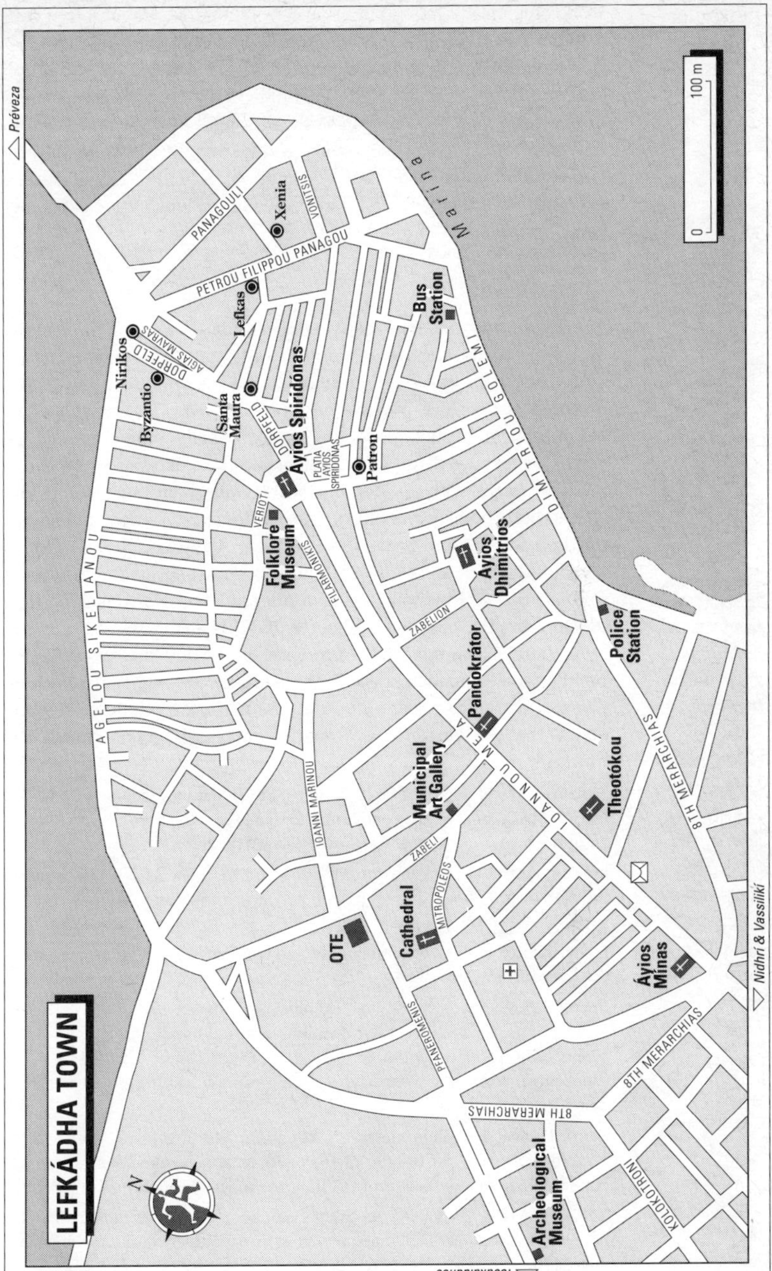
LEFKÁDHA TOWN
Préveza
Yira
Tsoukaladhes
Nidhri & Vassilikí
0
100 m
Marina
Xenia
Nirikos
Byzantio
Lefkas
Santa Maura
Ayios Spiridónas
Patron
Bus Station
Folklore Museum
Áyios Dhimítrios
Pandokrátor
Police Station
Municipal Art Gallery
Theotókou
OTE
Cathedral
Áyios Minas
Archeological Museum
PANAGOULI
VONITSIS
PETROU FILIPPOU PANAGOU
AGIAS MAVRAS
DORPFELD
VERIOTI
PLATIA AYIOS SPIRIDONAS
FILARMONIKIS
ZABELION
DIMITRIOU GOLEMI
AGELOU SIKELIANOU
IOANNI MARINOU
IOANNOU MELA
ZABELI
MITROPOLEOS
8TH MERARCHIAS
PFANEROMENIS
KOLOKOTRONI

stone only on the ground floor, and wood on the second, often with wooden balconies. The closely built houses with their small, elaborately planted gardens give this district the look of lanes you might find on Romney Marsh or Fire Island, perhaps even the flatter parts of old San Francisco.You can walk the length of the whole town in ten minutes, and traverse it in around five, but despite its size Lefkádha Town is surprisingly cosmopolitan, with a cinema, some excellent tavernas, cocktail bars, clubs and a small but hectic souvenir bazaar.

Accommodation

The few **rooms** that are available in Lefkádha Town tend to be in the dormitory area on the west side of town, between Odhós Dörpfeld and the lagoon. Few houses have telephones, so most accommodation has to be found on foot. If your Greek isn't up to negotiating a room, householders are usually happy to find an English-speaking neighbour to translate. Rooms tend to be cheap and very basic, with wooden floors and walls, spare furnishing, and shared bathrooms with cold running water only. To book ahead, try the Lefkádha Room-owners Association, based in Nidhrí (Odhós Megálo Vlachí 8; ☎0645/92 701 or 92 027; ②–③) or the *Pinepolis Rooms*, Odhós Pinépolis, a small alley off the seafront two short blocks from the pontoon bridge (☎0645/24 175; ②).

There's no campsite in Lefkádha Town, now that Camping Fryni *has closed down; head for the bus station where you can catch a bus 5km south to* La Pissina Camping *at Kariótes (see p.129).*

As there is little space for expansion on the outskirts of Lefkádha, building has remained static in the town for several years, with no new **hotels** built in over a decade. The half-dozen that do exist are all at the northern tip of town, from Platía Áyios Spiridónas upwards:

Byzantio, Dörpfeld 40 (☎0645/22 629). Small and basic modern hotel, but less of a bargain than the comparable *Patron*. Located above its own taverna in the busiest section of town, with shared facilities. ②.

Lefkas, Petroú Filípa Panáyou 2 (☎0645/23 916, fax 24 579). In a prime location overlooking the lagoon, with excellent rooms and facilities. ⑤.

Nirikos, Áyias Mávras (☎0645/24 132–3, fax 23 756). Very comfortable modern hotel, with its own restaurant and bar, and en-suite rooms overlooking the causeway. ④.

Patron, Platía Áyios Spiridónas (☎0645/22 359). A bargain, with clean, basic rooms, shared hot-water facilities and cold water in rooms. Some rooms have wonderful views of the *platía*, which can be a mixed blessing, especially in high season, when you can forget about getting any sleep before 2am. ②.

Santa Maura, Spiridhón Viánta 2 (☎0645/22 342 or 22 552, fax 26 253). Tucked in an alley off the top of Dörpfeld, smart en-suite rooms, with air-conditioning and double-glazing to fight the town's heat and noise. ③.

Xenia, Panágou 2 (☎0645/24 762–3, fax 25 129). Large modern B-class hotel, with restaurants and bars, aimed at the wealthier tourist and business market. ④.

The Town

Lefkádha Town is the most walkable of all the island capitals. Indeed, given the difficulty of actually getting a vehicle into the centre, it's almost obligatory. Nightlife and tavernas are clustered around the top of Dörpfeld, and most of the churches and museums are either on or near Dörpfeld or Ioánnou Méla, the street it runs into south of the Italianate Platía Áyios Spiridónas at the heart of town.

The Folklore Museum and Municipal Art Gallery

Located in the warren of streets to the west of Platía Áyios Spiridónas, the **Folklore Museum** houses a modest collection of traditional artefacts, but its series of photographs of the town before the 1953 earthquake is fascinating, and it contains some interesting models of Dörpfeld's excavations on the island (see p.119). The displays of domestic items – furniture, beds, cookware and clothes, including some beautiful women's costume wear for island festivals – take up three rooms and could, at a pinch, provide an hour's diversion from the heat or rain. For a different slant on Lefkadhan life, you might check out the **Municipal Art Gallery** on Mitropoléos, which occasionally features interesting exhibitions by local artists.

The Folklore Museum on Filarmoníkis is open Mon–Fri 9am–9pm; 200dr.

Churches

A number of small private **churches** dotted around the town, mostly dating from the eighteenth century, have so far survived the earthquakes, but even these have had to take the precaution of erecting free-standing bell towers built of iron. Modest in size, their architecture is atypical of the region in abandoning Byzantine design for simple, single-aisled rectangular buildings that would survive earthquakes.

The churches are opulently decorated with screens and icons by painters of the **Ionian School**, including its founder, **Panayiotis Doxaras**. Born on Zákinthos in 1662, Doxaras studied in Italy and introduced Renaissance influences, including those of Leonardo da Vinci, into his work, while simultaneously abandoning the traditions of Byzantine painting. Doxaras taught painting, and also produced his own translation of Andrea Pozzo's book, *Concise Instructions of the Painting of Frescoes*. The Ionian School, which has been described as a regional school of Italian painting, flourished under Doxaras and his son, Nikolaos. The school's work is typified by naturalistic representation of their subject matter – the saints – often in workaday settings. Doxaras senior, who also painted the original ceilings of Áyios Spirídhon in Corfu which were destroyed by damp, was responsible for the paintings in the church of **Áyios Dhimítrios** on Zabélion, his son for the ceiling paintings of **Áyios Mínas**, at the crossroads of Méla and Merárchias. The latter church has a striking metal clock tower and some of the best examples of the Ionian School, including work by Nikolaos Koutouzis and Lefkádha's most famous pupil of the school, Spiridon Ventouris.

Most of Lefkádha Town's pre-quake churches are privately owned by island families, and open and close erratically; before and after morning and evening services are the best times to visit.

The church of the **Pandokrátor**, on Ioánnou Méla, is owned by the family of the poet and politician Aristotelis Valaoritis (1824–1879), who rivals the Zakinthian poet Solomos for the title of father of modern Greek literature, and is entombed behind the altar of the church. Further down Ioánnou Méla is the church of the **Theotókou** (or Presentation of the Virgin), which has ceiling friezes copied from the work of Raphael by Lefkadhan painter Spiridon Gazis, and the only remaining stone bell tower in Lefkádha.

The Archeological Museum

The Archeological Museum is open Tues–Sun 9am–1pm; free.

A five-minute walk west of Áyios Mínas on Pfaneroménis is the **Archeological Museum**, a modest one-room collection of artefacts unearthed by Dörpfeld. Most of the important finds have been taken to Athens, but there remain here details of columns, axes, jewellery, pottery and lamps, as well as photographs of Dörpfeld at work at Nidhrí when it was little more than a collection of huts. Unfortunately, the labelling is limited to Greek and German.

Eating and drinking

Much of Lefkádha's evening entertainment is centred on Dörpfeld and its surrounding streets and alleys, and in particular the small elegant square of Áyios Spiridónas church. Surrounded on three sides by bars and restaurants, busking musicians, jugglers and fire-eaters often perform here on summer evenings. However, with the exception of old-fashioned *Ouzeria Thalassina* in the square itself, establishments in this area are the priciest in town. The north end of Dörpfeld is as hectic as London's West End in high season, with garish souvenir shops and tourists spilling out of cafés and bars onto the streets.

Less expensive **bars** are to be found away from the centre, particularly along the southerly end of Ioánnou Méla. The best of these is the *Cafe Karfakis*, an old-style *kafenío* with straw-upholstered wooden seats, and ancient phonographs and 78s decorating the interior. Staff are helpful and in the evenings provide generous servings of *mezédhes* (often resembling miniature meals) with drinks, a tradition that has all but died out in most tourist bars. The hippest watering hole on Lefkádha is the difficult-to-find *Vengera Club*, tucked away on tiny Odhós Maxáira (signposted up an alley one block down Dimítriou Golémi from the bus station). This little-known hangout has a cool jazz and funk music policy, reasonably priced drinks and snacks, and a quiet walled garden away from the crowds on Dörpfeld.

Lefkádha Town's best local **restaurants** are hidden away in the alleys west of Dörpfeld by Áyios Spiridónas. *Taverna Reganto*, on tiny Dimarkoú Venióti and signposted by the church, is the favourite here: island cuisine at its best, in a simple, friendly setting that's always full of locals. In high season its opening hours can be erratic, so if it's closed head for the *Lighthouse*, on Filarmoníkis, which has its own

The Lefkádha Festival of Language and Arts

Each August, Lefkádha hosts a three-week **folk arts festival**, which attracts performers and visitors from around the world (so it's not a good time for finding rooms). Troupes come from eastern and western Europe, South America and elsewhere, performing mainly in Lefkádha Town, but also in villages around the island. The island and mainland Greece respond with troupes of their own musicians and dancers, as well as concerts and theatre performances: the 1996 festival, for example, featured a dramatization of Antoine de Saint-Exupéry's novel, *The Little Prince*, and a production of Brecht's *The Good Woman of Szechuan*. For details, call ☎0645/23 352.

small garden and a range of succulent, freshly cooked taverna dishes. Larger and more tourist-oriented is the *Romantika* on Mitropoléos, with eyebrow-raising, almost postmodern decor, a small garden at the rear, and a vast menu of grills, seafood, salads and oven-baked staples. In season, the *Romantika* hosts nightly performances of Lefkadhan *kantáthes*; if you'd prefer a quieter evening, try the *Taverna Vitsounis* opposite. The smartest restaurant in town is the *Adriatica*, at the corner of Pfaneroménis and Merárchias, a rather barn-like establishment with a mixture of Greek and international dishes, where people tend to dress up to eat. There are also a couple of upmarket restaurants facing the yacht quay on Golémi, the international-style *Sto Molo*, and the more traditional *psistariá O Karavoulias*. Both are favoured by the yachting fraternity, although the view is marred by incessant traffic and, in summer, the smell of drains. If the melee of Dörpfeld is your preferred backdrop for a lively evening meal, the *Eftikia* by the *Hotel Santa Maura* is recommended. For a pastry or breakfast, try the *Gustoso Zaharoplastio* at the south end of Méla.

Listings

Banks Both the Ionian Bank and the National Bank of Greece have branches on Ioánnou Méla, the former at the southern end, the latter midway down. The Agricultural Bank of Greece is situated in the corner of Platía Áyios Spiridónas. Banks only open mornings (Mon–Fri 8am–1.30pm); outside these hours, the post office, larger hotels and travel agencies will change travellers' cheques but not always at bank rates.

Bookshops There are no dedicated English-language bookshops on the island, although some Greek bookshops stock foreign-language guides and paperback fiction in English, German and Dutch. Most accessible are the *Katopodis*, *Konidaris*, *Mataragas* and *Tsiribasis* stores, all of them on Ioánnou Méla.

Car rental EuroHire, Golémi 5 (☎0645/267 76), a few doors from the bus station, is the best bet for car and motorbike hire.

Cinema The *Cinema Eleni*, beyond the Archeological Museum on Pfaneroménis, is the only outdoor cinema in the Ionians, set in a small, overgrown garden with a large screen attached to a handy block of flats. Its fare is mostly subtitled English-language films, with programmes changed daily (9pm

& 11pm; 1200dr); as well as the usual parade of American blockbusters, it can also startle with the occasional art-house movie. Be sure to wear long clothes and/or mosquito repellent.

Hospital Corner of Mitropoléos and Zabélion (☎0645/22 336).

Laundries There are two laundries/drycleaners on Ioánnou Méla, but laundry doesn't come cheap – you can expect to pay 200dr and upwards per item, more if you want it ironed.

Library Ioánni Marínou (Tues–Sat 8.30am–1.30pm).

OTE Corner of Zabélion and Pfaneroménis (daily 7am–10pm).

Police Golémi 1 (☎0645/22 100).

Post office Ioánnou Méla (Mon–Fri 7am–2.30pm).

Around Lefkádha Town

The main point of interest in the immediate vicinity of Lefkádha Town is the impressive semi-ruined **castle of Santa Maura**, squatting on the other side of the causeway to the mainland, a ten-minute walk from the north end of Odhós Dörpfeld. The fort, which now comprises three structures – Santa Maura itself, and the George and Alexander forts built during the Russian occupation – was started in the fourteenth century by the Orsini family, and was extensively rebuilt by the Venetians in the eighteenth century. However, much of the interior was destroyed when an explosives magazine accidentally blew up in 1888, and bombing during World War II further damaged the structure. Parts of what remains of the fortifications are open to the public daily, and are used as a spectacular backdrop to performances during the arts festival (see p.127).

Yíra beach

Lefkádha Town has an excellent boomerang-shaped beach, **Yíra**, on the seaward side of the lagoon. You can catch a bus there during high season from the bus station (hourly 9am–4pm), or it's a pleasant forty-minute walk from town, heading out westwards along Sikeliánou; alternatively, you can walk there along the sea road on the opposite side of the pontoon bridge, perhaps combining it with a visit to Santa Maura Castle.

Roughly 4km long, the shingle beach is often virtually deserted even in high season, save for the occasional cuddling couple or nudist bather hiding in its most secluded spots – which, paradoxically, are in the centre (look out for the flagpole with an anemometer on top). The beach is bookended by two **tavernas**, and at the western end there are a couple of **bars**: one is housed in the first of four renovated windmills, while the larger *Club Milos* also serves as a restaurant by day and a club by night, where the local kids and the odd windsurfer while away afternoons and nights to the accompaniment of nosebleed techno and other rave culture imports. The presence of the windmills attests to the power of the prevailing winds here, which can produce small, choppy surf, although few windsurfers seem to have caught on to Yíra, opting for the flatter Vassilikí instead.

Faneroméni monastery

Easily accessible on foot from Lefkádha Town, or from the south end of Yíra beach, the picture-postcard **Faneroméni monastery** is the major ecclestiastical attraction on the island. From the outside, it resembles a large Swiss ski chalet, but this effect disappears once inside the spacious courtyard, which houses a chapel with beautiful stained glass windows, a crammed museum, small and austere monks' cells, a bookshop and even public toilets. The monastery was originally built in the seventeenth century, but was destroyed by fire and rebuilt in the last century. During the German occupation of the island in World War II, the monks were forbidden to sound bells lest this be used as a code. They resorted to sounding a large wooden log, which hangs in the main entrance; nowadays, a solitary monk tends the building. Skimpy clothing is frowned on, though women can borrow capes (hanging on hooks by the entrance) to cover their shoulders. Near the main entrance to the monastery are some excellent shady walks along signed paths through the pine woods.

Faneroméni monastery is open daily 8am–2pm & 4–8pm; free. The quickest way to reach it from town is to walk along Pfaneroménis and up the lane from the hamlet of Fríni, which gives excellent views over town, lagoon and mainland (30min).

The east coast to Vassilikí

Lefkádha's east coast is the most accessible part of the island, and in parts is beginning to resemble Corfu's east coast, as the small resorts strung along the coast road expand and merge into one another. Most people head for, or find themselves deposited in, the major settlements of **Nidhrí** or **Vassilikí**, but there are also a number of more remote resorts, such as **Sívota** and **Mikrós Yialós**, and some fine walking routes around **Mount Stavróta**.

Kariótes and Ligiá

Travelling south out of Lefkádha, the first village you'll arrive at, barely 3km from town, is **KARIÓTES**, now more of a satellite suburb and with no seafront beyond the *álykes* (salt pans) outside the village – which, like their namesakes on Zákinthos, are as fascinating as, well, watching salt dry. Kariótes does, however, have the best **campsite** on Lefkádha: *La Pissina*, a small site hard by the coast road south of the village, but set back on lush grass beneath olive trees, with washing facilities, a shop, bar, restaurant and a small pool (☎0645/71 103). There's little else around it, but the island buses stop just outside.

The first stop of note on the route south is **LIGIÁ**, a working fishing harbour, with views across to the ruined castle of Áyios Yióryios on the mainland, and a couple of narrow but clean shingle beaches on its outskirts – the best bet is **Tempéli**, just south of the port, with a beach bar and shady pines. There's little here to detain the independent traveller, though the choice of **accommodation** is reasonable, including the *Konaki* (☎0645/71 267 or 71 397, fax 71 125; ③), a smart B-class hotel on the edge of the village with pool and gardens. If you prefer an apartment (all ③) try *Marios Mezzinis* (☎0645/71 332), *Maura* (☎0645/22 649 or 24 587) or *Verde Apartments* (☎0645/22 536); for village rooms, contact Katina Gourzi (☎0645/71 105; ②) or the *psistariá, O Yannis* (☎0645/71 336; ②). The fishing trade supplies a number of excellent **tavernas**, such as *O Zouras* on the quay, *Paradisos* above Tempéli beach and *Marios* on the road out of town, and there are a couple of **bars**, *Xenis* and the oddly named *Arts Club*.

Epískopos and Nikianá

Two kilometres on is the shallow pebbly bay of **EPÍSKOPOS**, which shelters *Episcopos Beach* (☎0645/71 388), a basic but shady **campsite** with a shop, restaurant, grill and bar, and wash facilities. It shares the beach with the *Dukato* (☎0645/71 122; ⑥), a stylish **hotel** with gardens overlooking the bay.

Epískopos may shortly become a suburb of the port of **NIKIANÁ**, which is smaller than Ligiá but shows more signs of development. It too has a working harbour, with a beach just beyond. The beach is another narrow strand of shingle, with rocky outcrops; far better is the strand on the other side of the bay, accessible from the main road but with no facilities. Nikianá has two **hotels**, the newly built and family-run *Pegasos* (☎0645/71 766, fax 25 290; ⑥), with gardens and en-suite rooms that have sea views, and the smarter, but smaller *Ionion* (☎0645/71 720; ④). There are also a number of apartment developments: *Philigros* (☎0645/24 310) has studios built around an overgrown garden off the main road; *Vicky Apartments* (☎0645/71 555) is a small, upmarket establishment, with its own gardens and bar, but overlooking the road. There are three **tavernas** overlooking the small harbour, of which the best is the *Pantazis Psistaria*, which also has rooms to let.

Nidhrí

Beyond Nikianá, a series of small coves leads on to the hamlet of Perigiálli, where the sprawling resort of **NIDHRÍ** begins. Nidhrí is where most package travellers to Lefkádha will find themselves, and offers boat trips to Meganíssi and the satellite islands. It's also the prettiest of the resorts along this coast, with some fine pebble beaches and a lovely setting, at the mouth of a three-kilometre-long inlet, facing out towards the Gení peninsula and the islands of Madhourí, Spartí and Skórpios. Just as breathtaking as the sea views in Nidhrí, however, are the car fumes. Some high-season mornings and evenings, when two whistle-wielding traffic cops are fielded to massage traffic flow, the town actually develops its own smog problem. And, on top of the traffic congestion, the centre is scarred by the ugly, unchecked development along the main road, with many hotel rooms just metres from the traffic, which is busy day and night.

Fortunately, there's a tailor-made escape in the form of Nidhrí's very own **waterfall**, about a 45-minute walk inland (5min by car). On the road beyond the hamlet of Ráhi, a signposted track leads to a small waterfall on the left, which shouldn't be mistaken for the main fall, further along the path. Depending on the weather, the waterfall's pool can be big enough to swim in and makes a great place for a picnic. The walk from Nidhrí is pleasant and on level ground, through a rocky gorge with overhanging rocks and a flood-stream strewn with snowy-white boulders. There's some shade en route, but the walk is best attempted in the cool of early morning or late afternoon.

Accommodation

Hotels tend to fill up fast in Nidhrí and generally aren't cheap, but the town does boast one of the best places to stay on the island: the *Hotel Gorgona* (☎0645/92 268 or 923 74, fax 92 558; ②), which offers an unbeatable mix of position (away from the busy main road), price and welcome. It's set in its own lush, subtropical garden, signposted two minutes' walk along the road to Ráhi, and offers good, modern en-suite rooms with balconies at bargain rates. You'll have to speak some Greek, but the owner, Maria Gazi, and her staff are unfailingly friendly and helpful.

Much of the accommodation in and around the village is run by travel agents, who can offer a wider choice of rooms, apartments and villas than the individual room-owners – see "Listings" on p.132 for details.

Nidhrí also has a number of hotels on the beach, notably the two *Nidrion Beach Hotels*, the second of which is in fact an extension of the first (☎0645/92 400 or 92 401, fax 92 151; ⑤). They offer modern, C-class comfort in en-suite rooms, some with good views of the islands. In the centre of town, the smart *Bel Air* apartment hotel is air-conditioned and double-glazed against the noise, and has its own pool, bar and other facilities (☎0645/92 125; ④). Of the **rooms** to let, Emilios Gazis (☎0645/92 703; ②) and Athanasios Konidaris (☎0645/92 749; ③), both in the centre of Nidhrí, provide some of the best.

Eating and drinking

Nidhrí's core is the dozen or so tavernas and bars that line its quay, the grandly named **Ákti Aristotéli Onási** – now mostly used as a car park, but the view just about compensates for this sorry waste of one of the island's prime sites. At night, the quay comes alive: day-trip boats string lights in their rigging and there's usually a street market offering anything from books and toys to palmistry and tarot readings. Some of the most popular restaurants have queues for tables; others have hired greeters to lure punters off the pavement.

The *Barrel* **taverna** here dishes up an interesting variety of local dishes and north European food, especially fish, with exotica such as bream (a local speciality) cooked in a whisky sauce. The *Bistro* has a simpler mix of Greek and international, as well as snacks, and an amusingly cheeky line in self-promotion. *Il Sappore* lays on a vast range of pizzas and pasta, but if you want a quieter meal head for the beachfront *Agra Beach* taverna, under the hotel of the same name, which specializes in traditional Ionian dishes like *pastítsio* and is very popular with Greeks. Nightlife is limited to **bars** like *No Name* and *Byblos*, and the *Sail Inn Club*, a music bar-disco which claims to stay open 22 hours a day.

Boat trips

For more on Lefkádha's satellite islands, see p.142.

Most people staying in Nidhrí seem to spend a lot of their time trying to leave it, if only on the myriad **boat trips** heading out to the islands of Madhourí, Spartí, Skórpios and Meganíssi. The boats line up along the quay each morning, ready for departure between 9 and 10am (around 3000dr per person), returning late afternoon. Most craft are interchangeable: small fibreglass *kaíkia*, with small bars and toilets, and open seating areas on the top deck or aft. Where they do differ, however, is in their itinerary – some will take in the sea caves of Meganíssi, others not, so it's advisable to check. The islands are all close to each other, so the journeys between them are short and sheltered. One of the best alternatives to these fibreglass buckets is the large wooden *Motor Sailer Panagiota*, a handsome old-fashioned *kaíki* run by and moored behind the *Barrel* taverna; the *Barrel* also offers day-trips on yachts that can take up to sixteen people. *Athos Travel* just south of the Ráhi turning (☎0645/92 185) organize unusual night-time star-watching excursions, as well as other themed boat trips.

Listings

Car rental As well as from the travel agencies mentioned below, car rental is available from branches of Eurohire (☎0645/26 776), Avis (☎0645/92 136) and Hertz (☎0645/92 289), all in the centre of Nidhrí.

Doctor Surgery by the town hall (Mon–Fri mornings only).

Exchange There are no banks in Nidhrí – most travel agencies offer bank rates, and the post office (see below) changes travellers' cheques.

Laundrette The island's sole self-service laundry, *Sunclean*, is situated at the southern end of town, opposite the *Athos Hotel*, and opens till late.

Post office A bright-yellow travelling post office parks by the town hall in the centre of the village Mon–Fri 9am–2pm.

Travel agents Nidhrí's travel agencies are all close to each other on the main road. Biggest is the island-wide *Samba Tours* (☎0645/92 658 or 92 035, fax 92 659) which offers rooms, as well as the usual range of travel, car rental and exchange services. Similarily, *Nidri Travel* (☎0645/92 514, fax 92 256) offers rooms and apartments, car rental and tickets, and can also arrange sailing-boat charters and jeep safaris to the more inaccessible parts of the island.

Homer (☎0645/92 554; fax 92 627) rents out rooms, apartments and a wide range of cars and bikes (motor or pedal).

Vlihós and the Géni peninsula

When Nidhrí finally peters out, the country reverts to flat olive groves. Just outside the village limits, near the hamlet of Kámbos, are the main set of **excavations** by Dörpfeld, a small circle of Mycenean burial chambers, which produced some of the finds displayed in the Archeological Museum in Lefkádha Town. A kilometre beyond the Dörpfeld site is the turning for the small hamlet of Haradiátika, which is one of the main routes up onto the island's highest mountain, **Mount Stavróta**. Haradiátika is erratically served by the Vassilikí bus, has just one taverna, but is a favourite with walkers, who use the rough road to the even smaller hamlet of Áyios Illías to reach the 1100-metre summit.

About 3km from Nidhrí, the main road comes to **VLIHÓS**, which looks out over the marshy flats at the bottom of the inlet – a veritable mosquito factory in summer. Vlihós is popular with freelance and bareboat yacht sailors, but has no hotels and little to detain the traveller, apart from a few rooms and a handful of tavernas like *O Thalassolikos* on the seafront by the village's tiny square.

From Vlihós, a minor road leads round to the **Géni peninsula**, where those who want to enjoy the view of the inlet but escape the madness of Nidhrí can find **accommodation**: *Villa Maria Rooms* (☎0645/95 153; ③), *Ilios Club* apartments (☎0645/95 612; ②) and *Australias* apartments (☎0645/95 521; ③). The road ends after 3km at the tiny chapel of Áyia Kiriáki, where Dörpfeld is buried, and which has excellent views of Nidhrí and the hills beyond.

Over the saddle of the Géni peninsula, **Dessími bay** is a large expanse of blue water cutting deep into high green hills, behind which it loses the sun early. It's flanked by two neighbouring **campsites** which, confusingly, are reached by two different (and steep) lanes, even though only a fence separates them. *Santa Maura Camping* (☎0645/95 007, 95 493 or 95 270; fax 26 087), the further and larger of the two, is a basic site with washing facilities, shop, bar and a simple taverna-snack bar, but it's shady, with a fair sprinkling of olive trees. The beach in front is narrow, pebbly and, in high summer, tangled with the lines from innumerable powered inflatables in the water. The similar *Dessimi Beach Camping* (☎0645/95 374, 95 225 or 95 328), which gives onto a wider and cleaner stretch of beach, has a better taverna, but in high season is packed bumper to bumper with large RVs.

Póros and Mikrós Yialós

From Vlihós, the main road south winds sharply up into the hills, passing through the quiet hamlets of Katohóri and Paliokatoúna, where a turning leads down to the attractive village of **PÓROS** and on to the small resort of Mikrós Yialós. Don't mistake Póros's presence on the map as a sign of tourism development – it's quiet even at the height of the season, and its few tavernas and bars close during the daytime. **MIKRÓS YIALÓS** is a four-kilometre trek downhill (the twice-daily bus from Lefkádha Town turns back at Póros), and the number of cars using the road is a sign that this isn't the quiet beach you may have hoped for. The small bay boasts a handful of **tavernas**, a few rooms at *Oceanis Studios* (☎0654/95 095–6, fax 95 095; ②), plus the upmarket *Poros Beach Camping* (☎0654/23 203), which has bungalows (②), shops and a pool. The pebble beach is clean, and the lack of any waterborne traffic in the long Rouda Bay that leads out to the open sea keeps the water clear. The *Mermaid* taverna is expanding into a small hotel here, and Mikrós Yialós looks set to start climbing back up the hill.

Inland to Sívros

About 2km on from Paliokatoúna, a right turn off the main road leads up into the hills, shortly passing the untouched village of **FTÉRNO**. The village *kafenío* and the *psistariá*, *O Haris*, are good spots to break your journey, though the sight of a tourist is still enough to draw a small crowd of bemused children and the odd inquisitive adult.

Ftérno itself is quite literally a dead end, but further on from the Ftérno turning, along spectacular and sometimes vertiginous mountain roads, are the neighbouring villages of **VOURNIKÁS** and **SÍVROS**. The former sports a pretty town square and fountain, one taverna and two cafés. There's no advertised accommodation, but rooms are sometimes available through the taverna or the cafés. Similarly, Sívros, which has stunning views down over the farming plain behind Vassilikí, is a quiet hill town with one taverna, one cafe and no visible accommodation. There are some private rooms here, but they're difficult to find: enquire in the taverna or café, or ask for the village taxi driver, who might be able to help. There are few facilities in either village, but either could make an excellent walking base, perhaps after an initial investigative trip, away from the hubbub of Vassilikí.

Sívota

The next bay round from Mikrós Yialós – though 14km away by road – is **SÍVOTA**, a long, crooked and beautiful inlet where the sea is not actually visible from the village. Already, however, apartment developments are appearing on the hills around the harbour, and Sívota has become a favourite with yachties, visited by flotillas of the British tour op Sunsail. Nights can be lively, but during the day, even in high season, the place tends to remain fairly quiet. Thom Skliros (☎0645/31 151 or 31 347; ②), at the furthest supermarket on the right of the harbour, has a few **rooms** and there's an unofficial campsite by the bus stop at the edge of the village. The list of facilities extends to two shops, bars, bike and car rental, a pizzeria, and a number of excellent **tavernas**: the *Ionion* is the most popular, but the *Delfinia* and *Kavos* are also good. Sívota has no real beach, just a thin pebbly strand that can be reached by taking an overgrown path along the north side of the harbour. Only two **buses** a day (6.30am and 2.30pm) thread their way down from Lefkádha Town; beyond that you're stuck here, unless you're prepared to negotiate the two-kilometre hike up to the main road to hail down the Vassilikí bus.

Vassilikí and around

Visitors tend to either love or loathe **VASSILIKÍ**. It's nightlife and water sports make it very popular with a young crowd, but island-hopper purists shudder at the intensity of commercialization along its narrow streets and quayside. Nevertheless, the crowds and traffic congestion – eased a little by a one-way system around the village – can't entirely obliterate the charm of its waterfront bars and tavernas, or the view out over its huge bay and spectacular mountains. Be warned, however, that in high season Vassilikí can simply overload with tourists, to the extent that frustrated visitors sometimes have to take a taxi back to Nidhrí, or even up to Sívros, to find a bed for the night. Here, even more than at Lefkádha Town or Nidhrí, it's crucial to phone ahead to book accommodation.

There are no banks in Vassilikí, but the post office at the back of the village and the travel agencies listed below will change travellers' cheques.

Accommodation

Much of Vassilikí's **accommodation** is on or around the one-way system at the centre of the village, which tends to be both busy and noisy. A better bet is to go **beyond the ferry dock** on the northern spur of the harbour, along the road that leads along the back of the beach towards Póndi. The *Paradise* (☎0645/32 156; ②), a basic but friendly hotel overlooking the small rocky beach beyond the dock, is the best bargain here. Also good value for its class is the upmarket *Hotel Apollo* (☎0645/31 122 or 31 141, fax 31 142; ④). Rooms and apartments are available along the beach road to Póndi either through *Pension Holidays* beyond the dock (☎0645/31 011 or 31 426), or approached individually: *Billy's House* (☎0645/31 418 or 39 363), *Christina Politi's Rooms* (☎0645/31 440) and the *Samba Pension* (☎0645/31 555) are smart and purpose-built, though not particularly cheap (all ②–③). Vassilikí's only **campsite**, the large *Camping Vassiliki Beach* (☎0645/31 308 or 31 457, fax 31 458), is about 500m along the beach road. It has its own restaurant, bar and shop, but is comparatively expensive.

In the **centre of town**, the two main hotels are the *Vassiliki Bay Hotel* (☎0645/23 567, fax 22 131; ③), which is quite reasonably priced for its stylish, modern en-suite rooms with balconies and views; and the *Hotel Lefkátas* (☎0645/31 801–3, fax 31 804; ③), a large, modern building with bar, restaurant and disco, overlooking the busiest road in town.

Cars can also be rented from GM Rental *(☎0645/31 650–1, fax 31 651) and* Chris and Alex's *(☎0645/31 580), both near the Póndi turn.*

Rooms in the centre of town tend to disappear into the maw of the package companies who bring clients here. With such a premium on accommodation, few private room-owners are prepared to rent for just one night; many refuse to negotiate for less than a week. Worth trying, preferably in advance, are Yioryios Krisovitsanos (☎0645/31 002; ②), Yioryios Politis (☎0645/31 455; ③) and the upmarket *Pension Kalias* (☎0645/31 003; ④). Or get in touch with one of the local **travel agencies**, which keep a range of accommodation on their books: *Samba Tours* on the road running down to the quay (☎0645/31 520, fax 31 522), *Hirtis Travel* by the Póndi turn (☎0645/31 414, fax 31 127) or *Vassilikí Travel* near *Samba Tours* (☎0645/95 414–5), all of which also offer **car rental**, exchange facilities and a variety of other tourism services.

The beaches

Vassilikí's **beach** is a disappointment, at least for those hoping to spend time on it, as opposed to windsurfing off it. Much of it is stony and pebbly, although it improves towards Póndi (see opposite). The deep bay, protected by an eight-kilometre promontory leading to Cape Lefkátas and by Cape Lipsó on its eastern side, is ideal for **windsurfing**. Prevailing northwesterly winds and local topography produce a fairly stable pattern of onshore winds in the morning and increasing cross-shore winds in the afternoon. Three windsurfing centres now ply their trade on the beach, including *Club Vassiliki*, which claims to be the largest in the world. It offers boards, equipment and tuition from beginner to advanced levels, with simulator boards and video tuition in its club house. Half-day board hire costs 6000dr in the morning (9am–1pm) and around 7000dr in the afternoon (2–6pm).

Club Vassiliki *and* Fanatic Board Centre *can offer complete windsurfing packages to Vassilikí through agents in Britain – see p.6.*

The number of boards on the water at Vassilikí makes swimming slightly hazardous, so most people join the morning queues for the *kaíkia* that ply between the quayside and the excellent sandy beaches of Egrémni and Pórto Katsíki, on the wild, uninhabited west coast of Cape Lefkátas (see p.140).

Eating, drinking and nightlife

Vassilikí's quayside **tavernas** are difficult to differentiate, but standouts include the *Dolphin Psistaria*, near the bus stop on the quay, which offers a large selection of fish and seafood; the glitzier *Restaurant Miramare* at the end of the quay, which has a similar menu, though its outside tables are exposed to prevailing winds; and the *Penguin* in the centre, which specializes in lobster, swordfish and steaks served with exotic sauces. If you're looking for somewhere more peaceful, head for the *Sapfo* taverna-grill near the *Vassiliki Bay Hotel*; for something more unusual, try the *Pirate's Place*, on the one-way system out of the centre, which conjures up dishes ranging from *pastítsio* and fish in beer batter, to stir-fries and curries.

Vassilikí's **nightlife** has developed along with its fashionability among high spenders, although a cynic might diagnose style outstripping content. Where to drink tends to depend on the size of crowds and your taste in music: bars along the front specialize in terms of music policy and develop faithful followings. Amazingly, one of the cheapest places to drink on the entire island is in the centre of the L-shaped quay: the no-name *kafenío* next to the bakery, with tables on the edge of the harbour, which is much favoured by Greeks. There's one club, *Remezzo*, on the beach, which gets more than its fair share of poseurs and designer beefcakes, and flyers sometimes advertise raves on the beach at Pórto Katsíki.

Póndi

Barely a twenty-minute walk along either the beach or the road, the micro-resort of **PÓNDI** has become a quieter alternative to Vassilikí. It has a better, less crowded beach, which even has some patches of sand on the foreshore, though you'll find little **accommodation** here and only a handful of tavernas. About a five-minute walk up from the beach, the *Ponti Beach Hotel* (☎0645/31 572–5, fax 31 576; ④) is very popular with Greek visitors. It has en-suite rooms with excellent views of the bay, a tiny pool, and a bar and restaurant that are open to non-residents. Cheaper rooms are available on the beach at the *Pondi* (☎0645/31 888; ③), and the tour operator Manos Holidays brings clients here.

The west coast

The mountainous and often sheer west coast is the least developed part of Lefkádha, but is blessed with the best beaches, such as picturesque **Aï Nikítas** and **Káthisma**, and some of the island's most interesting villages, clinging to the high mountain roads. **Buses** from Lefkádha Town travel as far as the small, remote village of Atháni, from where a newly metalled road continues 14km to Cape Lefkátas.

Tsoukaládhes and Pefkoúlia beach

TSOUKALÁDHES, just 6km from Lefkádha, is beginning to develop a roadside tourism business, with some tavernas and bars, a small, basic **campsite**, and two sandy beaches a couple of kilometres' hike below the hamlet. Given its proximity to Lefkádha Town, however, and its dull appearance, there's very little reason to stay here.

Four kilometres on, the road plunges down to the sand-and-pebble **Pefkoúlia beach**, one of the longest on the island, with a taverna, *Oinilos*, that has rooms at the north end, and unofficial camping down at the other end, about 3km away. Buses to points further down the west coast stop at either end.

Aï Nikítas

Jammed into a gorge between Pefkoúlia and the next beach, Mýlos, is **AÏ NIKÍTAS**, the prettiest resort on Lefkádha, its wood-clad buildings jumbled together claustrophobically. The beach is small and pebbly, and loses the sun before 6pm even in high season, but it's blessed with crystal-clear water last seen in a David Hockney painting. Sea taxis ply from here to the difficult-to-reach, kilometre-long sandy beach at Mýlos (1000dr return). The back of the village, however, has been left as an ugly, dust-blown car park, which rather detracts from the appeal of the pleasant, if basic, *O Aï Nikitas* **campsite** (☎0645/97 301), set in terraced olive groves.

Accommodation

In between the car park and beach is a short, steep lane of shops, bars and tavernas; most **accommodation** is situated in the alleys that run off this lane. Tourism here is determinedly upmarket, and consequently there are few if any bargains to be had. The best bets are the *Pansion Aphrodite* (☎0645/97 372; ③), the small *Hotel Selene* (☎0645/97 369; ③), and the purpose-built wooden apartments owned by Spiros Verikios (☎0645/97 380; ③). A quieter option is the *Olive Tree* (☎0645/97 453; ③), tucked away on the south side of the village, a friendly, wood-clad hotel with en-suite rooms and balconies, accessible either from the village or the road above it. In the middle of the village, the newly built *Hotel Nefeli* (☎0645/97 400, fax 97 402; ④) and the *Hotel Kalypso* (☎0645/97 332, fax 97 333; ④) offer some of the smartest accommodation, but top of the range is the *Hotel Agios Nikitas* (☎0645/97 460, fax 97 462; ⑤), which has rooms spread through three small balconied buildings built around beautiful gardens. By far the most attractive option, however, has to be the *Pension Ostria* (☎0645/97 483 or 25 318; ④), a beautiful blue and white building above the village with a restaurant-bar overlooking the bay, decorated in a mix of beachcomber and ecclesiastical (driftwood, stones, church relics). The rather small en-suite rooms have similar views of garden and sea, and the bar and restaurant are open to non-residents, making this a good spot to relax if you're just passing through.

Aï Nikítas is within walking distance of both Káthisma (3km) and Kalamítsi (5km), along the dramatic coastal road.

Eating and drinking

Teetering just above the beach, the taverna *Sapfo* offers the best views in Aï Nikítas and a choice of seafood, pasta, grills and salads. The *Taverna Portoni* in the village's one tiny high street also juggles a wide range of fish, pasta and traditional Greek dishes. Tucked up an alley on the north side of the village is the quieter and cheaper *Agnantia*, with an extensive menu and views over village and sea.

Aï Nikítas has a Europcar *rental agency at the top of the village (☎0645/23 581).*

Káthisma beach and Kalamítsi

Beyond Mylos beach is the first of this coast's magnificent beaches, **Káthisma**, served by five daily buses from Lefkádha Town. Viewed from the cliffs above, the beach is stunning, a perfect line of gold sand and dazzling blue sea with a creamy turquoise wash at the water's edge. Close up, the reality is a little more prosaic, and in high season the beach can be scruffy, with no likelihood of improving until the winter storms hoover the Ionian. There's one vast, barn-like **taverna** on the beach, dubbed, obviously after a great deal of deliberation, *Kathisma Beach*, and above the beach a bar, the *Balcony*, and a smaller taverna, the *Sunset*, which has **rooms** to rent (☎0645/24 142 or 23 600; ③). A large sign on the beach insists "Camping strictly forbidden", although there remain signs of discreet freelance camping at the far end of the beach. While Káthisma is very popular with islanders, there are no beach facilities other than the free showers offered to bathers by the *Kathisma Beach Taverna*, and little shade.

From here the coast road takes on a series of spectacular hairpin bends on the way to the mountainside village of **KALAMÍTSI**, the last tourist-oriented settlement on the coast before distant Athání. Most of the houses here are the barely modernized shells of cramped peasant cottages, although tourist **accommodation** tends to be in purpose-built two-storey houses. Basic rooms are available through Spiro Karelis (☎0645/99 214; ②) and Spiro Verginis (☎0645/99 411; ②), larger rooms and apartments at *Hermes* (☎0645/99 417; ②), the *Blue and White House* (☎0645/99 269; ②) and *Deili Rooms and Studios* (☎0645/99 456 or 26 210; ③). There are a few shops and bars, as well as a couple of **tavernas**: the *Paradeisos*, in its own garden with fountain, and the more basic *Ionio*. Just outside the north end of the village, the aptly titled *Panorama View* restaurant offers a good selection of decently priced seafood, pasta, grills and taverna staples. Three kilometres' hike down a rough track is the village's quiet sandy beach.

South to Athání and beyond

Beyond Kalamítsi, the road first climbs the mountainside then dips into a valley behind the cliffs. Past Hortáta (barely a turning in the road, with a couple of tavernas) and Komíli (one taverna and a couple of ruined houses), the landscape becomes eerily empty, although the 4km between Komíli and Dhrágano, with its magnificent near-deserted wheat-farming landscape, makes for an excellent walk.

Take care if visiting Athání on public transport – the last bus back to Lefkádha Town leaves early in the afternoon.

Some guides speak misleadingly of **ATHÁNI** as a "centre" for this region of the island. In fact, it's a bit of a dead end – three tavernas, two shops and a public phone – though a very pleasant one. Most visitors head for the *Panorama* (☎0645/33 291 or 33 476; ②), which, as well as a **restaurant** with balcony, has an upstairs cocktail bar and

rooms with, as the title justifiably claims, panoramic views over the sea as far as Cape Lefkátas and, on clear days, Kefalloniá in the south. *O Alekos* (☎0656/33 484; ②) is a more traditional taverna, also with rooms, but if you want a quieter lunch or dinner, head for the family-run *Lefkatas* taverna on the edge of town.

From Athání, the road – now decently surfaced – continues for about 4km along the barren Lefkátas peninsula to a signpost for the steep path down to **Egrémni beach**, and a further 5km to the beach at **Pórto Katsíki**. Sandy and shady, these are two of the most picturesque beaches on the island, though any dreams of solitude will be shattered as hundreds of *kaíkia* full of day-trippers come puttering in mid-morning from Vassilikí.

Cape Lefkátas

Cape Lefkátas is a shadeless 14km from Athání and, while the terrain is suitably rugged and majestic, you'll find little to celebrate here beyond a lighthouse and a sense of achievement for actually having made it this far. The cape, which can be quite fearsome in bad weather, rises an almost sheer 60m on its west coast, and is little gentler on the protected east side. It has numerous mythological associations, not to mention a barely recognized role as one of the key sites in early queer history.

The rocks have been identified as the site of human sacrifices as long ago as 1200 BC. By the fourth century BC the ritual victims were criminals, with feathers and even live birds tied to them to help ease their descent, and boats at hand in the sea below – if the victims survived the plunge, their lives were spared. By this time, the promontory was the site of a temple of Apollo, who was believed to take care of seafarers and whose cult promoted the idea of leaping from the cliff to cleanse mind and body – not only from the stain of crimes, but also from the torment of unrequited love. Aphrodite is said to have been the first to go over the edge, in response to the death of her lover, Adonis. Byron describes the cape in *Childe Harold's Pilgrimage* as "the lover's refuge, and the lesbian's grave" – a reference to **Sappho**, who according to local myth threw herself over the edge of Cape Lefkátas out of frustrated love for a man, Phaon. Nineteenth-century engravings of her suicide tend to figure the iconic lesbian in a state of bliss, lyre clasped to her bosom, eyes closed and raised to the heavens, fearless on the western precipice and about to jump. Perhaps the greatest irony, however, is that despite the untold number of tavernas and bars that sport her name, Sappho probably never actually visited Lefkádha at all: the suicide is inferred from literalist readings of the few remaining fragments of her poetry, and the boyfriend was written into the story by historians mortified at the fact that she dated girls. Still, with all the testosterone wafting over from Vassilikí, the island could do with the odd coachload of carousing dykes.

Kariá and the interior

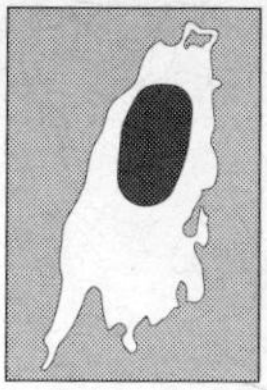

No one should leave Lefkádha without venturing into its **interior** at least once. Whereas the interiors of the other Ionian islands are either too easily accessible or just plain dull, inland Lefkádha can startle with panoramic hillscapes or hidden valleys which nurture the island's wheat industry. The elephantine hump of **Mount Stavróta** blocks communication across the island, so that communities such as Sívros and Vournikás (see p.134) have to be approached from the south, though the majority of the inland villages can be easily reached from Lefkádha Town itself (buses visit most villages at least once a day).

Kariá

The road south from Lefkádha forks at the city limits, the right-hand prong rising into the hills to enter the district of **Sfakiótes**, a conglomerate of some half a dozen tiny villages. The beautiful town square and cafés of Lazaráta, 8km south of Lefkádha Town, merit a break in your journey here. About 5km beyond Lazaráta is **KARIÁ**, which also boasts a lovely main square, shaded by plane trees, with excellent views out over the Ligiá/Nikianá coast to Akarnanía on the mainland. As well as a post office and gas station, the village is noted for the number of shops selling carpets and other woven goods, and **lace embroidery**. This timeworn tradition is celebrated in the tiny but fascinating **folklore museum** on the edge of the village, run by the family of one of Kariá's greatest lacemakers (daily 9am–6pm; 500dr). Even if the notion of lacemaking causes your eyes to glaze over, this renovated peasant home is worth a visit for its wealth of social detail, with eating, sleeping and living quarters carefullly reconstructed, and clothing, implements and lacework artfully arranged around the house.

Practicalities

The *Karia Village Hotel* (☎0645/51 030; ④), tucked away 200m along the first lane rising above the village, is a surprisingly large and modern **hotel** for its setting, with balconied en-suite rooms, a swimming pool, bar and restaurant. **Rooms** are available (all ②–③) from Haritini Vlachou (☎0645/41 634), the Kakiousis family (☎0645/61 136), Olga Lazari (☎0645/61 547) and Michael Chalikias (☎0645/61 026).

Kariá's square, which also serves as the village bus stop, is an excellent place for lunch or dinner, or just chilling out. As well as a number of *kafenía*, it has a popular *psistariá*, *La Platania*, while just off the square is the smarter *O Rousos* taverna. Curiously, the village also boasts a German-style beer cellar, the *Alt Kelerei*, hidden away on the northern edge.

Around Kariá

To the south of Kariá, rising up the slopes of Stavróta, are two of the oldest villages on the island, with architecture dating back to the sixteenth century. **VAFKÉRI** is nearly deserted today, but there's a useful rough road linking it to Nidhrí on the east coast. **EGLOÚVI**, the highest village on Lefkádha, with spectacular views, is the centre of the island's lentil crop. Less than a kilometre outside the village, a small cave barred to the public is claimed to have been the cave of the *Odyssey*'s one-eyed giant, Polyphemus, although only a liberal reading of the tale would identify it as the place. From Egloúvi, a track, signposted at the south end of the village, leads circuitously up to the 1100-metre summit of Mount Stavróta – a good half-day's round trip.

Three kilometres north of Kariá, the pretty vine-growing village of **ASPROGERAKÁTA** has a small **hotel**, the *Santa Maura* (☎0645/61 136; ③), and a number of tavernas around a small town square. Beyond here, rough roads skirt the lesser peak of Mount Pyrgós to reach the two main west coast villages, **DHRIMÓNAS** and, 3km further, **EXANTHIÁ**, high above the beaches of Káthisma and Kalamítsi. Clinging to the side of the mountain, both villages have enough shops and cafés serving local people, but little to detain the traveller, apart from spectacular views of the sunset out at sea.

Lefkádha's satellites

Lefkádha's four main satellite islands lie a short way off its east coast and can be reached – or at least viewed – by day-trip boat from Nidhrí (see p.132). **Meganíssi**, the largest and most interesting, can also be reached by regular ferry. The nearest, tiny **Madhourí**, is owned by the family of nineteenth-century poet and political hero Aristotelis Valaoritis, and is off limits to visitors. **Spartí** is deserted and covered in scrub. **Skórpios**, purchased in the 1960s by Aristotle Onassis, is held in trust for Athina Onassis, daughter of the late Christina, and is patrolled by armed guards. Daily tours pass close by – some even stop to let you swim off the boat in a sheltered bay – and you can spot a few buildings through the trees from the Meganíssi ferry, but the island, where Onassis and Jackie Kennedy were married, is virtually a ghost estate. Over fifteen different *kaíkia* circle the islands daily, which must make life for the inhabitants rather like living in a zoo.

Lefkádha's more distant satellites, the near-deserted islands of Kálamos, Kástos and Átokos, are in fact closer to the Greek mainland. Nowadays, none of them can be reached from Lefkádha, and only **Kálamos** has a regular ferry service, from Mítikas on the mainland (south of Vónitsa on the coast road between Préveza and Astakós). **Kástos** has a small village and harbour, but can only be reached by finding a lift with an independent yacht heading in that direction or by hiring a *kaíki* to take you – enquire in Mítikas or Kálamos. **Átokos**, to the southwest of Kástos, is now deserted, and attended by rumours of forced evacuation after an outbreak of disease.

Meganíssi

Almost barren **MEGANÍSSI** has remained a well-kept secret for many years, kept quiet by visitors who like their islands nearly deserted. Little has changed over the decades, although there are the first small signs of development, suggesting that Meganíssi should be visited before it's sucked into the mainstream of Greek tourism. An excellent, year-round (weather permitting) **ferry** service connects Nidhrí with the small port of **Spilió** and the main port of **Vathí**. The ferry takes under half an hour (single 420dr) and exists to serve the inhabitants of Meganíssi, which is why the first services leave Meganíssi, and the last Nidhrí (see also p.132).

Spilió and Spartohóri

The first port, **SPILIÓ**, is little more than a landing stage and a pebble beach, though it does have a couple of **tavernas**, a very basic **campsite**, and a public telephone. The campsite is next door to, and provided by, the *Star Taverna* (☎0645/51 107, fax 51 186), and is free, although only on the basis of a one- or two-night stay. There's a basic shop and washing facilities.

Five minutes up the hill from Spilió is the small, whitewashed village of **SPARTOHÓRI**. Unspoilt for decades, Spartohóri now has a souvenir shop and a couple of new **restaurants**: a pizza place, the *Tropicana*, which can direct you to **rooms** (☎0645/51 425; ②), and the *Rooftop Cafe*, which serves up a wide range of Greek and international dishes on a balcony with panoramic views over the satellite islands and Lefkádha. The one constant is the traditional taverna *Lafkis*, in the centre of the village (open evenings only). Apart from a few shops, this is all there is to this quiet, pretty village – walk too fast and you'll find yourself out in open country in minutes.

Katoméri and Vathí

The island's only road rises over the hills to the east of Spartohóri, giving panoramic views, notably of the wild, narrow peninsula to the south. Traffic is rare, and the silence and sense of isolation at the centre of the island are to be savoured, especially if you've just escaped the craziness of Nidhrí. After about an hour's walk, you'll reach the main village of **KATOMÉRI**, which can lay claim to a couple of bars and *kafenía*, and the island's one **hotel**, the *Meganisi*, a small and comfortable place with en-suite rooms and balconies, a restaurant, bar and terraces (☎0645/51 240, fax 51 639; ③; open year round).

The port of **VATHÍ** is a ten-minute walk down from Katoméri. While unremarkable, and lacking any swimming facilities, it's still a very attractive place, with a deep bay and very little development beyond a handful of tavernas and bars, and one or two villas on the surrounding hills. There's now **accommodation** in Vathí – although villagers still have to rack their brains for it when asked – at the waterfront *Different Studios* (☎0645/22 170; ③). The *Rose Garden Taverna*, with a surprisingly varied menu, vies for custom with the basic *Restaurant Greco*, but the favourite among Greek visitors – where Lefkadhans flock for Sunday lunch – is the waterside *Porto Vathi*, which serves vast portions of locally caught seafood. The most popular of Meganíssi's beaches is **Ambelákia**, to the east of Vathí, but accessible only by the path which heads east and then north out of Katoméri.

Kálamos

KÁLAMOS is another drowned mountain, mostly bare but with some evergreen woods reaching down as far as its pebbly beaches. It's mainly seen as a stopping-off point for bareboat sailors, some of whom favour it above any other small island in the region. A **ferry** leaves mainland Mítikas – which sports one hotel, the *Simos* (☎0646/81 380; ③) – once a day at noon for the voyage to the island.

Kálamos has just one village, **HÓRA**, with some **rooms**, although these are often booked through the summer. The ferry doesn't return to Mítikas until 7am, so you should enquire at the *Simos* in Mítikas about accommodation on the island before leaving, or come prepared to camp. Hóra is spread out above the small harbour, and is one of the few villages in the area that survived the 1953 earthquake, whose epicentre was quite close by. There's a basic *kafenío*-cum-taverna, a mini-market and a post office (which will change money), as well as a couple of snack bars and cafés. The nearest beach, a shingle strip, is a short walk southwest, and is served by a couple of bar-tavernas; further along the beach, freelance camping, if discreet and safe, is fairly easy.

With just one road winding around the mountain top, Kálamos provides an excellent, if limited, walking terrain. The fortified former capital, Kástro, now deserted and overgrown, is a ninety-minute walk from Hóra near the summit. Better beaches are to be found on the north coast, between Hóra and Epískopi, although almost all involve a hair-raising scramble down through the woods. The longest walk on the island, to the deserted village of Pórto Leóne, abandoned since the 1953 earthquake, is a two-hour hike across the mountainside with fantastic views over Kástos.

Travel details

Buses

Lefkádha Town to: Aï Nikítas (6 daily; 1hr 15min); Atháni (2 daily; 2hr); Athens (5 daily; 7hr); Kalamítsi (2 daily; 1hr 15min); Kariá (7 daily, 2 on Sun; 1hr); Káthisma (5 daily; 1hr 15min); Katohóri (2 daily; 1hr); Nidhrí (16 daily, 5 on Sun; 45min); Póros (2 daily; 1hr 30min); Préveza (4 daily, 3 on Sun; 30min); Sívota (2 daily; 1hr 45min); Sívros (2 daily, 1 on Sun; 1hr 30min);

Thessaloníki (Tues & Thurs only; 12hr); Vassilikí (5 daily; 2hr); Vlihós (16 daily, 5 on Sun; 45min); Yíra (8 daily, 5 on Sun; 15min).

Ferries

In season, there are connecting services on from the destinations detailed below with the *Four Islands Ferry* company (in Nidhrí ☎0645/92 528; in Vassilikí ☎0645/31 520).

Nidhrí to: Fiskárdho, Kefalloniá (1 daily; 1hr 30min); Fríkes, Ithráki (1 daily; 2hr); Meganíssi (7 daily; 30min).

Vassilikí to: Fiskárdho, Kefalloniá (2–4 daily; 1hr); Fríkes, Itháki (1 daily; 1hr).

Chapter 4

Itháki

Odysseus' legendary homeland, **Itháki (Ithaca)**, is the least spoilt of all the Ionian islands, but precisely because of that it is also the most difficult for visitors to get onto. Accommodation is scarce (there are only four small hotels on the entire island), much of it prebooked by overseas travel operators, which only increases competition for the remaining beds. The Homer/Odysseus industry has led to an orgy of theming, but otherwise there are few signs of the commercialism that has blighted other islands. There are no burger joints on Itháki, no theme pubs or video bars named after British sitcoms, yet it is very Anglophone – much more so than Lefkádha, for example – not to say Anglophile.

The island's landscape, much of it almost vertical, precludes any significant development. Like its larger neighbour, Kefalloniá, Itháki is essentially a series of drowned mountains – here three of them, joined by a tall, narrow isthmus, with human settlements on a number of plateaux around the peaks. The capital, **Váthi**, is separated from the three outlying villages, **Stavrós**, **Fríkes** and **Kióni**, by a journey of over 20km along the one main road, making getting around surprisingly difficult for such a small island. Its **beaches** are almost entirely pebble, with some sand deposits and sandy seabeds. The best are in

Accommodation price codes

Rooms and hotels listed in this book have been price-coded according to the scale outlined below. The rates quoted represent the cheapest available double room in high season. Out of season, rates can drop by as much as fifty percent or more, especially if you negotiate for a stay of three or more nights. Single rooms, where available, cost around seventy percent of the price of a double. For further information, see p.32.

① up to 4000dr
② 4000–8000dr
③ 8000–12,000dr
④ 12,000–16,000dr
⑤ 16,000–20,000dr
⑥ 20,000–30,000dr
⑦ 30,000dr upwards

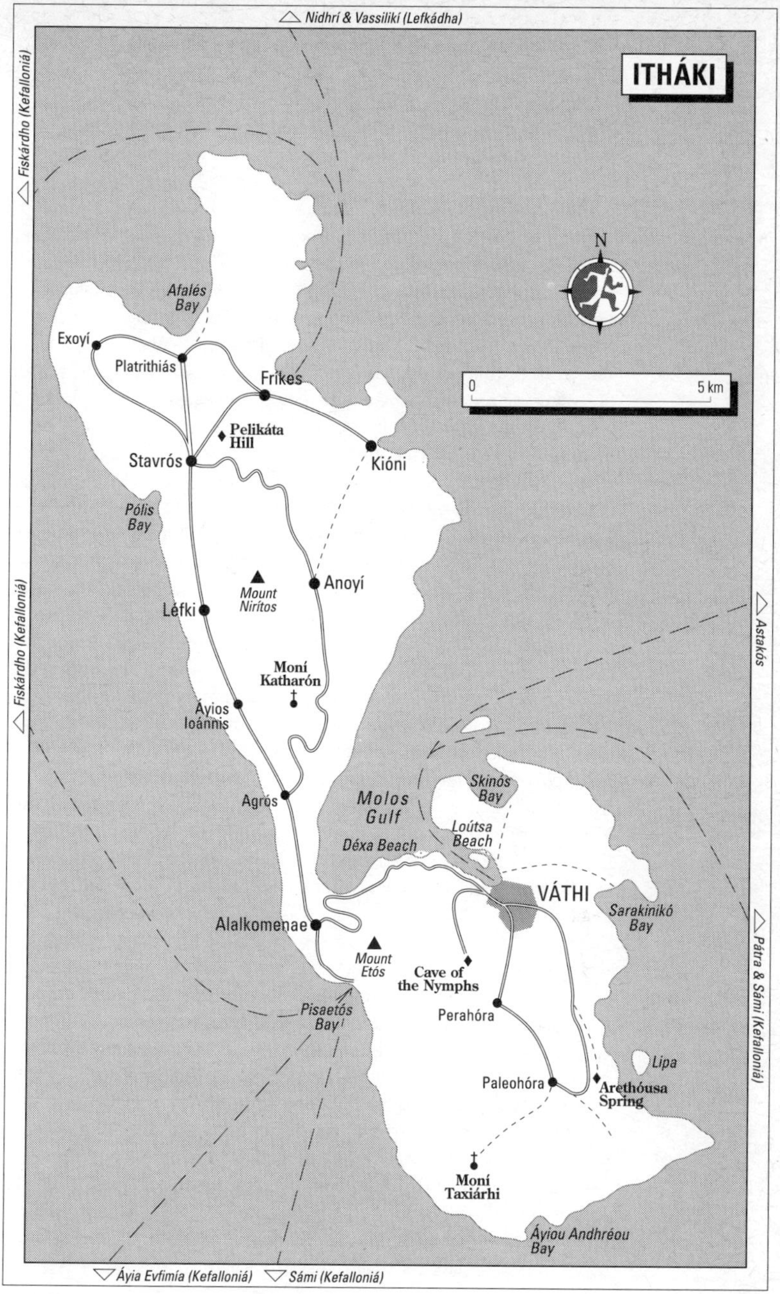
Nidhrí & Vassilikí (Lefkádha)
ITHÁKI
Fiskárdho (Kefalloniá)
N
0
5 km
Afalés Bay
Exoyí
Platrithiás
Fríkes
Pelikáta Hill
Stavrós
Kióni
Pólis Bay
Anoyí
Mount Nirítos
Léfki
Astakós
Moní Katharón
Fiskárdho (Kefalloniá)
Áyios Ioánnis
Skinós Bay
Molos Gulf
Agrós
Loútsa Beach
Déxa Beach
VÁTHI
Sarakinikó Bay
Alalkomenae
Mount Etós
Cave of the Nymphs
Pátra & Sámi (Kefalloniá)
Perahóra
Pisaetós Bay
Lipa
Paleohóra
Arethóusa Spring
Moní Taxiárhi
Áyiou Andhréou Bay
Áyia Evfimía (Kefalloniá)
Sámi (Kefalloniá)

the south, around Váthi, although there are some decent stretches between Fríkes and Kióni, and others accessible by boat.

Some history

Itháki is known to have been inhabited since at least 3000 BC from Neolithic finds in the north of the island. One local history suggests more than half a dozen possible origins for the island's **name**; from the ancient mythical figure Ithacus, son of the sea god Poseidon, through a variety of possible Phoenician, Turkish and Venetian roots. Its first settlers lived in the north, but by 1500 BC the south was also inhabited. During the Mycenean period, Itháki became the seat of power for the Kefallonian state, which extended over the other Ionian islands and parts of the Akarnanian mainland as well. The peak of this period, prior to 1000 BC, probably coincides with the composition of the much-disputed **Odyssey** (see the box on p.153); archeological finds from this period, which have been used to support a reading of the epic as a literal description of historical events, can be seen in Váthi's archeological museum.

In 1000 BC, Itháki fell under Dorian rule, and slipped from its position of power. Under Corinth (800–180 BC) it became a political backwater, and was similarly undisturbed when power transferred to Rome. During the Byzantine era (394–1185 AD), Itháki was annexed to Kefalloniá, and from then on shared much of its larger neighbour's history. However, the smaller, unprotected island fell prey to repeated attacks by pirates and Turkish invaders, and in the 1470s was sacked by Turkish forces. Most survivors abandoned the island, and the new Venetian rulers were forced to offer land and tax exemptions to lure settlers back. By the 1570s, the island had a new, fortified coastal capital, **Váthi**, set on a generous natural harbour from which it derives its name (meaning "deep" in Greek). Under Venetian rule, the population on the island rose from only 60 families in the 1560s to an estimated 12,000 people in the 1790s.

Ithakans were prominent among the activists who, led by the Friendly Society, fomented the War of Independence against the Turkish rulers on mainland Greece in 1821. In the early part of the nineteenth century, growing emigration saw Ithakans travelling around the world and gaining a widespread reputation for their **seafaring** skills. This in turn transformed Itháki into a wealthy and powerful island. As well as building the Neoclassical mansions that can be seen in Váthi today, Itháki's middle class financed a strong and vibrant social and cultural infrastructure. However, maritime success abroad ultimately led to further emigration, initiating an economic decline that only began to bottom out in recent decades. During World War II, Itháki was overrun by Axis forces, first the Italians (1941–43), and then the Germans (1943–44). Like neighbouring Kefalloniá, Lefkádha and Zákinthos, the island was devastated by the earthquakes of 1953 (see p.168).

Arrival and getting around

There isn't a flat piece of ground on Itháki that's long or straight enough to land anything other than a helicopter, so everyone visiting the island arrives by sea. Package tourists will frequently find themselves **flying into Kefalloniá**, where they are bused, rather tediously, to Fiskárdho in the north, and then transported by ferry to **Fríkes** at the northernmost point of Itháki. With bus journey, embarkation and transfers to accommodation, this can add at least two or three hours to your journey. If you're flying to Kefalloniá independently, it's better to sail from Sámi, where ferries are more frequent, to the capital, **Váthi**, a sensible place to stop and get your bearings on Itháki.

If you find yourself being bused to Fiskárdho to transfer to Itháki, sit on the left of the bus for the best views.

Island-hoppers have the choice of arriving at Váthi (from Sámi), Fríkes (from Fiskárdho on Kefalloniá, or Nidhrí on Lefkádha), or Pisaetós (from Fiskárdho, Sámi or Áyia Evfimía on Kefalloniá). The only other options, short of parachuting in, are the connections with Pátra and Astakós (see box below) on the mainland.

In high season, four **buses** run daily between Váthi, Fríkes and Kióni. Travel agencies in all three villages can arrange moped or bike **rental**, and larger agencies car rental, although given the size of the island this is of questionable value: there are relatively few navigable roads – to Perahóra and Pisaetós in the south and Anoyí and Exoyí in the north – and it would probably be cheaper to go by taxi. In any case, apart from the journey between Váthi and Stavrós, most points on the island are within reasonable walking distance of each other.

Astakós

Itháki's shortest link with mainland Greece, the daily ferry to **ASTAKÓS**, is a poor option both in terms of travel connections and accommodation. The one good reason to travel via this small coastal resort is if you are heading inland by bus or car, towards Athens or into the interior – or, of course, in the opposite direction towards Itháki. Journeys south to Pátra and beyond, however, and northwards via Lefkádha and Préveza are quicker and more comfortable by sea. The bus journey north to Igoumenítsa, for example, though admittedly scenic, involves two changes of bus and a complicated diversion via Agrínio, Árta and Ioánnina, taking twelve hours or more.

Astakós is a growing resort, despite having no beach to speak of beyond a thin strand of pebble and sand. Its convenience makes it popular with mainlanders, and there's a growing presence from foreign travel operators. Buses are timed to meet ferries, and the KTEL **bus office** is in the ancient *kafenío* at the near end of the seafront. The town has one decent **hotel**, the *Stratos* (☎0646/41 096; ③), with balconied en-suite rooms overlooking the seafront. There are also **rooms** available, mainly through seafront businesses: try the *Dina*, the first taverna you'll come to (☎0664/42 042; ②). As ever, the best bet for **eating or drinking** is to follow the Greeks – to the *Cafe Skorpios* for lunch or drinks, or the *Spyros* taverna for more substantial fare.

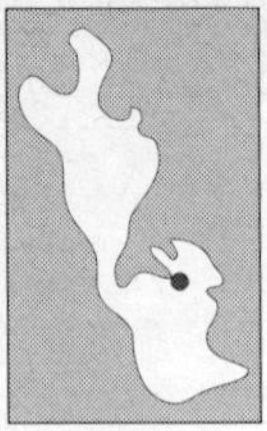

Váthi

Itháki's capital has the most idyllic setting of any port in the archipelago. Ships approaching **VÁTHI** have to turn into a large outer bay, and again into a smaller one, then pass between headlands into an interior bay, where the town sits at the crux. Váthi is entirely hidden from the open sea, in such convoluted folds of terrain that visitors sometimes fail to realize that the mountains in the distance are in fact the northern half of the island. It was for this reason that islanders chose the bay as the site of their first major sea port in the sixteenth century, when the threat of piracy had been largely eliminated with the help of the Venetians.

Accommodation

Except at the very height of the season, townspeople still meet ferries offering **rooms**. Most are in the quieter backstreets rising into the hills above the town, and in this large pedestrian warren of alleys, they can be hard to find if you're by yourself. There are also a few, rather pricey rooms within stumbling distance of the ferry ramp on the south side of the harbour, amidst the yacht moorings. Especially worth seeking out are the rooms owned by Vassili Vlassopoulou (☎0674/32 119; ②) – surrounded by pleasant gardens, they're clearly visible from the bay on the Venetian steps leading from behind the ferry quay towards the church. Also within easy access are those owned by Sotiris Maroulis at Odhós Odysseus 29, near the Perahóra road (☎0674/28 300; ②).

Váthi only has two **hotels**, and there's no sign of another being built. They're on the quay at either end of town. Nearer and cheaper is the *Odysseus* (☎0674/32 381; ③), a good, basic hotel with en-suite rooms above its own taverna, set back from the street but slightly troubled by traffic on the nearby main road out of town. Topped by a big neon sign at the far end of the quay, the *Mentor* (☎0674/32 433, fax 32 293; ③) has en-suite rooms with balconies, some with full-on sea views, and takes most credit cards. It's open year round, but even out of season, it's a favourite with walking tour companies, and can sometimes fill up. The hotel has its own restaurant and bar, much favoured at night for its illuminated patio.

Váthi's two main travel agencies, *Polyctor Tours* and *Delas Tours* (see p.152), offer a range of rooms, apartments and villas in town and across the island. If none of the above have space, or can make alternative suggestions, the town's taxi drivers, lined up along the quay by the bus stop, may be able to help. Private rooms are sometimes available in the suburb/village of Perahóra above Váthi, but it's a long way to go to be disappointed.

The Town

Much of Váthi was destroyed by the 1953 earthquake, leaving only a few of its magnificent Neoclassical mansions and a number of churches, including the small **Cathedral** and the church of the **Taxiárhi**, which contains an icon of the crucifixion believed to be the work of El Greco. However, the modest size of the town and the comparative wealth of its seafaring population seem to have worked in its favour after the earthquake: it was reconstructed far more sympathetically than either Zákinthos Town or Argostóli. And a preservation order passed in 1978, forbidding unsightly development, has protected the town from excessive commercialization. Its boutiques, souvenir shops, tavernas, *kafenía*, cafés and cocktail bars are all discreetly housed in vernacular architecture.

Váthi Archeological Museum

While many of the best finds have been taken to Athens, or simply looted by unscrupulous north European archeologists, Váthi's **Archeological Museum** maintains a decent collection of exhibits related to the *Odyssey* myth. Mainly domestic wares, they include Mycenean tripods which support the theory that Odysseus's home was indeed on Itháki. The museum is linked to the **Library**, which has an extensive and often bizarre collection of editions of Homer, including one in Chinese.

The Archeological Museum, opposite the bus stop, is open Tues–Sun 8.30am–2pm; free.

Beaches

If you're staying in Váthi or, perhaps more importantly, visiting from Kefalloniá with only a few hours to spare, it's good to know that there are decent beaches within fifteen minutes' walk in either direction around the bay. Biggest, and busiest, is **Déxa** on the western side of the bay, over the hill along the main road rising above the ferry quay. This long pebble strip offers water sports and a snack bar, and has been claimed as the site of Phorcys (it's actually signposted "Forkinos Bay"), the beach where the Phaeacians deposited the sleeping Odysseus.

Nearest and smallest is the beach at **Loútsa**, on the opposite side of the bay to the ferry quay, a small sandy cove with a snack bar in season. Loútsa is also the site of one of the few surviving Venetian fortifications, whose cannon emplacements are visible on a low bluff above the beach. A very narrow path leads on from Loútsa past some microscopic coves towards the headland.

The track that strikes off to the right and uphill before Loútsa leads over the headlands towards the superior deserted pebble beach in **Skinós bay**. An even longer track, leaving the centre of town, trails over the hills to **Sarakinikó bay**, which is a good hour's hike but, like Skinós, worth the effort for the swimming. The one drawback to this part of the coastline, though, is the noisy industrial plant overlooking Sarakinikó which fills the area with an insistent drone that can be heard as far as the Arethóusa Spring.

Eating and drinking

Váthi's nightlife unfolds around its tightly packed seafront and the few short streets behind it. There is little to differentiate between the **cafés and bars** on the main drag facing the fishing quay – here it's perhaps best to follow the locals to the *kafenío* in the middle of the strip. For a yet more traditional atmosphere, seek out the ancient *kafenío* tucked behind the seafront near the National Bank – though unaccompanied women may find the predominantly male atmosphere unwelcoming. An excellent alternative is the magnificent Neoclassical mansion on the seafront that's recently been transformed into the *Itháki Yacht Club*. The grounds, with a curious seawater pond connected to the bay by a tunnel under the road, are spread with tables during the summer, and the large bar inside, though it looks like some sort of swank gentlemen's club, is open to all.

For dinner, most visitors head off around the bay – with a torch – to one of a trio of **tavernas**: *Gregory's*, popular for its lamb and fish, and the more traditional *Tziribis* and *Vlachos* nearby. The views back across to Váthi are excellent, but bills usually reflect the setting. On the way you'll pass the *Mylos Creperie*, a hip music, booze and snacks hangout that's popular with townies and visitors alike.

In town, *O Nikos*, tucked behind the strip of cafés, is an excellent point-at-what-you-want-to-eat taverna, and its few tables fill early. A few doors away, the *Sirenes Itháki Yacht Club* takes a similar menu up market in a nautical theme restaurant: Smyrna meat balls with a red sauce, fish in rosemary and raisins, shrimps in lemon and mustard sauce, and others. The food is good and the price reasonable for the slightly outlandish setting.

Listings

Banks The National Bank of Greece is visible from the junction of the two quayside roads; the Commercial Bank and the Agricultural Bank are just behind it (all Mon–Fri 8am–1pm). Hotels and travel agencies will change currency and travellers' cheques, but shop around for the best deal or, if possible, the "Bank rates offered" sign.

First aid As well as the first aid clinic on the seafront towards the ferry quay (☎0642/32 282), the pharmacy on the quay by the bus stop is able to give advice on minor ailments.

OTE On the seafront (Mon–Fri 7.30am–10pm).

Police station On the seafront (☎0664/32 205).

Post office On the seafront (Mon–Fri 8am–2pm).

Shopping Váthi has many well-stocked mini-markets, a bakery, fish and meat stores, as well as other shops, including a couple of excellent local art galleries and craft outlets.

Travel agencies There is no tourist information office in Váthi or elsewhere on Itháki, but commercial travel agencies and hotels are usually happy to provide information. Polyctor Tours in the town centre (☎0674/33 120, fax 33 130) is the agent for most ferries (as well as Olympic Airways, useful if returning to

Athens via Kefalloniá), and operates a ticket office opposite the ferry quay for most sailings. Polyctor's smaller neighbour, Delas Tours (☎0674/321 104, fax 33 031) offers accommodation as well as other travel services.

Odysseus sites

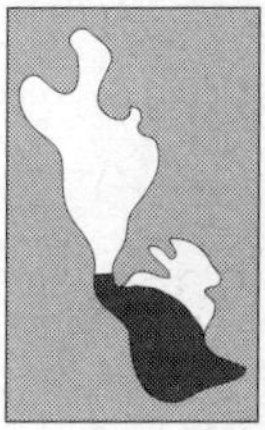

The **Odysseus sites** at this end of the island – the Arethoúsa Spring, the Cave of the Nymphs and Alalkomenae, suggested location of Odysseus' castle – are all within reach of Váthi, the first two on foot, the third by bus or taxi. Trips to either (but not both) the Cave of the Nymphs and Arethoúsa Spring can be fitted into a day-trip from Kefalloniá, Alalkomenae only if you take a cab (a return fare should be no more than 5000dr).

Homer, the *Odyssey* and Itháki

Anyone travelling in the Ionian will soon become either confused or cynical about the sheer number of places – from Paleokastrítsa in northern Corfu to Alalkomenae on Itháki – competing to be accepted as the actual sites of events in the **Odyssey**. Classical authorities still take a dim view of arguments for placing so much of Homer's epic in Greece, preferring the traditional reading, which identifies sites as far afield as Gozo, the Messina Straits between Italy and Sicily, Italy's Aeolian islands and Tunisia. Indeed, some interpretations of the story have taken it entirely outside the Mediterranean basin, to such improbable locales as Iceland. The safest interpretation is that Homer – whose single authorship is itself questioned by theories that hold the *Odyssey* to be a group effort put together over the centuries – was mixing myth and legend with actual historical and geographical detail.

Explorer Tim Severin, however, in his book *The Ulysses Voyage: Sea Search for the Odyssey*, comes down in favour of siting Odysseus' adventures around Itháki, the island that names his home in the epic – even if German archeologist Wilhelm Dörpfeld (see p.119) tried unsucessfully to cart it off to Lefkádha. In 1985, following earlier expeditions to reconstruct Jason's search for the Golden Fleece, Severin and a group of fellow explorers set off on a full-scale model of a Bronze Age galley, to retrace Odysseus' journey home from Troy. Using estimated times of journeys described in the *Odyssey*, and matching descriptions of landscape and astronavigational details, Severin pieced together Odysseus' adventures around Itháki and neighbouring islands.

Among Severin's key propositions is that King Alcinous' castle was probably sited at Paleokastrítsa on Corfu, and that Odysseus was washed ashore at Érmones. Severin cites Paxí, in particular Harámi beach in Lákka bay, as the likely position of Circe's home of Aeaea, which concurs with the local nickname of Circe's Grove for a glade at nearby Ipapánti. He speculates that Scylla and Charybdis may have been natural features in the landscape at the northern tip of Lefkádha, and further suggests Déxa bay on Itháki as the likely site of the Cave of the Nymphs, Pelikáta as Odysseus' castle, and Arethóusa as the site of the spring where Eumaeus watered his swine. Ultimately, however, even Severin concedes to the many ambiguities surrounding the text, and Homer's tale resists the attempt to moor it definitively to dry land.

Odysseus sites

The Arethóusa Spring

The walk to the **Arethóusa Spring** – allegedly the place where Eumaeus, Odysseus' faithful swineherd, brought his pigs to drink – is a three-hour trip there and back, setting off along a signposted track out of Váthi next to the OTE. The isolation and the sea views along the way are magnificent, but the walk crosses some slippery inclines and might best be avoided if you're nervous of heights. The route, particularly where it turns off the rough track onto a narrow path, is shadeless, so take a hat and plenty of liquids in summer. When the weather's fine it's worth taking a picnic, but the route shouldn't be attempted in poor weather and isn't recommended for lone walkers.

Near the top of the lane leading to the spring path, a signpost points up to what is said to have been the **Cave of Eumaeus** – if you're tempted, the tortuous path zigzags up to just below the bluff high above, and the cave is a large single hollow with a tree growing up through a hole in the roof.

The route to the spring continues along the track for a few hundred metres, and then branches off onto a narrow footpath through the maquis that covers the sloping cliffs. Parts of the final downhill track involve scrambling across rock fields (follow the splashes of green paint), and care should be taken around the small but vertiginous ravine that houses the spring. The geographical features around the spring, which is sited at the head of the ravine below a crag known as Kórax (the raven), compare to Homer's description of the meeting between Odysseus and Eumaeus, lending themselves to literalist claims. However, the spring itself is distinctly underwhelming – in summer it's just a dribble of water sounding like a kitchen leak in a shallow cave. It's worth pointing out that the spring is a dead end – the only way out is back the way you came. A small pebble beach a short way down from the spring, reached by a steep, narrow path, is good for a swim if time allows.

If you feel a little uneasy about the gradients involved in reaching the spring, it's still worth continuing along the main track that runs above it, a journey up through woodlands that provides excellent sea views. The track loops round and heads back into the village of **Perahóra** above Váthi, which has views as far as Lefkádha to the north. On the way, you'll pass **Paleohóra**, the ruined medieval capital abandoned centuries ago, but with vestiges of houses fortified against pirate attacks and some churches still retaining details of Byzantine frescoes of the saints. Around 3km southwest of Paleohóra, through densely forested highlands, is the site of the sixteenth-century **Móni Taxiárhi**. The monastery was destroyed in the 1953 earthquakes, but its small church has since been rebuilt.

The Cave of the Nymphs

The **Cave of the Nymphs** (known locally as *Marmarospíli*), is about 2.5km up a rough track signposted on the brow of the hill above

Déxa beach. The cave is atmospheric but underwhelming compared to the caverns of neighbouring Kefalloniá, and these days is illuminated with coloured lights. The claim that this is the *Odyssey*'s Grotto of the Nymphs, where the returning Odysseus concealed the gifts given to him by King Alcinous, is enhanced by the proximity of Déxa beach (see p.151), although there is some evidence suggesting that a cave above the beach, which was unwittingly demolished during quarrying many years ago, was the "true" Cave of the Nymphs.

Odysseus sites

Alalkomenae and Pisaetós

Alalkomenae, Schliemann's much-vaunted "Castle of Odysseus", is signposted on the Váthi–Pisaetós road, on the saddle between Déxa bay and Pisaetós, with views over both sides of the island. The actual site, however, some 300m uphill, is little more than foundations spread about in the maquis. Schliemann's excavations unearthed a Mycenean burial chamber, and domestic items such as vases, figurines and utensils (to be seen in the archeological museum), but sections of Cyclopean wall, and the remains of what has been suggested is a temple to Apollo, date from three centuries after Homer. In fact, the most likely contender for the site of Odysseus' castle is above the village of Stavrós in the north, and intriguingly close to the site of the ruined ancient capital of Pólis.

The road (though not buses) continues to the harbour of **Pisaetós**, about 2km below, with a large pebble beach that's good for swimming though popular with local rod-and-line fishermen. A couple of tavernas here largely serve the ferries from Fiskárdho, Sámi and Áyia Evfimía on Kefalloniá.

Northern Itháki

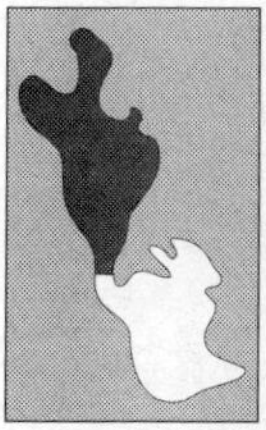

The road to the north of the island rides high on the side of **Mount Nirítos**, affording breathtaking views of neighbouring Kefalloniá. At the hamlets of Agrós and Áyios Ioánnis, new tracks are gradually appearing which allow access to small remote beaches along this hitherto wild stretch of coastline. The only facilities along this road are the shops and *kafenía* of Léfki, halfway to Stavrós, which was a notable centre of Resistance organization in the Ionians during World War II.

Stavrós and around

STAVRÓS is the second largest town on the island, although its inland position and distance from any decent beaches – the nearest, a steep 2km below the town, shares Pólis bay with a small fishing harbour – make it a less than ideal place to stay. It's a pleasant enough town none the less, with *kafenía* edging a small square that's dominated by a rather fierce statue of Odysseus – the only such public monument dedicated to him in the islands – and a tiny **museum** (Tues–Sun 9am–3pm) displaying local archeological finds. Stavrós's Homeric site is on the side of **Pelikáta Hill**, where remains of roads, walls and other structures have been suggested as the possible site of Odysseus's Castle. Items from the site, including part of a mask engraved "*EUCHN ODUSSEI*" (Dedicated to Odysseus), can be seen at the museum.

Stavrós is probably only useful as a base if both Fríkes and Kióni are full up, and is an obvious stopping-off point for exploring the northern hamlets and the road up to the medieval village of Anóyi on Mount Nirítos. Both *Polyctor* and *Delas* (see p.152) handle **accommodation** in Stavrós, and a number of the town's traditional tavernas, including the *Petra* (☎0674/31 596), offer rooms.

Anoyí

A mountainous and highly scenic road leads some 5km southeast from Stavrós to **ANOYÍ**, whose apt name roughly translates as "upper land". It was once the second most important settlement on the island, but is almost deserted today. The centre of the village is dominated by a free-standing Venetian campanile, built to serve the (usually locked) church of the **Panayía**; enquire at the one *kafenío* about access to the church, and its frescoes and striking reredos, originally painted in Byzantine times but mostly replaced after earthquake damage over the intervening centuries. On the outskirts of the village are the foundations of a ruined **medieval prison**, and in the surrounding countryside, some extremely strange **rock formations**, the biggest being the eight-metre-high Arakles (Heracles) rock, just east of the village.

The **monastery of Katharón**, 3km further south along the road, has stunning views down over Váthi and the south of the island. The monastery houses an icon of the *Panayía* – Virgin Mary – discovered by peasants who were clearing scrub land in the area. Local mythology claims that a temple to Artemis stood on the site, and suggests a link to the medieval Cathar sect. Byron is said to have stayed at the monastery in 1823, during his final voyage to Messolónghi. Every year the monastery celebrates its own festival on September 8, when the icon is displayed and everyone sings and dances.

North of Stavrós

Three roads leave Stavrós heading north: one, to the right, heads 2km down to Fríkes, while the main road, to the left, loops around the hill village of Exoyí, and on to **PLATRÍTHIAS** (the middle of the three roads is a minor short cut to Platríthias). On the outskirts of Platríthias, signposted off the main road from Exóyi, Mycenean graves and buildings establish that the area was inhabited at the time of Homer. A track leads down from Platríthias to **Afáles**, the largest bay on the entire island, with an unspoilt and little-visited pebble beach. Among a group of tiny settlements above Platríthias are the abandoned hamlet of Kalamós, 3km north, and Kolliéri just a kilometre away, with its curious folklore monument – a towering column of millstones, next to a stone mill with wheels and grinding channel intact. The landscape around here, thickly forested in parts and dotted with vineyards, makes excellent walking terrain.

Fríkes

Viewed from the daily ferries that leave Lefkádha or Kefalloniá, or from the island bus as it trundles through en route to Kióni, **FRÍKES** doesn't appear to have much going for it. You could sprint around its tiny harbourfront in under a minute, and find yourself in open country towards Stavrós in five. Wedged in a valley between two steep hills, Fríkes was only settled in the sixteenth century when the threat from pirate raids had diminished. Waves of emigration in the nineteenth century have further capped its size – as few as 200 people are estimated to live here today – but its maritime prowess and proximity to other islands have made it a natural trading post and year-round port. Consequently, it stays open for tourism far later in the season than its neighbour Kióni, and at present has a better range of tavernas. There are no beaches in the village, but plenty of good, if small, pebble strands a short walk away towards Kióni. When the ferries and their cargoes have departed, Fríkes falls quiet and this is its real charm: a downbeat but cool place to lie low from the touristic rat race.

Fríkes' one **hotel**, the rather pricey *Nostos* (☎0674/31 644, fax 31 716; ③), is a small but smart family-run affair, with en-suite rooms, a bar, restaurant and small garden; it's about a hundred metres from the quay, along the right turning of the two roads leaving town. The seafront *Kiki Travel* (☎0674/31 726) has **rooms** and other accommodation, and also offers vehicle rental and other travel services. The Fríkes office of island-wide *Polyctor Travel* on the quay (☎0674/31 771) can offer mostly upmarket studios, apartments and villas in and around the village, as well as handling ferry tickets. Phoning ahead is advisable, but if you turn up here without a reservation, both the *Ulysses* taverna-*kafenío* on the front and the neighbouring, and nameless, souvenir shop have rooms available.

For such a small place, Fríkes has a wealth of good seafront **tavernas**. *Symposium* has a variety of grill and oven dishes, seafood and some unusual vegetarian options, such as baked beetroots and potatoes. The *Kirki Grill* is a straightforward taverna with an obvious specialization, while the *Ulysses*, an equally basic taverna-cum-*kafenío*, is the funkiest place to drink. The neighbouring *Penelope* is also geared up market, with a varied menu covering north European and Greek.

Kióni

KIÓNI sits at a dead end in the road, 5km southeast of Fríkes (although a rough path ascends towards Anoyí from the back of the village). It too was only established in the sixteenth century, when settlers from Anoyí felt it was safe to move down from the hills. On the same geological base as the northern tip of Kefalloniá, it avoided the very worst of the 1953 earthquakes, and so retains some fine examples of pre-twentieth-century architecture. It's an extremely pretty village, wrapped around a tiny harbour, comparable in prospect and features to Longós on Paxí and Fiskárdho on Kefalloniá. Tourism here is dominated by British blue-chip travel companies, and by flotilla and bareboat sailors.

Kióni's bay has a **beach** of sorts, 1km along its south side, a small sand and pebble strand below a summer-only snack bar. Better pebble beaches can be found within walking distance northwards towards Fríkes, where bizarre rock formations along the roadside are sometimes stacked upright like matchsticks. You can also hire a boat from the Moraitis boat rental agency (from around 3000dr – see below) to explore quiet nearby bays and coves, and larger *kaíki* trips to further beaches are occasionally organized.

There are two major dates in Kióni's summer calendar: June 24 when the church of **Áyios Ioánnis** celebrates its saint's day, and anyone called Ioannis has his name day; and July 20, the festival of Áyios Ílias, when the village's 200 or so inhabitants set off in boats to attend a service at a small chapel that sits on Kióni bay's southern promontory.

While the best **accommodation** has been snaffled by the Brits, some local businesses have rooms and apartments to let, among them *Apostolis* (☎0674/31 072), *Dellaportas* (☎0674/31 481, fax 31 090) and *Kioni Vacations* (☎0674/31 668). A quieter option, just a short walk uphill on the main road in the tiny hamlet of Ráhi, are the rooms and studios run by Captain Theofilos Karatzis and his family (☎0674/31 679; ③), with panoramic views over the area. Alternatively, seek out or phone the very helpful Yioryíos Moraitis (☎0674/31 464, fax 31 702), whose boat rental company has access to accommodation in Kióni. Propellerheads can even visit Yioryíos' website at http://www.travel-greece.com:80/ionian/ithaki/boatren – though it's a drastically simple site.

For all its blue-chip tone, Kióni is poorly served for **restaurants**, with just two waterfront tavernas – the traditional *Avra* and the *Kioni*, which mixes European and Greek – a pizzeria and, one block back in the village, the upmarket *Calipso* restaurant. Village facilities stretch to two well-stocked shops, a post office, and a couple of bars and cafés. Back up the hill towards the hamlet of Ráhi there's also the small, bunker-like *Kioni* cocktail bar and nightclub.

Travel details

Buses

Váthi to: Kióni (4 daily; 1hr).

Ferries

The frequencies of the ferry services given below apply in season, from May to September; out of season, there is one daily service on each route. All the ferries carry vehicles.

Fríkes to: Fiskárdho, Kefalloniá (1 daily; 1hr); Nidhrí, Lefkádha (1 daily; 2hr); Vassilikí, Lefkádha (1 daily; 1hr).

Pisaetós to: Fiskárdho, Kefalloniá (1 daily; 1hr); Sámi, Kefalloniá (3 daily; 1hr 30min); Áyia Evfimía, Kefalloniá (1 daily; 30min).

Váthi to: Sámi, Kefalloniá (4 daily; 1hr); Astakós (2 daily; 1hr 30min); Pátra (2 daily; 5hr).

Chapter 5

Kefalloniá

Rugged, mountainous and blessed with some of the most dramatic scenery in the region, **Kefalloniá** is the largest Ionian island, but has resisted the sort of development that has overtaken Corfu and some of the other islands. The island is variously known as Kefalloniá, **Kefallinía** and **Cephalonia** – the first is the phonetic transliteration of the present Greek name, the second the modern version of its ancient moniker (which also names its airport), and the third the Anglicized version. Like its tiny neighbour, Itháki, it's little more than a series of mountain tops piercing the waves – **Mount Énos**, which looms over the south of the island, is one of the highest in Greece – with towns and villages sheltering in the valleys and on the lower slopes. Despite its landmass, there are only three towns of any size: the handsome and spacious capital, **Argostóli**; the main ferry port, **Sámi**, a nondescript enclave on the eastern coast; and **Lixoúri**, virtually a suburb of Argostóli but, because of the convoluted landscape, 35km away by road yet only thirty minutes by ferry.

Kefalloniá's seaside resorts are all based around small villages and ports. The **beaches** in the south tend to be sandy, those in the north, pebble, including the exquisite white crescent of **Mírtos**, one of the most famous and most photographed beaches in the entire Ionian.

Accommodation price codes

Rooms and hotels listed in this book have been price-coded according to the scale outlined below. The rates quoted represent the cheapest available double room in high season. Out of season, rates can drop by as much as fifty percent or more, especially if you negotiate for a stay of three or more nights. Single rooms, where available, cost around seventy percent of the price of a double. For further information, see p.32.

① up to 4000dr
② 4000–8000dr
③ 8000–12,000dr
④ 12,000–16,000dr
⑤ 16,000–20,000dr
⑥ 20,000–30,000dr
⑦ 30,000dr upwards

Below the thumbnail of limestone around the popular port and resort of **Fiskárdho**, much of the northern coastline is sheer cliff, with the most terrifying mountain roads in the archipelago and some of the most breathtaking views. Kefalloniá also conceals two unmissable geological quirks, the **Dhrogaráti cave system** and the **Melissáni underground lake**, as well as some minor archeological sites and some more locations said to be associated with the Odysseus myth.

The island sits close to the fault line that has given this area of the Ionian a history of cataclysmic **earthquakes**. The most violent ever recorded, in 1953, levelled its graceful capital, Argostóli, destroyed almost all of its outlying villages, and in some parts killed up to eighty percent of the population (see the box on p.168). Argostóli was rebuilt with overseas help, not quite to its former elegance, though it remains a pleasant town. Most of the interior villages were rebuilt, often beside earthquake ruins which can still be seen today. Many Kefallonians were forced or chose to live abroad after the earthquake, but a large number have returned, bringing languages and a sophistication absent in some other parts of the Ionian.

Kefalloniá's **bus** system is basic but expanding, and with a little legwork it can be used to get you almost anywhere on the island. Key routes connect Argostóli with Sámi, Fiskárdho, **Skála**, a small development with a long sandy beach and pine woods, and **Póros,** a slightly shabby resort built around a fishing port. There's also a useful connection on from Sámi to the tiny resort of **Áyios Evfimía**, which attracts many package travellers. The island has a plethora of **ferry** connections, principally from Fiskárdho to Lefkádha and Itháki, and from Sámi to Lefkádha, Itháki and the mainland, as well as links to Zákinthos, Killíni and Pátra.

Some history

Remains excavated around Kefalloniá, and now on display in Argostóli's archeological museum, have established that there were settlements on the island as long ago as 50,000 BC – before the modern Mediterranean began to take shape. Kefalloniá was once covered in fir trees – **abies cephalonica**, named after the island – which formed a large part of its trade in ancient times: *cephalonica* wood has been discovered in the structure of the Minoan Palace at Knossós on Crete. The island is believed to have acquired its **name** from legendary king Cephalus, whose escapades were recorded by Hesiod, Ovid, Apollodorus and others. Son of Hermes and Herse, he was known above all as a hunter – an activity keenly pursued by modern Kefallonians, to the chagrin of animal lovers and walkers harassed by hunting dogs.

By the seventh century BC, the island had split into four democratic cities; the most famous of them was Same (modern-day Sámi), named in Thucydides and Homer, who records that Odysseus sailed for the the Trojan War with twelve ships from the city. During the

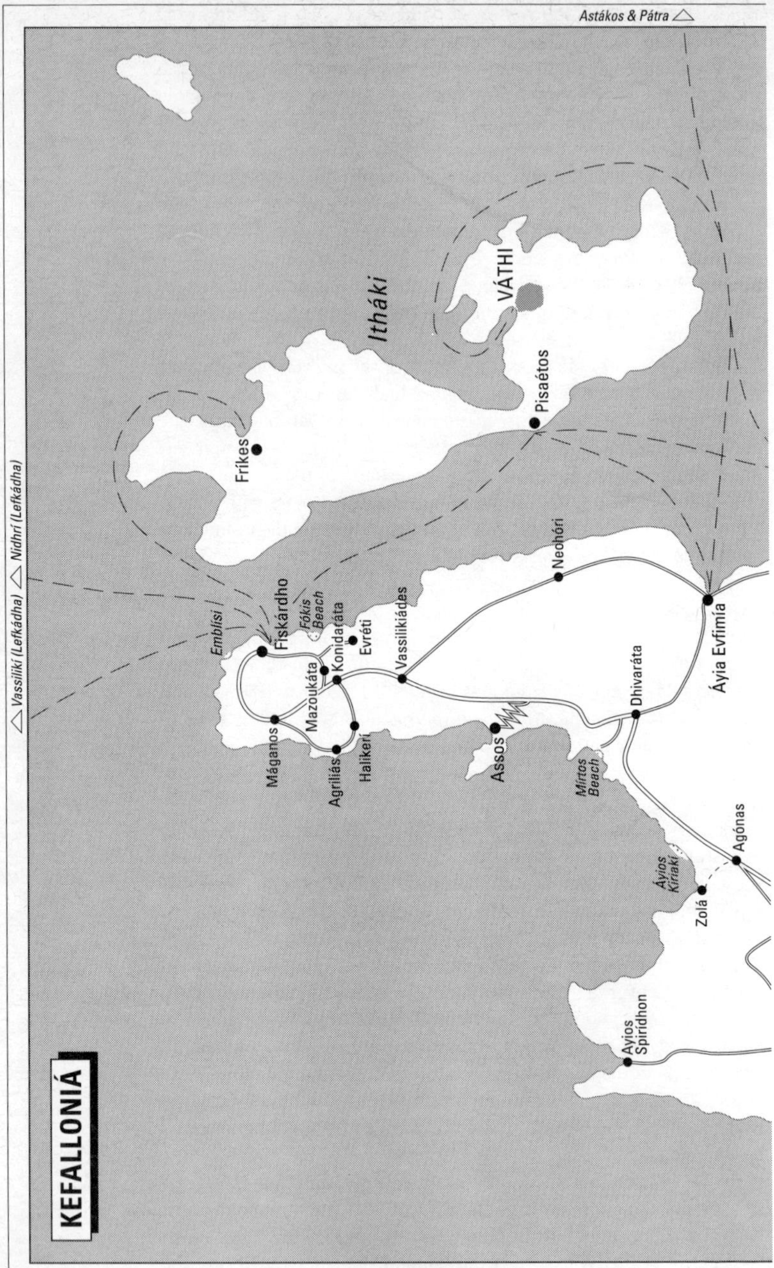
KEFALLONIÁ
Vassilikí (Lefkádha)
Nidhrí (Lefkádha)
Astákos & Pátra
Itháki
VÁTHI
Pisaétos
Fríkes
Neohóri
Emblísi
Fiskárdho
Fókis Beach
Konidaráta
Evréti
Vassilikiádes
Mazoukáta
Máganos
Agriliás
Halikerí
Assos
Dhivaráta
Áyia Evfimía
Mírtos Beach
Agónas
Áyios Kiriakí
Zolá
Ayios Spirídhon

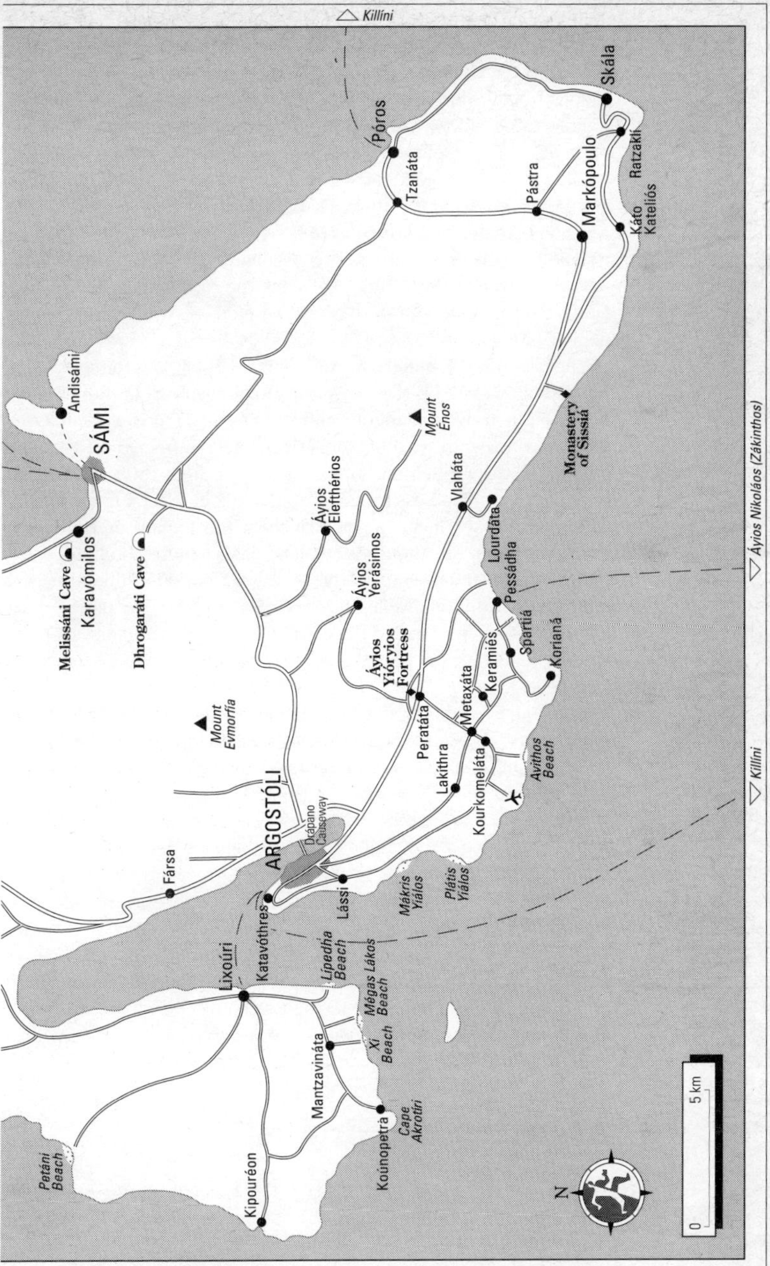
Killíni
Póros
Skála
Tzanáta
Pástra
Markópoulo
Ratzaklí
Káto Kateliós
Andisámi
SÁMI
Mount Énos
Monastery of Sissiá
Áyios Nikoláos (Zákinthos)
Melissáni Cave
Karavómilos
Dhrogaráti Cave
Áyios Elefthérios
Vlaháta
Lourdáta
Áyios Yerásimos
Pessádha
Spartiá
Áyios Yióryios Fortress
Keramiés
Korianá
Mount Evmorfía
Metaxáta
Peratáta
Lakíthra
Kourkomeláta
Ávithos Beach
Killíni
ARGOSTÓLI
Drápano Causeway
Fársa
Lássi
Mákris Yiálos
Plátis Yiálos
Katavóthres
Lixoúri
Lípedha Beach
Mégas Lákos Beach
Xi Beach
Mantzavináta
Cape Akrotíri
Kounopetra
Kipouréon
Petáni Beach
N
0
5 km

Peloponnesian War (431–404 BC), Kefalloniá was overrun by Athens which, while an ally, distrusted the island and seized it to use as a base for attacks on Corinth to the east – to no avail, as the Ionian islands fell to Sparta at the end of the war. In the Byzantine period, Kefalloniá became the seat of the "theme", or administrative district, of the islands. Out of the mainstream of Byzantine politics, however, it – like the rest of the Ionian islands – fell prone to attack by pirates and other opportunists. In 1082, the Ionians were attacked by the Normans, under Robert Guiscard. When his son failed to take Kefalloniá, Guiscard and his forces sailed from Corfu to back him, but within weeks of reaching the island the Norman leader had succumbed to plague. The port where he died, Fiskárdho, derives its name from his.

The island was handed over to Venice in 1204, and for some time was administered by the powerful Orsini dynasty of Rome, who imported their own aristocrats and introduced a feudal system. Over the following centuries, Kefalloniá ricocheted between the Turks, the Venetians, the French and the Russians, until in 1809 the **British** took over in a bloodless invasion. Kefalloniá became a focus for the widespread resentment of the British in the Ionian: in 1848, this erupted in open rebellion, with violent clashes in Argostóli, followed by heavy jail sentences for activists. A brief period of liberal parliamentary reform followed, but was overturned by a new British administration, who exiled the editors of radical island newspapers. Britain finally ceded Kefalloniá and the other Ionian islands to Greece in 1864.

Kefalloniá was taken over by the **Germans** in World War II in a particularly gruesome fashion. The island had been seized by the Italians, who controlled it briefly prior to the fall of Mussolini and Italy's capitulation in September 1943. At this moment of administrative confusion, with contradictory orders to both surrender and repel the Germans, the Italians were left helpless and hopelessly outnumbered. Rather than herd them into POW camps, the Germans, according to Ionian historian Arthur Foss, "decided in cold blood to massacre their former allies". In villages on the slopes of Mount Énos, and out near the sea mills of Katovóthres at Argostóli, over 5000 Italian soldiers were shot and their bodies burnt. The massacre is a key event in Louis de Bernière's novel, *Captain Corelli's Mandolin*, a tragicomic epic spanning the start of Greece's involvement in World War II up to the present day.

Argostóli and around

Despite the 1953 earthquakes, **ARGOSTÓLI** is a very attractive town, with some remaining pre-quake architecture, a large and airy main square, and a busy waterfront facing east across the Koutávos lagoon to the wooded slopes of Mount Evmorfía. The waterfront dou-

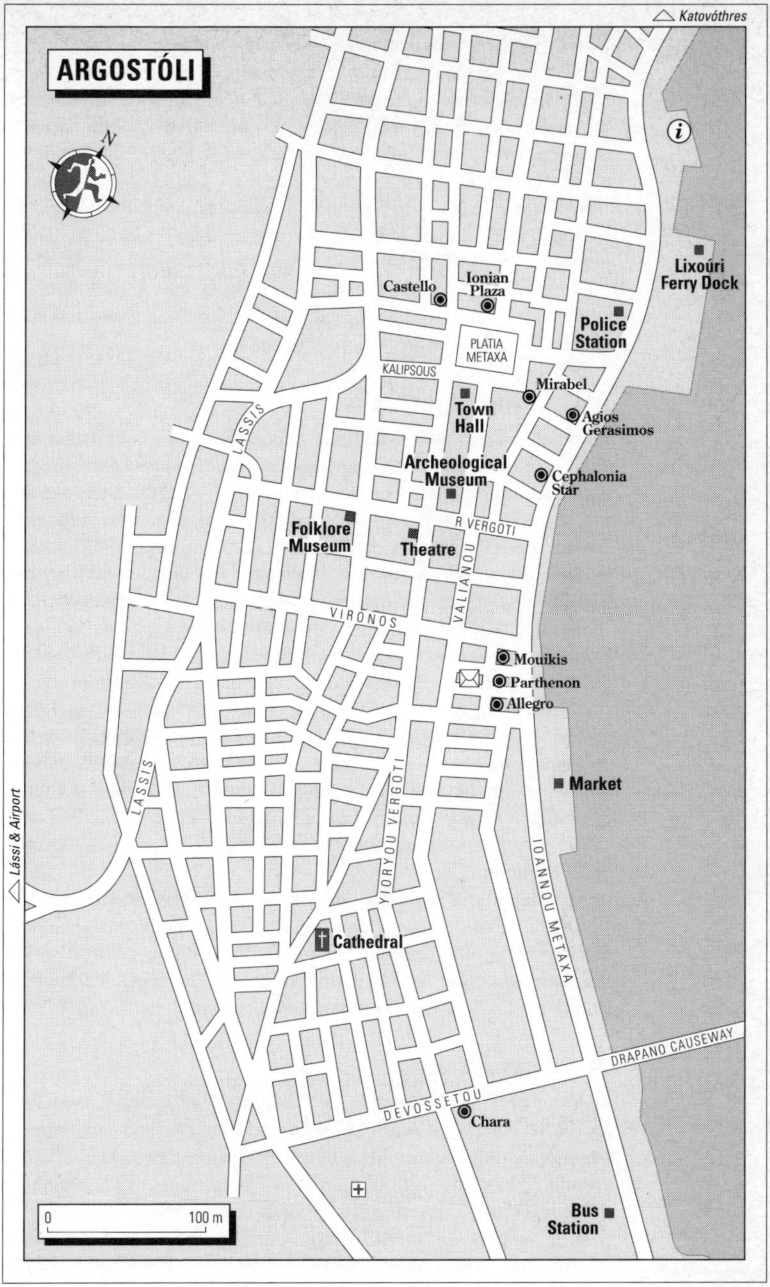

ARGOSTÓLI
N
Katovóthres
Lixoúri Ferry Dock
Castello
Ionian Plaza
Police Station
PLATIA METAXA
KALIPSOUS
Mirabel
Town Hall
Agios Gerasimos
LASSIS
Archeological Museum
Cephalonia Star
Folklore Museum
Theatre
R VERGOTI
VALIANOU
VIRONOS
Mouikis
Parthenon
Allegro
Market
LASSIS
Lássi & Airport
YIORYOU VERGOTI
IOANNOU METAXA
Cathedral
DRAPANO CAUSEWAY
DEVOSSETOU
Chara
0
100 m
Bus Station

bles as a working quayside used by fishermen and freighters, and an illuminated promenade at night. Day and evening tour craft line the parts of the quay not used by working boats. The lagoon is traversed by the Drápano bridge, a remarkable feat of engineering overseen by the Swiss-born soldier and politician, Charles Philippe de Bosset, British governor of Kefalloniá from 1810 to 1814. Originally built of wood, the bridge caused some controversy among islanders, who feared that it might help potential invaders. Although most package tourists to Kefalloniá will find themselves based along the Lassí peninsula (a twenty-minute walk from or into Argostóli) or at outlying resorts such as Skála, Póros, Áyios Evfimía or Fiskárdho, there is still a high level of tourism based in town, and restaurants and bars which cater to both townspeople and visitors.

Arrival and information

Argostólí's shiny new **Kefallinía airport** lies 11km south of town. There are no airport buses, and suburban bus routes to nearby villages like Svoronáta are so infrequent there is little point in recommending that you try to connect with them. As with every airport in the Ionian, expensive taxi rides into town (around 3500dr) have become an unofficial tourism surcharge. Kefalloniá's taxi drivers have a cute twist on the custom, though: they also charge per piece of luggage. Negotiate a price beforehand and *always* feign disbelief. Apart from a bar-café and an exchange booth which opens to meet international flights, there are no other facilities at the airport.

Those arriving in Argostóli by bus from other parts of the island will wind up at the brand-new KTEL **bus station**, a minute from the Drápano causeway, which sports a café-bar and modern toilets. Unless you're booked into a hotel or travelling straight on from Argostóli, it's best to head for the main square, **Platía Metaxá**, if only to get your bearings, or to dump your bags at a bar and look for a hotel or room.

Argostóli's **tourist office**, the friendliest in the Ionian, is at the north end of the seafront, in a one-storey building next to the port authority. The office has information about rooms, and can advise on transport and other resorts around the island (☎0671/22 248 or 24 466; Mon–Fri 8am–2pm, in August until 10pm).

Accommodation

Argostóli never seems a particularly busy town, but its **accommodation** can be full even at the dead end of the tourism season and in the winter, when some of the hotels around Platía Metaxá remain open. Yet compared to cities like Pátra or Corfu, and other island capitals such as Zákinthos or Lefkádha, Argostóli's hotels are very reasonable.

In a working town with a large permanent population, **private rooms** aren't too plentiful, but the tourist office has a list of what's available. Some of the best bargains can be found through waterfront tavernas, such as the *Kalafatis* (☎0671/22 627; ②), nearest to the Drápano bridge on the Metaxá waterfront, the *Tzivras* (☎0671/22 628; ②) on Vandórou, just off the centre of the waterfront, or *Spiro Rouhotas* taverna (☎0671/23 941; ②), opposite the Lixoúri ferry ramp. A number of travel agencies also offer rooms, apartments and villas: try *Ionian Options* (☎0671/22 054) on XXI Máiou, by the Lixoúri ferry, or *Filoxenos Travel* (☎0671/23 055/6) on R. Vergóti.

The town's one **campsite**, *Argostoli Camping* (☎0671/23 487), lies 2km north of the centre, just beyond the Katovóthres sea mills. The site has basic amenities, a shop, restaurant-bar and, surprisingly, what it describes as a "music hall". Despite the presence of a bus stop, there's only an infrequent service in high season, so you'll probably have to walk.

Budget hotels

Allegro, Andréa Choída 2 (☎0671/22 268). A block from the front, in an alley off the middle of Ioánnou Metaxá, basic but decent rooms with a choice of en-suite or shared bathrooms. ③.

Chara, Devossetoú (☎0671/22 427). A small and drastically simple rooming house, but only three blocks up from the Drápano bridge and a minute from the bus station. ②.

Parthenon, Zakynthoú 4 (☎0671/22 246). The bargain stay in Argostóli: a small, friendly and old-fashioned hotel tucked in an alley along from the *Mouikis Hotel*, best approached from the waterfront. ②.

Moderate hotels

Ayios Gerasimos, Áyios Gerásimos 6 (☎0671/24 113, fax 28 697). Compact, modern hotel with comfortable en-suite rooms, in an alley between Vergóti and XXI Máiou off the waterfront. Open year-round. ③.

Mirabel, Platía Metaxá (☎0671/25 381–3, fax 25 384). Tucked into the south-west corner of the main square, with large and comfortable air-conditioned en-suite rooms. Good value for its position, open year-round and takes credit cards. ③.

Mouikis, Vironós 3 (☎0671/23 454–6). The mid-price favourite: anonymous decor but very comfortable en-suite rooms with air-conditioning, balcony, phone and TV. Comparable to *Mirabel* but in a quieter setting. Busy year-round, so booking advisable, and takes credit cards. ③.

Expensive hotels

Castello, Platía Metaxá (☎0671/23 250). Small but stylish hotel with en-suite rooms overlooking the *platía*. Café and bar. Open year-round. ④.

Cephalonia Star, Ioánnou Metaxá 50 (☎0671/23 181, fax 23 180). Large waterfront hotel, with spacious en-suite rooms whose balconies overlook lagoon and hills. Restaurant and bar. Tends to be heavily booked by British travel companies, but rooms should be available throughout the season. ④.

Ionian Plaza, Platía Metaxá (☎0671/25 581, fax 25 585). Possibly the ritziest hotel in the archipelago, and surprisingly cheap for what it is – designer decor down to its swagged curtains and chic bathroom fixtures. If it's in your budget, this is a pampered capitalist's bargain. ⑤.

The Town

The mansions on the palm-lined boulevard of V. Geórgiou leaving the north side of Platía Metaxá give an idea of the elegance and wealth of Argostóli before the 1953 earthquakes. The *platía* is the focus of town life, although, typically, its restaurants and bars are the most expensive in town. The square's southwest corner, next to the small park, makes a useful landmark as it leads off both towards Lassí and the nearest beaches. Argostóli's main retail and administrative streets, where you'll find shops, banks and the post office, run south of the square.

The archeological museum

Argostóli Archeological Museum, on R. Vergóti, is open Tues–Sun 8.30am–2pm; 500dr.

Modest if compared to Corfu Town's, the **archeological museum** at Argostóli nevertheless runs to two spacious rooms containing a plethora of artefacts excavated on the island, mainly pottery, jewellery, glassware and other domestic items, some dating from the Mycenean period. There are also fragments of architectural details, funerary relics and some statuary, including a ribald Pan figure

Earthquakes in the Ionian

Three **tectonic plates** meet in the region of Kefalloniá, Itháki and Zákinthos: the Eurasian Plate, which carries Italy, parts of northern Greece and the Balkans; the Turkish–Hellenic Plate, which carries southern Greece and the Aegean, as well as Turkey and Cyprus; and the African Plate, which supports most of the southern Mediterranean. These plates are in constant, minute motion, part of a process called subduction which is causing Greece to sink slowly into the Aegean. The tension between the plates causes continual, usually minor **seismic activity**. Major earthquakes occur only a few times each century, and the twentieth seems to have had its quota, notably in the violent upheavals of 1948 and 1953.

The worst quake on record, in **August 1953**, wreaked destruction across Kefalloniá, Itháki, Lefkádha and Zákinthos, and inspired an international aid campaign by America, Britain and France. No less than 113 distinct tremors or aftershocks hit the islands over a period of five days from August 9 to 14. Argostóli and Zákinthos Town were virtually razed to the ground, with roads piled up like waves and huge vents opened up in the landscape. Over six hundred islanders died and thousands more were injured. An estimated seventy percent of buildings throughout the islands were destroyed, and some communities were wiped out altogether. Argostóli's Archeological Museum exhibits some remarkable photographic records of the event.

Tremors are common throughout the Ionian every year, but normally so minor that they go unnoticed. Islanders are generally phlegmatic about the threat of another major earthquake; beyond limiting the height of buildings and reinforcing foundations, there is nothing else they can do. Your chances of experiencing a tremor, less still an earthquake, while on holiday here are very slim.

found at the Melissáni cave shrine, who was once obviously priapic but is now in a state of blunt detumescence. If underwhelming, the collection does suggest that prehistoric Kefalloniá was culturally advanced compared to neighbouring islands.

The folklore museum

The **Korgialenío History and Folklore Museum**, on Ilía Zervoú behind the Municipal Theatre, is rich in detail of domestic life and island culture over the centuries. Its collection of furniture, clothing and other memorabilia is presented in a series of mock rooms from various eras and social strata: from a peasant kitchen to the drawing room of a wealthy family's mansion. Most fascinating is its extensive collection of photographs of the island before and after the 1953 earthquakes, which record both the sophistication of Kefallonian architecture and culture, and the extent of the devastation after the tremors.

The Korgialenío History and Folklore Museum is open Tues–Sun 8.30am–2pm; 500dr.

The sea mills

The disused **sea mills** at Katovóthres, an intriguing geological oddity forty minutes' walk north through pine woods from the centre of Argostóli, have become something of a tourist trap, dominated by a large multiroomed taverna and music hall to which coachloads of tourists are bused in shifts starting at 6pm. During the day, though, anyone can walk into the concreted-over complex of pools and (disused) water wheel. The view of Lixoúri, the Gulf of Argostóli and the mountains is magnificent, as are the sunsets. The sink holes at the tip of the peninsula into which seawater drains were first discovered in the 1830s, and before World War II were harnessed to provide electricity. However, it took until the 1960s for scientists to discover where the water went: they dumped green dye into the sink holes, and two weeks later the traces started to appear in the Melissáni cave and in springs along the Sámi–Áyia Evfimía coast. Moving at something like 1km a day, the water seeps under the mountains to reappear 20km away on the other side of the island.

Nearby is the **Áyios Theodóros lighthouse**, no more than a small Doric rotunda with a light on its roof. It was built by Charles Napier, governor of the island from 1822 to 1830, and resident during Byron's brief visit prior to his fateful journey to Messolónghi (the original was in fact destroyed by an earthquake in 1875, but rebuilt to the same design). Curiously, it resembles a smaller version of the Maitland rotunda in Corfu Town, built only a few years before, which might suggest a certain rivalry between the two men.

There are some small, pebbly coves towards and around Katovóthres, but most Greeks and tourists based in town either walk or take the bus to the beach at Lassí.

Eating and drinking

If you want to eat with the Greeks, your first destination should be either the aforementioned *Tzivras* or *Kalafatis* **tavernas**: the former has an impressive range of taverna staples with a lot of vegetarian options like *briám* (potato and courgette bake), helpings of which tend to be large and should probably be ordered on their own. *Kalafatis* has a more conventional menu, but succulently done. Either is the likely place to find a bona fide Kefallonian meat pie, a traditional dish with a pudding-like crust, and meat stuffing mixed with rice and vegetables. Both are extremely popular, so if thwarted head for the neighbouring *Anonymous* or *Sapfo* tavernas.

Eating in Platía Metaxá is an altogether different matter, usually done to the accompaniment of tinkling stemware under candlelight. The *Ionian Plaza Hotel*'s *Palazzino* restaurant has a good, if not particularly cheap, range of exotic pasta dishes, and the *Kefalos* opposite is recommended for decent breakfasts and lunch, and evening staples like spaghetti, steak, salads. *The Captain's Table*, the smartest in town – it actually has a greeter – is recommended for a splurge and for anyone keen to experience the little-heard Kefallonian style of *kantáthes* singing (nightly from 9pm).

Zaharoplastía around the square and on the waterfront serve continental breakfasts, but at a price. The best is the *Igloo* on Andréa Choída, a few blocks south of the *Mouikis Hotel* and a block from the waterfront, which is also good for a quiet evening drink. Alternatively, the waterfront fruit and veg **market** is a great place to assemble your own breakfast or lunch, with provisions from the bakeries and supermarkets opposite.

Platía Metaxá is the main attraction in the evenings, for a meal, drink or just a *vólta*, but it's also prone to overspill from two loud and competing music **bars** – fab if you like your Human League remixes laced with blasts of grunge, not so great if you don't. Local poseurs prefer to loll at the *Da Cappo* café-bar, the *Flonitiko* café and the *Koukos* club-bar, on V. Geórgiou near the square – all very stylish but none of them cheap. You'll find a quieter and cheaper drink on the waterfront in the bars towards the Lixoúri ferry – *Spiro Rouhotas*'s is ideal – or, in the opposite direction, head for the best-sited bar in the whole of Argostóli, the modest but welcoming *kafeníо* right by the Drápano bridge, with a view other bar-owners would kill for.

Listings

Banks and exchange The Ionian Bank, Andóniou Trítsi 73; the Bank of Greece on Valiánou; the National Bank, corner of Konstantínou and Sitebórou (all Mon–Fri 8am–1.30pm). The post office also changes travellers' cheques, and the *Hotel Mouikis* offers bank rates.

Car and bike rental Recommended is the island-wide *Sunbird* agency, which has an office at Andóniou Trítsi 84 (☎0671/23 723). *Budget* can be found at Lassí 3 (☎0671/24 232), and *Ford* car rental has offices in Argostóli on Ioánnou Metaxá (☎0671/22 338) and on the main drag at Lassí (☎0671/25 471–2), as well as Skála and Póros.

Ferries The *Bartholomos* agency by the Lixoúri ferry dock (☎0671/28 853) is the main agent for Greece–Italy lines. The *Vassilatos* agency, Ioánnou Metaxá 54 (☎0671/22 618 or 28 000), also handles international ferry bookings.

Hospital On the corner of Devossetoú and Souídias (☎0671/22 434 or 24 641).

Laundry There's a self-service laundromat on the Lassí road, three blocks up from the Napier Gardens (daily 8am–10pm); the mini-market opposite sells tokens for the machines, and individual one-wash bags of powder. There's also a *plindírio*/dry-cleaner on Krítis, behind the *Mouikis* hotel.

Olympic Airways G. Vergóti 1 (☎0671/28 808).

OTE R. Vergóti (daily 7am–midnight).

Performing arts The growth of video appears to have killed off the town's *Rex* cinema on V. Georgíou, but the imposing blue and white *Municipal Theatre* on G. Vergóti opens occasionally for special performances of music and drama.

Police Metaxá, by the Lixoúri ferry jetty (☎0671/22 300).

Post office Konstantínou (Mon–Fri 8am–1pm).

Lixoúri and the Lixoúrion peninsula

LIXOÚRI was flattened in the 1953 earthquake, and little of it has risen above two or three storeys since. The waterfront it presents to ferries arriving from Argostóli is uninspiring: a smattering of tavernas and bars on either side of the town square, Platía Petrítsi, but all of it rather dowdy. It has many fans, however, who use it as a base for the quiet sandy beaches on the way to Cape Akrotíri, and for exploring the mountainous central and northern sections of the peninsula by car or motorbike.

Ferries run between the northern end of Argostóli's quayside and Lixoúri in half an hour (Mon–Sat hourly, Sun every two hours; one-way 200dr, vehicle 500dr).

Like its larger neighbour, Lixoúri consists of a long, narrow grid of alleys stretched along the seafront, with little beyond apart from a few hotels in the dormitory area at the back of town. The beach immediately to the south is narrow but sandy and popular with families. Better beaches can be found 2km south, at **Lípedha**, with its rich red sand and unusual sandstone rock formations. While there are rooms within a kilometre of Lípedha (see below), the only facilities so far at this embryonic resort are two beach bars.

Lixoúri practicalities

Lixoúri has a small strip of beachside **hotels** a few hundred metres south along the coast road leaving the waterfront. The two main establishments here, the *Poseidon* (☎0671/92 518 or 92 519; ③) and *Summery* (☎0671/91 771 or 91 871, fax 91 062; ③), are both reasonable value and, though heavily booked by British tour operators, should have rooms free through most of the season for independent travellers. Both have en-suite rooms with balconies and views; the former has gardens giving onto the beach, the latter a pool and tennis courts. The best bargain for accommodation in Lixoúri, however – if prices hold – is the *Giardino* (☎0671/92 505 or 92 382, fax 92 525; ②), four blocks back from the front – take the road leaving the right-hand corner at the back of Platía Petrítsi – which has en-suite rooms, pool, restaurant and bar. This too is used by package tours, but if you phone ahead you'll often find that it has availability.

Perdikis Travel (☎0671/91 097 or 93 077, fax 92 503) on the ferry quay is an agent for **rooms** in Lixoúri and outside town, as is the very friendly *A.D. Travel* (☎0671/93 142 or 92 663), based a few blocks back behind the north end of the town square, just by the bridge over the dry riverbed. An attractive if out-of-the-way alternative is the *Taverna Apolafsi* rooms and studios (☎0671/91 691, fax 91 572; ②). Blissfully quiet except on music nights, the taverna is a twenty-minute walk south from Lixoúri towards Lípedha beach.

If you're **eating** in Lixoúri, the first place to head for is the *Akrogiali* on the seafront. It's not cheap, but this authentic island taverna has an extensive menu and attracts customers from all over the island. Nearby *Antoni's* mixes traditional dishes with a line of steaks and European food, while *Maria's*, a block back and behind the square to the south, is a large, cheap and basic family taverna. South of the square, the *Archipelagos* restaurant-*ouzerí* has a good range of seafood and pasta, and doubles as a bar in the evenings. At night, drinkers tend to congregate in the square and in the pricey seafront **bars**, but the funkiest place to drink in Lixoúri is the small and friendly *kafenío* facing the ferry dock.

The south coast of the peninsula

The flatter southern part of the peninsula, known locally as **Kátoi**, still bears some of the most dramatic scars of the 1953 earthquake. This farming region was one of the worst hit on the island, and in places there remain eerie landscapes of subsided fields and orchards, and small hills shunted up out of the earth. Flocks of bell-laden sheep graze on the weird tumuli left by the quake, sending crazy gamelan music drifting across the countryside. The only **bus** service on the peninsula connects Lixoúri with Xi beach, 6km away to the south, three times a day. On the way it detours to **Mégas Lákos**, where the beach is narrow but a rich, almost silky, red, set below low cliffs and served by a couple of tavernas.

Xi itself has a beach bar, a couple of snack bar-tavernas, and serried ranks of sun loungers on the beach in front of the *Cephalonia Palace* **hotel** (☎0671/91 111–2 or 93 134, fax 92 638; ⑥). Popular with British tourists, this has all the typical facilities of a large, self-contained resort hotel – vast pool, restaurants, bars, shops, gardens – which is just as well, because the landscape between it and the nearest village, Mantzavináta, 2km north, is a desert-like moonscape.

A road also leads from Mantzavináta 4km southwest to the quieter beach at **Koúnopetra**, site of a curious rock formation. Until the 1953 earthquake, this rocking stone had a strange rhythmic movement that could be measured by placing a knife into a gap between the rock and its base. However, after the quake the rock became motionless.

The west coast of the peninsula

The peninsula has one of the finest vantage points for sunsets on the entire island: the **monastery of Kipouréon**, hefted up on the cliffs above the wild west coast some 14km from Lixoúri. The views are magnificent, but the monastery itself is minor, most of it having been rebuilt in the 1970s. Like the rest of the west coast of the peninsula, Kipouréon is only really accessible by private vehicle, and across some fairly rough terrain.

If you have your own transport, you could also reach the magnificent beach at **Petáni**, 14km northwest of Lixoúri, a dramatic two-kilometre stretch of sand that's possibly the finest, and certainly the remotest, on the island. The **Áyios Spirídhon** inlet, 16km from Lixoúri at the north of the promontory, has a sandy beach that's safe for swimming, though it seems to be unfortunately positioned to catch seaborne garbage.

Lassí

LASSÍ, a twenty-minute walk south from the centre of Argostóli, is an unattractive package resort that sprawls along the edge of a busy four-lane highway and suffers from being right under the flight path to the airport. The beaches, to be fair, are well maintained, although their modest size and the concentration of tourism in the area means they are very busy even in low season. Lassí's ribbon development has a number of good **restaurants** – the *Il Gabbiano* pizzeria, the *Panorama* taverna, and the upmarket *Trata* and *Sirtaki psistariés* – to serve those holidaying here, but given that there are far superior beaches around the southeastern tip of Kefalloniá, the independent traveller would be wasting time staying here. Immediately beyond Lassí, **Makrís Yiálos** and **Platís Yiálos** are good sandy beaches for a day out if you're staying in Argostóli, with snack bars and restaurants in the hotels overlooking the beach.

The Livátho peninsula

The **Livátho hills** to the southeast of Argostóli, beyond and inland from the beaches at Makrís Yiálos and Platís Yiálos, are ideal for gentle walking. This lush green range of rolling farmland and tree-shaded country roads slopes down to some fine beaches, most notably at Ávithos. The network of pretty little villages that dot the hills between Lakíthra and Pessádha are home to many wealthy islanders, which gives places like Kourkomeláta the air of chintzy suburbs – though there is surprisingly little in the way of facilities. The walking hereabouts is excellent, except in hunting season (Sept 25–Feb 28), when the threat of attack by off-leash hunting dogs has to be taken seriously (if possible, take a walking stick). Five **buses** a day run to Kourkomeláta, stopping at Lakíthra, Metaxáta and Svoronáta.

Ten kilometres southeast of Argostóli, the well-preserved village of **METAXÁTA** boasts a number of large, pre-earthquake mansions shaded by ancient palm trees, and a bust of Byron in its small, deserted town square, on the site of a house where the poet stayed. Substantially rebuilt after the 1953 earthquake, **KOURKOMELÁTA**, 1km to the southwest, sits on a bluff overlooking the coast. The *Marina* **café-bar** here, with a garden and excellent views, is virtually the only such establishment between Lakíthra and Spartía. Kourkomeláta also has a large, impressive church, Áyios Gerásimos (usually locked), and a Neoclassical Cultural Centre, used occasionally for special events. Just downhill from Kourkomeláta is **KALIGÁTA**, dominated by a beautiful blue and white campanile attached to its Baroque church. The village is home to the Calliga winery, which produces the island's excellent Robola wines. **Ávithos beach**, a gentle two-kilometre walk south of Kaligáta, is in fact two large coves, with a solitary beach taverna and views out to Diás island. It's the last sign of sand before the pebbles of Loúrdha bay to the east and offers good, safe swimming.

East of Metaxáta, the terrain alters from green woodland to flat farmland and, north towards Peratáta, the scrubby lower slopes of Mount Énos. Two kilometres on, **KERAMÍES** is a working country town, with a large square and fountain, although oddly quiescent: its one *kafenío* was closed and up for sale in 1996. On the coast at Loúrdha bay, **SPARTÍA** sits above a small harbour with a smattering of holiday bungalows and a taverna. **PESSÁDHA**, further round the bay, is equally uninspiring: apart from a couple of tavernas, it's notable solely for its daily summer ferry connection with Zákinthos.

Áyios Yióryios fortress

Although an earthquake destroyed much of its interior detail in the seventeenth century, the Venetian fortress at **Áyios Yióryios** is one of the best-preserved structures of its kind in the archipelago. The *kástro* is reached by a steep one-kilometre walk up the lane signposted at the centre of the town of Peratáta, 7km from Argostóli and on the bus routes to both Skála and Póros. The remaining walls and battlements command spectacular views out over the entire Livátho region, Argostóli itself and Mount Énos to the east.

It's estimated that a defensive structure has existed on the rocky pinnacle since the fourth century AD, and the fortress was established as the island's capital by the Normans in the twelfth century. It was extensively expanded by the Orsinis in the thirteenth century, and remained the centre of island life for several centuries, with a population of as many as 15,000, as a bulwark against repeated Ottoman attacks.

Áyios Yióryios fortress is open Tues–Sat 8am–8pm, Sun 8am–2pm; 500dr.

While much of the interior is ruined, the walls, towers and subterranean features such as dungeons remain. Most remarkable is a secret **tunnel**, some 9km long, leading from the *kástro* to a point on the road around the south of the Koutávos lagoon. Now disused, the tunnel was dug as an escape route in case the *kástro* were ever overrun. It was last used in 1943, when a group of Italian soldiers, besieged inside the *kástro* by German soldiers, were spirited out of it by sympathetic islanders.

Mount Énos

Mount Énos, the vast hogback mountain that dominates the south of the island, has been declared a national park, mainly to protect wildlife rather than attract visitors. Facilities are nonexistent and, at 15km from the Argostóli–Sámi road, walking to the summit isn't much of an option.

Minor routes lead up onto the mountain from the south, at Astoupádes and Áyios Yióryios, and from the north at Digaléto, but the most direct approach is to take the signposted turning some 14km from Argostóli on the main Sámi road (4km beyond the turning signposted for the hamlet of Frangáta). From the turn-off, it's 3km to the hamlet of Áyios Eleftérios, and 12km further by rough road to the highest peak (1628m).

As well as being one of the highest mountains in Greece, Énos is also unusual for the amount of vegetation, notably the indigenous *abies cephalonica* firs. Despite vast fires and animal deforestation over the centuries, the mountain remains one of the largest areas of forest in the archipelago. A herd of a dozen or so wild horses forage in the woodlands, but tend to avoid humans. Falcons, eagles and other raptors are common sights. The views are the best in the entire Ionian, reaching as far north as the mountains of Corfu, across to the Peloponnese, and to nearby Zákinthos, Lefkádha and Itháki. It's essential to take local advice on weather before setting out for the mountain, particularly out of season, when conditions can deteriorate very quickly.

Southeast Kefalloniá

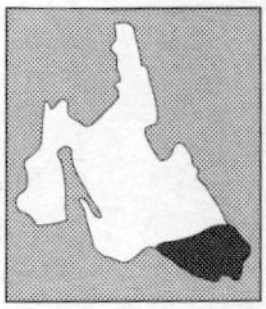

The main coast road to the east of Peratáta yields few places to stay or even stop, although the vast **Kateliós bay** to the west of Skála has the finest sandy beaches on Kefalloniá. The resort of **Skála** is the best package destination at this end of the island, as its neighbour **Póros**, with a narrow pebble beach and crumbling concrete seafront, has begun to look a little careworn recently.

Vlaháta and Lourdáta

The first stop of any note beyond Peratáta is the village of **VLAHÁTA**, which is slowly blending with the micro-resort of Lourdáta on the coast below. Vlaháta has some rooms (*Maria Studios*, ☎0671/31 055) and a good taverna, the *Dionysus*, but you would be better off continuing to **LOURDÁTA**, 2km south. This growing seaside hamlet has a fine shingle beach, a kilometre or so long, and a couple of

tavernas on a tiny plane-shaded village square – the *New World* and the *Diamond*, which has a large range of vegetarian alternatives to standard fare – as well as the smarter *Spiros* steak and grill house just above the village. *Adonis* (☎0671/31 206; ②) and *Ramona* (☎0671/31 032; ②) have **rooms** just outside the village, on the road down, while the one **hotel**, the *Lara* (☎0671/31 157, fax 31 156; ③), down by the beach, has comfortable en-suite rooms with sea views, a restaurant and bar. Most of its clientele are British package tourists, booked by the week or fortnight, but it also has rooms for independent travellers at most times in the season. Beyond this, Lourdáta's facilities stretch only as far as a couple of shops, a bike rental place, *Yamata* (☎0671/31 311), and the *Adonis* cocktail bar.

Sissiá and Markópoulo

Beyond Vlaháta, the road passes beneath the peak of Énos, through primeval mountainscapes and boulder fields veined with flood drains to channel the sometimes apocalyptic winter storms. Four kilometres from Vlaháta, a lane leads 1km down towards the sea and the ruins of the thirteenth-century **monastery of Sissiá**, associated in myth with a visit by St Francis of Assisi, who is said to have been forced ashore here in a storm. The original building was abandoned centuries ago, and demolished in the 1953 earthquakes. A new and rather nondescript monastery was built after the quake.

Three kilometres on, the main road forks – left to Póros, right to Skála. The villages in this region are small and mostly resistant to tourism, although **MARKÓPOULO**, 5km along the Póros road, is noteworthy for two curious reasons. On the one hand, it is claimed by local wags to be the birthplace of the eponymous adventurer. More importantly, every August 15, for the festival of the Assumption of the Virgin Mary, its church of the **Panayía of Langouvárda** is the site of a bizarre **snake-handling ritual**. The church stands on the site of the monastery of Our Lady of Langouvárda, destroyed in the earthquake, which in turn had been first established as a nunnery. The story goes that when the nunnery was attacked by pirates, the nuns prayed to be transformed into snakes to avoid being taken prisoner. Their prayers were answered, and each year the "return" of a swarm of small, harmless black snakes is meant to bring the villagers good luck. As Mother Nature is unlikely to keep such a schedule, some discreet snake breeding on the part of the village priests must be suspected.

Katelió s

Along the Skála fork of the coast road, the mountain landscape opens out into a wide, empty valley around **KATELIÓS** and the neighbouring resort of **KÁTO KATELIÓS**, which are rapidly preparing for expansion. Manos Holidays already brings clients here, and the telltale skeletons of apartment developments are appearing across the valley. However, they have yet to have an impact on the wild landscape here, and so far few tourists have arrived to begin to occupy the long sandy beaches. There's one **hotel**, the smart, modern *Odyssia* (☎0671/81 614; ④), and a small development of spanking new self-contained **apartments**, available through the stylish *Arbouro* **taverna** (☎0671/81 192; ③). The beaches looping around eastwards to Kaminía, below the village of Ratzaklí, are loggerhead turtle nesting grounds, so care should be taken to avoid nests and the usual guidelines followed (see box on p.204). Because of the turtle presence, freelance camping isn't advisable here; you would, in any case, face a strenuous hike to Ratzaklí to find water, toilets or shops.

Southeast Kefalloniá

Skála

The popular resort of **SKÁLA** attracts a sizeable return clientele, who keep it busy into October when other resorts (including its neighbour Póros) have all but closed down. It can boast the finest beaches at this end of the island, running away for several kilometres in either direction and backed by a sweep of native Kefallonian pines, which give the place an oddly un-Mediterranean feel, more akin to parts of the Scottish or New England coastline. A small **Roman villa**, signed on a path above the beach just by the *Golden Beach Palace* rooms, was excavated in the 1950s to reveal a pair of well-preserved mosaics, one of a man being attacked by wild cats, the other a scene around a sacrificial altar. The mosaics are protected in a modern wood and glass structure, and a modest entrance fee (300dr) is charged.

Rebuilt after the 1953 earthquake, the compact village spreads out from a small square, with the main action on the short high street that runs down to the beach. Much **accommodation** is prebooked well in advance, and private rooms are scarce, although Dennis Zapantis has studios and apartments at his *Dionysus Rooms* (☎0671/83 283; ②), a block south of the high street, and rooms can be found at the *Golden Beach Palace*, 100m south of the seafront square (☎0671/83 327; ②). More upmarket, the *Tara Beach Hotel* (☎0671/83 250 or 83 341–3, fax 83 344; ④) can offer comfortable en-suite rooms or individual bungalows in lush gardens on the edge of the beach. If all else fails, try *Skalina Tours* (☎0671/83 175 or 83 275), one of a number of agencies which offer accommodation and car/bike **rental** in the village; *Ford* car rental has an office just off the main drag (☎0671/03 276).

Skála falls behind neighbouring Póros in terms of seafood restaurants, but it does have a number of good eating options. Try the *Pines*, which is split between the beach (serving snacks and salads) and the road above the beach, where it becomes a fully fledged restaurant veering between north European and local dishes; or the *Flamingo*, which offers a mix of seafood, steaks and island dishes like Kefallonian meat pie. The beach also has two conventional tavernas, the *Paspalis* and *Sunset*, both good for lunches. *The Loft* is a hip late-night cocktail **bar** near the town square, and the beachside *Pikiona* pool and music bar stays open until the small hours.

Póros

With stamina and a spare three or four hours, it's possible to reach **PÓROS** on foot from Skála, along 13km of rough coastal road through fairly wild undeveloped countryside; 1km out of Skála, you'll pass the vestigial remains of a Roman temple. Only two buses a day (Mon–Sat) run between the resorts, so the journey is most easily covered by car or motorbike, over the final hump of Mount Énos, through the hill towns of Áyios Yióryios and **TZANÁTA**. The latter is worth a halt (at 4km – uphill – it's also walkable from Póros) to visit the large Mycenean burial chamber unearthed outside the village. The chamber, a lined circular underground vault with entranceway, was only excavated in 1991, and is believed to be the last resting place of a local Bronze Age chieftain. Archeological investigations are continuing, as this is another site contending for the crown of Homer's "real" Ithaca. Beyond here, the road to Póros plunges down through a small but dramatic gorge which carries a river (usually dry) through the town.

Póros in fact comprises two bays: the first you'll come to is the centre of tourist activities; the second, a five-minute walk over the small headland to the south, is the port proper, which has ferry connections with Zákinthos Town and Killíni on the mainland. After the three main towns, Póros is the largest development on the island, and there's certainly plenty to do and consume. Away from high and mid-season, however, when the bus services dwindle, Póros is geographically isolated, and anyone holidaying here without their own transport may feel they've picked the short straw.

These days, Póros looks distinctly frayed at the edges, with a scruffy concrete seafront in the first bay, which is where most package tourists will find themselves billeted, and a narrow, kilometre-long pebble beach stretching to the north. Paths off the road south to the port lead down to inviting blue-water swimming off rocks. Most of the action takes places in the main street running down to the seafront, and along the seafront itself.

Practicalities

Póros has plenty of **rooms**, **apartments** and a few **hotels**, although many of these places are block-booked by tour operators. The *Pension Astir* (☎0674/72 443; ②) has good-value en-suite rooms on the seafront, while the elegant new *Odysseus Palace*, on the crossroads at the back of town (☎0674/72 036, fax 72 148; ⑥), has very stylish en-suite rooms with balconies, and has offered bargain discounts of over fifty percent to British visitors in recent summers (halving the listed room price to 12,500dr a night). Rooms and apartments tend to cluster around the bridge crossing the riverbed:

try *Blue Bay* apartments (☎0674/72 500), *George's Rooms* (☎0674/72 508) or the *Macedonia Studios* (☎0674/72 840–2). Among **travel agents**, *Poros Travel* on the seafront (☎0674/72 476 or 72 284) offers a range of accommodation, as well as services such as car rental and ferry bookings. Neighbouring *Sarafis Shipping* (☎0674/72 555 or 72 556, fax 72 557), agents for various domestic and international ferry services, and for yacht charters, also has accommodation in the area. Ford car rental has an office on the main drag (☎0674/72 675).

The main seafront has the majority of the **restaurants**, and Póros's one nightclub, *J&A's*, overlooking the beach. At night, however, the old port is quieter and has more atmosphere, with tavernas such as *Tzivas* and the *Dionysus* that are strong on locally caught seafood.

Sámi and around

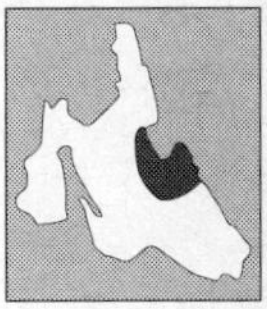

The former capital, **SÁMI**, is where the majority of island-hoppers will arrive on Kefalloniá. It's the only surviving settlement of the island's four ancient city-states, although little remains from this time beyond fragments of foundations dotted about the hill above the modern town. Initially, there seems to be little about Sámi to entice you to stay: the town is drab and functional, and the long sand-and-pebble beach it shares with Karavómilos is serviceable at best. However, there is a fine, near-deserted pebble beach 2km east at **Andisámos** and, more importantly, Sámi is the natural jumping-off point for the two major tourist attractions on the island, the **Drogharáti** cave system and the underground lake of **Melissáni**. Given the frequency of ferries between Sámi and Itháki, day-trips to the latter's capital, Váthi, are also easily manageable.

Sámi comprises a long, L-shaped seafront, with a small harbour to the east, and a compact grid of dormitory roads behind it. Most bars and restaurants are close to the crossroads – rather grandly dubbed Platía Kyproú – at the centre of the seafront. Hotels and rooms tend to be in the streets behind the seafront, and on the roads out of town: the main road to Argostóli, and the coast road north towards Áyia Evfimía.

Daily **ferries** arrive in Sámi from Váthi and Pisaetós on Itháki, and Astakós on the mainland, and there are connections from Italy and Pátra (*Strintzis Lines* has an office on the waterfront). **Taxis** meet ferries and congregate on Platía Kyproú. There are daily **bus** services between Sámi and Argostóli, although the last leaves at 3pm. In season, there are also two buses a day (Mon–Sat) from Sámi to Fiskárdho via Áyia Evfimía, and twice a week (Mon & Fri) to Ássos. Buses stop on the seafront just by Platía Kyproú. For renting a car or scooter, the handiest agency is *Karavomilos Hire* by the crossroads (☎0674/22 034).

Accommodation

Sámi has a good, though not particularly cheap, range of accommodation. Conveniently, the two *períptera* on the front handle basic **rooms** in town, as does the *Sami Supermarket* (☎0674/22 803; ②), whose vast sign is visible from the seafront, and the stylish *Cafe Riviera* on the front with offices in the *Kastro Hotel* (☎0674/22 656 or 22 282; ②); both café and hotel have good, if compact, rooms with all mod cons. If you arrive in high season and find these full, head for the miniature suburb just north of the town centre, which has walk-up signs for rooms in private homes. It's also worth considering the small, if rather dull, suburb of Karavómilos, around the bay from Sámi itself, for rooms: try the new, purpose-built *Calypso Apartments* (☎0674/22 933; ③) attached to the pottery workshop.

Given the prices of rooms in Sámi, you might just as well opt for a **hotel**. The *Kyma* (☎0674/22 064; ②) on Platía Kyproú is very basic and old-fashioned, but within spitting distance of the quay. More upmarket, the *Ionion* (☎0674/22 035 or 22 412; ③) has modern ensuite rooms, as does the smarter *Athina* (☎0674/23 066; ③). However, the best mid-range option is the *Melissani* (☎0674/22 064; ③), a small, friendly modern hotel signposted behind the main parade of quayside tavernas, which takes a range of credit cards. Sámi also has two top-of-the-range hotels: the *Sami Beach* (☎0674/22 802 or 22 824, fax 22 846; ⑤), with pool, bar, restaurant, and rooms overlooking the hotel gardens and the beach; and the quieter *Pericles* (☎0674/22 780–5, fax 22 787; ④), 500m back from the quay, which is popular with British tourists and has extensive grounds, with two pools and sports facilities, restaurant, bar and entertainment.

Sámi's one **campsite**, *Camping Karavomilos Beach* (☎0674/22 480, fax 22 932), is a short walk along the path above the beach towards Karavómilos, with a taverna, bar and shop. The site has over 300 pitches on flat, shady ground, and its gate leads directly onto the beach.

Eating and drinking

Sámi doesn't have a great many **tavernas** beyond those on the seafront. Visitors tend to doughnut around the smart *Adonis Restaurant*, which serves up a mixture of European cuisines, but the best bet is to follow the Greeks themselves to *Delfinia*, which produces succulent fresh fish and meat dishes, as well as a variety of vegetable options such as *briám* and *yígandes* beans, dished up in Desperate Dan-size portions.

The *Riviera* is the favourite **bar** in the evenings, and its *zaharoplastío* is great for after-dinner sweets or **breakfast**. The best place for a snack breakfast, however, is *Captain Jimmy's*, which is also recommended to anyone who has to feed a Häagen-Dasz habit.

Melissáni and Dhrogaráti caves

These two small but dramatic cave systems are both within walking distance of Sámi. At Melissáni, 5km away off the Áyia Evfimía road, there's an underground lake, illuminated by sunlight falling through a large hole in the ceiling. Dhrogaráti is a conventional cave tunnel system, but with a large central cavern. If you're stuck for time and have to choose, Melissáni is the more spectacular of the two.

Melissáni

The Melissáni cave is open daily 8am–6pm; 800dr. Carry a windcheater or lightweight waterproof – the cave is chilly even on hot days.

Melissáni cave is at least 30,000 years old, with stalactites that have been dated at around 20,000 years. Although it was only opened to tourists in the 1960s, it is known to have been used as a shrine to Pan in prehistoric times; artefacts from the shrine, including a risqué Pan figure, are displayed in Argostóli's archeological museum. From the entry in a small car park off the Sámi–Áyia Evfimía road, stairs lead down to a short tunnel sloping to a small balcony overlooking the underground lake, which is filled with water from the sinkholes at Katovóthres on the other side of the island (see p.169). Water exits Melissáni into the so-called Karavómilos Lake, which is actually a salt-water duckpond at Karavómilos beach, 500m away. The roof of the cave collapsed during the 1953 earthquake, providing a light that turns the water brilliant turquoise. For an extra fee (500dr per person seems to be the unofficial average), boatmen take groups out into the middle of the lake, and through to an interior chamber, where the Pan shrine is believed to have been. The lake is best seen around midday in high summer, with the sun overhead filling the cave with light, but it's just as impressive on a sunny October afternoon.

Dhrogaráti

The Dhrogaráti caves are open daily 8am–6pm; 800dr.

The **Dhrogaráti** caves are a good 3km along the main road out of Sámi and then 2km along a signposted track inland. Guides take small groups through a series of illuminated cave sections, leading to the stunning, cathedral-like central chamber. As well as an impressive array of illuminated stalactites and stalagmites, the chamber has extraordinary acoustics, and has been used for musical performances in the past, including, it's claimed, a concert by Maria Callas.

Áyia Evfimía

Built around a small port, 9km northwest of Sámi, **ÁYIA EVFIMÍA** is an amiable little town in which to lie low, although its beaches are among the worst on the island. The main one – laughably called Paradise – is a pebble cove barely 20m in length; those who find Paradise too tiny to squeeze onto will, however, find quieter coves along the road to Sámi. The town comprises an L-shaped quay around a tiny harbour, with a handful of backstreets and terraced alleys mounting the hillside above. Virtually all the action takes place on the quay, or just behind it.

In low season, Áyia Evfimía isn't a place to get stuck in without wheels. In summer, however, there are two **buses** a day to Sámi and to Fiskárdho, timed to enable you to spend the day in either, and two a week (Mon & Fri) to Ássos. It's easily possible to make a day-trip on the **ferries** to Váthi on Itháki, with enough time to make it to the Arethoúsa spring and back for lunch before the boat returns. There are also daily ferries on the short hop to Pisaetós (30min), which has a couple of tavernas, with the Homeric site of Alalkomenae an aerobic hour's hike uphill from the bay.

Practicalities

The *Dendrinos Taverna*'s **rooms** (☎0674/61 392; ②), at the northern end of town, are the bargain stay in Áyia Evfimía, although (as with all taverna rooms) they're prone to the heat and noise of the establishment. Both Dionysios Logaras (☎0674/61 202 or 61 349; ③) and Gerasimos Raftopolous (☎0674/61 216; ③) have comfortable modern rooms and apartments available in the centre. But at those prices you might as well check into either of Áyia Evfimía's two small, friendly **hotels**, *Pilaros* (☎0674/61 210; ③) and *Moustakis* (☎0674/61 030; ③), both of which have modern en-suite rooms a block back from the quay.

The *Dendrinos* **taverna**, above Paradise beach, is the best place to go for authentic island cuisine and barrel wine; the long-established *Pergola Restaurant* in the centre also has a wide range of island specialities and standard Greek dishes. Its neighbour, the newer *Finikas* taverna, offers a mix of fish, steaks and international cuisine, and the owners may be able to help with accommodation. Hipsters head straight for the *Cafe Triton* at night, died-in-the-wool philhellenes to the *Asteria Kafenio*, which doubles as the town barber. The *Strawberry zaharoplastío* is the place for a decadent breakfast, and *Gerolimatos Rentacar* (☎0674/61 036, fax 61 516) can supply a getaway vehicle.

Northern Kefalloniá

If heading north by bus from Argostóli, sit on the left to get the best sea views.

Kefalloniá's northern tip is most easily reached along the main road north from Argostóli, which provides some jaw-dropping views (the link road from Áyia Evfimía on the east coast to Dhivaráta sees fewer buses, though it's easily manageable if you're making a loop by car or motorbike). Heading out of the island capital, the road climbs above the Gulf of Argostóli into a series of small mountain villages. The first, **FÁRSA** (which has a *kafenío* and snack bar), was rebuilt after the earthquake, and the original village can be seen, in ruins, just above. Apart from the hamlet of Agónas, which leads off to the village of Zolá and the long, near-deserted sandy beach of **Áyios Kíriaki** below it, there is little else of note here until Mírtos Beach.

Mírtos

From the near-sheer cliffs above it, **Mírtos** appears as a dazzling crescent of white pebble next to a turquoise sea – though if you have to make the four-kilometre trip down from Dhivaráta on foot it loses a little of its sparkle. Buses only stop at Dhivaráta, although with your own transport you can drive all the way down to the beach. There's just one **restaurant** on the beach, which, along with a cave in the cliffs, provides the only shade for most of the day. The west-facing beach is a great place to catch the sunset, although given the bus times this is the preserve of the motorist or biker – or anyone prepared to rough it in the **rooms** at the no-name taverna in Dhivaráta.

Ássos

ÁSSOS should not be missed, even if you have to do it on one of the coach trips that swing through nearly every afternoon. The most atmospheric village on the island, it clings to a tiny isthmus leading to a huge fortified rock, which protects the pocket-sized harbour and pebbly beach. Ruined walls of pre-quake mansions surround the plane-shaded village square, dubbed "Paris" by villagers in honour of the French, who financed its reconstruction after the 1953 earthquakes. A path, zigzagging up through woodland and terraces, leads into the ruins of the **Venetian fortress**, which itself contains the ruins of three small churches, including the Catholic church of Áyios Markós. Until 1815, part of the fortress was Kefalloniá's version of Alcatraz, a virtually inescapable prison whose foundations are visible today.

Unfortunately, Ássos is also one of the most difficult places on the island to get to. Driving there is possible, although the access road down from the main Fiskárdho road is hair-raising even on the few KTEL **buses** that visit: three a week from Argostóli, and two from Sámi. Otherwise, Fiskárdho buses stop at the Ássos turning if you ask, and the early afternoon bus from Argostóli sometimes detours down to the village if it has school students to drop off. Early (10am) buses out of Argostóli and the afternoon (5pm) bus back from Fiskárdho make it easy to spend a day in Ássos if you allow time and energy for the walks down and up (a good hour each way).

Practicalities

Staying in Ássos is not easy, as much of the **accommodation** is block-booked throughout the season. The best place to start is with Andreas Roukis (☎0674/51 523; ②), whose rooms are on the right-hand side entering the village, with a telltale NTOG plaque outside (enquiries in the village are invariably directed towards him, anyway). If he's full, he should be able to point you elsewhere. The

Myrtos taverna, towards the fortress, may also be able to help with accommodation.

Ássos is cut off from the rest of Kefalloniá and charges accordingly. It has a number of good but pricey **restaurants**, including the *Nefeli Garden* on Platía Páris, the basic *Platanis Grill*, and the blue *psistariá* at the end of the quay. There are a couple of shops for basics, and fruit and vegetables can be bought from a small truck that stops in the village most afternoons. It's likely that staying for any length of time here might begin to feel like living in a goldfish bowl, but Ássos lacks the development of somewhere like Fiskárdho, and in low season it can be truly idyllic.

Fiskárdho

Beyond Ássos, the road heads inland and the terrain begins to alter. The northern tip of the island around **FISKÁRDHO** sits on a bed of limestone which buffered it against the worst effects of the 1953 earthquakes, and the coastline here is reminiscent of the tree-lined pebble coves of Paxí. Fiskárdho is the island's premier resort, a small fishing port built around a horseshoe bay lined with handsome old houses – most of them restaurants, bars or boutiques – with *kaíkia* and yachts moored at the quay. Day or night, the scene is picture-postcard pretty, its only drawback the lack of a beach in the bay. After Sámi, Fiskárdho is Kefallonia's busiest passenger port, with daily **ferry** connections to Itháki and Lefkádha (the ferry from Vassilikí also connects with Sámi to the south).

Fiskárdho has an upmarket reputation, with prices to match, and its boutiques teeter on the edge of flat-out chichi. As one restaurateur proudly boasts, "we attract mainly middle- and upper-class English people", which could either hasten your step or send you screaming in the opposite direction. At night it's a very vibey place, even in low season, though it tends towards claustrophobia: village rivalries run very close to the surface, and some visitors love playing doll's house with the Greeks and with other tourists. Although the village remains small and development is fairly contained, it's also the busiest resort, and remains so up until the last days of October. Much of the prime accommodation was snapped up years ago by blue-chip travel companies like Greek Islands Club and Simply Ionian, though everyone and her sister seems to have rooms to rent in Fiskárdho.

Accommodation

The best bargain for **private rooms** in Fiskárdho is *Regina's* (no phone; ②), at the back of the village beyond the *Sirene* music bar and the baker: rooms are decent but basic, the owners friendly, and *Regina's* has the benefit of being some distance from the village's night-time revels. On the north side of the harbour, the large *Nicola's Terrace* taverna has good, modern rooms, also away from the front and with the best views of the village (☎0674/41 307; ③). For much the same price, the central *Theodora's Cafe Bar* has rooms in two whitewashed houses at the far end of the quay (☎0674/41 297 or 41 310; ②), while, moving up a notch, the *Koria* handicraft shop in the centre of the village has rooms on the seafront (☎0674/41 270; ③). For a quieter position in the village, in the alley to the side of Nikos's bike rental on the quay, try the *Nitsa Rooms* (☎0674/41 327; ③), which are set in an exquisite alley-garden full of the owner's pot plants. At the top of the price range, *Fiskardhona* (☎0674/41 436; ④), opposite the post office, and *Philoxenia* (☎0674/41 319; ④), next to Nikos's bike rental, offer rooms in renovated traditional island homes in the village.

Around the bay and towards Fókis beach, there are a number of **apartment** buildings, although some of these are for three, four or more people. *Stella Apartments* (☎0647/41 211, fax 41 262; ④) have kitchens and lounge/dining areas, and balconies with views of Lefkádha; *Kiki* (☎0674/41 208, fax 41 278; ④) can offer studios and apartments overlooking a small beach.

Pama Travel (☎0674/41 306), on the southern quay opposite the lighthouses, is the main **travel agency** in town, run by the impeccably well-connected Tassos Matsoukis, an elder statesman of Fiskárdho's tourism industry and owner of the village's oldest tourist restaurant, *The Captain's Cabin. Pama* handles rooms in Fiskárdho, and also offers accommodation in the Matsoukis family village, Mazoukáta, a short walk or drive into the hills above town. *Fiskardho Travel* on the quay (☎0674/41 315, fax 41 352) also has rooms in Fiskárdho, among a wide range of services, including yacht charter, car and boat rental, ferry tickets, tours and excursions.

If you're having difficulty finding accommodation, try Vassilikiádes, 10km south on the main road, which has a few tavernas and St Ferentinos *rooms (☎0674/51 281; ②).*

The Town

The northern tip of Fiskárdho bay is guarded by the remains of a Venetian **lighthouse**, and above it on the headland are the crumbling ruins of what is believed to have been a Norman **church**. Arthur Foss, in his *The Ionian Islands*, speculates that the structure might have been part of plans for an eleventh-century settlement here under Norman invader Robert Guiscard. Guiscard, however, died of the plague a few weeks after arriving, and the settlement was probably abandoned, although the port derives its name from his. Below the church on the north shore of the bay, a Friends of the Ionian **nature trail**, reached through a low gate below the *Nicola's Terrace* taverna, runs through the shady woods, where you can bathe from the rocks. The trail can be followed with an FOI self-guide leaflet, available in the village shops or from the *Simply Ionian* office on the quay. There are two excellent pebble **beaches** within a few minutes' walk on either side of the village: **Emblísi**, signed down a turning off the main road into Fiskárdho (slightly marred by a humming electricity sub-station at the back of the beach, where the island's power line comes ashore); and **Fókis**, set in a beautiful fjord-like cove ten minutes' walk south of the village, with a summer taverna above the beach.

Eating and drinking

Fiskárdho's **restaurant** culture seems to have achieved the ecological balance that has disastrously eluded places like Lákka on Paxí: no two are alike and, while menus overlap, all are distinct from each other. The **seafront** is dominated by the *Tassia Psistaria*, which has to have the widest choice of fish on Kefalloniá, ranging from lobster and red mullet, to fish in Kefallonian garlic sauce, squid and fish soup. It's popular and busy at lunchtime and evenings, but not cheap – be sure to specify what weight of fish you want. *The Captain's Cabin* is the only other quayside restaurant of note, with Greek and Kefallonian specialities like *keftédhes* succulently done. This too can be terrifically busy, even in low season: it's a favourite with British tourists, and the place where flotilla folk knock back incendiary sambuca cocktails into the small hours.

Away from the front, the *Alexis* bar-restaurant strays off the conventional Greek menu with curries and chicken in sauces. Set in its own small square, it also has a cheap and quiet bar independent of the restaurant. The *Lagonderia* specializes in grills, and is fairly secluded at the back of the village. *Nicola's Terrace*, alone on the north side of the bay, is a noisy, barn-like taverna with a vast menu and a balcony blessed with a stunning night-time view of the village.

The best place to **drink** has to be the quayside *kafenío*, which produces magnificent *mezédhes* – miniature meals of fish, vegetables or meat – in the evening. Carousing tends to end late in Fiskárdho: most popular are the *Captain's Cabin* and the louche *Sirene* music bar. Hidden at the back of the alley containing the post office, the *Polia tou Peirati* is a quiet and friendly bar away from the hubbub, though it's not cheap.

Around Fiskárdho

Fiskárdho sits at the knot of three pleasant **walks** along the lanes circling the limestone northern peninsula, with excellent sea views on either side of the promontory. The easiest, heading beyond Fókis beach, cuts up into the hills overlooking Itháki to Mazoukáta (4km; taverna and *kafenío*), before rejoining the main Argostóli–Fiskárdho road at Mánganos 1km further on. The second follows the same route to begin with, before veering south after 2km at the partly ruined village of Tselentáta; after another 2km you'll reach the dead-end hamlet of Evretí, which has views over the Daskalía island, claimed to be the place where Penelope's suitors set their ambush for the returning Odysseus. The third heads up the main road from Fiskárdho to Mánganos (5km), before veering off southwest to the villages of Agriliás (1km on) and Halikerí (2km on), above small coves on the west coast. You'll reach the main road again at Konidaráta (3km on), where if you time it right you can catch a bus back to Fiskárdho; otherwise it's around 8km (downhill) on foot.

Travel details

Buses

Argostóli to: Ássos (3 weekly, Mon, Wed & Fri; 1hr 30min); Fiskárdho (Mon–Sat 2 daily; 2hr); Kourkomeláta (4 daily; 45min); Póros (4 daily, 2 on Sun; 1hr 30min); Sámi (4 daily, 1 on Sun; 1hr 30min); Skála (2 daily, 1 on Sun; 1hr 30min).

Lixoúri to: Xi beach (3 daily; 30min).

Póros to: Skála (Mon–Sat 2 daily; 1hr).

Sámi to: Fiskárdho, via Áyios Evfimía (Mon–Sat 2 daily; 1hr 30min); Ássos, via Áyios Evfimía (2 weekly, Mon & Fri; 1hr).

Ferries

Argostóli to: Killíni (2 daily; 2hr 30min); Lixoúri (12 daily, 8 on Sun; 30min).

Áyia Evfimía to: Pisaetós, Itháki (1 daily; 30min); Váthi, Itháki (1 daily; 1hr).

Fiskárdho to: Fríkes, Itháki (1 daily; 1hr); Nidhrí, Lefkádha (1 daily; 1hr 30min); Pisaetós, Itháki (1 daily; 1hr); Vassilikí, Lefkádha (4 daily; 2hr).

Pessádha to: Áyios Nikoláos, Zákinthos (2 daily; 1hr 30min).

Póros to: Killíni (2 daily; 1hr 30min).

Sámi to: Astakós (1 daily; 2hr); Pátra (1 daily; 5hr); Pisaetós, Itháki (1 daily; 30min); Vassilikí (Lefkádha), via Pisaetós and Fiskárdho (1 daily; 3hr); Váthi, Itháki (4 daily; 1hr).

Chapter 6

Zákinthos

Second largest of the Ionian islands after Kefalloniá, **Zákinthos** has three distinct landscapes: the deserted, mountainous north and west coasts, the undulating central plain, which with its green rolling hills and red-roofed hamlets resembles parts of Tuscany, and the extremely busy southern coasts which in parts could be Blackpool or Coney Island without the rides. Its tourism industry, based in a few resorts in the south, is one of the most developed in Greece, but elsewhere the island is untouched by commerce. Indeed, while **Laganás** is the most commercialized resort in the entire archipelago, a few kilometres away there are ancient hill villages as pristine as any to be found on Paxí or Kefalloniá. The capital, **Zákinthos Town**, rebuilt after the disastrous 1953 earthquakes, has lost almost all of its Venetian architecture but remains a pleasant town to visit or to stay in. The **Vassilikós peninsula** south of the town has some fine countryside and beaches, culminating in exquisite **Yérakas**, probably the best beach in the entire Ionian. Virtually all the accommodation is confined to the busier centres, so those seeking a quiet retreat should consider the island's northern neighbours instead.

Like the rest of the archipelago, Zákinthos owes much of its history to the Venetians, who after their invasion in the fourteenth centu-

Accommodation price codes

Rooms and hotels listed in this book have been price-coded according to the scale outlined below. The rates quoted represent the cheapest available double room in high season. Out of season, rates can drop by as much as fifty percent or more, especially if you negotiate for a stay of three or more nights. Single rooms, where available, cost around seventy percent of the price of a double. For further information, see p.32.

① up to 4000dr	⑤ 16,000–20,000dr
② 4000–8000dr	⑥ 20,000–30,000dr
③ 8000–12,000dr	⑦ 30,000dr upwards
④ 12,000–16,000dr	

ry planted the island's conspicuous olive trees. Its main agricultural business, however, has traditionally been **raisins**, to which, at the peak of the industry in the eighteenth century, two-thirds of the island's cultivated land was devoted, creating fortunes for its aristocracy. The Venetians called the island **Zante** (dubbing it *fior di Levante*, "flower of the Levant", because of the luxurious vegetation), and even today islanders slip between either name. The island has in effect two springs: early in the year, and again between October and November, when autumn rains revive cyclamen, irises, lilies and wild orchids. Some local **wines**, such as the white Popolaro, compare with the best in the archipelago, and Zákinthos produces its own brand of the sticky, white *mandoláto* **nougat**, commonly sweetened with sugar but also available in its superior honey-sweetened variant. The best local **cheese** is the pungent *grapéria*, which may be a little too strong for milder northern palates.

Two things have shaped modern-day Zákinthos: an **earthquake** and an airport. This area of the Ionian Sea is a site of fairly constant seismic activity (see p.168), most of it minor and largely indiscernible. However, on August 9, 1953, an earthquake comparable to that of 1992 in San Francisco hit the region at midday. Thousands died or were seriously injured, and in some rural areas whole communities were wiped out. The force was such that an estimated seventy per cent of buildings on Zákinthos were destroyed. Zákinthos Town, which had won the nickname of "Venice of the South" for its elegant architecture, was further damaged by fires that spread from taverna kitchens; contemporary photographs in the Zákinthos Museum show the town's streets heaped up like waves.

After the earthquake, Zákinthos had to rebuild itself from the ground up, and this has had a curious effect on the island's **maps**. Many villages had to be abandoned and rebuilt away from the quake ruins, so few places now stand where they were originally built (Zákinthos Town is the obvious exception). Village names are now officially held to refer to "areas" rather than specific places, but the disorientation is only increased by haphazard road signage. Anyone planning trips on the island should bear this in mind, as some maps imply a settlement where the visitor will find only desert or forest.

The earthquake also left Zákinthos clear to rebuild itself for the tourism boom, which in the last decade has taken hold of parts of the island with a vengeance. Thanks to the presence of the only international **airport** in the Ionian islands outside Corfu, over 360,000 Britons alone visited Zákinthos in 1995 – compared to an indigenous population of roughly 30,000. This has given rise to certain unspoken cultural tensions, but many islanders seem to be profiting from the building explosion that is threatening to engulf the southeast and much of the central plain as well. Despite the seasonal invasion – a fair number of Dutch, German and Scandinavian visitors add to the British crowds – much of Zákinthos remains relatively unspoilt. The party

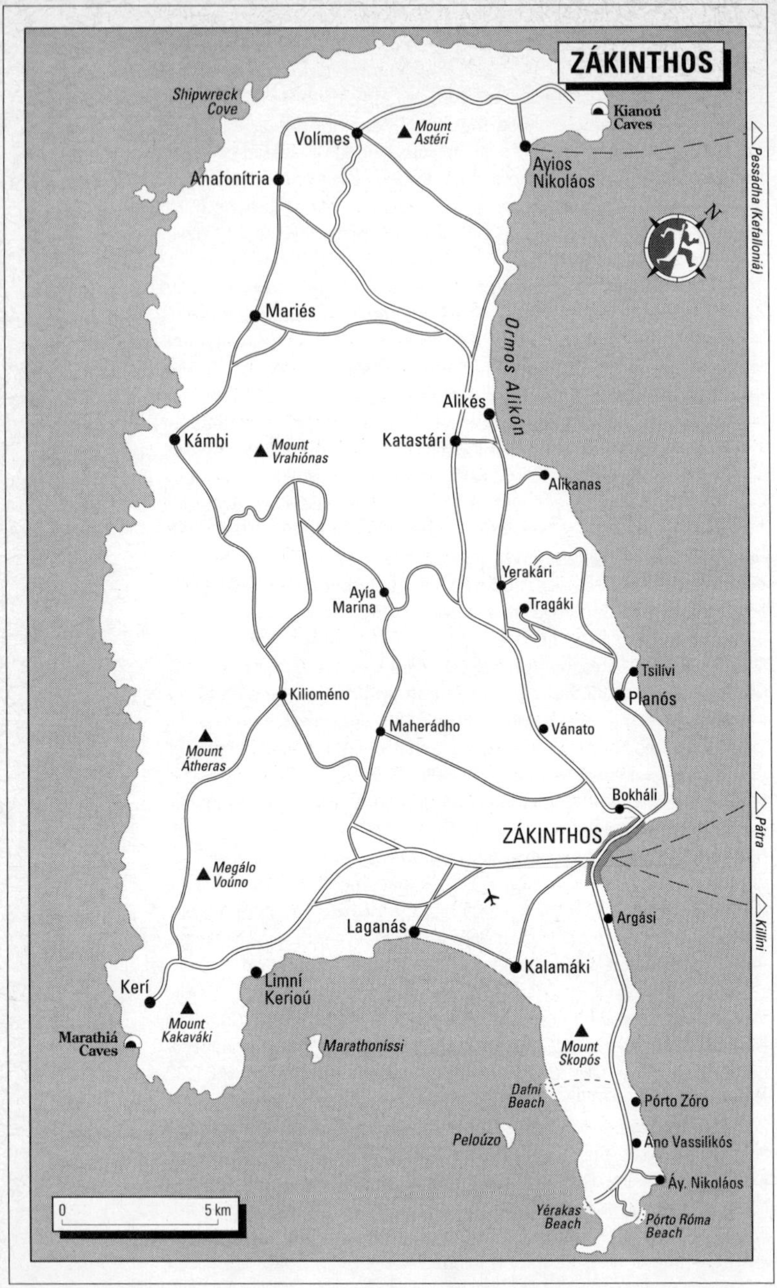
ZÁKINTHOS
Shipwreck Cove
Kianoú Caves
Volímes
Mount Astéri
Ayios Nikoláos
Pessádha (Kefalloniá)
Anafonítria
N
Mariés
Ormos Alikón
Alikés
Kámbi
Mount Vrahiónas
Katastári
Alíkanas
Yerakári
Ayía Marina
Tragáki
Tsilívi
Planós
Kilioméno
Maherádho
Vánato
Mount Átheras
Bokháli
ZÁKINTHOS
Pátra
Megálo Voúno
Argási
Kilíni
Laganás
Kalamáki
Kerí
Limní Kerioú
Mount Kakaváki
Marathiá Caves
Marathoníssi
Mount Skopós
Dafni Beach
Pórto Zóro
Peloúzo
Áno Vassilikós
Áy. Nikoláos
0
5 km
Yérakas Beach
Pórto Róma Beach

resort of Laganás and its more refined neighbour, **Kalamáki**, as well as eastern resorts like **Tsilívi**, are all fairly self-contained. The dismal public transport system – combined with some of the most hair-raising driving in Greece – doesn't encourage mobility among visitors (indeed, walking anywhere on the roads of southern Zákinthos might count as a high-risk sport). Some of the beaches aren't served by public transport at all and don't even have a taverna or a beach bar, but **Áyios Nikólaos** on the Vassilikós peninsula has cleverly launched its own free bus service, luring tourists away from other resorts.

Some history

Zákinthos was first settled by Achaeans from what is now the northern Peloponnese in the Mesolithic era (12,000–3000 BC), and earned a brief mention in the *Odyssey*: Homer refers to "woody Zákinthos" and includes twenty young men from the island among the small army of doomed suitors who proposed marriage to Penelope. Zantiots fought alongside the Athenians in the Pelopponesian War (431–404 BC), but the island was subsequently overrun by the victorious Spartans, who were themselves supplanted by successive waves of invading Macedonians and Romans. The latter gave way to the Byzantine Empire, which ruled the region from the second to the twelfth century AD. In 1185, Zákinthos and neighbouring Kefalloniá broke away from Byzantine rule and formed a semi-independent palatinate, ruled by a succession of regional aristocrats sanctioned by Rome. The complex game of regional politics and warfare between city-states saw the islands frequently change hands between Rome, Venice, Naples and Ioánnina, capital of the northern mainland region of Epirus. After years of skirmishes, the Turks took the region in 1479, but were expelled by the Venetians in 1485. One local history describes the Turkish onslaught on Zákinthos as a "holocaust". Few islanders survived, and the Venetians began a campaign of settlement.

Under Venetian rule, Zákinthos expanded beyond the port to establish settlements elsewhere on the island. The Venetians imported their own stratified social system, with the names of the nobility inscribed in the *Libro d'Oro* (golden book), which became the social register of Zákinthos society and a despised symbol of privilege and power. This caste system created great wealth for Zákinthos's dynasties, but was clearly hated by the impoverished majority, who staged an uprising in 1628 that was bloodily put down by the Venetians. When they were finally unseated by the French in 1797, the *Libro d'Oro* was burnt by jubilant crowds in Platía Áyios Markoú. The French were ousted by a Russian–Turkish alliance in 1798, and in 1800 the Russians and Turks signed a treaty to establish the Eptaníssos (Seven Islands) state of the Ionian islands. The new constitution still favoured the island's elite, however, and the Zakinthians once again rebelled, unsuccessfully, raising the Union

Jack on the Venetian fort as an appeal to the expansionist trading partner from the north. In 1807, the island was briefly handed to the French again, but in 1809 the British took Zákinthos. The island remained a British protectorate until the archipelago was ceded to Greece in 1864. Zákinthos was overrun by the Italians and then by the Germans in World War II, although it didn't suffer as badly as neighbouring Kefalloniá.

Pátra

The busiest mainland port after Pireás, **PÁTRA** is a major stopping-off point for travellers moving between the islands and mainland. It is convenient for Zákinthos and Kefalloniá, and has train (6 daily; 4hr; OSE ☎061 22 1311 or 27 7441) and bus (26 daily; 6hr) connections with Athens – though, oddly, no airport of any decent size. It is also a major terminal for ferries to Italy, many of which call at Igoumenítsa and Corfu. Pátra itself has little to detain the traveller, although if you find yourself in between connections it's not an unattractive city. There are no beaches or major historical sites in the immediate vicinity, but Pátra is handy for ancient **Olympia**, 2hr away by regular bus or train.

Buses and **trains** arrive within a few hundred metres of the ferries on Óthonos Amalías, in an area that resembles a rail shunting yard. The only **tourist office** is in the ferry terminal building, and keeps local maps and accommodation info. If you're passing through with time to spare, the railway station has a handy **left luggage** office.

Pátra is built on a grid system, much of it one-way. The long cross-streets are very busy, so it's best to try for accommodation off the main roads and away from the seafront. **Hotels** are often booked out, even in low season, so expect to have to shop around. Handy mid-range places include the *Galaxy*, Áyios Nikólaos 9 (☎061/27 8815 or 27 5981; ③), the *Mediterranee*, nearby at no. 18 (☎061/27 9602 or 27 9624; ④), and the *Adonis*, Kapsáli 8 (☎061/22 4213 or 22 4235; ③). There is also a **youth hostel** at Iróon Politehníou 68 (☎061/42 7278). **Banks** and exchanges abound, and there are 24-hour foreign exchange machines at the corner of Óthonos Amalías and Patréos, and on Áyios Nikólaos next to the *Galaxy* hotel.

While the seafront and central Platía Tríon Simonoú have cafés, bars and a few shops, much of Pátra life goes on some blocks back from the port. The town centre is Platía Yióryiou, which houses the city's main Apíllon Theatre. Town youth congregate around Platía Ólgas; families and couples among the many bars and tavernas around the pleasant Psilá Alónia park, some ten (short) blocks from the sea. The two main sights, visible from most parts of the city, are the **Kástro**, some 193 steps up from the top of Áyios Nikoláos, whose ruins command stunning views north to Messolónghi and sometimes feature outdoor concerts; and the giant jelly-mould **basilica of Áyiou Andhréou** at the far end of town.

Nightlife is centred on Odhós Gerokostópolou, north of Yióryiou, which has a number of music bars and **restaurants**. For a drink away from the obvious places, try the popular and curiously titled *Beer Society*, tucked in an alley off Ríga Ferréou near Érmou and Kolokotróni. One to avoid is the pricey bar at the end of the pier at Simonoú.

Arrival

Most visitors arrive at the island **airport**, equidistant from Laganás and Kalamáki in Kólpos Laganá (Laganás Bay) on the southern coast. It's tiny, even by Ionian standards (the check-in queue starts in the car park), and has very limited facilities. There's no dedicated bus service from here, although the Laganás–Zákinthos Town bus does pass the bottom of the road leading away from the airport every few hours. Taxis into Zákinthos Town or to Laganás cost around 2000dr – it is possible to haggle, but the drivers, who are as likely to be expat Brits as Greeks, know you're stuck without them. It's just about feasible to walk to either Zákinthos Town, 5km or so to the north, or Laganás, 4km south, but most independent travellers tend to give in to the taxi drivers.

Ferries from the mainland ports of Pátra (summer only) and Killíni (the main year-round point of access) arrive at **Zákinthos Town**. Oddly, there is no regular ferry connection between Zákinthos Town itself and the rest of the Ionian islands to the north, except via Killíni/Pátra. An unreliable daily ferry sails between Pessádha on Kefalloniá and the port of **Áyios Nikólaos** in the north of Zákinthos (not to be confused with the beach complex of the same name in the south) in the summer, and is met by a KTEL bus to Zákinthos Town.

Local transport

The island's skeletal **bus** system radiates out from Zákinthos Town to serve the larger resorts and some outlying villages, but little else. The KTEL bus station – with spectacularly unhelpful staff – is on Odhós Filíta, one block back from the seafront, and buses usually run on time, though the timetable is subject to change without notice.

There are **taxi stands** in Zákinthos Town and some of the larger resorts; taxis also cruise the smaller resorts when they're in the area (but tend to disappear during the siesta). You could try phoning for a taxi (see p.199) from a bar or hotel, but this is more expensive than flagging one down; drivers often charge for the journey to pick

Zákinthos Town and around

ZÁKINTHOS TOWN is a small, busy working port that has made few concessions to tourism. However, it is the only sensible place to base yourself if you want to explore the island by public transport. There are sufficient hotels, a few private rooms, bars and restaurants for visitors who do choose to stay, as well as a number of museums and historic buildings – notably the **Kástro** that towers above the town. The seafront restaurants and bars give onto a busy main road, and are prone to its noise and fumes. A further drawback to this part of Zákinthos Town is its one-way system, which has the novel effect of speeding up the already crazy traffic. After school and in the evenings bored teens race each other on bikes and mopeds around the town centre until late, giving even the smartest of restaurants the ambience of a racetrack. The best advice for those seeking reasonable accommodation or a decent meal is to head north beyond Platía Solómou.

There is no tourist office in Zákinthos Town or indeed elsewhere on the island. The **tourist police** (beyond Mitsis travel agency on the seafront) are said to have tourism info but usually feign ignorance. Hotels and travel businesses can help with information, and some have free maps to supplement those on sale in the shops.

Accommodation

There is a limited range of hotels and rooms on the seafront, which are convenient if you arrive late but hardly cheap. Bargain-hunters are advised to seek out the *Zenith* and *Oasis*, at the back of town, although not without the help of a map. Anyone planning to stay more than a day or so is advised to head for the district of Repára, just beyond Platía Solómou. This end of town is relatively quiet, because little traffic has business in the suburb of Akrotíri beyond it.

Perhaps due to the earthquake and the subsequent explosion in building, **rooms** in Zákinthos Town and outside are almost never named. It's easy to spend half a day trekking around looking for the elusive "*Enikiázontai Domatia*" (Rooms to Let) sign, so it's probably best to take up an offer from the room-owners who meet incoming ferries in summer. Otherwise, there are rooms next to the *Egli Hotel* on the seafront (☎0695/23 963; ②); at the *Ypsarias* (☎0695/42 884) and *Green Boat* (☎0695/45 992) *psistariés* on Odhós Krionéri beyond Platía Solómou; and next door to the *Hotel Oasis* (see below; ☎0695/45 194 or 51 034).

Budget hotels

Deithnes, Áyiou Lazaroú (☎0695/22 286). Double rooms only, with en-suite baths. ②.

Egli, Loútzi (☎0695/28 317). Tucked in at the side of the plush *Strada Marina*, a traditional Greek family hotel offering the same views as its smarter neighbour. All rooms with en-suite bathrooms, balconies and sea view. ②.

Oasis, Koutoúzi (☎0695/22 287). Very small, basic rooms, tucked away in an alley above tiny Platía Áyia Saránda. ②.

Omonia, Xanthopoúlou (☎0695/22 113). Simple, old-fashioned hotel, given a makeover a few years ago. ②.

Pension Zenith, Tertséti (☎0695/22 134). Small apartment hotel with en-suite rooms, slightly upmarket from the *Oasis*. ②.

Upmarket hotels

Bitzaro, Dionissiou Róma (☎0695/23 644). Fairly smart C-class hotel in Repára area, with en-suite bathrooms, balconies and a roof terrace. ③.

Palatino, Kolokotróni/Kolyva (☎& fax 0695/45 400). Upmarket and tucked away from the seafront in the Repára area. TV, air-conditioning, bar. Open year-round. ④.

Plaza, Kolokotróni (☎0695/48 909, fax 45 278). Small hotel in the Repára area with en-suite bathrooms and balconies, some with sea views. ④.

Reparo, Dionίssiou Róma/Voúltsou (☎0695/23 578). A friendly and modern (if a little frayed) purpose-built hotel, which promises and usually delivers "B-class service at C-class prices". All rooms are en suite, with balconies and some sea views. Bar/breakfast room. ③.

Strada Marina, Stráta Marína seafront, at the Platía Solómou end (☎0695/42 761–3, fax 28 733). The smartest in town and probably the only hotel in the "international" league: air-conditioning and TV in the rooms, 24-hour restaurant, bar, coffee shop, and a rooftop pool and restaurant. Wheelchair access. ⑤.

The Town

The obvious first port of call in Zákinthos Town is **Platía Solómou**, which was named after the island's most famous son, **Dionissios Solomos** (1798–1857). Considered Greece's foremost poet of the modern period, Solomos wrote the *Hímnos yía Eleftһería* (Hymn of Freedom) which became the Greek national anthem, and was responsible for establishing demotic Greek as a literary idiom. The *platía* is flanked by the town hall, which occasionally doubles as a cinema; the **Library** (Mon–Wed noon–7.30pm, Thurs–Sat 7am–2.30pm), which features an interesting display of photographs of old Zákinthos; and the small Byzantine Museum (see below).

Museums

Zákinthos Town's three museums are close to each other in Platía Solómou and adjoining Platía Áyiou Márkou. None of them is worth going out of your way for, but the **Byzantine Museum** is marginally more interesting than the other two. On display here are examples of the **Ionian School** of painting, though not as good as those in the churches of Lefkádha Town. Chiefly influenced by painters of the Renaissance, the school flourished on Zákinthos in the seventeenth and eighteenth centuries, and was noted for a distinctly realist approach to its religious subject matter. Saints and other figures are represented in workaday settings and in distinctly earthbound form, far removed from the sunbursts and wings beloved of earlier religious imagery.

The Byzantine Museum is open Tues–Sun 8.30am–3pm; 400dr.

The **Solomos Museum** on Platía Áyiou Márkou contains some of the poet's effects and manuscripts – the collection is split between Zákinthos and Corfu, where he spent most of his working life – and what is said to be part of the tree under which he sat and composed the *Hymn of Freedom*. The museum also contains memorabilia of two other noted Zantiot poets, Ugo Foskolo and Andreas Kalvos.

The Solomos Museum is open Mon–Sat 9am–noon; free. The Zákinthos Museum is open Tues–Sun 8.30am–3pm; 400dr.

Next door to the Solomos Museum, the **Zákinthos Museum** is a small local history collection that includes minor antiquities and tra-

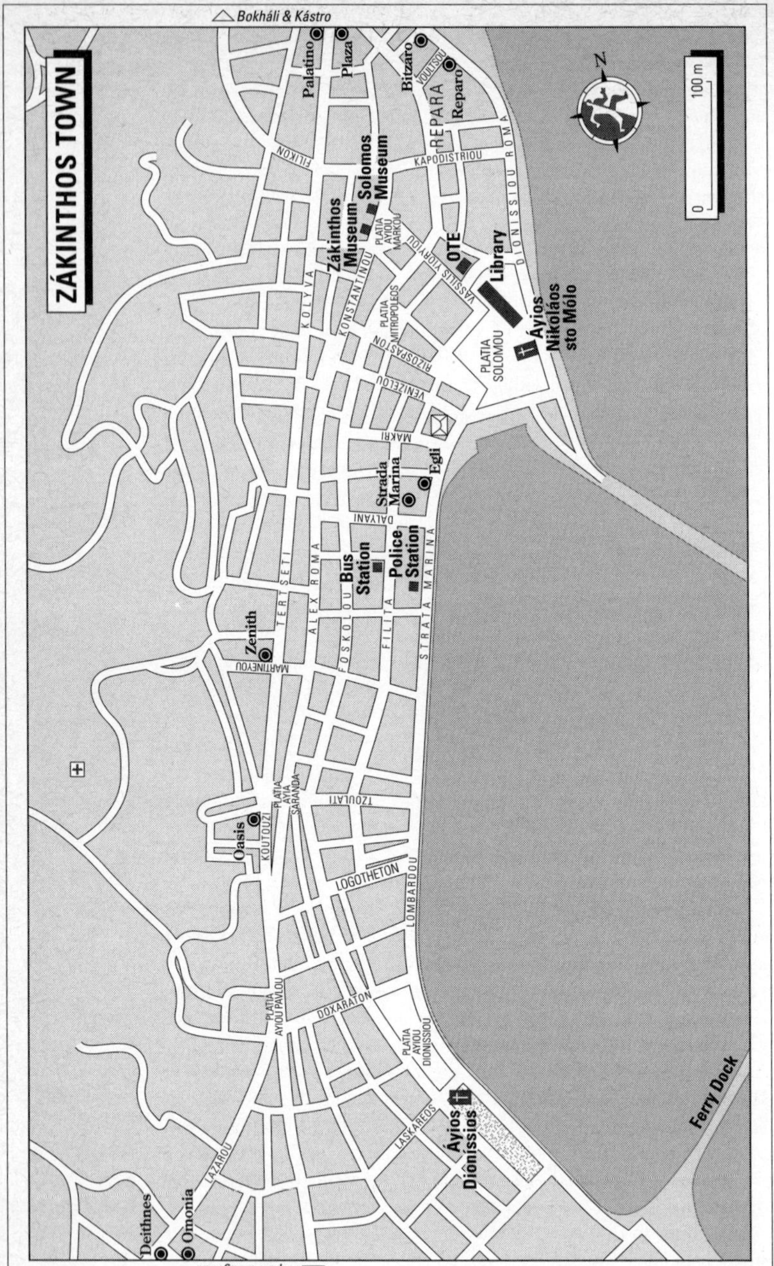
ZÁKINTHOS TOWN
Bokháli & Kástro
Airport & Laganás
100 m
0
N
Palatino
Plaza
Bitzaro
Reparo
VOULTSOU
REPARA
FILIKON
KAPODISTRIOU
ROMA
DIONISSIOU ROMA
Solomos Museum
Zákinthos Museum
PLATIA AYIOU MARKOU
KONSTANTINOU
KOLYVA
OTE
VASSILIS VIORYIOU
Library
Áyios Nikoláos sto Mólo
PLATIA SOLOMOU
PLATIA MITROPOLEOS
RIZOSPASTON
VENIZELOU
MAKRI
Egli
Strada Marina
DALYANI
Bus Station
Police Station
TERTSETI
ALEX ROMA
FOSKOLOU
FILITA
STRATA MARINA
Zenith
MARTINEYOU
PLATIA AYIA SARANDA
TZOULATI
Oasis
KOUTOUZI
LOGOTHETON
LOMBARDOU
PLATIA AYIOU PAVLOU
DOXARATON
PLATIA AYIOU DIONISSIOU
LASKAREOS
Áyios Dionissios
Ferry Dock
LAZAROU
Deithnes
Omonia

ditional artefacts from everyday Zantiot life, as well as a reconstruction of the prehistoric settlement of Zákinthos Town.

Churches

Few of the town's churches survived the 1953 earthquake. **Áyios Nikoláos sto Mólo** (St Nicholas of the Mole), a former fishermen's chapel at the edge of Platía Solómou, is the only one to have been renovated after the quake using its original stones (though the interior was restructured using modern materials). Inside are the vestments of the island's saint, Dionissios, patron saint of fishermen, who preached here in the sixteenth century. More spectacular is the church of **Áyios Dioníssios** itself, at the other end of the seafront to Platía Solómou, lit at night like a fairground ride. The church contains some remarkable icons of the saint's life, as well as a magnificent carved silver coffin. Built of concrete in 1948, with a bell tower modelled on St Mark's in Venice, it survived the earthquake more or less intact.

The Kástro

The Kástro is open daily 8am–4pm; 400dr.

Zákinthos Town's only major historic site is the **Kástro**, a huge, ruined Venetian fortress to the north of town, sited on a bluff which was a defensive enclave from the Byzantine era onwards. Little of the original structure remains beyond a few minor outbuildings (mostly from the seventeenth century), some foundations and ruins of the massive walls, but it is a remarkable piece of stone engineering, with stunning views in almost every direction. Long ago overrun by firs, the keep now has the air of a small walled forest. It's an ideal spot for a picnic or a quiet afternoon in the shade, under an hour's walk from the centre of town, on the edge of the small hamlet of Bokháli. There are no public facilities, however, beyond the few tavernas in Bokháli, and in season the Kástro is inundated with coach parties.

Eating and drinking

Zákinthos Town is the best place for **eating** on the island, although that isn't saying much. Travellers on a budget can snack in the cheap *psistariés* and takeaways on the backstreets around Filíta, Alex Róma and Konstantinou. The seafront *tavernas* offer reasonable fare, but the smartest restaurants are in elegant Platía Áyios Márkou, along with some seriously hip and ferociously expensive music bars. The best food, however, is to be found at *Alivizos* and *Arekia* along the shadowy sea road beyond Platía Solómou.

Alivizos, Dioníssiou Róma. The first taverna along the sea road to Akrotíri offers a wide range of sophisticated staples and is very popular with Zantiots. Open later in season and, unusually, during the siesta. Live music most evenings.

Arekia, Dioníssiou Róma. If you eat only one meal in Zákinthos Town, eat it here. This small, family-run taverna performs miracles with traditional dishes:

Kantáthes and arékia

Venetian influence is notable not only in the architecture of Zákinthos Town, but also in two popular song forms unique to the island. The Zákinthos opera house may have disappeared in the 1953 earthquake, never to be replaced, but a hybrid of Italian bel canto and Greek folk styles, imported by a wave of refugees who fled Crete following the Cretan War of 1669, survives to this day. The two dominant forms of this hybrid are **kantáthes** and **arékia**, quite distinct from the traditional, eastern-tinged *syrtáki* or *rembétika* "blues" heard in other parts of Greece. *Kantáthes* displays a more direct lineage from light operatic ballads, sung in trios and quartets, predominantly male (although women do join in), and often romantic or comic. *Arékia* tends to be quieter, more reflective, sometimes sung by a single voice, and often takes the form of love ballads or a lament for family or home. Both can be heard in more traditional tavernas in Zákinthos Town (*Alivizos* and, best of all, *Arekia*), the tavernas in Bokháli (*Panorama* and *Kastro*), Laganás (*Zougraz*) and elsewhere. Local variants, songs invented for specific festivals and family events such as weddings, can also be heard during celebrations in hill villages such as Kerí and Katastári. It's a difficult music to find in recorded form, although authentic recordings of traditional songs by Zákinthian composer Dimitris Lagios are available in many shops in town.

succulent meat and fish, mouthwatering meatballs and small *tiropittákia* to die for. Jealously guarded by Zantiots, who throng for its nightly free *kantáthes* and *arékia* sessions (10pm). Open evenings only; go early weekends.

Bukios, Platía Áyiou Márkou. The best of the square's restaurants. Wide range of traditional taverna dishes, international and vegetarian.

Fioro di Levante, Platía Solómou. Priced on a par with the smart Áyios Márkou restaurants, but an unmissable setting for a snack or dessert.

Kastro, Bokháli (☎0695/23 401). A lengthy menu of island and typical Greek dishes, authentic *kantáthes* and views over the town. Worth booking ahead.

Molos, Stráta Marína. The most reasonable of the seafront tavernas offering full meals and snacks, but the pavement seating can become busy.

Panorama, Bokháli (☎0695/288 62). Upmarket neighbour to *Kastro*, with a more sophisticated menu (and prices), but with stunning views over Zákinthos Town. Booking advisable.

Village Inn, Stráta Marína. Well-prepared Greek and Italian dishes, but one of the more expensive restaurants in town. Worth a visit for its bizarre decor: German baronial meets Polynesian, with a miniature jungle at the rear.

Nightlife

More conventional night-club-discos can be found 4km south in Argási *– see p.202.*

The hub of nightlife in Zákinthos is Platía Áyiou Márkou – the most expensive place to eat or drink in town, with prices matching London's West End. A favourite with local and visiting youth is *The Base*, at the centre of the square, a bar which usually has a DJ playing anything from dance imports to Miles Davis or Philip Glass. The town has a small but energetic hard-core dance culture that's unique in the Ionian. It's based on a number of bars around Áyiou Márkou and in nearby streets, and on two record stores, *Music Magazi* on Delyssa and *Kokos* on Tertséti, which are the best places to find out about new nightclubs and one-offs (most schools of house, techno, trance, hip/trip-hop have arrived on Zákinthos). The *Jazz Café* on Tertséti has borrowed the logo and bouncing typography of the London jazz venue, but is actually a small and friendly disco-bar with a 200dr cover charge and house/techno DJ.

Listings

Banks and exchange Most of the main regional Greek banks are on Konstantínou, and there's a foreign exchange cash autoteller at the Ergo Bank on Vassilís Yióryiou (Leofóros Dhimokratías on some maps). A number of travel agencies, such as *Konstantakos* on the corner of Filíta and Kiriákou Xénou, offer "no commission" exchanges on travellers' cheques. The post office also offers exchange services. The Ergo Bank represents Western Union; there is no American Express representation on Zákinthos.

Beaches The only beach in Zákinthos Town is the scruffy, pebble private concession beyond Platía Solómou, which has changing rooms, toilets and showers (entry 200dr). The taverna-bar *Asteria* further along also has bathing facilities for its customers. Otherwise, the nearest beaches are south at Argási and north at Tsilívi.

Bike and car rental *Sky* on Vassilís Yióryiou (☎0695/26 278) and *Ionian* on Makri (☎0695/28 946 or 51 797) hire pedal bikes, as well as cars and motorbikes; *Moto-Saki* on Vassilís Yióryiou (☎0695/23 928) has motorbikes.

Boat trips At least half a dozen boats circumnavigate the island, visiting spots like the otherwise inaccessible Smuggler's (Shipwreck) Cove, two to three times a week in season; all depart from Zákinthos Town's quayside in the morning. You can pay on board or in the offices along the quay; tickets are also sold by agencies at outlying resorts, who arrange transport into town to join the cruises. One of the best is the MV *Pelargos*, which visits six coastal sites (2000–3000dr, depending on season). The boat trips make much of the Kianoú Caves at Cape Skinári on the northernmost tip of the island (the so-called "blue caves"), but not all trips actually take you into them – and those that do often employ outboard dinghies, involving a precarious transfer from the main vessel. Otherwise, be prepared for eight hours' enforced sunbathing; many just get drunk or sleep most of the trip.

Hospital Above town on the continuation of Marteláou and Martinéyou (☎0695/22 514–5). The outpatients and casualty departments regularly deal with tourists.

Laundry There's a tiny old-fashioned *plindírio* tucked away at the far end of Áyios Tavoulári, between Platía Áyiou Pavloú and Platía Áyia Saránda.

Olympic Airways Konstantínou 16 (☎0695/28 611).

OTE Vassilís Yióryiou (daily 7am–midnight).

Taxis Taxi ranks on Platía Solómou and Stráta Marína by Odhós Dalvani; also available by phone (☎0695/48 400, 23 623 or 24 036).

Vice-consulate Britain, Vicky Vitsou Kitsoni, Foskolos 5 (☎0695/48 030, fax 23 769).

Around Zákinthos Town

As the number of visitors grow, more and more accommodation appears, with newer beach resorts springing up along Zákinthos's **east coast** wherever enterprising businesspeople can bulldoze a path down to something that might pass muster as a beach. Here, as on the other Ionian islands, the east coast is green, fairly flat and protected from the open sea to the west. Unfortunately, Zákinthos's eastern beaches are sometimes prone to oil and tar pollution. Despite this, the beaches are safe and the water's fairly clean, although often at the mercy of prevailing northwesterly winds, which increase in strength in the afternoon. To the north of Zákinthos Town, villas and apartments block-booked by British tour operators make up the bulk of accommodation, but this area – on an island not noted for good walking – is a good bet for some relatively quiet walking among small hill hamlets.

Tsilívi and Planós

Five kilometres north of Zákinthos Town, **TSILÍVI** is the first real resort on this coastline, a fairly quiet, family-oriented place with a number of good sandy beaches offering water sports. Most accommodation is in **PLANÓS**, nearly a kilometre back from the beach, and ranges from good, purpose-built **rooms** – try *Gregory's* (☎0695/61 853; ③) or *Dolphin* (☎0695/27 425; ③) – to smarter **hotels** such as the large *Mediterranee* (☎0695/26 100–4; ④) which has en-suite rooms, a restaurant and a pool. There's also a good basic **campsite**, *Zante Camping* (☎0695/24 754), 1km further on from Planós, beyond the tiny Boúka harbour, above the beach and away from any other settlements. There seems little reason to base yourself here unless as part of a package, although it might make a short-term base if you want to explore the northern half of the central plain, which starts west of here.

Alikés

The largest beach in the region is at **ALIKÉS**, a resort that's even quieter and less developed than Tsilívi – though as a consequence its season is short and accommodation sparse. It's known for its salt pans, which give the back of the village the appearance of a moonscape, while its long beach, perhaps due to a steep seabed, experiences lively surf created by the prevailing winds. There are **rooms** on the beach (try the *Golden Dolphin* taverna), and a couple of **hotels** set back from the village, but with sea views: the *Ionian Star* (☎0695/83 416; ④), a small friendly place with its own restaurant and garden, and the *Montreal* (☎0695/83 241; ④). *Spring Tours* (☎0695/83 035) can arrange rooms and apartments here and in nearby Katastári, the village visible on a hillside to the south. The choice of **places to eat** is limited to a pizzeria, a popular *psistariá*, *Zorba's*, and two traditional tavernas. The bus system gives out at

Alikés, but it would make a reasonable beach base for those exploring the north with their own transport.

Yerakári and Tragáki

Inland from these beach resorts is a network of tiny villages that are well worth exploring on foot or bicycle. Zákinthos Town's hellish traffic dies away at Vanáto, and northwest of here lie some beautiful traditional hamlets where tourism has barely begun to intrude. Particularly recommended are the **YERAKÁRI** "trio", 10km from Zákinthos Town and within a fifteen-minute walk of each other: hilltop Áno (Upper) Yerakári, whose Italianate campanile is visible from miles around, neighbouring Méso (Middle) Yerakári, and Káto (Lower) Yerakári. Three rather roundabout kilometres to the east, off a minor road towards Tsilívi, is **TRAGÁKI**, which boasts some surviving examples of pre-earthquake architecture (Friends of the Ionian has produced a detailed historical trail around the village). It's a working village with courtyarded houses, a still-functioning olive press, an ancient well and, on the outskirts, ruins of Venetian houses. Apart from a friendly *kafenío*, and two shops supplying villagers' needs, it makes absolutely no concessions to tourism.

Argási

ARGÁSI, 4km southeast of Zákinthos Town, is the closest large resort to the island capital, with hotel complexes now climbing the lower slopes of Mount Skopós. Commercialization is rampant, and might be measured by the mildly surreal vision of an English café that proudly announces a "Greek night" every Saturday. The beach, however, is skimpy – in parts no more than a few metres wide – and there's little of note in the village beyond a ruined church, now being rebuilt of concrete, and, hidden away near the beach (just behind the *Life's a Beach* snack bar), a tiny but beautiful Venetian chapel.

There is little reason to base yourself here unless you're on a cheap package or want to spend time exploring the Vassilikós peninsula to the south. **Rooms** can be had at *Pension Vaso* (☎0695/44 599; ③) and *Andro* (☎0695/22 190; ③) on the main road in the centre of the village, and the seafront boasts some smart hotels: the *Locanda* (☎0695/45 386; ④) and the larger *Iliessa Beach* (☎0695/45 345; ④), for example, both have en-suite rooms, some with sea views, as well as pools and gardens overlooking the beach.

Eating out in Argási is an indifferent affair, and those staying here would be better off heading into Zákinthos Town in the evening. The *Enato* and *Papillon* tavernas both serve a bland mix of Greek and international food. Slightly more promising are the *Three Brothers*, which specializes in fish, and the *Big Plate*, which can offer some good vegetarian alternatives. For a complete change of scene, there's a Chinese, the *Genting*, tucked down an alley near the crossroads in the centre of town. Argási is also home to three of the island's main **discos**, *Byblos*, on the road to Zákinthos Town, and *Thamous* and the garish *Mykonos Town* in the opposite direction; entry is normally free, with prices reflected in drinks, and things rarely get going before midnight.

Argási is the main point of access for **Mount Skopós**, via a signposted path leaving the coast road at the first hairpin bend out of town to the south. It's a long day's hike to the summit and back, over some fairly rough terrain, and the view of the mainland and Kefalloniá to the north, while spectacular, can sometimes be misty.

The Vassilikós peninsula

The **Vassilikós peninsula**, stretching southeast of Zákinthos Town, is the most beautiful part of the island, with untouched countryside and forest, the island's two best beaches and, for early risers, great sunrises over the Peloponnese. Most tourism in the area is through island-based companies or overseas villa companies such as Simply Ionian, and often dependent on rented transport: the KTEL **bus** from Zákinthos Town visits only three times a day, though there is a free daily private bus from Laganás to Áyios Nikólaos (see opposite). There's usually a taverna or two in walking distance of most accommodation, but otherwise you're pretty much stranded – which makes the peninsula perfect for dropouts, but not so great for those who crave company or amenities.

To add to the sense of isolation, Vassilikós, in the wake of the 1953 earthquake, is the most confusingly named area on the island. The whole peninsula to the southeast of Argási, some 14km of it, is in fact Vassilikós, and the original village, Áno Vassilikós, is barely a few hundred metres of road halfway down the peninsula, but the name Vassilikós is attributed to various hamlets on the peninsula on different maps of the island; haphazard road signs only add to the confusion.

Pórto Zóro and Áno Vassilikós

The road south from Argási rises up into the foothills of Mount Skopós, passing a signposted turn-off for the first beach on the peninsula, **Porto Zoro**, after 6km. This access road, however, soon becomes impassable except on foot; if you have your own transport, it's better to continue along the main road for half a kilometre to the turning unofficially signed "The Beach with Rocks and Flowers", which will bring you to Pórto Zóro after five minutes' driving down a steep, rough track. The beach is clean and sandy and, with the promised topography and flora, very picturesque. There's a **taverna** and bar, the *Porto Zoro* (☎0695/35 304; ③), with basic but modern **rooms** overlooking the beach, which would make Zóro an excellent place to chill out for a while.

The small hamlet of **ÁNO VASSILIKÓS** straggles along the road above a small beach which is part sand, part pebble, with deposits of sea grass. There are **rooms** at *Vassilikos Apartments* (☎0695/35 277; ③) and a couple of **bar-restaurants**, *Harry's Place* and the more traditional *Fanaria Psistaria*, but little else. Just to the south is one of the peninsula's more commercial beaches, mystifyingly named Banana, which has two small bars, dunes and a firm, though very narrow, strip of sand.

Áyios Nikólaos

About 3km from Áno Vassilikós, **ÁYIOS NIKÓLAOS** boasts the most attractive beach on this side of the peninsula: a small stretch of sand cleft in the middle by a rock outcrop crowned with a bar. The resort is set in a rocky, almost desert-like landscape in a remote area of the peninsula, and at first sight may appear to be little more than a single complex: the *Vasilikos Beach* (☎0695/24 114; ④), a large, modern, if rather boxy, three-storey **hotel** set back from the beach, with restaurant, pool and bar. The hotel is responsible for a free **bus service** from other resorts, a clever loss leader which picks up at Laganás (10am), Kalamáki (10.15am) and Argási (10.30am), returning late afternoon. The resort also offers various water-sports activities, a Hawaiian-style beach **restaurant** and, in a small but inevitably expanding cluster of businesses, two very modern **apartment** developments with all mod cons, the *Christina* (☎0695/35 247; ③) and *Virginia* (☎0695/35 315; ③).

Pórto Róma and Yérakas

What some maps call Vassilikós village is in fact a barely inhabited junction in the middle of nowhere, where the bus from Zákinthos Town stops and turns. Here you'll find two tavernas, the *Blue Roses Music Bar*, and some houses and villas scattered in the surrounding countryside, which is lush, almost jungle-like. Lesser roads lead off to Pórto Róma on the left and Yérakas beach on the right.

The small cove of **Porto Roma** shelters a sand and pebble beach (which occasionally suffers from oil pollution), a bar and a taverna, but little else. There are some private rooms on the road down, and *Porto Roma Apartments* rents out apartments and studios in the area around the cove (☎0695/35 331; ④). There are also individual villas owned by companies such as *Friendly Tours*, based in Zákinthos Town (Fóskolos 5; ☎0695/48 030, fax 23 769).

Far preferable, however, is **Yérakas**, the island's finest beach, a long lazy crescent of golden sand and shallow waters protected from the open sea and prevailing winds by low sandy cliffs. A turtle breeding ground (see p.204), the beach heaves during the day in high summer, but is off limits between dusk and dawn; off season, Yérakas is a stunning haven. There are two tavernas set back from the beach, and one small snack bar on the sand, but as yet no other facilities. It is possible, however, to **stay** quite near the beach, and thus have it almost to yourself between curfew and crowds: *Liuba Apartments* (☎0695/35 372 or 35 313, fax 35 481; brochure available) has a field of small and basic self-catering cabins a few minutes' walk from Yérakas.

Laganás Bay

Laganás Bay is the first glimpse of Zákinthos most tourists get – on a jet coming in to land at the island's airport. **Laganás** itself is the largest single resort on the island, and the most popular, with the facilities, and problems, to match. Its bars and restaurants stretch for a kilometre along the beach, and a similar distance inland along

Loggerhead sea turtles

One night in September 1995, a bomb went off in the offices of Zákinthos architect, Nikos Lykouresis, a founder of the Zakinthian Ecological Movement. No one was hurt, but the attack, believed to have been carried out by opponents of the ecology movement, took the tension between conservationists and businesspeople to a new high. The subject of the tension is the **loggerhead sea turtle**, *Caretta caretta*, which breeds on two of the main beaches on Zákinthos and elsewhere on the island besides. The turtles are an endangered species, and this is one of their largest breeding grounds in Europe.

The tensions began in the early 1980s, just when the tourism boom was taking off. Environmentalists started a campaign to protect the turtle breeding grounds where, from May to October, the females come ashore at night to lay their eggs, bury them in the sand and return to the sea. The hatchlings most frequently come out at night, burrow out and head for the water, although they can sometimes be glimpsed scuttling down the beaches in early mornings.

Protecting the turtles would, however, adversely affect business on the beach: those bars and tavernas setting out tables and chairs on the sand, the sunbed franchises who plant bayonet umbrellas in the sand, the watersports companies whose propellers proved a threat to the slow-moving animals, and the discos and bars whose noise and lights would deter the females from laying and disorient the hatchlings.

The two factions, represented on one side by a coalition of ecological groups – the World Wildlife Fund, Sea Turtle Protection Society of Greece, the Zakinthian Ecological Movement, and Friends of the Ionian – and by local businesses on the other, have been battling over proposals to make Laganás Bay, the main breeding round, a protected marine park. If the conservationists win, some seafront operations will lose their businesses.

There have been three proposals for the future of Laganás Bay: one from the Greek government, which has been criticized by the Council of Europe for failing to protect the turtles; one from the environmentalists; and one from the local businesses, some of whom are coming to the real-

its main thoroughfare. Even in the last knockings of the season in late October, when Zákinthos can sometimes still be baking hot, Laganás continues partying around the clock while other island resorts are closing down. This is *not* a place to come for a quiet break or an early night. Its neighbouring resort to the east, **Kalamáki**, gives onto a superior section of the same beach and is much less developed – though not necessarily quieter, due to the proximity of the airport.

At nearly 9km, the beach in Laganás Bay is the longest on the island and, in spite of the crowds, one of the best. It has slightly muddy sand (but firm rather than sticky), and the sea is shallow and clear – though usually busy with bathers and pleasure craft at the Laganás end. The beach between Laganás and Kalamáki is one of the biggest breeding grounds for the **loggerhead sea turtle** in Greece, where a number of strict rules are enforced. Visitors are

---

ization that a marine park in one form or another is inevitable. The proposals have themselves become hostage to local government politics, as turtles don't win many votes on Zákinthos. Mounting pressure from the EU may force the government to agree to the environmentalists' demands, but that doesn't mean that the loggerheads will be safe. Previous orders to comply with court orders have been ignored, and some businesses flout basic rules of conservation on a daily basis.

Paradoxically, Greek tourism operators have discovered that a little anthropomorphism actually helps business, and the loggerhead has been pressed into the service of the merchandising industry: bars, restaurants, hotels and shops all borrow the name and image, and you can carry a memento of the imperilled reptile home on T-shirts, tea towels, paperweights, jewellery boxes, wall hangings, posters, matchboxes, decorative magnets and snowstorm shakers. It's possible that the animal itself might be killed off, only to live on as a fridge magnet.

There are a few simple things you can do to avoid disturbing the turtles' breeding habits. The World Wildlife Fund has issued the following list of **guidelines** for visitors:

1. Don't use the beaches of Laganás and Yérakas between sunset and sunrise.
2. Don't stick umbrellas in the sand in the marked nesting zones.
3. Take your rubbish away with you – it can obstruct the turtles.
4. Don't use lights near the beach at night – they can disturb the turtles, sometimes with fatal consequences.
5. Don't take any vehicle onto the protected beaches.
6. Don't dig up turtle nests – it's illegal.
7. Don't pick up the hatchlings or carry them to the water, as it's vital to their development that they reach the sea on their own.
8. Don't use speedboats in Laganás Bay – a 10kph speed limit is in force for vessels in the bay.

---

asked not to dig up or drive over the beach, and to stay off it at night (when, in season, the turtles come ashore to lay eggs). The presence of used condoms on the beach suggests that not everybody is getting this message.

Travel agencies in Laganás and Kalamáki can arrange day-trips, including coach transfers, on the tour boats based at Zákinthos Town (see p.199).

There are three **islands** in Laganás Bay, none of them inhabited and only two accessible. Boat trips to **Marathoníssi**, the largest, run every few hours from stalls on the beach (around 1000dr per person). The island has a small sandy beach, part of which is a turtle breeding ground (so don't disturb any sticks you see protruding from the sand), and offers an escape from the crowds of Laganás – though it's sometimes exposed to prevailing winds and has absolutely no facilities. **Áyios Sóstis**, a diminutive rock islet near the main beach, houses the *Cameo* discotheque, has a small pebbly beach and can be reached by a rickety wooden walkway a few hundred metres to the south of Laganás. The third island, **Peloúzo**, near the tip of the Vassilikós peninsula, is simply a large rock.

Laganás

Prior to the arrival of tourism, **LAGANÁS** was little more than a small hamlet near the mouth of a stream emptying into the bay. The bulk of accommodation here is new or purpose-built and prone to the vagaries of Greek plumbing and fittings. Roads are nameless, but you'll soon learn to navigate using familiar landmarks. Bars, restaurants and snack bars are all but interchangeable, although some do go out of their way to offer alternatives to what at times can look like an unending diet of junk food. Greek has become a second language here, which is how the predominantly Anglophone visitors like it; many businesses are in fact owned or staffed by expat or retired Brits. It has the widest range of beach amenities on the island, and provides off-beach attractions such as horse riding and ballooning. While hotels are mostly block-booked by package companies, competition has forced many of them to open their pools and grounds to outsiders – provided you use their bars or restaurants.

The resort is constructed on a simple grid plan. The two key thoroughfares are the main drag, which runs perpendicular to the beach, and the right-hand turning nearly a kilometre back from the sea, by *Dennis's Bikes*, where buses turn in the direction of Zákinthos Town.

Accommodation

While many of the places to stay in Laganás are monopolized by tour operators, there are still plenty of **rooms** and **apartments** to be had – although in high season it can be extremely busy, and anyone heading here should phone ahead. Accommodation is often smack in the middle of the party zone, though the southwesterly end of the resort tends to be quieter; numerous private houses offering walk-up room accommodation can be found on the road that leaves the centre of the main drag, opposite the *Time Out* bar, and curves round to the beach at the hamlet of Lithákia, at the southern end of Laganás Bay. There's a basic **campsite**, or rather, a field with facilities, just a short distance southwest of Laganás – it's signposted in town, but the quickest route is to walk south along the beach for 200m to the first turn-off road, which leads up to the site. Vehicles should follow the road sign opposite the *Time Out* bar to reach the campsite about 500m on.

Most of Laganás' **hotels** are either on the beach to the north of the main drag, or a few minutes' walk back from it. However, an increasing number now trail back towards the airport, causing some staying "in" Laganás to have to commute to the beach by bus.

Alexandros (☎0695/51 580). A small hotel, with en-suite rooms, balconies and sea views. At the quieter end of the north part of town, set back about 100m from the beach. ③.

Australia (☎0695/50 171). Small, set back from the beach, with a pool. ④.

Galaxy (☎0695/51 175). Friendly family-run hotel with gardens leading to the beach. ③.

Galazia Thalassa (☎0695/51 123). The cheapest in the area, a basic rooming hotel with doubles only, but close to the beach. ③.

Ionis (☎0695/51 141). Small hotel, away from the beach on the main drag, with en-suite rooms, balconies, a bar and pool. ③.

Poseidon (☎0695/51 199). Right on the beach, with a pool; air-conditioned en-suite rooms with balconies and sea views. ④.

Thalassi Avria (☎0695/51 110). Cheap and basic rooming hotel, a block back from the beach. ③.

Zante Beach (☎0695/51 130). The smartest in Laganás, set away from the party zone 500m towards Kalamáki and two blocks back from the beach. En-suite rooms, balconies, restaurant, bar and pool. Very popular with north European coach parties, so least likely to have vacancies. ⑤.

Eating and drinking

Good **food** isn't a big selling point in Laganás. Many of the seafront and main drag businesses specialize in snacks, junk food and versions of British staples (fish and chips and fry-ups). These are, however, only versions of the original: here fish will be a local white-meat, bonier, oilier but tastier than North Sea cod or haddock; and a Greek sausage (*loukánika*) doesn't taste anything like the British banger. Most restaurants are clustered around the centre of Laganás, where they compete shoulder to shoulder for passing trade. Competition keeps prices down, although the more stylish restaurants can get away with charging 3000dr a head, excluding drinks.

In the centre, the *Bee Garden* serves a wide range of Chinese food, and the *Pizzeria* offers pasta and pizzas made in a real pizza oven, while the *Apollo* and *Acropolis* tavernas have lengthy menus of Greek and international dishes. The latter also offers special themed Greek evenings with music and dance, as does the *Sarakino*, which has the added attraction of being set in the grounds of a ruined Venetian mansion, giving dinner the air of picnicking outside the fallen House of Usher. *Sarakino* is 2km inland, however, and accessible mainly by the restaurant's own free minibus which cruises Laganás touting for trade. Once committed, there's no escaping.

For a quieter and cheaper meal than can be found in the centre, head off **on the Kalamáki road** just past *Dennis's Bikes*. The *Chinese Ruby* and *House of India* have comprehensive menus prepared by native chefs, and the *Hollywood Diner* offers above-average burgers, as well as imaginative salads in season. The *Taverna Zougraz*, tucked away on the right leaving Laganás on this road, has a vast menu of pan and grilled fish and meat dishes, and also stages *kantáthes* performances at night.

On the beach, junk food reigns supreme, but the following offer a wider range, including salads, seafood and taverna dishes: *Harbour House*, *Greek Islands*, *Blue Waves*, *Koralli* and *Blue Sea*.

There's a **bar** about every dozen metres along Laganás' main thoroughfares. Prices are reasonable, but the chance of enjoying a quiet drink is scarce. It's a pity to have to issue this warning, but a few unscrupulous bars in Laganás sometimes play "swap the banknote" on tourists. It's advisable to double-check what you're handing over, as in some circumstances it can be impossible to negotiate. That said, Laganás is the only place you're likely to encounter this on Zákinthos.

Listings

Bike and motorbike rental *Dennis's*, by the Zákinthos Town turning at the back of the main drag.

Doctor There's a surgery, with English-speaking staff, on the main drag (daily 9.30am–2pm & 5–10pm; ☎0695/52 252).

Exchange There are no banks in Laganás, but plenty of travel agents will change cash and travellers' cheques.

Phones Besides the ubiquitous cardphones, many travel offices offer quieter metered phones, but check the tariff beforehand.

Kalamáki

KALAMÁKI is basically a baby version of Laganás, offering all the good features of the bay without the drawbacks of the main resort. It has a variety of accommodation and tavernas, and restrained nightlife, more upmarket than Laganás'. Just one street runs down to the sea, although a smattering of developments is springing up in lanes off it. The one minus is the proximity of the airport: the drone of aircraft waiting to take off is quite audible from the centre of the village.

Accommodation

Kalamáki has a number of small, quite smart **hotels** (recommendations listed below), as well as **rooms** owned by the proprietors of the two *Stanis* tavernas (☎0695/26 375 or 26 374; ③) towards the back of the village, and some small apartment complexes. *Zakyta Holidays*

(☎0695/27 080), in the centre of the village, handles a wide range of rooms, apartments and villas, and can change money.

Cavo Doro (☎0695/42 597). A comfortable low-rise hotel with its own taverna and bar, gardens and pool, near the bottom of the main street, close to the beach. ⑤.

Crystal Beach (☎0695/42 788, fax 42 917). Kalamáki's largest hotel is friendly, comfortable and excellent value, with an unrivalled setting overlooking the beach, at the bottom of the main street. Two restaurants and bars, and a pool. ④.

Exotica (☎0695/40 695). Probably the plushest hotel in the resort, away from the beach off the main street, with restaurant, bar and pool. ④.

Klelia (☎0695/27 056 or 41 288, fax 41 288). Smart, newly built forty-room hotel on the main street, but a bit soulless. ④.

Eating and drinking

Restaurants in Kalamáki tend to be aimed at people who like to dress up for dinner, with decor and prices to match. The two *Stanis* tavernas (one situated by the road to Laganás, the other on a picturesque knoll above the beach, with its own small menagerie loose in the garden) both have extensive menus of Greek and international dishes, although the beachside version is geared more to lunches and its sibling more to evening meals. Worthwhile alternatives include *Jools' Diner*, serving English and international dishes, and the *Merlis*, which mixes Greek bakes and grills and Italian dishes, mainly pasta and meat-based dishes. **Nightlife** tends to begin in bars like *All Satros*, and gravitates towards the *Byzantio Club* on the hillside above the village, which has a garden with breathtaking views over the bay and islands.

The west coast

Zákinthos's skeletal public transport service renders most of the hill villages in the west and north of the island off limits to those without transport. Local tour agencies do offer weekly island **coach tours** in season, starting at around 3000dr a head, but these are whistlestop tours with only a few breaks for meals, refreshment and sightseeing.

Kerí

Easily accessible is **KERÍ**, hidden in a fold above the cliffs at the island's southernmost tip. The village retains a number of pre-quake, Venetian buildings, including the church of the Panayía of Kerí – who is said to have saved the island from marauding pirates by hiding it in a sea mist. Kerí is also famous for a geological quirk, a series of small tar pools mentioned by both Pliny and Herodotus, but these have mysteriously dried up in recent years. A rough path leaving the southern end of the village leads 1km onto the lighthouse, whose surrounding cliff paths afford spectacular views of the sea and tree-tufted limestone sea arches and stacks.

Maherádho

Some 10km west of Zákinthos Town, **MAHERÁDHO** also boasts some impressive pre-earthquake architecture, and is set in beautiful arable uplands, surrounded by terraced olive and fruit groves. The magnificent church of **Ayía Mávra** has an impressive free-standing campanile, and inside a splendid carved iconostasis and icons by Zakinthian painter Nikolaos Latsis. The town's major festival – one of the biggest on the island – is for the saint's day, which conventionally falls on the first Sunday in June. The other notable church in town, that of the Panayía, commands breathtaking views over the central plain. The interior, however, has been denuded of most of its artwork, much of it moved to Ayía Mávra.

Kilioméno and Kámbi

Ascending into the bare mountainscape of the west coast on a rough country road from Maherádho, you'll reach, after 6km, **KILIOMÉNO**, the best place to see surviving pre-earthquake domestic architecture, in the form of the island's traditional two-storey houses. The town was originally named after its church, **Áyios Nikoláos**, whose impressive campanile, begun over a hundred years ago, still lacks a capped roof.

The road on from Kilioméno climbs 12km up into the island's highest western hills to reach the tiny clifftop hamlet of **KÁMBI**, the destination for numerous coach tours organized to catch sunset over the sea. The village contains a small **folk museum**, with a collection of domestic and agricultural artefacts, and local crafts such as embroidery. Its clifftop **taverna** has extraordinary views over the 300-metre-high cliffs and western horizon, although you're likely to find yourself sharing the sunset with a sizeable crowd of fellow visitors. On an incline above the village there's an imposing concrete cross, said to have been constructed in memory of islanders killed here by Nationalist soldiers during the Civil War – one lurid legend says that islanders were hurled from the cliffs. An alternative history of the cross claims it was erected to commemorate those killed by the Nazis during the island's wartime occupation.

Maríes and Volímes

Four kilometres north of Kámbi, following the bare mountain road north, **MARÍES** is the only village in the region with access down to the sea. A steep, rough track leads down 7km to the small rocky cove of **Stenítis Bay**, which has a waterfront taverna and dock. Maríes itself, protected in a wooded green valley, has an unusual three-aisled church dedicated to Mary Magdalene, who is said to have stopped here to preach en route to Rome. Tough hiking paths lead up onto the slopes of Mount Vrahiónas, the island's highest mountain, with views across the island and north to Kefallonía.

Ten kilometres north, **VOLÍMES** is the largest of the island's hill villages, and in fact comprises three smaller settlements: Káto (Lower), Méso (Middle) and Áno (Upper) Volímes, which are within a few minutes' drive of each other. Each is a small living museum of rural island architecture; Áno Volímes, built on a hillside surrounding the church of Ayíos Dimítrios, is probably the best-preserved village on the entire island. Volímes is the end destination of most island tours, mainly because of its reputation for fine embroidery and farm produce, notably cheese and honey. The Women's Agrotourism Cooperative here is a self-help organization established in 1988 as part of a national, government-sponsored initiative to involve rural women in tourism; its office in Áno Volímes can organize accommodation in private homes in the villages.

Travel details

Buses

Zákinthos Town to: Alikés (5 daily; 1hr); Argási (6 daily; 30min); Kalamáki (4 daily; 45min); Kerí (2 daily; 1hr); Laganás (12 daily; 50min); Tsilívi (9 daily; 45min); Vassilikós (2 daily; 1hr 15min); Volímes (2 daily; 1hr 45min).

There is also a bus connection in season all the way to Athens, via the daily ferry to Pátra (KTEL ☎0695/22 656).

Ferries

Áyios Nikoláos to: Pessádha on Kefalloniá (2 daily May–Sept; 1hr 30min).

Zákinthos Town to: Killíni (5 daily; 1hr 30min); Pátra (daily in season; 3hr).

Flights

Zákinthos airport to: Athens on Olympic (2 daily; 45min).

Contexts

The historical framework

This section is intended just to lend some perspective to travels in the Ionian Sea, and is weighted towards the era of the modern, post-independent nation – especially the twentieth century. Isolated off the west coast of Greece, perilously close to Italy, the history of the Ionian archipelago stands apart from that of the mainland and the Aegean until recent times.

The earliest cultures

The archipelago's isolation puts it on the sidelines of the historical narrative that produced the great archeological finds at Delphi, Mycenae, Olympia and elsewhere. However, evidence in the form of tools has been found on Corfu and Kefalloniá, suggesting that the region was inhabited by Paleolithic (early Stone Age) hunter-gatherers as long ago as 70,000–50,000 BC, prior to the last great Ice Age. At this time Corfu and the other islands were still part of a dry landmass, and what is now the northern Adriatic was covered by a vast forest. These people would originally have come from the eastern Mediterranean, finding themselves "islanded" when, during the period 14,000–10,000 BC, the ice thawed, raising the level of the Mediterranean by over 100 metres. Their communities would have been agrarian and self-supporting, producing pottery and handicrafts, and worshipping earth/fertility deities, clay figurines of which can be seen in some island museums. The development of agriculture, trade and sea travel would transform this civilization into one that learned to specialize, compete and, when it seemed advantageous, go to war.

Minoans and Mycenaeans

During the peak of the Bronze Age **Minoan civilization** (3000–1100 BC), which saw Crete rise to dominate the Aegean, it appears that while islands in the archipelago traded with the Minoans – wood from Kefalloniá's unique fir species, *abies cephalonica*, was used in the construction of the palace of Knossos – they stayed apart from Minoan culture. This was a period of fluctuating regional dominance for the whole of the Mediterranean basin, based upon sea power, with vast palaces serving as centres of administration. **Knossos** on Crete became the centre of the dominant Minoan civilization, but also important – and closer to the Ionian – were **Mycenae**, **Tiryns** and **Argos** in the Peloponnese. When Minoan culture went into decline, around 1400 BC, Mycenae, south of Corinth and 150km from what is modern-day Pátra, became the seat of power. For at least two centuries, Mycenae ruled the region – and in turn gave its name to the period – until it in turn collapsed around 1200 BC.

This is a period whose history and remains are bound up with **legends**, recounted most famously by **Homer**. Mycenae was the home of Agamemnon, engineer of the **Trojan War**, which was the subject of Homer's *Iliad*, and it was the end of the Trojan War that started Odysseus' long voyage home in the *Odyssey*. Debate continues over the provenance of the *Iliad* and *Odyssey*, both in terms of their authorship – it's likely that they were originally oral epics – and whether they were journalism, fiction, or both. They seem to have been based in fact, although the amount of detail accepted varies between rival authorities. They certainly reflect the prevalence of violence, revenge and war as part of the culture, instigated and aggravated by trade and territorial rivalry (one reading of the

Odyssey casts Odysseus as little more than a pirate and opportunist). The few surviving examples of architecture from this period – sections of vast fortifications seen on Corfu, Itháki, Kefalloniá and elsewhere, and known, with Homeric felicity, as Cyclopean walls – give a measure of the level of political tension and aggression in Mycenaean Greece.

At this time, and for centuries after, Greece was a collection of small independent regions, divided by clan loyalties and geography, vying for power, and forming and dissolving alliances as the power structure shifted. These miniature states succeeded or failed depending on their level of military or economic strength; Corfu, for example, established itself as a powerful naval force, and Kefalloniá was perfectly situated to become a trading post between the east and west Mediterranean.

The Dorian and Classical eras

As the circulation of trade and population around the Mediterranean increased, so these communities had to cope with the sudden and not always welcome arrival of new peoples and businesses that might supplant their economic power. The most radical alteration to the balance of power was the influx of northern **Dorians**: their unseating of Mycenaean rule was traditionally viewed as an "invasion" but is nowadays thought to have been a fundamental shift in the region's economy, which wrought drastic changes among the palace cultures and their naval forces in the eleventh century BC.

The Dorians imported their own religion, the twelve gods of **Olympus**, supplanting the widespread cult of Dionysus – deity of wine, fruitfulness and vegetation, and originally a goddess – and other female earth/fertility deities. The Dorian era was also notable for the appearance of a "Greek" **alphabet**, which is still recognizable alongside modern Greek and which replaced the "Linear A" script discovered on Crete, and the later "Linear B" Minoan/Mycenaean script.

City-states: Sparta, Athens and Corinth

The ninth century BC saw the birth of the Greek **city-state** (*polis*). Citizens – not just royalty or aristocracy – had a hand in government and community activities, and organized commerce and leisure. Economic and territorial expansionism increased, as did overseas trade, and this would shortly create a new class of manufacturers.

The city-state was defined by those who lived in it, and each state retained an individual identity and culture. Consequently, alliances between them were always temporary and tactical. Athens and Sparta, the Dorian city-state in the southern Peloponnese, were the two most powerful, and pursued a bitter rivalry for centuries.

Sparta was founded and run according to a militaristic regime which some today describe as fascistic. Males were subject to military service between the ages of 7 and 30, and young women were also expected to excel in athletics. **Athens** was the place that developed the – at the time, limited – notion of democracy. Its literal meaning, recognizable from modern Greek, is "people power", but this only applied to "freeborn" males, and not to women or slaves. As many as 40,000 Athenians were entitled to vote at the Assembly. Not only Athens, but every city-state had its **acropolis** or "high town", where polytheistic religious activity, under the aegis of Zeus, was focused.

After Athens and Sparta, **Corinth** was the next most powerful city-state, and the one that exercised the most influence on Corfu and the Ionian islands. Corinth was both a trading centre and a powerful naval force, with strong colonialist tendencies. As well as Corfu, it settled Syracuse (on Sicily) and Lefkádha, and would later seal tactical alliances with the city-states of Kefalloniá, notably Pale and Same. Affinities between regions and city-states shifted violently when it came to war: while Corfu prospered after it was colonized by Corinth in the eighth century BC, a fierce battle between the two was one of the causes of the **Peloponnesian Wars** in 431–404 BC. Similarly, during that war Kefalloniá's city-states were all allies of Athens, only to find themselves invaded by distrustful Athenians who used the island as a power base against Corinth.

Sparta emerged as nominal victors from the Peloponnesian Wars, but the years of warfare had drained all city-states of resources and commitment to the political system. The increasingly complex world of trade was subverting the older structures, and the invention and spread of **coinage** – an innovation as radical in its time as computerization today – was expanding and streamlining commercial life. A revitalized Athens, for example, was trading as far afield as the Black Sea, and Corfu had established trade links with Egypt.

Hellenistic and Roman Greece

The most important factor in the decline of the city-states was meanwhile developing beyond their boundaries, in the northern kingdom of **Macedonia** – a territory and title still fiercely contested today.

The Macedonian empire

Based at the Macedonian capital of Pella, **Philip II** (359–336 BC) forged a strong military and unitary force, extending his territories into Thrace. He then pushed south to take the rest of Greece (including the Ionian islands), in 338 BC defeating the Athenians and their allies at the decisive Battle of Chaironeia, just east of Delphi. On his death at the age of 23, Philip was succeeded by his son, **Alexander the Great**, whose extraordinary thirteen-year career extended the empire into Persia and Egypt and even parts of modern India.

These vast gains began to crumble almost immediately after the death of Alexander in 323 BC. The empire was divided up into the three Macedonian dynasties of **Hellenistic Greece**, though Corfu and the Ionian islands fell victim to a series of regional takeovers, including early incursions by the Romans.

Roman Greece

Corfu, fatefully positioned between the heel of Italy and the Greek mainland, was the first city-state seized by the **Romans**, in 229 BC. The Romans subdued the rest of Greece over some seventy years of campaigns, from 215 to 146 BC. However, Rome allowed considerable autonomy in terms of law, religion and language, and Greece and its overlords coexisted fairly peacefully for the next four centuries. While Athens and Corinth remained important cities, the emphasis of power shifted north – particularly to towns such as Salonica (Thessaloníki) along the new *Via Egnatia*, a military and civil road connecting Rome and Byzantium via the port of Brundisium (modern Brindisi).

The Byzantine Empire and medieval Greece

The shift in power towards the north of Greece was exacerbated by the decline of the Roman Empire and its division into eastern and western halves. In 330 AD the Emperor Constantine moved his capital to the Greek city of Byzantium and here emerged Constantinople (modern Istanbul), the "new Rome" and spiritual and political capital of the **Byzantine Empire**. While the last western Roman emperor was deposed by barbarian Goths in 476 AD, the oriental portion of the empire was to be the dominant Mediterranean power for some 700 years, and only in 1453 did it collapse completely.

Christianity

Although Christianity was formally introduced during the reign of Constantine, Christian preachers had been travelling in Greece since the first century AD – Corfu is believed to have first been evangelized in 37 AD. By the end of the fourth century, Christianity was the official state religion, its liturgies (still in use in the Greek Orthodox church), creed and New Testament all written in Greek.

In the seventh century, **Constantinople** was besieged by Persians, and later by Arabs, but the Byzantine Empire held, losing only Egypt, the least "Greek" of its territories. From the ninth to the eleventh century, it enjoyed a "golden age", both spiritual and political. Intrinsic in the Orthodox Byzantine faith was a sense of religious superiority, and the emperors saw Constantinople as a "new Jerusalem" for their "chosen people". This was the start of a diplomatic and ecclesiastical conflict with the Catholic west that would have disastrous consequences in subsequent centuries. As antagonism grew, the eastern and western patriarchs mutually excommunicated each other.

From the seventh through to the eleventh centuries, parts of **Byzantine Greece** became a rather provincial backwater. Administration was top-heavy and imperial taxation led to semi-autonomous provinces ruled by military generals, whose land was usually taken from bankrupt peasants. This alienation of the poor primed a disaffected populace for change, almost regardless of who implemented it.

Ionian and central Greece were particular vulnerable when waves of **Slavic raiders** staged numerous sorties from the Balkans in this period. At the same time, other groups moved down into the region from **central Europe** and were assimilated peaceably. From the thirteenth century on, immigrants from **Albania** fanned out across central Greece, the Peloponnese and nearby islands.

The Crusades, the Venetians and the Ottomans

With the Byzantine Empire in steady decline, the eleventh century saw dramatic rearrangements of the power structure, particularly in the western parts of Greece. The **Normans** landed first at Corfu in 1081 and occupied the rest of the Ionian over the next two years. They returned to the mainland, with papal approval, a decade later on their way to liberate Jerusalem. This was only a foretaste of regular incursions into the Ionian region by the **Crusaders** on their way to Asia Minor. Richard the Lionheart, for example, landed on Corfu in 1192, but hastily left, fearing arrest by Byzantine officials who regarded him an enemy of the Orthodox Church.

In the **Fourth Crusade** of 1204, Venetians, Franks and Germans turned their armies directly on Byzantium and sacked and occupied Constantinople. These Latin princes and their followers, seeking new lands and kingdoms, divided the best of the empire among themselves. All that remained of Byzantium were four small kingdoms or **despotates**: the most powerful in Nicaea in Asia Minor, Trebizond on the Black Sea, Mystra in the Pelopponese and Epirus, on the mainland opposite Corfu.

The Ionian archipelago fell under this last administration, although, crucially, **Venice** had demanded the islands when the spoils of Byzantium were being shared out. As in the rest of Greece, the region passed a turbulent century in which vying post-imperial factions assumed and relinquished power. Venice made an offer for the Ionian islands in 1350, but was refused. However, local lords and landowners on Corfu sensed the way power was moving in the region, and saw they would be safest with the Venetians. In 1386, Venice took advantage of an interregnum in the Ionians, sent an army to conquer, and was asked to "protect" the island by its leaders. Over the next century and more, Venice set its sights on subsuming the other Ionian islands and Párga – the only toehold the Venetians managed to get on the mainland – into its empire.

In the meantime, the **Ottoman Empire** grew more powerful in the east. Constantinople finally fell in 1453, and a decade later most of the former Byzantine Empire was in Turkish hands. Only the Cycladic islands, which had also been taken by the Venetians, and scattered enclaves such as the remote Máni region of the Peloponnese, Sfákia in Crete and Soúli in Epirus, were able to resist Ottoman rule. Even Zákinthos was seized for a time by the Turks, as were Kefalloniá and Itháki; tiny Paxí was sacked and most of its population enslaved by the Ottoman admiral, Barbarossa. Lefkádha passed between Turkish and Venetian rule several times, before finally joining the rest of the Ionian islands under Venice in 1684.

Under what Greeks refer to as the "Dark Ages" of Ottoman rule, much of present-day Greece passed into rural provincialism, taking refuge in a self-protective form of village life that has only recently been disrupted. Taxes and discipline, occasionally backed by acts of genocide against rebel communities, were inflicted by Turkish authorities, but estates passed into the hands of local chieftains, who often had considerable independence. Greek identity was sustained by the **Orthodox Church** which, despite instances of forced conversions to the Muslim faith, was allowed to continue. Monasteries organized schools, often secretly, and became the sole guardians of Byzantine culture, although many scholars and artists emigrated west, contributing to the Renaissance.

In contrast, the Ionian islands flourished under Venice. Extensive planting of olives established an industry that continues throughout the islands today. Venice's distinctive architecture, with its signature Lion of St Mark, was transposed to the towns of Corfu, Argostóli, Lefkádha and Zákinthos. Venice sustained the lords and landowners, and brutally crushed any attempts to propose land reform. This would eventually undermine them, particularly when islanders became involved in the **Filikí Etería**, or "Friendly Society", a secret group working to build opposition against the Turks.

The struggle for independence

As the Ottoman empire itself began showing signs of unravelling, opposition to Turkish rule became widespread, exemplified by the **Klephts** (brigands) of the mountains. It took until the nineteenth century, however, for a resistance movement to rally sufficient support and fire power to challenge the Turks. The French Revolution of 1789 gave fresh impetus to "freedom movements" and to the *Filikí Etería*, who were recruiting on the Ionian islands as well as among exiles living abroad. Napoleon's declaration of war on Venice fired visions of independence in the Ionian, but after he had defeated the Venetians in 1797 he sent emissaries to the archipelago to establish his own authority. Nevertheless, the **French** upended the social order and freed serfs, and jubilant crowds burnt the *Libro d'Oro* (the "Golden Book" that listed those aristocrats favoured by the Venetians) in impromptu celebrations in most of the Ionian capitals. In Corfu, the French embarked on an ambitious building programme, but this was cut short by Napoleon's downfall in 1814. Throughout the Ionian, the French were replaced by the administrators of a militarily imposed **British** protectorate. The British introduced their own judicial and education systems, and set about building roads, reservoirs and other civic projects. Despite the benefits of these innovations, British rule was marked by a high-handedness – along with a tendency to use brute force to quell dissent – that won them few friends.

The war of independence

By 1821, the *Filikí Etería* had assembled a rather motley coalition of Klephts and theorists, who launched their insurrection against the Turks at the monastery of **Áyia Lávra** near Kalávrita in the Peloponnese, where on March 21 the Greek banner was openly raised by the local bishop, Yermanos. Despite punitive resistance by their British rulers, the Ionian islands enthusiastically if surreptitiously supported the rebellion with money, weapons and manpower. While much of the detail of the ensuing **war of independence** is confusing – with landowners believing they were fighting to regain their traditional privileges, and peasants seeing it as a means of improving social conditions regardless of who was in power – the Greeks, through local and fragmented guerrilla campaigns, managed to present a coherent threat to Turkish rule.

Outside Greece, prestige and publicity for the insurrection was promoted by the arrival of a thousand or so **Philhellenes**, almost half of them German, though the most important was the English poet, **Lord Byron**, who died while training Greek forces at Messolónghi in April 1824. Byron's connections with the Ionian islands, in particular Kefalloniá, conferred on him an abiding heroic status here as elsewhere in Greece.

Greek guerrilla leaders such as **Theodhoros Kolokotronis** were responsible for the most significant military victories of the war, but the death of Byron had an immense effect on public opinion in the west. Originally, aid for the Greek struggle had come neither from Orthodox Russia, nor from the western powers of France and Britain, ravaged by the Napoleonic Wars. Yet when Messolónghi fell again to the Turks in 1827, these three powers finally agreed to seek autonomy for parts of Greece, and sent a combined fleet to confront the Turks, then sacking the Peloponnese. After an accidental sea battle in **Navarino Bay** destroyed almost the entire Turkish fleet, and heightened aggression from Russia, Turkey was forced to accept the existence of an autonomous Greece.

In 1830 Greek independence was confirmed by the western powers and borders were drawn. These included just 800,000 of the six million Greeks living within the Ottoman Empire, and the Greek territories were for the most part the poorest of the Classical and Byzantine lands, comprising Attica, the Peloponnese and the Argo-Saronic and Cycladic islands. The rich agricultural belt of Thessaly, Epirus in the west, and Macedonia in the north, remained in Turkish hands.

The emerging state

Modern Greece began as a republic, and its first president was a Corfiot. An aristocrat and career diplomat, **Ioannis Capodistrias** (1776–1831) had gained an impressive reputation negotiating with the British and Russians, and won widespread support for his defence of Lefkádha against the Epirus despot, Ali Pasha. Capodistrias concentrated on creating a viable structure for the emerging Greek state in the face of diverse protagonists from the independence struggle, though his later career was marred by unpopular acts of nepotism and autocracy. Almost inevitably, he was assassinated – in 1831, by chieftains from the Máni peninsula – and perhaps equally inevitably, the western powers who had forced the resolution of the independence issue stepped in. They created a monarchy and installed a Bavarian prince, **Otho**.

The new king proved to be autocratic and insensitive, giving official posts to fellow Germans and dismissing suggestions by the landless peasantry that the old estates be redistributed. A popular revolt forced him from the country in 1862, and the Europeans produced a new prince, this time from Denmark. Britain ceded the

Ionian islands to Greece as part of this arrangement, more or less as a sweetener. **George I** proved more capable than his predecessor: he built the first railways and roads, introduced limited land reforms in the Peloponnese, and oversaw the first expansion of the Greek borders.

The Megáli Idhéa and war

From the very beginning, the unquestioned motive force of Greek foreign policy was the **Megáli Idhéa** (Great Idea) of liberating Greek populations outside the country and incorporating the old territories of Byzantium into the kingdom. In 1878 **Thessaly**, along with southern Epirus, was ceded to Greece by the Turks. Less illustriously, the Greeks failed in 1897 to achieve *enosis* (union) with **Crete** by attacking Turkish forces on the mainland, and in the process virtually bankrupted the state. The island was, however, placed under a High Commissioner, appointed by the great powers, and in 1913 became a part of Greece.

It was from Crete, also, that the most distinguished Greek statesman emerged. **Eleftherios Venizelos**, having led a civilian campaign for his island's liberation, was in 1910 elected as Greek prime minister. Two years later he organized an alliance of Balkan powers to fight the **Balkan Wars** (1912–13), campaigns that saw the Turks virtually driven from Europe. With Greek borders extended to include the northeast Aegean, northern Thessaly, central Epirus and parts of Macedonia, the *Megáli Idhéa* was approaching reality. At the same time, Venizelos proved himself a shrewd manipulator of domestic public opinion by revising the constitution and introducing a series of liberal social reforms.

Division, however, was to appear with the outbreak of **World War I**. Venizelos urged Greek entry on the British side, seeing in the conflict possibilities for the "liberation" of Greeks in Thrace and Asia Minor, but the new king, Konstantinos I, married to a sister of the German Kaiser, imposed a policy of neutrality. Eventually Venizelos set up a revolutionary government in Thessaloníki, and in 1917 Greek troops entered the war to join the French, British and Serbians in the **Macedonian campaign**. On the capitulation of Bulgaria and Ottoman Turkey, the Greeks occupied Thrace, and Venizelos presented at Versailles demands for the predominantly Greek region of Smyrna on the Asia Minor coast.

It was the beginning of one of the most disastrous episodes in modern Greek history. Venizelos was authorized to move forces into Smyrna in 1919, but by then Allied support had evaporated and in Turkey itself a new nationalist movement was taking power under Mustafa Kemal, or **Atatürk** as he came to be known. In 1920 Venizelos lost the elections and monarchist factions took over, their aspirations unmitigated by the Cretan's skill in foreign diplomacy. Greek forces were ordered to advance upon Ankara in an attempt to bring Atatürk to terms.

The so-called **Anatolian campaign** ignominiously collapsed in summer 1922, when Turkish troops forced the Greeks back to the coast and a hurried evacuation from **Smyrna**. The Turks moved in and systematically massacred whatever remained of the Armenian and Greek populations before burning most of the city to the ground.

The exchange of populations

This ensuing Treaty of Lausanne in 1923 ordered the **exchange of religious minorities** from both countries. Turkey was to accept 390,000 Muslims from Greece. Greece, mobilized for a decade and with a population of less than five million, was faced with the resettlement of over 1,300,000 Christian refugees. The *Megáli Idhéa* ceased to be a viable blueprint.

The effect on Greek society was far-reaching. The great agricultural estates of Thessaly were finally redistributed, both to Greek tenants and refugee farmers, and huge shantytowns developed around Athens, Pireás and other cities, a spur to the country's then almost nonexistent industry.

Political reaction was swift. A group of army officers assembled after the retreat from Smyrna "invited" King Konstantinos to abdicate and executed five of his ministers. Democracy was nominally restored with the proclamation of a republic, but for much of the next decade changes in government were brought about by factions within the armed forces. Meanwhile, among the urban refugee population, unions were being formed and the Greek **Communist Party** (KKE) was established.

By 1936 the Communist Party had enough democratic support to hold the balance of power in parliament, and would have done so had not the army and the by then restored king decided otherwise. Yiorgos (George) II had been voted in by a plebiscite held – and almost certainly manipulated – the previous year, and so presided over an increasingly factionalized parliament.

The Metaxas dictatorship

In April 1936, George II appointed a Kefallonian, **General Ioannis Metaxas**, as prime minister, despite the fact that Metaxas only had the support of six elected deputies. Immediately a series of KKE-organized strikes broke out and the king, ignoring attempts to form a broad liberal coalition, dissolved parliament without setting a date for new elections. It was a blatantly unconstitutional move and opened the way for five years of ruthless and at times absurd dictatorship.

Metaxas averted a general strike with military force and proceeded to set up a state based on fascist models of the time. Left-wing and trade union opponents were imprisoned or forced into exile, a state youth movement and secret police set up, and rigid censorship, extending even to passages of Thucydides, imposed. It was, however, at least a Greek dictatorship, and though Metaxas was sympathetic to Nazi organization he completely opposed German or Italian domination.

World War II and the civil war

The Italians tried to provoke Greece into **World War II** by torpedoing the Greek cruiser *Elli* in Tínos harbour in August 1940. The Greeks made no response. However, when Mussolini occupied Albania and, on October 28, 1940, sent an ultimatum demanding passage through Greece for his troops, Metaxas' legendary rebuttal to the Italian foreign minister was *"óhi"* (no). (In fact, his response, in the mutually understood French, was *"C'est la guerre."*) The date marked the entry of Greece into the war, and Óhi Day is still celebrated as a national holiday.

Occupation and resistance

Fighting as a nation in a sudden unity of crisis, the Greeks drove Italian forces from the mainland and in the operation took control of the long-coveted and predominantly Greek-populated northern Epirus. The Ionian islands found themselves on the front line, and were taken by the Italians. The Greek army, however, lost its impetus during a harsh winter fighting in the mountains, and British backup never materialized.

In April the following year Nazi columns swept through Yugoslavia and across the Greek mainland, effectively reversing the only Axis defeat to date, and by the end of May 1941 airborne and seaborne **German invasion** forces had completed the occupation. Metaxas had died before their arrival, while King George and his new self-appointed ministers fled into exile in Cairo. Few Greeks of any political persuasion were sad to see them go.

The joint **Italian–German–Bulgarian Axis occupation** of Greece was among the bitterest experiences of the European war. Nearly half a million Greek civilians starved to death as all available food was requisitioned to feed occupying armies, and entire villages throughout the mainland and especially on Crete were burnt and slaughtered at the least hint of resistance activity. In the Ionian, even the olive crop was sequestered, driving the olive industry underground.

The Nazis supervised the deportation to concentration camps of virtually the entire **Greek Jewish population**. This was at the time a sizeable community. Thessaloníki – where former UN and Austrian president Kurt Waldheim worked for Nazi intelligence – contained the largest Jewish population of any Balkan city, and there were significant populations in all Greek mainland towns and on many islands. Over two thousand Jews were rounded up in Corfu Town alone for transportation; less than a hundred returned.

With a quisling government in Athens – and an unpopular, discredited Royalist group in Cairo – the focus of Greek political and military action over the next four years passed largely to the **EAM**, or National Liberation Front. By 1943 it was in virtual control of most areas of the country, working with the British on tactical operations, with its own army (**ELAS**), navy and both civil and secret police forces. On the whole, it commanded popular support, and it offered an obvious framework for the resumption of postwar government.

However, most of its membership was communist, and the British prime minister, **Churchill**, was determined to reinstate the monarchy. Even with two years of the war to run it became obvious that there could be no peaceable post-liberation regime other than an EAM-dominated republic. Accordingly, in August 1943 representatives from each of the main resistance movements – including two non-communist groups – flew from a makeshift airstrip in Thessaly to ask for guarantees from the "government" in Cairo that the king would not return unless a plebiscite had first voted in his favour. Neither the Greek nor British authorities would consider the proposal and the one possibility of averting civil war was lost.

The EAM contingent returned divided, as perhaps the British had intended, and a conflict broke out between those who favoured taking peaceful control of any government imposed after liberation, and the hardline Stalinist ideologues, who believed such a situation should not be allowed to develop.

In October 1943, with fears of an imminent British landing force and takeover, ELAS launched a full-scale attack upon its Greek rivals; by the following February, when a ceasefire was arranged, they had wiped out all but the EDES, a right-wing grouping suspected of collaboration with the Germans. At the same time other forces were at work, with both the British and Americans infiltrating units into Greece in order to prevent the establishment of communist government when the Germans began withdrawing their forces.

Civil war

In fact, as the Germans began to leave in October 1944, most of the EAM leadership agreed to join a British-sponsored "official" **interim government**. It quickly proved a tactical error, however, for with ninety percent of the countryside under their control the communists were given only one-third representation; the king showed no sign of renouncing his claims; and, in November, Allied forces ordered ELAS to disarm. On December 3 all pretences of civility or neutrality were dropped; the police fired on a communist demonstration in Athens and fighting broke out between ELAS and **British troops**, in the so-called **Dhekemvriána** battle of Athens.

A truce of sorts was negotiated at Várkiza the following spring, but the agreement was never implemented. The army, police and civil service remained in right-wing hands and, while collaborators were often allowed to retain their positions, left-wing sympathizers, many of whom were not communists, were systematically excluded. The elections of 1946 were won by the right-wing parties, followed by a plebiscite in favour of the king's return. By 1947 guerrilla activity had again reached the scale of a full **civil war**.

In the interim, King George had died and been succeeded by his brother Paul (with his consort Frederika), while the **Americans** had taken over the British role, and begun putting into action the cold war **Truman doctrine**. In 1947 they took virtual control of Greece, their first significant postwar experiment in anti-communist intervention. Massive economic and military aid was given to a client Greek government, with a prime minister whose documents had to be countersigned by the American Mission in order to become valid.

In the mountains US "military advisers" supervised **campaigns against ELAS**, and there were mass arrests, court martials and imprisonments – a kind of "White Terror" – lasting until 1951. Over three thousand executions were recorded, including a number of Jehovah's Witnesses, "a sect proved to be under communist domination", according to US Ambassador Grady.

In the autumn of 1949, with the Yugoslav–Greek border closed after Tito's rift with Stalin, the last ELAS guerrillas finally admitted defeat, retreating into Albania from their strongholds on Mount Grámmos. Atrocities had been committed on both sides, including, from the Left, wide-scale destruction of monasteries, and the dubious evacuation of children from "combat areas" (as told in Nicholas Gage's virulently anti-communist book, *Eleni*). Such errors, as well as the hopelessness of fighting an American-backed army, undoubtedly lost ELAS much support.

Reconstruction American-style: 1950–67

It was a demoralized, shattered Greece that emerged into the Western political orbit of the 1950s. It was also perforce American-dominated, enlisted into the Korean War in 1950 and NATO the following year. In domestic politics, the US Embassy – still giving the orders – installed a winner-take-all electoral system, which was to ensure victory for the Right over the next twelve years. All leftist activity was banned; those individuals who were not herded into political "re-education" camps or dispatched by firing squads, legal or vigilante, went into exile throughout Eastern Europe, to return only after 1974.

The American-backed, highly conservative "**Greek Rally**" party, led by General Papagos, won the first decisive post-civil war elections in 1952. After the general's death, the party's leadership was taken over – and to an extent liberalized –

by **Konstantinos Karamanlis**. Under his rule, stability of a kind was established and some economic advances registered, particularly after the revival of Greece's traditional German trade links. However, the 1950s was also a decade that saw wholesale **depopulation of the villages** as migrants sought work in Australia, America and western Europe, or the larger Greek cities.

The main crisis in foreign policy throughout this period was **Cyprus**, where a long terrorist campaign was waged by Greeks opposing British rule, and there was the sporadic threat of a new Greek–Turkish war. A temporary and unworkable solution was forced on the island by Britain in 1960, granting independence without the possibility of self-determination or union with Greece. Much of the traditional Greek–British goodwill was destroyed by the issue, with Britain seen to be acting with regard only for its two military bases (over which it still retains sovereignty).

By 1961, unemployment, the Cyprus issue and the imposition of US nuclear bases on Greek soil were changing the political climate, and when Karamanlis was again elected there was strong suspicion of a fraud arranged by the king and army. Strikes became frequent in industry and even agriculture, and King Paul and autocratic, fascist-inclined Queen Frederika were openly attacked in parliament and at protest demonstrations. The Far Right grew uneasy about **"communist insurgence"** and, losing confidence in their own electoral influence, arranged the assassination of left-wing deputy **Grigoris Lambrakis** in Thessaloníki in May 1963. (The assassination, and its subsequent cover-up, is the subject of Vassilis Vassilikos's thriller *Z*, filmed by Costa-Gavras.) It was against this volatile background that Karamanlis resigned, lost the subsequent elections and left the country.

The new government – the first controlled from outside the Greek Right since 1935 – was formed by **Yiorgos Papandreou's** Centre Union Party, and had a decisive majority of nearly fifty seats. It was to last, however, for under two years as conservative forces rallied to thwart its progress. In this the chief protagonists were the army officers and their constitutional commander-in-chief, the new king, 23-year-old **Konstantinos (Constantine) II**.

Since power in Greece depended on a pliant military as well as a network of political appointees, Papandreou's most urgent task in order to govern securely and effectively was to reform the armed forces. His first Minister of Defence proved incapable of the task and, while he was investigating the right-wing plot that was thought to have rigged the 1961 election, "evidence" was produced of a leftist conspiracy connected with Papandreou's son Andreas (himself a minister in the government).

The allegations grew to a crisis and Yiorgos Papandreou decided to assume the defence portfolio himself, a move for which the king refused to give the necessary sanction. He then resigned in order to gain approval at the polls, but the king would not order fresh elections, instead persuading members of the Centre Union – chief among them **Konstantinos Mitsotakis**, the recent Greek premier – to defect and organize a coalition government. Punctuated by strikes, resignations and mass demonstrations, this lasted for a year and a half until new elections were eventually set for May 28, 1967. They failed to take place.

The Colonels' Junta: 1967–74

It was a foregone conclusion that Papandreou's party would win popular support in the polls against the discredited coalition partners. And it was equally certain that there would be some sort of anti-democratic action to try and prevent them from taking power. Disturbed by the party's leftward shift, King Konstantinos was said to have briefed senior generals for a coup d'état, to take place ten days before the elections. However, he was caught by surprise, as was nearly everyone else by the **coup of April 21, 1967**, staged by a group of "unknown" colonels. It was, in the words of Andreas Papandreou, "the first successful CIA military putsch on the European continent".

The **Colonels' Junta**, having taken control of the means of power, was sworn in by the king and survived the half-hearted counter-coup which he subsequently attempted to organize. It was an overtly fascist regime, absurdly styling itself as the true "Revival of Greek Orthodoxy" against western "corrupting influences", though in reality its ideology was nothing more than warmed-up dogma from the Metaxas era.

All political activity was banned, trade unions were forbidden to recruit or meet, the press was so heavily censored that many papers stopped printing, and thousands of "communists" were arrested, imprisoned and often tortured. Among them were both Papandreous, the composer

Mikis Theodorakis (deemed "unfit to stand trial" after three months in custody) and Amalia Fleming (widow of Alexander). The best-known Greek actress, Melina Mercouri, was stripped of her citizenship *in absentia* and thousands of prominent Greeks joined her in exile. Culturally, the colonels put an end to popular music (closing down most of the *rembétika* clubs) and inflicted ludicrous censorship on literature and the theatre, including (as under Metaxas) a ban on production of the Classical tragedies.

The colonels lasted for seven years, opposed (especially after the first year) by the majority of the Greek people, excluded from the European community, but propped up and given massive aid by US presidents **Lyndon Johnson** and **Richard Nixon**. To them and the CIA the junta's Greece was not an unsuitable client state; human rights considerations were considered unimportant, orders were placed for sophisticated military technology, and foreign investment on terms highly unfavourable to Greece was open to multinational corporations.

Opposition was from the beginning voiced by exiled Greeks in London, the United States and western Europe, but only in 1973 did demonstrations break out openly in Greece. On November 17 the students of Athens **Polytechnic** began an occupation of their buildings. The ruling clique lost its nerve; armoured vehicles stormed the Polytechnic gates and a still-undetermined number of students were killed. Martial law was tightened and junta chief **Colonel Papadopoulos** was replaced by the even more noxious and reactionary **General Ioannides**, head of the secret police.

The return to civilian rule: 1975–81

The end of the ordeal, however, came within a year as the dictatorship embarked on a disastrous political adventure in **Cyprus**. By attempting to topple the Makarios government and impose *énosis* (union) on the island, they provoked a Turkish invasion and occupation of forty percent of the Cypriot territory. The army finally mutinied and **Konstantinos Karamanlis** was invited to return from Paris to take office again. He swiftly negotiated a ceasefire (but no solution) in Cyprus, withdrew temporarily from NATO, and warned that US bases would have to be removed except where they specifically served Greek interest. In November 1974 Karamanlis and his *Néa Dhimokratía* (New Democracy or ND) party was rewarded by a sizeable majority in elections, with a centrist and socialist opposition, including PASOK, a new party led by Andreas Papandreou.

The election of *Néa Dhimokratía* was in every sense a safe conservative option, but to Karamanlis' enduring credit it oversaw an effective and firm return to democratic stability, even legitimizing the KKE (Communist Party) for the first time in its history. Karamanlis also held a referendum on the monarchy – in which 59 percent of Greeks rejected the return of Constantine – and instituted in its place a French-style presidency, the post which he himself occupied from 1980 to 1985. Economically there were limited advances, although these were more than offset by inflationary defence spending (the result of renewed tension with Turkey), hastily negotiated entrance into the EC, and the decision to let the drachma float after decades of its being artificially fixed at thirty to the US dollar.

Crucially, though, Karamanlis failed to deliver on vital reforms in bureaucracy, social welfare and education and, though the worst figures of the junta were brought to trial, the ordinary faces of Greek political life and administration were little changed. By 1981 inflation was hovering around 25 percent, and it was estimated that tax evasion was depriving the state of one-third of its annual budget. In foreign policy the US bases had remained and it was felt that Greece, back in NATO, was still acting as little more than an American satellite. The traditional Right was demonstrably inadequate to the task at hand.

PASOK: 1981–89

Change – *allayí* – was the watchword of the election campaign which swept **Andreas Papandreou**'s Panhellenic Socialist Movement, better known by the acronym **PASOK**, to power on October 18, 1981. The victory meant a chance for Papandreou to form the first socialist government in Greek history and break a near fifty-year monopoly of authoritarian right-wing rule. With so much at stake the campaign had been passionate even by Greek standards, and PASOK's victory was greeted with euphoria both by the generation whose political voice had been silenced by defeat in the civil war and by a large proportion of the young. They were hopes which perhaps ran naively and dangerously high.

The victory, at least, was conclusive. PASOK won 174 of the 300 parliamentary seats and the Communist KKE returned another thirteen deputies, one of whom was the composer Mikis Theodorakis. *Néa Dhimokratía* moved into unaccustomed opposition. There appeared to be no obstacle to the implementation of a radical **socialist programme**: devolution of power to local authorities, the socialization of industry (though it was never clear how this was to be different from nationalization), improvement of the social services, a purge of bureaucratic inefficiency and malpractice, the end of bribery and corruption as a way of life, an independent and dignified foreign policy following expulsion of US bases, and withdrawal from NATO and the European Community.

A change of style was promised, too, replacing the country's long traditions of authoritarianism and bureaucracy with openness and dialogue. Even more radically, where Greek political parties had long been the personal followings of charismatic leaders, PASOK was to be a party of ideology and principle, dependent on no single individual member. Or so, at least, thought some of the youthful PASOK political enthusiasts.

The new era started with a bang. The wartime resistance was officially recognized; hitherto they hadn't been allowed to take part in any celebrations, wreath-layings or other ceremonies. Peasant women were granted pensions for the first time – 3000dr a month, the same as their outraged husbands – and wages were indexed to the cost of living. In addition, civil marriage was introduced, family law reformed in favour of wives and mothers, and equal rights legislation was put on the statute book.

These popular **reformist moves** seemed to mark a break with the past, and the atmosphere had indeed changed. Greeks no longer lowered their voices to discuss politics in public places or wrapped their opposition newspaper in the respectably conservative *Kathimeriní*. At first there were real fears that the climate would be too much for the military and they would once again intervene to choke a dangerous experiment in democracy, especially when Andreas Papandreou assumed the defence portfolio himself in a move strongly reminiscent of his father's attempt to remove the king's appointee in 1965. But he went out of his way to soothe **military susceptibilities**, increasing their salaries, buying new weaponry, and being super-fastidious in his attendance at military functions.

The end of the honeymoon

Nothing if not a populist, Papandreou promised a bonanza he must have known, as a skilled and experienced economist, he could not deliver. As a result he pleased nobody on the **economic** front.

He could not fairly be blamed for the inherited lack of investment, low productivity, deficiency in managerial and labour skills and other chronic problems besetting the Greek economy. On the other hand, he certainly aggravated the situation in the early days of his first government by allowing his supporters to indulge in violently anti-capitalist rhetoric, and by the prosecution and humiliation of the Tsatsos family, owners of one of Greece's few modern and profitable businesses – cement, in this case – for the illegal export of capital, something of which every Greek with any savings is guilty. These were cheap victories and were not backed by any programme of public investment, while the only "socializations" were of hopelessly lame-duck companies.

Faced with this sluggish economy, and burdened with the additional charges of (marginally) improved social benefits and wage indexing, Papandreou's government had also to cope with the effects of **world recession**, which always hit Greece with a delayed effect compared with its more advanced European partners. **Shipping**, the country's main foreign-currency earner, was devastated. Remittances from émigré workers fell off as they joined the lines of the unemployed in their host countries, and tourism receipts diminished under the dual impact of recession and Reagan's warning to Americans to stay away from insecure and terrorist-prone Athens airport.

With huge quantities of imported goods continuing to be sucked into the country in the absence of domestic production, the **foreign debt** topped £10 billion in 1986, with inflation at 25 percent and the balance of payments deficit approaching £1 billion. Greece also began to experience the social strains of **unemployment** for the first time. Not that it didn't exist before, but it had always been concealed as underemployment by the family and the rural structure of the economy – as well as by the absence of statistics.

The result of all this was that Papandreou had to eat his words. A modest spending spree, joy at the defeat of the Right, the popularity of his Greece-for-the-Greeks foreign policy, and some much-needed reforms saw him through into a **second term**, with an electoral victory in June

1985 scarcely less triumphant than the first. But the complacent and, frankly, dishonest slogan was "Vote PASOK for Even Better Days". By October they had imposed a two-year wage freeze and import restrictions, abolished the wage-indexing scheme and devalued the drachma by fifteen percent. Papandreou's fat was pulled out of the fire by none other than that former bogeyman, the **European Community**, which offered a huge two-part loan on condition that an IMF-style **austerity programme** was maintained.

The political fallout of such a classic right-wing deflation, accompanied by shameless soliciting for foreign investment, was the alienation of the Communists and most of PASOK's own political constituency. Increasingly autocratic – ironic given the early ideals of PASOK as a new kind of party – Papandreou's response to **dissent** was to fire recalcitrant trade union leaders and expel some three hundred members of his own party. Assailed by strikes, the government appeared to have lost direction completely. In local elections in October 1986 it lost a lot of ground to *Néa Dhimokratía*, including the mayoralties of the three major cities, Athens, Thessaloníki and Pátra.

Papandreou assured the nation that he had taken the message to heart but all that followed was a minor government reshuffle and a panicky attempt to undo the ill-feeling caused by an incredible freeing of **rent controls** at a time when all wage-earners were feeling the pinch badly. Early in 1987 he went further and sacked all the remaining PASOK veterans in his cabinet, including his son, though it is said, probably correctly, that this was a palliative to public opinion. The new cabinet was so un-Socialist that even the right-wing press called it **"centrist"**.

Similar about-turns took place in **foreign policy**. The initial anti-US, anti-NATO and anti-EC rhetoric was immensely popular, and understandable for a people shamelessly bullied by bigger powers for the past 150 years. There was some high-profile nose-thumbing, like refusing to join EC partners in condemning Jaruzelski's Polish regime, or the Soviet downing of a Korean airliner, or Syrian involvement in terrorist bomb-planting. There were some forgettable embarrassments, too, like suggesting Gaddafi's Libya provided a suitable model for alternative Socialist development, and the Mitterrand–Gaddafi–Papandreou "summit" in Crete, which an infuriated Mitterrand felt he had been inveigled into on false pretences.

Much was made of a strategic opening to the Arab world. Yasser Arafat, for example, was the first "head of state" to be received in Athens under the PASOK government. Given Greece's geographical position and historical ties, it was an imaginative and appropriate policy. But if Arab investment was hoped for, it never materialized.

In stark contrast to his early promises and rhetoric, the "realistic" policies that Papandreou pursued were far more conciliatory towards his big Western brothers. This was best exemplified by the fact that **US bases** remained in Greece, largely due to the fear that snubbing NATO would lead to Greece being exposed to Turkish aggression, still the only issue that unites the main parties to any degree. As for the once-reviled **European Community**, Greece had become an established beneficiary and its leader was hardly about to bite the hand that feeds.

Scandal

Even as late as mid-1988, despite the many betrayals of Papandreou, despite his failure to clean up the public services and do away with the system of patronage and corruption, and despite a level of popular displeasure that brought a million striking, demonstrating workers into the streets (February 1987), it seemed unlikely that PASOK would be toppled in the following year's **elections**.

This was due mainly to the lack of a credible alternative. Konstantinos Mitsotakis, a bitter personal enemy of Papandreou's since 1965, when his defection had brought down his father's government and set in train the events that culminated in the junta, was an unconvincing and unlikeable character at the helm of *Néa Dhimokratía*. Meanwhile, the liberal centre had disappeared and the main Communist party, KKE, appeared trapped in a Stalinist time warp under the leadership of Harilaos Florakis. Only the *Ellinikí Aristerá* (Greek Left), formerly the European wing of the KKE, seemed to offer any sensible alternative programme, and they had a precariously small following.

So PASOK could have been in a position to win a third term by default, as it were, when a combination of spectacular **own goals**, plus perhaps a general shift to the Right, influenced by the cataclysmic events in eastern Europe, conspired against them.

First came the extraordinary cavortings of the Prime Minister himself. Towards the end of 1988, the 70-year-old Papandreou was flown to Britain for open-heart surgery. He took the occasion, with fear of death presumably rocking his judgement, to make public a year-long liaison with a 34-year-old Olympic Airways hostess, **Dimitra "Mimi" Liani**. The international news pictures of an old man shuffling about after a young blonde, to the public humiliation of Margaret, his American-born wife, and his family, were not popular (Papandreou later divorced Margaret and married Mimi). His integrity was further questioned when he missed several important public engagements – including a ceremony commemorating the victims of the 1987 Kalamáta earthquake – and was pictured out with Mimi, reliving his youth in nightclubs.

The real damage, however, was done by **economic scandals**. It came to light that a PASOK minister had passed off Yugoslav corn as Greek in a sale to the EC. Then, far more seriously, it emerged that a self-made con man, **Yiorgos Koskotas**, director of the **Bank of Crete**, had embezzled £120 million of deposits and, worse still, slipped though the authorities' fingers and sought asylum in the US. Certain PASOK ministers and even Papandreou himself were implicated in the scandal. Further damage was done by allegations of illegal **arms dealings** by still more government ministers.

United in disgust at this corruption, the other Left parties – KKE and *Ellinikí Aristerá* – formed a coalition, the **Synaspismós**, taking support still further from PASOK.

Three bites at the cherry

In this climate of disaffection, an inconclusive result to the **June 1989 election** was no real surprise. What was less predictable, however, was the formation of a bizarre **"catharsis" coalition** of conservatives and communists, united in the avowed intent of cleansing PASOK's increasingly Augean stables. That this coalition emerged was basically down to Papandreou. The *Synaspismós* would have formed a government with PASOK but set one condition for doing so – that Papandreou stepped down as prime minister – and the old man would have none of it. In the deal finally cobbled together between the Left and *Néa Dhimokratía,* Mitsotakis was denied the premiership, too, having to make way for his compromise party colleague, **Tzanetakis**.

During the three months that the coalition lasted, the *kathársis* turned out to be largely a question of burying the knife as deeply as possible into the ailing body of PASOK. Andreas Papandreou and three other ministers were officially accused of involvement in the Koskotas affair – though there was no time to set up their **trial** before the Greek people returned once again to the polls. In any case, the chief witness and protagonist in the affair, Koskotas himself, was still imprisoned in America, awaiting extradition proceedings.

Contrary to the Right's hope that publicly accusing Papandreou and his cohorts of criminal behaviour would pave the way for a *Néa Dhimokratía* victory, PASOK actually made a slight recovery in the **November 1989 elections**, though the result was still inconclusive. This time the Left resolutely refused to do deals with anyone and the result was a consensus caretaker government under the neutral aegis of an academic called Zolotas, who was pushed into the prime minister's office, somewhat unwillingly it seemed, from Athens University. His only mandate was to see that the country didn't go off the rails completely while preparations were made for yet more elections. These took place in **April 1990** with the same captains at the command of their ships and with the *Synaspismós* having completed its about-turn to the extent that in the five single-seat constituencies (the other 295 seats are drawn from multiple-seat constituencies in a complicated system of reinforced proportional representation), they supported independent candidates jointly with PASOK. Greek communists are good at about-turns, though; after all, composer Mikis Theodorakis, musical torchbearer of the Left during the dark years of the junta, and formerly a KKE MP, was by now standing for *Néa Dhimokratía*.

On the night, *Néa Dhimokratía* scraped home with a majority of one, later doubled with the defection of a centrist, and **Mitsotakis** finally got to achieve his dream of becoming prime minister. The only other memorable feature of the election was the first parliamentary representation for a party of the Turkish minority in Thrace, and for the ecologists – a focus for many disaffected PASOK voters.

A return to the Right: Mitsotakis

On assuming power, Mitsotakis followed a course of **austerity measures** to try and revive the chronically ill economy. Little headway was made, though given the world recession it was hardly surprising. Greek inflation was still approaching twenty percent annually and, at nearly ten percent, unemployment remained a major problem. The latter has been exacerbated since 1990 by the arrival of thousands of impoverished **Albanians**, particularly in Epirus and the northern Ionian islands. They have formed something of an underclass, especially those who aren't ethnically Greek and are prey to vilification for all manner of ills. They have also led to the first real immigration measures in a country whose population is more used to being on the other side of such laws.

Other conservative measures introduced by Mitsotakis included laws to combat strikes and terrorism. The terrorist issue had been a perennial source of worry for Greeks since the appearance in the mid-1980s of a group called **Dhekatoévdhomo Noemvríou** ("November 17", the date of the Colonels' attack on the Polytechnic in 1973). They have killed a number of industrialists and attacked buildings of military attachés and airlines in Athens, so far without any police arrests. It hardly seemed likely that Mitsotakis' laws, however, were the solution. They stipulated that statements by the group could no longer be published, and led to one or two newspaper editors being jailed for a few days for defiance – much to everyone's embarrassment.

The **anti-strike laws** threatened severe penalties but were equally ineffectual, as breakdowns in public transport, electricity and rubbish collection all too frequently illustrated. As for the **Koskotas scandal**, the villain of the piece was eventually extradited and gave evidence for the prosecution against Papandreou and various of his ministers. The trial was televised and proved as popular as any soap opera, as indeed it should have been, given the twists of high drama – which included one of the defendants, Koutsoyiorgas, dying in court of a heart attack in front of the cameras. The case against Papandreou gradually petered out and he was officially acquitted in early 1992. The two other surviving ministers, Tsovolas and Petsos, were convicted and given short prison sentences.

The great showpiece trial thus went with a whimper rather than a bang, and did nothing to enhance Mitsotakis' position. If anything, it served to increase sympathy for Papandreou, who was felt to have been unfairly victimized. The real villain of the piece, Koskotas, was eventually convicted of major fraud and is now serving a lengthy sentence.

The Macedonian question

Increasingly unpopular because of the desperate austerity measures, and perceived as ineffective and out of his depth on the international scene, the last thing Mitsotakis needed was a major foreign policy headache. That is exactly what he got when, in 1991, one of the breakaway republics of the former Yugoslavia named itself **Macedonia**, thereby injuring Greek national pride and sparking off vehement protests at home and abroad. Diplomatically, the Greeks fought tooth and nail against the use of the name, but their position became increasingly isolated, and by 1993 the new country had gained official recognition, from both the EC and the UN – albeit under the convoluted title of the Former Yugoslav Republic of Macedonia (FYROM).

Salt was rubbed into Greek wounds when the FYROM started using the Star of Veryína as a national symbol on their new flag. Greece still refuses to call its northerly neighbour Macedonia, instead referring to it as *Ta Skópia* (Skopje) after the capital – and you can't go far in Greece these days without coming across officially placed protestations that "Macedonia was, is, and always will be Greek and only Greek!"

The pendulum swings back

In effect, the Macedonian problem more or less directly led to Mitsotakis' political demise. In the early summer of 1993 his ambitious young Foreign Minister, **Andonis Samaras**, disaffected with his leader, jumped on the bandwagon of resurgent Greek nationalism to set up his own party, **Politikí Ánixi** (Political Spring), after leaving *Néa Dhimokratía*. His platform, still right-wing, was largely based on action over Macedonia and during the summer of 1993 more ND MPs broke ranks, making *Politikí Ánixi* a force to be reckoned with. When Parliament was called upon to approve severe new budget proposals, it became clear that the government lacked support, and early elections were called for October 1993. Mitsotakis had also been plagued for nearly a year by accusations of phone-tapping, and had been linked with a nasty and complicated contracts scandal centred around a national company, AGET.

Many of ND's disillusioned supporters reverted directly to PASOK, and a frail-looking **Papandreou**, now well into his seventies, romped to election victory, becoming prime minister for the third time. PASOK immediately fulfilled two of its pre-election promises by removing restrictions on the reporting of statements by terrorist groups and renationalizing the Athens city bus company. The imposition of a trade embargo on Macedonia, however, landed the new government in hot water with the European Court of Justice. PASOK also set about improving the health system, and began to set the wheels in motion for Mitsotakis to be tried for his alleged misdemeanours – though all charges were mysteriously dropped in January 1995, apparently on the orders of Papandreou himself. Meanwhile, the Minister of Public Order, Papathemelis, made the government extremely unpopular with the youth and bar/restaurant owners by reintroducing licensing laws and imposing, for the first time, minimum age requirements.

Both the major parties received a good slap in the face at the **Euroelections** of June 1994, losing ground to the smaller parties. The major winner was Samaras, whose *Politikí Ánixi* almost doubled its share of the vote, while the two left-wing parties both fared quite well.

In the spring of 1995 presidential elections were held in parliament to designate a successor to the 88-year-old Karamanlis. The winner, with support from *Politikí Ánixi* and PASOK, was **Costis Stephanopoulos**, a former lawyer with a clean-cut reputation, who had been put forward by Samaras and welcomed by Papandreou in a deal that would allow his party to see out their four-year term.

In November 1995, Greece lifted its embargo on Macedonia, opening its mutual borders to tourism and trade; in return for this, the Macedonians agreed to drop controversial clauses from their constitution and replace the offending star in their flag. Relationships were almost instantly normalized, with only the name still moot: current favourites are "New Macedonia" or "Upper Macedonia".

However, the emerging critical issue was the 76-year-old Papandreou's continued stewardship of PASOK and the country, as he clung obstinately to power despite obvious signs of dotage. Numerous senior members of PASOK became increasingly bold and vocal in their criticism, no longer fearing expulsion or the sack as in the past.

Late in November 1995, Papandreou was stricken with severe lung and kidney infections, and rushed to intensive care at the Onassis Hospital. The country was essentially rudderless for two months, as there was no provision in the constitution for replacing an infirm prime minister. At last, in mid-January 1996, the conscious but groggy Papandreou was pressurized to sign a letter **resigning** as prime minister (though not, at that time, of PASOK); thus departed the last "dinosaur" of post-1974 politics. The "palace clique", consisting of Mimi Liani and entourage, were beaten off in the parliamentary replacement vote, in favour of the allegedly colourless but widely respected technocrat **Costas Simitis**, who seems to be just what Greece needs after years of incompetent flamboyance.

The current situation

General elections are due for autumn 1997; the goals of the two main parties are now virtually indistinguishable, with the main differences being methodology and, as ever, personalities. One of the many reasons for Mitsotakis' eventual failure was his lack of "bedside manner", which consistently alienated those naturally predisposed to support him, not to mention the outraging of opponents. PASOK's inherent advantage lies in its ability to convince its labour union constituency of the need occasionally to swallow bitter pills. If Simitis does not last out his term of office, the odds are on a prime ministerial contest between PASOK's **Vasso Papandreou** (no relation) and the increasingly popular ND mayor of Athens, **Dhimitris Avramopoulos**.

Greece now languishes in the EU's economic cellar, ranked below Portugal, though recent critical earmarks are vastly encouraging. The austerity programmes and a **"hard drachma"** programme have finally driven inflation down into single figures for the first time in decades. Increasingly amicable relations with its northern Balkan neighbours – Greece is the principal foreign investor in Bulgaria, for example – promise to generate jobs and drive down unemployment, currently just over nine percent.

Tourism, accounting for seven percent of GNP, was down twenty percent across the nation in 1995, leading the new government to promise renewed efforts to improve infrastructure, especially on the islands. Long-promised yacht marinas and roads are finally being completed with

EU assistance – opening up some islands, such as Lefkádha, as never before – while spas, casinos and golf courses are to be built or renovated. The renovation of Corfu Town for the 1993 economic summit is expected to extend into some of its run-down coastal resorts in the late 1990s. Cheap flight-only and backpacker tourism will be strongly discouraged in favour of special-interest, high-spending visitors such as walkers, divers, cavers and so on. The era of Greece as a cheap place to get to and a cheap place to stay in has probably gone forever. It is clear, though – in the Ionian and elsewhere – that the boom in cheap tourism had turned sour, and was beginning to harm both the local economy and the enjoyment of its visitors. It seems likely, however, that the tourism economy still has further to fall before it bottoms out.

Wildlife

Apart from the flora and fauna blown, washed or otherwise carried here, nature on the islands has developed from what was here over 10,000 years ago, when the icecaps melted and stranded these drowned mountains out at sea off the coastline of mainland Greece. Thanks partly to the Venetian invaders – whose extensive olive-planting programmes, at a time of general deforestation in the Mediterranean basin, bound and held much of the islands' topsoil – the Ionian islands are atypically green and fertile compared to most Greek islands.

Before the inundation at the end of the last Ice Age, great forests stretched across much of Italy, what is now the Adriatic Sea, and east across the north of Greece. Extensive deforestation for fuel, building and to clear land for cultivation and grazing utterly transformed this landscape on mainland Greece, far less so on the Ionian islands. The difference can be observed on any ferry journey in the region, simply by comparing the bare brown hills of the mainland with the olive groves and pine woodlands that cover most of the eastern coastlines and lower hillsides of the islands.

Modern Greece has escaped some of the worst effects of the intensification of agriculture, but there are signs that it may be succumbing. Pesticides and chemical fertilizers are now playing a larger part in farming, controversial (and possibly carcinogenic) olive sprays are gaining ground on Corfu and Paxí, and factory fishing threatens what is an already depleted fish stock, as well as the livelihood of independent fishing workers. Ugly and exploitative development has destroyed swaths of the countryside and coastline and, despite the eco-friendly sound bites of politicians and businessfolk, many Greeks (and, it has to be said, many visitors) regard the environment as little more than a convenient garbage dump.

Nevertheless, Greece's environment has yet to approach the state of parts of northern Europe; away from developed areas, it's still possible to find landscapes almost untouched by mankind. Rainy winters make the islands a great draw for botanists, especially in spring, and the vegetation in turn attracts ornithologists and their prey.

Flora

The Ionian archipelago follows a different biological clock from northern Europe or America, particularly noticeable in the development of its **flowers**. Despite being among the most northerly of the Greek islands, the Ionians see daffodils and crocuses in January, freesias and antirrhinums in March, and by Easter most woodlands and domestic gardens are in full bloom. Hot summers – not always guaranteed in this region – tend to blast most plant life, only for autumn rains to produce a second growth among some plants, such as dwarf cyclamen.

The best time to visit is spring, ideally around **Easter** – much of the plant life will have died back before most charter flights begin arriving in the region. By Easter, wild and cultivated carnations, geraniums, garlic, valerian and bush angelica are in flower, as is the slightly sinister bell-like datura. Country walks are likely to be scented with wild rosemary, oregano, thyme (parts of Lefkádha are smothered in this herb; beekeepers park hives in it to flavour the honey) and sage, as well as eucalyptus and myrtle, the last of which is used to line the streets in some Easter parades, giving off a heady aroma as the procession tramples over it.

The onset of **summer** brings yellow broom and, in flowering years, the tiny white star-like flowers of the olive tree. Scarlet pimpernels, anemones, camomile, campanula and love-in-a-mist abound. This is also the time that the region's two sturdiest blooms, the oleander and bougainvillea, appear. Wild orchids can materialize almost overnight. As summer progresses, new growth tends to be on the hills and lower slopes of the mountains. Hollyhocks, asphodel, pinks and grape hyacinths are common at high altitudes.

While the more mountainous islands are largely bare of **trees** at higher altitudes, the lower slopes of Lefkádha and Kefalloniá are notable for impressive stands of Aleppo pine, holm oak and, on the latter, the native Cephallonian fir (*abies cephalonica*) – which can also be found at even lower levels, notably the beaches of Skála. The ubiquitous **olive tree** (*Olea europea*), unlike its pruned mainland relative, is allowed to grow to unmanageable sizes on the islands; some of those on Corfu and Paxí may be as much as 500 years old. As well as commonplace fruits such as apple, orange, lemon, lime, pear and cherry, figs and prickly pears are also found throughout the islands.

Birds

Despite the unwanted attention of thousands of Greek gun-owners, who seem to regard the Ionian skies as one big funfair rifle range, a great variety of **birds** breed on the islands and migrate through them. Greece is a natural stopping-off point for species that winter in Africa but breed in northern Europe. Visitors in May should catch some of the northbound swarms; the late autumn return journey is less concentrated.

After the starling, the **housemartin** is probably the commonest bird in the Ionian, visiting in summer. As well as wheeling in great clouds over Corfu Town, it builds its mud nests in handy niches around the roofs of buildings, often under exposed eaves, where the parents can be observed feeding the young. Some canny birds simply nest in taverna awnings.

Blue tits, bullfinches, greenfinches and goldfinches are common in woodland and orchards, and in marshland and coastal dunes it's quite common to spot the avocet, bee-eater, sandpiper, grey heron, kingfisher and oystercatcher. In farmland and scrub you are also likely to glimpse the woodchat shrike, Sardinian warbler, the cirl bunting and the crested skylark. The golden oriole is one of the prettiest visitors to the islands, although if Paxí is anything to go by, its commonest habitat seems to be the deepfreeze – islanders apparently consider them great delicacies.

Most dramatically, there are a number of **predatory birds** common in the islands. Peregrine falcons can be spotted in more remote areas, often in pairs, usually turning endless circles on guard above a nest. Kestrels are a regular sight, hovering on thermals while hunting. Buzzards, griffons and Egyptian vultures and, in more solitary mountainous areas, the golden eagle, can also be seen, though rarely these days. It's not uncommon to spot pelicans as well.

At night, you're likely to to hear nightingales in less developed areas, as well as the tiny Scops owl; barn owls nest here, but are rarely seen.

Mammals

The Ionian islands share the more run-of-the-mill **mammals** common throughout Greece – rats, mice, voles, squirrels and foxes – but tend to lack the larger predators of the mainland's mountainous areas. The **jackal** is still said to be found in the remotest parts of Corfu, although with some difficulty, as it is shy and mainly nocturnal. On Kefalloniá, visitors to Mount Énos might possibly glimpse the dozen or so **wild horses** still at large on the mountain's slopes.

Hedgehogs are fairly common, and though shy will often forage in gardens. Similarly, pine martens and stone martens may also be glimpsed in fairly developed areas. At dusk, you're likely to spot an airborne mammal, the tiny pipistrelle bat.

The region's two aquatic mammals – the **dolphin** and **monk seal** – are very rare. The former can sometimes be seen, particularly around Paxí (early morning is usually the best time), when they race or play around ferries and other boats. Monk seals are rarer still, but are known to breed in caves around Paxí and other island coastlines. They are very shy, and should not be approached. As well as being endangered, the seal is easily scared away from its own habitat, although in breeding season it can also be quite protective.

Reptiles and amphibians

The summer heat and dry, rocky landscape of parts of the islands provide an ideal habitat for reptiles. Yet even **reptiles** avoid the intense heat; best times to catch them are mornings in spring, before the sun begins to bake.

Most of the islands have their own subspecies of **lizard**. On Corfu and Paxí, the most common is the Dalmatian algyroides, around 15cm long, with a red-brown body and dazzling blue under its lower jaw. The Balkan wall lizard, green/brown-coloured with a long tail, is seen throughout the islands, particularly Kefalloniá and Zákinthos. In the countryside south of Corfu Town, it's sometimes possible to spot the black/grey spiny agama or Rhodes dragon (this is the only place in the Ionian this resident of the Dodecanese has ever been seen).

Most dramatic of the lizards is the **Balkan green lizard**, which can be seen in open or uncultivated countryside (and sometimes the wilder gardens). This bright-green animal can grow up to half a metre in length, most of which is its tail, a crucial balance in its party-piece of running on its hind legs, from one hiding place to another. Looking like miniature tyrannosaurs, they can sometimes be spotted legging it around the gardens of the *Corfu Palace Hotel*.

A distant relative of the lizard, the **gecko**, is a common sight indoors throughout the islands, particularly at night. They cling to walls and ceilings with adhesive pads on their feet, and are both harmless and terrified of humans. Two species, the pink-tinged Turkish gecko and the brown/grey Moorish gecko, are common to the Ionian. You'll most often see them on walls or around light fittings, which attract the flies and mosquitoes on which they feed.

Tortoises can often be found on Corfu, Zákinthos and Kefalloniá. The Hermann's tortoise breeds on all three islands, and favours gentle grassy terrain. The best time to spot them is mid-morning, when they are likely to be basking between hiding places.

Two of the tortoise's smaller aquatic relatives, the European pond terrapin and stripe-necked terrapin, can be found in ponds, rivers and other freshwater environments. The European tends to be black with gold splotches, the stripe-necked grey or brown.

A somewhat larger version of the terrapin, the sea turtle, is common in the Ionian from Corfu down to Zákinthos. The **loggerhead turtle** (*Caretta caretta*) is now a protected species (see p.204), although anyone visiting Zákinthos will see that flagrant breaches of the rules regarding loggerheads are an almost daily occurrence. Like Schrödinger's cat, it seems likely that the very act of looking at the turtles endangers them. Leatherback and green turtles also breed in the region, but are rarely sighted.

Among **snakes**, there are adders on most of the islands (if you're unfortunate enough to frighten one into biting you, note that they're not poisonous). Large – up to two metres – brown snakes are probably Montpellier snakes, a slightly poisonous snake that feeds on rats and other small mammals. Grass snakes are also quite common, and harmless. The one dangerous species is the nose-horned viper, a short snake with zigzag marks down its back, and one of the most poisonous in Europe.

In springtime, the islands are alive with frogs and toads. The **green toad** announces itself with a curious throaty noise and its remarkable bright-green and grey marbled skin. Also common is the small **tree frog**, green or brown in colour – it can alter like a chameleon – and with adhesive suckers on its feet that enable it to climb. Its mountaineering skills and love of water sometimes lead it into bathrooms, where it does similar insect-catching work to the gecko.

Insects

Grasshoppers and crickets are common in Greece, but not as prevalent as the **cicada**, whose distinctive noise typifies and evokes a Mediterranean afternoon for many visitors. Whereas the grasshopper and cricket produce their sounds by rubbing limbs together, the (male) cicada produces its rasping sussurus by rapidly vibrating cavities on either side of its body. The cicada has a green, cricket-like body, hard to find in trees and shrubs, especially as they tend to fall silent when approached.

The islands are also home to over forty species of **butterfly**, best seen in spring or early summer. Migrant butterflies that will be recognized from northern European environments include the red admiral, large and small whites and the painted lady. One of the largest butterflies in Greece, the orange-yellow two-tailed pasha, is a rare sighting but remarkable; some are the size of a small bird. Cleopatras, with their large yellow wings, and the green hairstreak, a small vivid-green butterfly, can also be spotted. Most remarkable, however, are the swallowtails, with their yellow and black colouring and telltale trailing wing tips.

Books

Where separate editions exist in the UK and USA, publishers are separated by a semicolon in the listing below, with the UK company given first. Where books are published in one country only, this – or the city where the publisher is based – follows the publisher's name. University Press is abbreviated as UP; o/p signifies an out-of-print – but still highly recommended – book.

Travel and general accounts

Peter Bull *It Isn't All Greek to Me* (Peter Owen, o/p); *Life's a Cucumber* (Peter Owen, o/p). British actor Bull's two books about his love affair with Greece, in particular Lákka on Paxí. Some characters are still alive on the island today, and the tiny house he built three decades ago stands on the cliffs overlooking Lákka bay.

Gerald Durrell *My Family and Other Animals* (Penguin; Viking). Very funny anecdotal memoir of Durrell's childhood on Corfu half a century ago. Excellent on the (now vanished) landscape and Durrell's passion for island fauna; big brother Larry also makes an appearance.

Lawrence Durrell *Prospero's Cell* (Faber & Faber; Penguin, o/p). The first of his islands trilogy (which includes *Reflections on a Marine Venus*, on Rhodes, and *Bitter Lemons*, on Cyprus), this has hardly been out of print since it was published in 1945. Durrell's magical diary of his time on Corfu in the year before World War II is highly recommended for visitors to the island, and mandatory for those visiting Kalámi.

Lawrence Durrell *Spirit of Place* (Faber & Faber; Penguin, o/p). Durrell's collected shorter prose pieces include recollections of Corfu and travels in the Ionian, including a return visit after the war.

Martin Garrett *Greece: A Literary Companion* (John Murray, UK). Extracts of travel writing and the classics, arranged by region. Enjoyable and frustrating in equal measure.

Edward Lear *The Corfu Years* (Denise Harvey, Athens). Superbly illustrated journals of the nonsense versifier and noted landscape painter, whose paintings and sketches of Corfu, Paxí and elsewhere offer a rare glimpse of the Ionian landscape in the nineteenth century.

Henry Miller *The Colossus of Maroussi* (Minerva; New Directions). The perfect companion volume to *Prospero's Cell*: writing in Paris in 1939, Miller was invited to holiday in Kalámi with the Durrells on the eve of World War II. Much of the book covers journeys elsewhere, but the stranger's view of Corfu (and the Durrells) is wonderfully over-the-top.

James Pettifer *The Greeks: The Land and People Since the War* (Penguin; Viking). The best introduction to contemporary Greece, its recent history, as well as politics, culture and topics such as the impact of tourism. Having worked as a reporter in Greece and the Balkans, Pettifer eschews clichés for a complex and unsparing portrait of the modern state.

Terence Spencer *Fair Greece, Sad Relic: Literary Philhellenism from Shakespeare to Byron* (Denise Harvey, Athens; Scholarly Press, US). Greece from the fall of Constantinople to the war of independence, through the eyes of English poets, essayists and travellers.

Richard Stoneman *A Literary Companion to Greece* (J. Paul Getty Museum). Extracts from the classics, but also some more modern fare, including Cavafy's famed poem "Return to Ithaca" and Wilde on Zákinthos. Over 21 pages on the Ionian, although oddly no mention of Byron's "Childe Harold's Pilgrimage".

History and the Classics

A good general history is *A Traveller's History of Greece* by **Timothy Boatswain and Colin Nicolson**

(Windrush Press; Interlink), which gives a slightly dated but well-written overview of all periods Greek. The only specific history of any of the Ionian islands in English is *Old Corfu: History and Culture* by **Nondas Stamatopoulos** (KM Typografia), an incredibly detailed, labour-of-love history of the island and town, concentrating on antiquities.

The Classics

Many of the Classics make excellent companion reading while travelling around Greece – not least Homer's *Odyssey*, even though its geographical links with the Ionian islands have become confused rather than confirmed over the centuries. Thucydides' *History of the Peloponnesian War* should also prove illuminating for those travelling in the Ionian islands, which were embroiled in the war. The following are all available in Penguin Classic editions:

Herodotus *The Histories*.

Homer *The Odyssey; The Iliad*.

Pausanias *The Guide to Greece* (2 vols).

Plutarch *The Age of Alexander; Plutarch on Sparta; The Rise and Fall of Athens*.

Thucydides *The History of the Peloponnesian War*.

Xenophon *The History of My Times*.

Ancient history

A R Burn *History of Greece* (Penguin). Probably the best general introduction to ancient Greece, though for fuller and more interesting analysis you'll do better with one or other of the following.

M I Finley *The World of Odysseus* (Penguin). Good on the interrelation of Mycenaean myth and fact.

John Kenyon Davies *Democracy and Classical Greece* (Fontana; Harvard UP). Established and accessible account of the period and its political developments.

Oswyn Murray *Early Greece* (Fontana; Harvard UP). The Greek story from the Mycenaeans and Minoans to the onset of the Classical period.

F W Walbank *The Hellenistic World* (Fontana; Harvard UP). Greece under the sway of the Macedonian and Roman empires.

Byzantine, medieval and Ottoman

Nicholas Cheetham *Medieval Greece* (Yale UP, o/p in US). General survey of the period and its infinite convolutions in Greece, with Frankish, Catalan, Venetian, Byzantine and Ottoman struggles for power.

John Julius Norwich *Byzantium: The Early Centuries* and *Byzantium: The Apogee* (both Penguin; Knopf). Perhaps the main surprise for first-time travellers to Greece is the fascination of Byzantine monuments. These first two volumes of Norwich's history of the empire are terrific narrative accounts.

Timothy Callisto Ware *The Orthodox Church* (Penguin). Good introduction to what is effectively the established religion of Greece.

Modern Greece

Richard Clogg *A Concise History of Greece* (Cambridge UP). A remarkably clear and well-illustrated account of Greece from the decline of Byzantium to 1991, stressing recent decades.

Mark Mazower *Inside Hitler's Greece: The Experience of Occupation 1941–44* (Yale UP). Scholarly and well-illustrated history of Greece during the war, which demonstrates how the complete demoralization of the country and incompetence of conventional politicians led to the rise of ELAS and the onset of civil war.

C M Woodhouse *Modern Greece, A Short History* (Faber & Faber). Woodhouse was active in the Greek resistance during World War II. Writing from a right-wing perspective, his history is briefer and a bit drier than Clogg's, but he is scrupulous with facts.

Archeology and art

John Beckwith *Early Christian and Byzantine Art* (Penguin; Yale UP). Illustrated study placing Byzantine art within a wider context.

John Boardman *Greek Art* (Thames & Hudson, UK). A very good concise introduction to the art of the ancient world in the "World of Art" series.

Reynold Higgins *Minoan and Mycenaean Art* (Thames & Hudson). A clear, well-illustrated roundup.

Sinclair Hood *The Arts in Prehistoric Greece* (Penguin; Yale UP). Sound introduction to the subject.

Gisela Richter *A Handbook of Greek Art* (Phaidon; Da Capo). Exhaustive survey of the visual arts of ancient Greece.

Suzanne Slesin et al *Greek Style* (Thames & Hudson; Crown). Stunning and stylish domestic architecture and interiors, including Corfu and elsewhere in the islands.

R R R Smith *Hellenic Culture* (Thames & Hudson, UK). Modern reappraisal of the art of Greece under Alexander and his successors.

Peter Warren *The Aegean Civilizations* (Phaidon Books; P Bedrick Books, o/p). Illustrated account of the Minoan and Mycenaean cultures.

Modern fiction

Louis de Bernières *Captain Corelli's Mandolin* (Minerva; Pantheon). De Bernières' wonderful tragicomic epic of life on Kefalloniá during World War II and after became almost a fashion accessory among visitors to the island in recent summers. His take on historic detail has also won praise from Greek intellectuals, which should complete the recommendation. The later narrative is telescoped wildly, but the novel deserves the plaudits plastered on the cover.

Stratis Haviaras *When the Tree Sings* (Picador, o/p; Simon & Schuster, o/p); *The Heroic Age* (Penguin, o/p). Although unrelated to the region, these two remarkable novels are recommended for their quasi-autobiographical treatment of two periods in recent Greek history: the former a magic-realist vision of the Nazi occupation of a small Aegean island; the latter a personal history of the civil war, both seen through a boy's eyes.

Russell Hoban *The Medusa Frequency* (Picador; Harcourt Brace, o/p). While much of Hoban's avant-garde mystery takes place in the circuitry of the narrator's word processor, it also involves a journey into an underworld region which can only be accessed by a rather unusual gateway: an olive tree in the hills of Paxí.

Specific guides

Arthur Foss *The Ionian Islands* (Faber, o/p). Published in 1969, on the cusp of the region's development, this elegant and erudite guide to the islands mixes description with a comprehensive knowledge of the archipelago's history and culture. Copies fetch fancy prices in the second-hand book market, so try your library.

Noel Rochford *Landscapes of Paxos* and *Landscapes of Corfu* (Sunflower Books, UK). Seasoned hiker Rochford has a rather dense prose style, but these are excellent pocket guides to walks around the two islands.

Hilary Whitton Paipeti *The Second Book of Corfu Walks* (Hermes Press). A more leisurely, but no less extensive, guide to walking on the island, written by a knowledgeable long-term resident.

Flora and fauna

Marjorie Blainey and Christopher Grey-Wilson *Mediterranean Wild Flowers* (HarperCollins, UK). Comprehensive field guide.

Corbet and Ovenden *Collins Guide to the Mammals of Europe* (Collins; Stephen Green Press). The best guide on the subject.

Higgins and Riley *A Field Guide to the Butterflies of Britain and Europe* (Collins; Stephen Green Press). A field guide that sorts out all the butterflies you're likely to see, although it's a bit detailed for the casual observer.

Anthony Huxley and William Taylor *Flowers of Greece and the Aegean* (Hogarth Press, UK). The best book for flower identification, an excellent general guide with good photographic illustrations.

Petersen, Mountfort and Hollom *Field Guide to the Birds of Britain and Europe* (Collins; Stephen Green Press); **Heinzel, Fitter and Parslow** *Collins Guide to the Birds of Britain and Europe* (Collins; Stephen Green Press). There are no specific reference books on Greek birds, but these two European guides have the best coverage.

Language

So many Greeks have lived or worked abroad in America, Australia and, to a much lesser extent, Britain, that you will find someone who speaks English in the tiniest island village. Add to that the thousands attending language schools or working in the tourist industry – English is the lingua franca of most resorts, with German second – and it is easy to see how so many visitors come back having learned only half a dozen restaurant words between them.

You can certainly get by this way, but it isn't very satisfying, and the willingness to say even a few words will upgrade your status from that of dumb *turístas* to the honourable one of *ksénos*, a word that can mean foreigner, traveller and guest all rolled into one.

Learning basic Greek

Greek is not an easy language for English-speakers, but it is a very beautiful one, and even a brief acquaintance will give you some idea of the debt owed to it by western European languages. On top of the usual difficulties of learning a new language, Greek presents the additional problem of an entirely separate **alphabet**. Despite initial appearances, this is fairly easily mastered – a skill that will help enormously if you are going to get around independently (see the box on p.238). In addition, certain combinations of letters have unexpected results. This book's transliteration system should help you make intelligible noises, but you have to remember that the correct **stress** (marked throughout the book with an acute accent) is crucial to getting yourself understood.

Greek **grammar** is more complicated still: nouns are divided into three genders, all with dif-

Language-learning materials

TEACH-YOURSELF GREEK COURSES

Breakthrough Greece (Pan Macmillan; book and two cassettes). Excellent, basic teach-yourself course – completely outclasses the competition.

Greek Language and People (BBC Publications, UK; book and cassette available). More limited in scope, but good for acquiring the essentials and the confidence to try them.

Anne Farmakides *A Manual of Modern Greek* (Yale UP/McGill UP; 3 vols). If you have the discipline and motivation, this is one of the best for learning proper, grammatical Greek; indeed, mastery of just the first volume will get you a long way.

PHRASEBOOKS

Greek, A Rough Guide Phrasebook (Rough Guides). For an up-to-date, accurate pocket phrase book not full of "plume de ma tante"-type expressions, look no further than Rough Guide's very own; English-to-Greek is sensibly phonetic, though the Greek-to-English section, while transliterated, requires mastery of the Greek alphabet.

DICTIONARIES

The Oxford Dictionary of Modern Greek (Oxford University Press). A bit bulky but generally considered the best Greek–English, English–Greek dictionary.

Collins Pocket Greek Dictionary (HarperCollins). Very nearly as complete as the *Oxford* and probably better value for money.

Oxford Learner's Dictionary (Oxford University Press). If you're planning a prolonged stay, this pricey two-volume set is unbeatable for usage and vocabulary. There's also a more portable one-volume *Learner's Pocket Dictionary*.

ferent case endings in the singular and in the plural, and all adjectives and articles have to agree with these in gender, number and case. (All adjectives are arbitrarily cited in the neuter form in the following lists.) Verbs are even worse, with active verbs in several conjugations, passive ones, and passive ones used actively(!). To begin with at least, the best thing is simply to say what you know the way you know it, and never mind the niceties. Even "Eat meat hungry" should get a result; if you worry about your mistakes, you'll never say anything.

Katharévoussa and dhimotikí

Greek may seem complicated enough in itself, but problems are multiplied when you consider

The Greek alphabet

Greek	Transliteration	Pronounced
Α, α	a	a as in father
Β, β	v	v as in vet
Γ, γ	y/g	y as in yes, except before consonants and a, o or long i, when it's a throaty version of the g in gap
Δ, δ	dh	th as in then
Ε, ε	e	e as in get
Ζ, ζ	z	z sound
Η, η	i	i as in ski
Θ, θ	th	th as in theme
Ι, ι	i	i as in ski
Κ, κ	k	k sound
Λ, λ	l	l sound
Μ, μ	m	m sound
Ν, ν	n	n sound
Ξ, ξ	ks	ks sound
Ο, ο	o	o as in toad
Π, π	p	p sound
Ρ, ρ	r	r sound
Σ, σ, ς	s	s sound
Τ, τ	t	t sound
Υ, υ	i	indistinguishable from η
Φ, φ	f	f sound
Χ, χ	h/kh	harsh h sound, like ch in loch
Ψ, ψ	ps	ps as in lips
Ω, ω	o	o as in toad, indistinguishable from o

Combinations and diphthongs

ΑΙ, αι	e	e as in get
ΑΥ, αυ	av/af	av or af, depending on following consonant
ΕΙ, ει	i	long i, exactly like η
ΕΥ, ευ	ev/ef	ev or ef, depending on following consonant
ΟΙ, οι	i	long i, identical again
ΟΥ, ου	ou	ou as in tourist
ΓΓ, γγ	ng	ng as in angle; always medial
ΓΚ, γκ	g/ng	g as in goat at the beginning of a word; ng in the middle
ΜΠ, μπ	b	b at the beginning of a word; mb in the middle
ΝΤ, ντ	d/nd	d at the beginning of a word; nd in the middle
ΤΣ, τσ	ts	ts as in hits
ΤΖ, τξ	tz	j as in jam

that for the last century there has been an ongoing dispute between two versions of the language: *katharévoussa* and *dhimotikí*.

When Greece first achieved independence in the nineteenth century, its people were almost universally illiterate, and the language they spoke – *dhimotikí*, "demotic" or "popular" Greek – had undergone enormous change since the days of the Byzantine Empire and Classical times. The vocabulary had assimilated countless borrowings from the languages of the various invaders and conquerors, namely the Turks, Venetians, Albanians and Slavs.

The finance and inspiration for the new Greek state, and its early leaders, came largely from the Greek **diaspora** – Orthodox families who had been living in the sophisticated cities of central and eastern Europe, or in Russia. With their European notions about the grandeur of Greece's past, and lofty conception of Hellenism, they set about obliterating the memory of subjugation to foreigners in every possible field. And what better way to start than by purging the language of its foreign accretions and reviving its Classical purity? They accordingly devised what was in effect a new form of the language, **katharévoussa** (literally "cleansed" Greek). The complexities of Classical grammar and syntax were reinstated, and Classical words were dusted off and resuscitated. To the country's great detriment, *katharévoussa* became the language of the schools and the prestigious professions, government, business, the law, newspapers and academia. Everyone aspiring to membership in the elite strove to master it – even though there was no consensus on how many of the words should be pronounced.

The *katharévoussa*/*dhimotikí* debate has been a highly contentious issue through most of this century. Writers – from Sikelianos and Seferis to Kazantzakis and Ritsos – have all championed the demotic in their literature, as has the political Left in its rhetoric, while crackpot right-wing governments forcibly (re)instated *katharévoussa* at every opportunity. Most recently, the Colonels' Junta of 1967–74 reversed a decision of the previous government to teach in *dhimotikí* in the schools, bringing back *katharévoussa*, even on sweet wrappers, as part of their ragbag of notions about racial purity and heroic ages.

Dhimotikí returned once more after the fall of the colonels and now seems here to stay. It is used in schools, on radio and TV, after a fashion by newspapers (with the exception of the extreme right-wing *Estia*) and in most official business. The only institutions that refuse to bring themselves up to date are the Church and the legal professions – so beware rental contracts.

This is not to suggest that there is now any less confusion. The Metaxas dictatorship of the 1930s changed scores of village names from Slavic to Classical forms, and these official place names still hold sway on most road signs and maps – even though the local people may use the *dhimotikí* form. Thus you may see "Plomárion" or "Innoússai" written on officially authorized maps or road signs, while everyone actually says Plomári or Inoússes.

Greek words and phrases

Essentials

Yes	*Néh*
Certainly	*Málista*
No	*Óhi*
Please	*Parakaló*
OK, agreed	*Endáksi*
Thank you (very much)	*Efharistó (polí)*
I (don't) understand	*(Dhen) Katalavéno*
Excuse me, do you speak English?	*Parakaló, mípos miláteh angliká?*
Sorry/Excuse me	*Signómi*
Today	*Símera*
Tomorrow	*Ávrio*
Yesterday	*Khthés*
Now	*Tóra*
Later	*Argótera*
Open	*Aniktó*
Closed	*Klistó*
Day	*Méra*
Night	*Níkhta*
In the morning	*Tóh proï*
In the afternoon	*Tóh apóyevma*
In the evening	*Tóh vrádhi*
Here	*Edhó*
There	*Ekí*
This one	*Aftó*
That one	*Ekíno*
Good	*Kaló*
Bad	*Kakó*
Big	*Megálo*
Small	*Mikró*
More	*Perisótero*
Less	*Ligótero*
A little	*Lígo*
A lot	*Polí*
Cheap	*Ftinó*
Expensive	*Akrivó*
Hot	*Zestó*
Cold	*Krío*
With	*Mazí*
Without	*Horís*
Quickly	*Grígora*
Slowly	*Sigá*
Mr/Mrs	*Kírios/Kiría*
Miss	*Dhespinís*

Other needs

To eat/drink	*Trógo/Píno*
Bakery	*Foúrnos, psomádhiko*
Pharmacy	*Farmakío*
Post office	*Tahidhromío*
Stamp	*Gramatósima*
Petrol station	*Venzinádhiko*
Bank	*Trápeza*
Money	*Leftá/Hrímata*
Toilet	*Toualéta*
Police	*Astinomía*
Doctor	*Iatrós*
Hospital	*Nosokomío*

Requests and questions

To ask a question, it's simplest to start with *parakaló*, then name the thing you want in an interrogative tone.

Where is the bakery?	*Parakaló, o foúrnos?*
Can you show me the road to . . . ?	*Parakaló, o dhrómos ya . . ?*
We'd like a room for two	*Parakaló, éna dhomátio ya dhío átoma?*
May I have a kilo of oranges?	*Parakaló, éna kiló portokália?*
Where?	*Poú?*
How?	*Pós?*
How many?	*Póssi* or *pósses?*
How much?	*Póso?*
When?	*Póteh?*
Why?	*Yatí?*
At what time . . . ?	*Tí óra . . . ?*
What is/Which is . . . ?	*Tí íneh/Pió íneh..?*
How much (does it cost)?	*Póso káni?*
What time does it open?	*Tí óra aníyi?*
What time does it close?	*Tí óra klíni?*

Talking to people

Greek makes the distinction between the informal (*esí*) and formal (*esís*) second person, as French does with *tu* and *vous*. Young people, older people and country people nearly always use *esí* even with total strangers. In any event, no one will be too bothered if you get it wrong. By far the most common greeting, on meeting and parting, is *Yá sou/Yá sas* – literally "Health to you".

Hello	*Khérete*
Good morning	*Kalí méra*
Good evening	*Kalí spéra*
Good night	*Kalí níkhta*
Goodbye	*Adío*
How are you?	*Tí kánis?/Ti káneteh?*
I'm fine	*Kalá ímeh*
And you?	*Keh esís?*
What's your name?	*Pos se léneh?*
My name is . . .	*Meh léneh . . .*
Speak slower, please	*Parakaló, miláte pió sigá*
How do you say it in Greek?	*Pos léyeteh sta Eliniká?*

Talking to people (cont.)

I don't know	*Dhén kséro*
See you tomorrow	*Tha se dhó ávrio*
See you soon	*Kalí andámosi*
Let's go!	*Pámeh!*
Please help me	*Parakaló, na me voïthísteh*

Greeks' Greek

There are numerous words and phrases which you will hear constantly, even if you rarely have the chance to use them. These are a few of the most common.

Éla!	Come (literally) but also Speak to me! You don't say! etc.
Orísteh?	What can I do for you?
Embrós! or *Léyeteh!*	Standard phone responses
Ti néa?	What's new?
Ti yíneteh?	What's going on (here)?
Étsi k'étsi	So-so
Pó-pó-pó!	Expression of dismay or concern, like French "O la la!"
Pedhí moú	My boy/girl, sonny, friend, etc.
Maláka(s)	Literally "wanker", but often used (don't try it!) as an informal address.
Sigá sigá	Take your time, slow down
Kaló taxídhi	Bon voyage
Ópa!	Whoops! Watch it!

On the move

Aeroplane	*Aeropláno*
Bus	*Leoforío*
Car	*Aftokínito*
Motorbike, moped	*Mihanáki, papáki*
Taxi	*Taksí*
Ship	*Plío/Vapóri/Karávi*
Bicycle	*Podhílato*
Hitching	*Otostóp*
On foot	*Méh tá pódhia*
Trail	*Monopáti*
Bus station	*Praktorío leoforíon*
Bus stop	*Stássi*
Harbour	*Limáni*
What time does it leave?	*Tí óra févyi?*
What time does it arrive?	*Tí óra fthâni?*
How many kilometres?	*Pósa hiliómetra?*
How many hours?	*Pósses óres?*
Where are you going?	*Pou pas?*
I'm going to . . .	*Páo stó . . .*
I want to get off at . . .	*Thélo ná katévo stó . . .*
The road to . . .	*Ó dhrómos yía . . .*
Near	*Kondá*
Far	*Makriá*
Left	*Aristerá*
Right	*Dheksiá*
Straight ahead	*Katefthía*
A ticket to . . .	*Éna isitírio ya . . .*
A return ticket	*Éna isitírio me epistrofí*
Beach	*Paralía*
Cave	*Spiliá*
Centre (of town)	*Kéndro*
Church	*Eklissía*
Sea	*Thálassa*
Village	*Horió*

Accommodation

Hotel	*Ksenodhohío*
A room . . .	*Éna dhomátio . . .*
for one/two/three people	*yía éna/dhío/tría átoma*
for one/two/three nights	*yía mía/dhío/trís vradhiés*
with a double bed	*méh megálo kreváti*
with a shower	*méh doús*
Hot water	*Zestó neró*
Cold water	*Krío neró*
Can I see it?	*Boró ná tóh dho?*
Can we camp here?	*Boróume na váloumeh tín skiní edhó?*
Campsite	*Kámping/Kataskínosi*
Tent	*Skiní*
Youth hostel	*Ksenón neótitos*

The time and days of the week

Sunday	*Kiriakí*
Monday	*Dheftéra*
Tuesday	*Tríti*
Wednesday	*Tetárti*
Thursday	*Pémpti*
Friday	*Paraskeví*
Saturday	*Sávato*
What time is it?	*Tí óra ínheh?*
One o'clock	*Mía íy óra*
Two/three o'clock	*Dhío/trís íy óra*
Twenty to four	*Tésseres pará íkosi*
Five minutes past eight	*Októ kéh pénde*
Half past eleven	*Éndheka kéh misí*
In half an hour	*Séh misí óra*
In a quarter-hour	*S'éna tétarto*

Months and seasonal terms

January	*Yennári*
February	*Fleváris*
March	*Mártis*
April	*Aprílis*
May	*Maïos*

continued overleaf

Months and seasonal terms (cont.)

June	*Ioúnios*
July	*Ioúlios*
August	*Avgoustos*
September	*Septémvris*
October	*Októvris*
November	*Noémvris*
December	*Dhekémvris*
Summer schedule	*Therinó dhromolóyio*
Winter schedule	*Himerinó dhromolóyio*

Numbers

1	*énos éna/mía*
2	*dhío*
3	*trís/tría*
4	*tésseres/téssera*
5	*pénde*
6	*éksi*
7	*eftá*
8	*okhtó*
9	*enyá*
10	*dhéka*
11	*éndheka*
12	*dhódheka*
13	*dhekatrís*
14	*dhekatésseres*
20	*íkosi*
21	*íkosi éna*
30	*triánda*
40	*saránda*
50	*penínda*
60	*eksínda*
70	*evdhomínda*
80	*ogdhónda*
90	*enenínda*
100	*ekató*
150	*ekatón penínda*
200	*dhiakóssies/ia*
500	*pendakóssies/ia*
1000	*hílies/hília*
2000	*dhío hiliádhes*
1,000,000	*éna ekatomírio*
first	*próto*
second	*dhéftero*
third	*tríto*

Index

direct orders from

Amsterdam	1-85828-218-7	£8.99	US$14.95	CAN$19.99
Andalucia	1-85828-219-5	9.99	16.95	22.99
Australia	1-85828-141-5	12.99	19.95	25.99
Bali	1-85828-134-2	8.99	14.95	19.99
Barcelona	1-85828-221-7	8.99	14.95	19.99
Berlin	1-85828-129-6	8.99	14.95	19.99
Belgium & Luxembourg	1-85828-222-5	10.99	17.95	23.99
Brazil	1-85828-102-4	9.99	15.95	19.99
Britain	1-85828-208-X	12.99	19.95	25.99
Brittany & Normandy	1-85828-224-1	9.99	16.95	22.99
Bulgaria	1-85828-183-0	9.99	16.95	22.99
California	1-85828-181-4	10.99	16.95	22.99
Canada	1-85828-130-X	10.99	14.95	19.99
China	1-85828-225-X	15.99	24.95	32.99
Corfu	1-85828-226-8	8.99	14.95	19.99
Corsica	1-85828-227-6	9.99	16.95	22.99
Costa Rica	1-85828-136-9	9.99	15.95	21.99
Crete	1-85828-132-6	8.99	14.95	18.99
Cyprus	1-85828-182-2	9.99	16.95	22.99
Czech & Slovak Republics	1-85828-121-0	9.99	16.95	22.99
Egypt	1-85828-188-1	10.99	17.95	23.99
Europe	1-85828-159-8	14.99	19.95	25.99
England	1-85828-160-1	10.99	17.95	23.99
First Time Europe	1-85828-270-5	7.99	9.95	12.99
Florida	1-85828-184-4	10.99	16.95	22.99
France	1-85828-228-4	12.99	19.95	25.99
Germany	1-85828-128-8	11.99	17.95	23.99
Goa	1-85828-156-3	8.99	14.95	19.99
Greece	1-85828-131-8	9.99	16.95	20.99
Greek Islands	1-85828-163-6	8.99	14.95	19.99
Guatemala	1-85828-189-X	10.99	16.95	22.99
Hawaii: Big Island	1-85828-158-X	8.99	12.95	16.99
Hawaii	1-85828-206-3	10.99	16.95	22.99
Holland	1-85828-229-2	10.99	17.95	23.99
Hong Kong	1-85828-187-3	8.99	14.95	19.99
Hungary	1-85828-123-7	8.99	14.95	19.99
India	1-85828-200-4	14.99	23.95	31.99
Ireland	1-85828-179-2	10.99	17.95	23.99
Italy	1-85828-167-9	12.99	19.95	25.99
Kenya	1-85828-192-X	11.99	18.95	24.99
London	1-85828-231-4	9.99	15.95	21.99
Mallorca & Menorca	1-85828-165-2	8.99	14.95	19.99
Malaysia, Singapore & Brunei	1-85828-103-2	9.99	16.95	20.99
Mexico	1-85828-044-3	10.99	16.95	22.99
Morocco	1-85828-040-0	9.99	16.95	21.99
Moscow	1-85828-118-0	8.99	14.95	19.99
Nepal	1-85828-190-3	10.99	17.95	23.99
New York	1-85828-171-7	9.99	15.95	21.99
Norway	1-85828-234-9	10.99	17.95	23.99
Pacific Northwest	1-85828-092-3	9.99	14.95	19.99

In the UK, Rough Guides are available from all good bookstores, but can be obtained from Penguin by contacting: Penguin Direct, Penguin Books Ltd, Bath Road, Harmondsworth, West Drayton, Middlesex UB7 0DA; or telephone the credit line on 0181-899 4036 (9am–5pm) and ask for Penguin Direct. Visa, Access and Amex accepted. Delivery will normally be within 14 working days. Penguin Direct ordering facilities are only available in the UK and the USA. The availability and published prices quoted are correct at the time of going to press but are subject to alteration without prior notice.

around the world

Paris	1-85828-235-7	8.99	14.95	19.99
Poland	1-85828-168-7	10.99	17.95	23.99
Portugal	1-85828-180-6	9.99	16.95	22.99
Prague	1-85828-122-9	8.99	14.95	19.99
Provence	1-85828-127-X	9.99	16.95	22.99
Pyrenees	1-85828-093-1	8.99	15.95	19.99
Rhodes & the Dodecanese	1-85828-120-2	8.99	14.95	19.99
Romania	1-85828-097-4	9.99	15.95	21.99
San Francisco	1-85828-185-7	8.99	14.95	19.99
Scandinavia	1-85828-236-5	12.99	20.95	27.99
Scotland	1-85828-166-0	9.99	16.95	22.99
Sicily	1-85828-178-4	9.99	16.95	22.99
Singapore	1-85828-135-0	8.99	14.95	19.99
Spain	1-85828-240-3	11.99	18.95	24.99
St Petersburg	1-85828-133-4	8.99	14.95	19.99
Sweden	1-85828-241-1	10.99	17.95	23.99
Thailand	1-85828-140-7	10.99	17.95	24.99
Tunisia	1-85828-139-3	10.99	17.95	24.99
Turkey	1-85828-242-X	12.99	19.95	25.99
Tuscany & Umbria	1-85828-243-8	10.99	17.95	23.99
USA	1-85828-161-X	14.99	19.95	25.99
Venice	1-85828-170-9	8.99	14.95	19.99
Vietnam	1-85828-191-1	9.99	15.95	21.99
Wales	1-85828-245-4	10.99	17.95	23.99
Washington DC	1-85828-246-2	8.99	14.95	19.99
West Africa	1-85828-101-6	15.99	24.95	34.99
More Women Travel	1-85828-098-2	10.99	16.95	22.99
Zimbabwe & Botswana	1-85828-186-5	11.99	18.95	24.99

Phrasebooks

Czech	1-85828-148-2	3.50	5.00	7.00
French	1-85828-144-X	3.50	5.00	7.00
German	1-85828-146-6	3.50	5.00	7.00
Greek	1-85828-145-8	3.50	5.00	7.00
Italian	1-85828-143-1	3.50	5.00	7.00
Mexican	1-85828-176-8	3.50	5.00	7.00
Portuguese	1-85828-175-X	3.50	5.00	7.00
Polish	1-85828-174-1	3.50	5.00	7.00
Spanish	1-85828-147-4	3.50	5.00	7.00
Thai	1-85828-177-6	3.50	5.00	7.00
Turkish	1-85828-173-3	3.50	5.00	7.00
Vietnamese	1-85828-172-5	3.50	5.00	7.00

Reference

Classical Music	1-85828-113-X	12.99	19.95	25.99
Internet	1-85828-198-9	5.00	8.00	10.00
Jazz	1-85828-137-7	16.99	24.95	34.99
Opera	1-85828-138-5	16.99	24.95	34.99
Rock	1-85828-201-2	17.99	26.95	35.00
World Music	1-85828-017-6	16.99	22.95	29.99

In the USA, or for international orders, charge your order by Master Card or Visa (US$15.00 minimum order): call 1-800-253-6476; or send orders, with complete name, address and zip code, and list price, plus $2.00 shipping and handling per order to: Consumer Sales, Penguin USA, PO Box 999 – Dept #17109, Bergenfield, NJ 07621. No COD. Prepay foreign orders by international money order, a cheque drawn on a US bank, or US currency. No postage stamps are accepted. All orders are subject to stock availability at the time they are processed. Refunds will be made for books not available at that time. Please allow a minimum of four weeks for delivery.

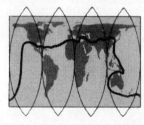

A heavyweight insurance for those who travel light.
Our 'hassle-free' insurance includes instant cover, medical, personal liability, legal expenses, cancellation, passport and much more.
For details call
0171-375 0011
Lines open: 8am-8pm Mon-Fri, 9am-4pm Sat.
COLUMBUS DIRECT
TRAVEL INSURANCE
2 MINS FROM LIVERPOOL STREET STATION
Visit us at 17 DEVONSHIRE SQUARE, LONDON EC2M 4SQ
VISA
MasterCard
SWITCH